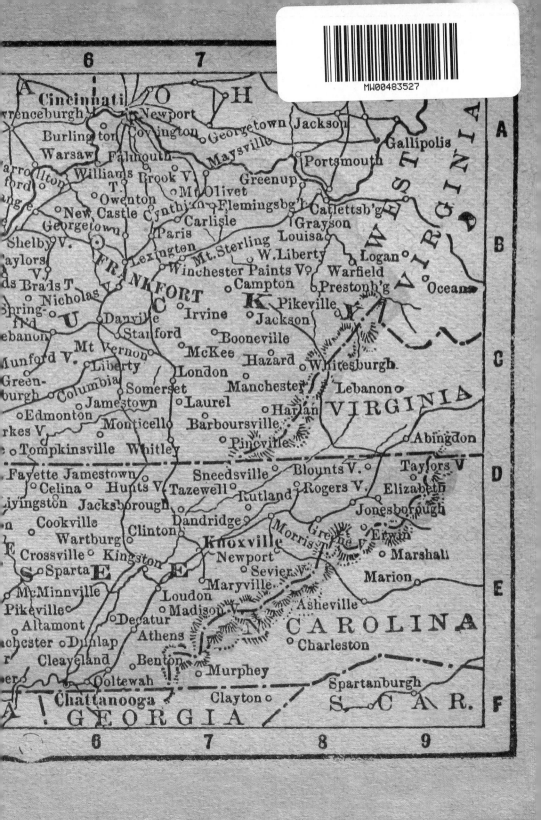

BIG WHISKEY

Kentucky Bourbon, Tennessee Whiskey,
the Rebirth of Rye, and the Distilleries
of America's Premier Spirits Region

BY
CARLO DeVITO

WITH
RICHARD THOMAS AND EMILY WEST

PHOTOGRAPHY BY
JOHN WHALEN

CIDER MILL PRESS

BOOK
PUBLISHERS
KENNEBUNKPORT, MAINE

13-Digit ISBN: 978-1-64643-096-3
10-Digit ISBN: 1-64643-096-4

This book may be ordered by mail from the publisher. Please include $5.99 for postage and handling. Please support your local bookseller first!

Books published by Cider Mill Press Book Publishers are available at special discounts for bulk purchases in the United States by corporations, institutions, and other organizations. For more information, please contact the publisher.

Cider Mill Press Book Publishers
"Where good books are ready for press"
PO Box 454
12 Spring Street
Kennebunkport, Maine 04046
Visit us online!
cidermillpress.com

Typography: Adobe Garamond, Akkurat, Historycal, Warnock Pro, Whiskey Label
Image Credits: page 630

Printed in China
1 2 3 4 5 6 7 8 9 0
First Edition

Bringing Home Kentucky and Tennessee Whiskey

If ever there was a time to quote legendary newspaper editor and publisher Horace Greeley, it is now: "Go West, young man!" But for our purposes here, we'll be more specific: "Go to Kentucky and Tennessee!" There has never been a richer time in either state's history. Construction in both states is at an all-time high. Business is booming! Kentucky and Tennessee are being handed out on a silver platter. And what's on the platter? A bottle of Kentucky bourbon and a bottle of Tennessee whiskey!

Investment in the region's distilleries is in the hundreds of millions of dollars. In both states, small towns that were moribund for years have suddenly sprung new life. Young people from all over the country are gathering there. And all the associated industries are going along for the ride.

There is no question that this is the whiskey capital of America. Kentucky and Tennessee form the heart of the largest distilling region in the United States.There are four main whiskeys that are strongly associated with this region: Kentucky bourbon, Tennessee whiskey, rye whiskey, and moonshine, or white whiskey.

Like a pair of siblings, wherein you can see one family's lineage in similarly shaped lips or cheeks, the two states are undeniably connected by similarity and rivalry. The mash bills for the Tennessee whiskeys and Kentucky bourbons are very similar in most cases. Ironically, the corn whiskey, or moonshine, also shares many similar recipes and grains. Kentuckians take immense pride in their bourbon, and Tennesseans are beginning to appreciate their state's own version of whiskey in a whole new way. And both sides make rye and moonshine.

The differences are just as startling. Kentucky seems to have fewer distilleries. But many of the distilleries they do have are much, much, much bigger than most distilleries in the United States. One distillery in Kentucky may have anywhere from one to thirty brands that it represents and produces.

And, of course, in Kentucky, bourbon is king. And these days, that kingdom of bourbon continues to expand. Distillery improvements and new construction are up in crazy numbers. And everyone seems to have been, is now, or will be involved in this robust industry.

Kentucky is a company town when it comes to distilling and horse racing. Both industries share storied pasts. Both are steeped in history, and both industries are chockablock with families that have been in their respective businesses for two, three, or four generations.

Tennessee—a leader in distilling production before Prohibition—is in the middle of one of the biggest booms in the state's history. Millions and millions of dollars are being poured into new distilleries—both large and small. Craft spirit distilling, while small in overall size, is a much bigger trend in Tennessee.

In 2009, Tennessee had three distilleries, but today there are more than forty. The two biggest are the large and iconic Jack Daniel's and George Dickel. But with the excitement that is brewing, Tennessee whiskey should be one of the hottest new categories in the next half-decade and beyond. In the meantime, a phalanx of new Tennessee moonshines, vodkas, and gins are being crafted across the state. The excitement in the industry is palpable. And the desire to compete with their now-bigger brother to the north has never been hotter.

For many years, Tennessee has been known as the center of country music. The state is awash with references to it. The other major export has been Tennessee whiskey. Now, more than ever before, whiskey is in the ascendancy. And soon, like its neighbors to the north, Tennessee will have a second industry that is as dominant as the one that put it on the map.

Maybe you can't move to Tennessee or Kentucky. The good news is you can always bring a little bit of Kentucky home, and celebrate with a mint julep and a souvenir from Keeneland or Churchill Downs, or raise a glass of Tennessee whiskey and toast Graceland or the Grand Ole Opry. The only movement required is a visit to your local purveyor of fine liquors, where you can procure some of the best whiskeys in the world and add them to you home bar.

Share a little Southern hospitality and spend time with friends and family over a good glass of whiskey. That's why whiskey is really so popular— sharing it with loved ones, bringing back memories, and making new ones. Doesn't matter if you're a Louisville Cardinals fan, a Kentucky Wildcat fan, a Tennessee Volunteers fan, or a fan of a far-flung team, you can always sit down with a bottle, pour a couple of glasses (maybe over a small amount of ice), lean back, and laugh. That's really what great whiskey is all about!

INTRODUCTION

Whiskey, Bourbon, Rye: What's the Difference?

Here's how it works: bourbon, rye, Tennessee whiskey, and some moonshine are whiskey. "Whiskey" is the term used to describe an aged spirit that is distilled from grain.

All bourbon, rye, and Tennessee whiskey come from grain—primarily corn, rye, malted barley, and wheat.

CORN WHISKEY (also known as moonshine or white whiskey) is the base spirit most Kentucky and Tennessee whiskeys are made from. It is the distillate with water added back (usually), which comes from grain and some variable amount of corn. Some are made from 100 percent corn. It is usually clear. Most are not aged, but a few are "rested" in oak for a short period so that they can be called whiskey. Some moonshine contains cane sugar as part of the mash bill.

BOURBON is a whiskey made from at least 51 percent (but no more than 80 percent) corn, with the rest made up of rye, wheat and/or malted barley. It must be made in the United States, and aged in new charred oak barrels. The final product must be at least 80 proof. Although there is no minimum aging requirement for bourbon, any bourbon younger than four years must have an age statement on the label. Furthermore, the age statement of any bourbon must be according to the youngest whiskey in the bottle.

STRAIGHT BOURBON is American bourbon aged a minimum of two years, as mandated by law. This same requirement applies to any other whiskey labeled "straight." Moreover, any "bottled in bond" bourbon must also be a straight bourbon, and aged for at least four years (not to mention that it must come from a single distilling season, and be distilled by one distiller at one distillery, then aged at a federally bonded warehouse). Blended bourbon must contain at least 51 percent straight bourbon, but may also include other spirits, flavoring, and color.

RYE WHISKEY, like bourbon, is an American invention and must also be aged in new charred oak and bottled at least 80 proof. Made from at least 51 percent rye grain, rye whiskey is spicier and drier than other varieties. Once common throughout the northeastern United States, rye whiskey almost died out after Prohibition, but is currently seeing a resurgence. Canadian whisky is also often called rye whisky, but most contemporary Canadian whiskies don't contain a majority of rye in their mash bill, or any at all.

CONTINUED ON NEXT PAGE >

TENNESSEE WHISKEY is made using the same method and ingredients as most bourbons, but features an extra step, a charcoal "mellowing" known as the Lincoln County Process, where the distillate is passed through heavily charred American maple chips before it is put into new American oak barrels for aging. Although there are no legal guidelines as to how much charcoal the distillate must pass through to qualify as Tennessee whiskey, Jack Daniel's and George Dickel filter their whiskeys through massive 10- and 13-foot vats of charcoal, respectively.

Whiskey is also a generic term, meaning the mash bill does not fulfill any of the above requirements—i.e. a distillate resulting from a mash bill of 25 percent corn, 25 percent rye, 25 percent malted barley, and 25 percent wheat is considered a generic whiskey. It might be very tasty, but it does not fulfill the requirements for bourbon, rye, or Tennessee whiskey.

GRAIN

There are four main grains we are concerned with:
corn, malted barley, rye, and wheat. These four grains, in some
combination or another, make up the greater part of bourbon, rye,
or Tennessee whiskey. They are the backbone of the industry.

CORN

Corn is the foundation of both Kentucky bourbon and Tennessee whiskey. White, sweet corn is the coin of the realm, and the cornfields of the South and Midwest feed a steady stream of corn to distilleries throughout these two states. Why corn? Because it helps offer that hint of sweetness that makes bourbon so popular in the United States. Corn is where it all began!

RYE

The backbone of 90 percent of the bourbon and Tennessee whiskey market comes from rye. Rye offers the spicy notes that one associates with bourbon and whiskey. It lends a gingersnap-like quality, blending lots of spices with a peppery finish. The more rye in the mash bill, the drier and spicier the whiskey will be. Rye is one of the hardiest and easiest crops to farm, which is what made it the most popular grain grown for distillation before Prohibition.

MALTED BARLEY

Malted barley is almost always in the mix. Malted barley provides several different elements. It adds another texture or flavor profile to the whiskey. Because it is malted, which means it has been wetted and started to germinate, it provides enzymes that will help break down the grains, and help the yeast turn sugars and carbohydrates into alcohol.

WHEAT

Most distillers use a red winter wheat in their mash. Wheat often lends a softer touch to whiskey, giving a soft, even sweet flavor not unlike that which oatmeal lends to a beer. Any whiskey with 51 percent or more wheat in its mash is a wheat whiskey, and bourbons that replace rye in the mash bill with wheat are "wheated" bourbons. Both lack the characteristic bite that comes from rye, and may have floral or grassy notes.

Mash and Wash

The mash is the blend of grains used to make the base of whiskey. In bourbon, the mash bill, or recipe, must be predominantly corn. In Kentucky, the percentage of corn ranges from 70 percent to 90 percent of the final mash bill. Buffalo Trace has a mash bill with corn making up as much as 90 percent of the recipe, while Jack Daniel's and George Dickel are both in the low 80s. After that, most of the industry is around the 70-something mark.

The mash bill in some instances is guarded like a state secret, while other distilleries are happy to share. Suffice to say, it is an immeasurably important part of the makeup of the final product.

Malted barley is the next constant, with that portion of recipes averaging anywhere from a low of 5 percent to a high of 15 percent.

The other portion is usually rye, but there are a few bourbons that substitute wheat for rye.

With the mash bill perfected, the next step is making mash, or distiller's beer. The grains are cooked. The corn is usually cooked first, and then the barley and other grains are added after the corn has come to a boil. The final product smells and tastes like Cream of Wheat, or to be more precise, cream of corn. It smells like breakfast. It has all the flavor and sweetness of a sweet corn porridge. After the full boil has been executed, and the grains are fully cooked, distillers have that liquid they refer to as mash.

The mash is then moved to a big open-topped tank called a fermenter. After it has had a chance to cool, yeast is added to this soupy mess.

Here is where recipes differ. Some mashes are fermented in three days. Others four or five. Some as long as seven days. How long the mash ferments directly relates to flavor. The longer it takes the yeast to turn cream of corn into an alcoholic porridge can, and does, determine the flavor profile of the whiskey. Woodford Reserve has five-day fermentations, and master distiller Chris Morris absolutely believes that the stone fruit, apple, and pear notes in this whiskey are a direct result of the cooking time.

Yeast works in the fermentation tank a lot like it does in a beer tank. The hungry yeast races through the slurry of sugar and carbohydrates and voraciously feasts, turning the sugar and carbs into alcohol. The result of this hunger turns the mash into distiller's beer, or wash.

Some distillers are looking for high-alcohol beers, while others are looking for lower alcohol content. It all depends on what flavor a particular distiller is trying to produce.

WHAT KIND OF FERMENTER DO YOU HAVE?

Most fermenters in the industry are stainless steel. However, some fermenters are made of wood, much in the way rooftop, wooden water tanks are made. They are open-topped, and usually made of the wood from cypress trees. Many distillers who use the wooden fermenters are very proud to show them off. They are very sexy indeed, and impart an old-timey note to the operation. But their draw goes beyond the surface—some distillers swear that the interaction of their mash bill with the wood helps the flavor profile of their spirits.

DISTILLING

Distilling is the process by which the distiller's beer or wash is turned into distillate. The mash, once it has been cooked, is ready to be turned into a distillate.

HEADS AND TAILS

Heads and tails are terms used to describe the front and back of the whiskey distilling process. The distiller will make cuts as the liquid passes through the still.

The distiller checks the volume of alcohol at the beginning of the run. The alcohol level is not sufficiently high enough, and the front of the run contains compounds and elements, such as methanol, that are not ingestible. Imbibing of the heads and/or tails may result in severe sickness, partial blindness, or even death. As the process continues, the liquid begins to process more efficiently, producing a higher alcohol content. The impurities in the liquid decrease as the alcohol increases. Thus the first "cut" is made. Simply put, the distiller shifts the direction of the liquid. The heads are usually sent off to the "low wine" tank, where they will again be run through a still to be refined and rendered drinkable.

Once the liquid is at a high enough alcohol content, the main run begins. The liquid is sent to a spirits tank that will hold it until it is ready to make its way to barrels and become bourbon, rye, Tennessee whiskey, whiskey, or remain a neutral grain spirit.

As the run starts to wind down, the alcohol level begins to drop, and the distiller makes another "cut." This particular cut is called tails. Like heads, the dangerous compounds begin to reappear because the process is not running efficiently. The distiller sends the tails off to the "low wine" tank for reprocessing. This is the end of the first run for the whiskey.

The whiskey is usually redistilled. In the bigger distilleries, the column still feeds a "doubler," or another still, where it will be run through for a second time. In most cases, distilleries feed their whiskey through a pot still or a combination pot/column still. In smaller places, it's run through the same still once again. In order to make gin or vodka, it's run through a taller column still, often called a stripping column, which will have anywhere from 15 to 20 distilling plates. These plates create a clear, odorless, tasteless spirit that provides the base for gins and vodkas.

Now the liquid is ready for barreling.

CLAPPING FOR CREDIT

Often, if you are lucky enough to see it, a distiller will pour distillate on his hands, rub them vigorously, and then smell them. Generally they will do this three times in a row. It's what the old moonshiners used to do. But why?

The first time they rub their hands together and smell them, they are trying to gauge the amount of alcohol in the distillate. The second time they do it, they are looking to see if the corn (or the dominant grain) comes through on the nose. The final time is to check if they can detect the nose of their yeast. Science has since replaced this brand of from-the-hip testing, but many distillers still do it.

Barrels

The barrel is an incredibly important part of the whiskey process, especially when making bourbon. It is the barrel that imparts color and additional flavor to the whiskey. How it's stored, where it's stored, and when it's moved or pulled all help determine the final flavor of the whiskey.

The most popularly used tree for barrels in the distilling world is American white oak. White oak, also known as *quercus alba*, produces one of the most highly regarded hardwoods in North America. The tree can be found as far north as Quebec, and as far south as northern Florida.

As far as the whiskey industry is concerned, the most valuable white oak comes from Arkansas. It produces fine-grained, pale sapwood that is strong, tough, heavy, and durable.

Barrels are made at cooperages by coopers who still execute their craft by hand. Due to the increased popularity of whiskey around the world and the influx of craft distillers in the United States and internationally, the barrel industry has swelled to an all-time high. The most commonly used barrels in Kentucky and Tennessee come from Kelvin Cooperage, Speyside Cooperage, Independent Stave, and Canton.

The wood is harvested and rough cut into strips. The wood is then stacked in interlocking piles and left outside to age, generally, for about two or three years. It is then milled into the pieces that make up a barrel. Each piece of lengthwise wood is called a stave. There are 32 staves in a 53-gallon barrel. The ends are called heads, or barrelheads.

Most barrels used in the craft beverage industry are fired in one way, shape, or form. Coopers place half-finished barrels over an open flame in order to affect what flavors the barrels will impart. Wine barrels are toasted; whiskey barrels are charred.

"People have suggested that the inside of barrels was originally burnt to remove the leftover flavors of goods previously stored within, which sounds reasonable enough.

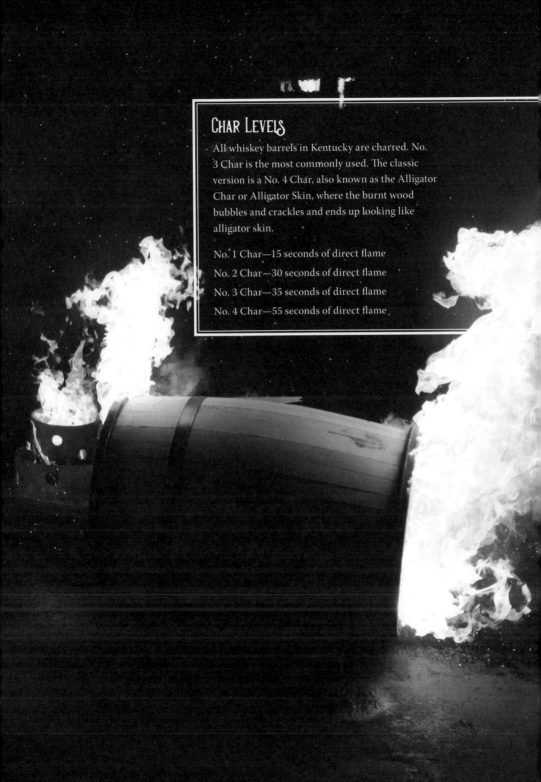

Char Levels

All whiskey barrels in Kentucky are charred. No. 3 Char is the most commonly used. The classic version is a No. 4 Char, also known as the Alligator Char or Alligator Skin, where the burnt wood bubbles and crackles and ends up looking like alligator skin.

No. 1 Char—15 seconds of direct flame
No. 2 Char—30 seconds of direct flame
No. 3 Char—35 seconds of direct flame
No. 4 Char—55 seconds of direct flame

Barrel Clocking

As each barrel is slotted to be rolled into its rack next to other barrels, it must be positioned properly so that when it arrives at its spot the bung is at 12 o'clock. The idea is that it reduces the chance of the whiskey leaking out near the bung entrance. This practice is called "clocking" or "barrel clocking."

There's also some evidence that the practice goes back as far as the 15th century amongst French cognac distillers, but no one really knows how the practice began," say the folks at Angel's Envy Distillery. "Because we only use new barrels, and nobody really stores fish or hog parts in them these days, we don't have to worry about scorching previous flavors out of our casks. So why do barrel coopers still char the interior? Charring the wood actually primes the wood, which impacts the spirit's flavor in several important ways that have nothing to do with smokiness."

Why charred barrels today? Barrels contain sap. Sap that is boiled becomes caramelized. Basically, it's the same concept as boiling sap to make syrup. When the whiskey settles into the wood, the boiled sap, now a sweet, caramel-like solid, interacts with the aging whiskey, imparting lovely caramel and vanilla flavors. The oak, and the burnt oak, also help color the whiskey, providing it its lovely, rich hue. That sounds like plenty of work, but that's not all: this wood helps take impurities out of the whiskey, as well.

SIZE MATTERS

These barrels come in a number of sizes: 5-, 10-, 15-, 25-, 30-, and 53-gallon barrels are among the most commonly used in the United States and around the world. In most cases, distillers large and small agree that the best, and most even, productivity comes from the 53-gallon barrels. They produce the flavor, color, and mixture of spices associated with classic, high-quality bourbon. Where a barrel is stored also has immense importance. Barrels are often stored in classic, seven-story rickhouses, or warehouses. The hotter the temperature, the shorter amount of time that a barrel needs to stay in the rickhouse. The cooler it is, the longer a barrel needs to remain.

TRADITIONAL BARRELS VS. PALLETIZED BARRELS

Traditional barrels are well known. The have the classic barrel shape, with the bulge in the middle and tapped at both ends, with a bung hole placed half way down one of the wider staves on the side of the barrel. These barrels are stored on their sides, bung hole up, and corked.

However, a new barrel is one the rise. The shape is pretty much the same, however, the bung hole is placed on one of the heads. The barrels are not placed in traditional rickhouses but in climate controlled warehouses, and are stored standing up.

Proponents of traditional barrels insist that time-honored methods are the best. But a new generation of distillers has seen the value proposition of the new barrels. They can be palletized, meaning it is safer and easier to move them with a forklift. Proponents of palletized barrels also argue that there is no discernible difference in how the final product tastes. The battle rages on.

THE ROLE OF THE RUBBER TIRE

When unloading a massive truckload of barrels at the distillery, the barrels are usually stacked three high in the back of large tractor trailer rigs. The barrels fit tightly, and so cannot be moved by fork lifts. The warehouse workers need to pull them down manually. But a barrel dropped from that height to a cement floor will surely crack. Enter the rubber tire. A large tire is placed at the bottom of the large wall of barrels and the top barrels are gently pulled out and bounced off the tire onto the factory floor. This happens until all the third-tier barrels are bounced off the truck.

WHISKEY RING

After the whiskey has been dumped, some barrels are disassembled, and the staves are sold in the distillery retail store. Viewing the stave from the side, one can see how far the whiskey penetrated into the wood. The idea is that whiskey literally expands into the wood when it is hot, and contracts when it is cold, taking some color and flavor with it. The trace of this expansion and contraction is called the whiskey ring.

However, during a distillery tour, one will see many differently sized barrels. The small craft distillers, especially the newest ones, tend to use smaller barrels. First, they just don't produce enough to require larger ones. Second, they need the smaller barrels to age their whiskeys and get them to market faster. The idea is that smaller barrels offer more wood-to-liquid contact, resulting in faster maturing. Brown spirits are extremely popular and command more review attention, consumer desire, and higher prices. If you're a small craft distiller, small barrels are your friend.

Is there a taste difference? If the smaller barrels are handled properly, no. If not, there can be. The small-barreled whiskeys have a more aggressive oak profile. That doesn't make them bad. It just makes the notes of pepper, dark caramel, and spices more pronounced. Some of these whiskeys, like Hartfield & Co., Corsair, and Nelson's Green Brier all produce whiskeys with bigger wood noses, but also with bigger flavor, more chocolate brown malt, and bigger spice notes. These are exciting, fun whiskeys.

Fixing Full Barrels

The big distilleries like Buffalo Trace, Woodford, Jim Beam, Wild Turkey, and Jack Daniel's all use the 53-gallon variety. These places employ coopers on-site to fix leaking barrels. But how do they stop them from leaking? First, they use an awl, and hit the open spot with it and a hammer to make the pinholes larger. Then they hammer cone-shaped pieces of wood, somewhat like fat toothpicks, into the holes. Once the leak has been plugged, the cooper might chip off any wood still sticking out with a chisel. The barrel can then be confidently rolled into a rickhouse and stored.

HONEY BARRELS

Honey barrels (also called sugar barrels) are mythical, or unicorn, barrels smuggled away in rickhouses all through Kentucky. Honey barrels are those barrels that suddenly produce a barrel to be sold at "cask strength," producing whiskey that has a magical taste.

Wild Turkey and Buffalo Trace not only believe in these barrels, they claim they have found them. *Whisky Advocate* contributor Chuck Cowdery has said, "I've been around Kentucky distilleries for forty years and have always heard the term. It simply refers to a particularly good barrel, and there is nothing mythological about that. It's subjective, of course, and certainly prone to abuse if marketers start using it." On the other hand, Eddie Russell—the master distiller at Wild Turkey—believes!

It is generally thought that these barrels are found in the middle two floors of a rickhouse. Many are destined to become single barrel, cask strength bottlings, or end up being reserved for exclusive customers who buy barrels of whiskey.

FINISHING

So, while bourbon has to originally be stored in brand-new American white oak barrels in order to earn the title of bourbon, it can be finished in other kinds of oak. Angel's Envy, for example, is finished in old, port barrels. Maker's Mark 46 is finished with several types of toasted French oak, and Woodford Reserve has released several high-end expressions of bourbon aged in old, Chardonnay, sherry, and cognac barrels.

The idea behind this type of finishing is that these bourbons will mirror the high-end Scottish single malt whiskies, adding new notes and more complexities to the final product. These bourbons are in demand by collectors and the foreign markets of Europe and Asia, where it is a much more common practice.

SCOTLAND, HERE WE COME

All bourbon has to be stored in a new American white oak charred barrel. The barrels cannot be reused to age bourbon again. But most once-used bourbon barrels are sold at a premium on the secondary market. The number one consumer of used American white oak bourbon barrels is Scotland. The distillers who make Scotch whisky age all of their first-run, single malt Scotch in once-used bourbon barrels. In many cases, there are pre-arranged deals. For example, Glenmorangie gets most of its barrels from Jack Daniel's.

THE ANGEL'S SHARE

Every master distiller and distillery owner must suffer the theft of his or her whiskey on a regular basis. As whiskey matures in the cask, a portion of the liquid evaporates. Over the centuries, this has come to be known as The Angel's Share. This is as true in Scotland and Ireland as it is in Kentucky or Tennessee.

According to the Scottish distillers at Bruichladdich, "as much as 5 percent of the volume of the new spirit we put into a cask will be quickly absorbed into the thirsty wood when it is initially filled—but it does not stop there. A smaller proportion, up to 2 percent, will go right through the grain each year and out into the atmosphere to be lost forever, unless you are an angel. It is therefore not uncommon for a cask that is 15 years old to be half-empty by the time it is bottled." In Kentucky and Tennessee, they estimate that between 4 percent and 10 percent of their whiskey is lost to the angels.

There are numerous factors that play a part in evaporation, but temperature and moisture (or lack thereof) play the biggest roles. Counter to what might seem logical, smaller barrels lose more than larger ones, and the hotter parts of the warehouse race through more whiskey than the cooler ones.

KELVIN COOPERAGE

Seen from the outside, there is nothing particularly inspiring when you arrive at Kelvin Cooperage. The first thing you see is the massive loading dock, its doors might be open at any given time, with hard-working men covered in smoke and sweat rolling new and used 100-pound barrels into giant containers as if they're pillows. A little glassed off window shields the operations desks from the world outside. But then, there's what's behind the proverbial curtain.

Kelvin Cooperage has been family run since it was founded in 1963 by Ed McLaughlin on the banks of the River Kelvin in Glasgow, Scotland. Ed had just completed his four-year cooperage apprenticeship and decided to open up his own shop. In the beginning, Kelvin serviced only Scotch distilleries, finding, repairing, and shipping used barrels.

In 1991, Ed's son Kevin relocated to Louisville, Kentucky, in order to take advantage of Louisville's proximity to Bourbon Country. Kelvin is all about family. Kevin served his apprenticeship in Scotland, and has managed Kelvin's Louisville facility since it opened in 1991. Kevin is a graduate of Pepperdine University. Ed's other son Paul joined the family business in June 2001, as general counsel. Prior to joining Kelvin, Paul was an attorney, having received his bachelor's degree from Harvard and his J.D. from Notre Dame. Since 2001, Kelvin is the industry's top purveyor of barrels to the craft market. Kelvin now supplies new and used barrels to leading craft distilleries throughout the world. Kevin, who was well-loved in the industry, passed away in 2019. Paul now owns and operates Kelvin Cooperage.

The move in 1991 served two purposes. Kelvin could source more barrels directly, and the inspection and repair took place on the US side of the Atlantic before shipping. Since then Kelvin Cooperage's used barrel

operation has served the major distilleries in Scotland, Ireland, and beyond continuously since its formation.

But the new barrel business soon began to boom. And throughout Kentucky and Tennessee, there is an unmistakable and immediate consensus regarding Kelvin's absolute craft of barrel making. And when you get behind those loading docks doors, you immediately understand why.

First, Kelvin takes raw, aged oak and saws, steams, pounds, hammers, and fires these barrels all by hand. Because Kelvin is all handmade, they offer key benefits to craft distilleries at any stage of development and production. They are a full-service barrel provider. They can offer traditional 53-gallon barrels, traditional wine barrels, customized whiskey barrels, and offer a

wide range of used or refurbished barrels.

The staves are assembled in a group. A cooper (a carpenter who makes barrels) pulls from a wide swath of cut and trimmed timber, fitting the staves through a hoop to make sure they fit snuggly. No two staves are alike. All are individual. Yet there are 32 staves in a barrel. The bands are placed around the wood and a metal cable tightens the ends and the barrel rings are set down, giving the barrel it's shape. The barrels are fired before the heads are attached. Even the bung hole gets seared, and is sanded and given a final polish before it's ready to go out the door.

No words can explain the wonder of such a place. To say they have two giant industrial sheds is to reduce its absolute magic. To see the barrels fired. To see the barrels

take shape. To see all the hand work that it takes to make a barrel is as exhausting as it is amazing. You begin to realize, whether it's at the station where they put on the hoops, or the station where the barrels are fired, or sanded, or even where they test the barrels before they go out, that these men are not just performing jobs – assembly line though it might appear to be – but that these workers are craftsmen. And when you see what comes in at the front, and what gets ready to be loaded out the back is nothing shy of artistry.

"When I first joined here in 2001, there were only six or seven heritage bourbon brands here in Kentucky, so it didn't make any sense for us to even think about that market," said Paul. "All of their needs were being met by the big cooperage operations. It wasn't until 2010 or 2011 that we even looked at it again. Our focus has definitely changed. When we were doing wine barrel production, it was mostly seasonal. Wine has stayed fairly steady, but whiskey has vastly overtaken it in volume."

To watch in the giant firing area, as pole beams of blue light shine down from the shed ventilators through the darkness where the fire suddenly rages for 15 seconds; to watch the coopers select the wood; to see them make the barrel heads; to watch them plane the wood — all of it is awe inspiring.

Throughout our tour, Paul walks and chats, in his button-down shirt, and down vest, like some studied ringmaster, waving his arms with careful consideration, showing you one wonder after another, knowing how much you will be enthralled. He has perfected his turn as one of the whiskey industry's Willie Wonka's, and rarely fails to please. His self-effacing good humor, and jovial personality make him the perfect foil for this incredible operation.

Regardless of where you go in Kentucky and Tennessee, one of the most popular industry vendors is Vendome Copper & Brass Works of Louisville. It makes 90 percent of all the copper and brass works in the industry in this part of the world. Vendome can trace its lineage to a small company called Hoffman, Ahlers & Co., a Cincinnati manufacturer that dates back to the 1830s. Elmore Sherman, the eventual founder of Vendome, started as a bookkeeper in the St. Louis branch in 1901. By 1910, Sherman had risen to vice president, and when George Ahlers died Sherman took his customers to Louisville and founded Vendome. It was a major success up until the time of Prohibition.

The Temperance Movement crippled the company for a decade, as the distilling industry almost totally collapsed. However, after the repeal of Prohibition, Vendome saw more than 100 different distilleries place orders, and the company rebounded nicely, expanding its reach into other states and countries. By the 1970s, the company was doing a large majority of its business out of state.

Since the 1980s, the small-batch, craft boom has been a new area of growth for the company, although it still services large customers as well. With more than 250 new small-batch distilleries, Vendome's expertise and experience have become invaluable to the ever-expanding industry. But it continues to be highly prized by the Kentucky and Tennessee distillers as well, and has been called upon to make many new stills to cover the increased production.

In 2005, the Elmore Sherman family was inducted into the Kentucky Bourbon Hall of Fame, the first non-distillers to be so honored.

When you first approach the offices of Vendome, you are greeted by a charming, refurbished gray and white Victorian home, simple but elegant. The only thing to truly make it stand out, as one might expect, is a copper plaque with the simple inscription "Vendome Copper & Brass Works." It belies what happens there. The little Victorian homestead is bounded an all sides by large industrial sheds and garages set off in a little neighborhood of its own.

Vendome occupies more than an entire block in Louisville's Butchertown neighborhood and has over 75 employees. The company also makes stainless steel tanks and copper coils for huge companies like Anheuser-Busch and Archer Daniels Midland. In the years before the small distillery boom and the brown spirits boom, Vendome had to find new ways to keep the lights on as well as expand. They reached out to the chemical, food, and beverage industries.

Vendome vice president Michael Sherman is now a fourth-generation family member to run this business in its illustrious 110-year history. He is tall, with blue khakis and a runner's zip-up pullover. A smile and shock of salt-and-pepper hair, he is affable

and friendly. Before we enter the works, he reminds us never to forget that were are in an industrial workplace. It is had to forget.

Entering one of the big sheds, you are greeted by all kinds of metals. Some shiny, some dull, some scraped and scratched, some polished. There is scrap everywhere. But there are also men at work. They take huge sheets of metal that they bend, poke, weld, hammer, and polish until the raw materials resemble a work of art.

Vendome manufactures almost all of their own parts. As Michael offered, even the threads on pipes were not good enough, so now they thread their own pipes. They have all manner of machines, some of which date back more than 100 years, back to a time when factories were filled with such things. They are not archaic to Michael and his gang. He and one of his longtime machinists, Tim, described how they bought the century-old behemoth, a 10-ton metal press, at auction for $5,000. "It cost two or three times that just to ship it," he laughs and rolls his eyes. But it paid for itself in the first job they took on. Tim laughs and cracks wise. After we walk away, Michael says not to be fooled by Tim's demeanor. Tim keeps meticulous

records in his own notebooks, going back more than two decades.

The number and variety of apparatuses among the many floors is mind boggling. In one shop they are assembling a five-story tall continuous column, seemingly the size of a small submarine. Alongside it, there are two medium-sized, 500-gallon pot stills for some small craft distilleries. Another thirty-foot copper column has been disassembled, and is ready to ship. There is super-sized, custom industrial piping for a refinery that you could crawl inside of. And still in another shed is a bowl that will be part of a giant still for a chemical processing plant. The bowl is the size of a small cottage.

Chief among the skills for being employed at Vendome is welding. They have a standard test for tradesmen to show that they can do the four standard types – MIG, TIG, SMAW, and FCAW. Most important on the floor, however, is how they weld copper. Michael says they want good welders to whom they can teach their copper technique. Their welds have to hold, or people get hurt. And they have to look good. Vendome has its own in-house style, and all welders either get it, or they don't last.

Sparks fly everywhere. It's as if the Tin Man were being refurbished at Oz. From welding to grinding, the metal is worked. Scrap is everywhere. Copper shavings. Stainless steel shavings. Precision laser cut outs. You are struck not just by the fabrication, which is incredible, but the scraping and polishing that goes on. The metal does not shine when it comes in, but it glows and gleams when it's ready to go out. The men who make these high-pressured machines are not just metal workers. They are in fact artisans. And the art they produce is on display when it gets shipped to its new home.

Whether you're at Angel's Envy, Copper & Kings, Rabbit Hole, Kentucky Peerless, or a number of other distilleries around the US,

large and small, chances are, the still is from Vendome. And it's not just working — it's showcased! Lit. Polished. A shiny object of affection. A feature on the distillery tour.

The stills are almost all custom. There's no catalog to order from. Distillers like to add their own touches. And Vendome is happy to oblige. A distiller comes to meet with Michael and his staff, and they design it together. As Michael says, if there's a new distillery, we know about it a year or so before anyone else. Vendome has a year-and-a-half backlog in ordering.

BIG ASS FANS

If there is one thing that Vendome Stills and Kelvin Barrels share in common it's fans, big ones. Why? You're talking about an industry that shuts down two weeks in July or August because it is simply too hot to operate the systems. They usually close down and clean out their operations that time of year. Kentucky and Tennessee can get very hot. If you're working in a brewery or warehouse, as well as in a lot of bigger tasting rooms, chances are you will see a huge fan, or "big ass fan" if you will.

Big Ass Fans started in 1999, with the idea of creating safer, more productive work environments in industrial facilities. Carey Smith incorporated the Delta T. Corporation in Lexington, Kentucky. He had seen a "high-volume, low-speed" (HVLS) ceiling fan made by a company in California. Smith signed an exclusive distribution agreement with the company, and changed the name of his company to HVLS Fan Company. He shifted his company's focus almost exclusively to the sales of this fan. The company's first line of products included several iterations of HVLS fans for industrial and agricultural use. These fans use airfoils instead of flat blades and feature onboard variable-frequency drives.

In 2000, the company then known as HVLS Fan Company initiated a marketing campaign with mailers depicting the rear of a donkey, a fan with a 20-foot (6.1 m) blade span, and the caption "Big Ass Fan." Postmasters in seven states refused to distribute the advert cards. The response was immediate, and customers wanted to know if they had any of those "big ass fans" for sale. Sales shot up and Smith changed the name of his company to Big Ass Fans. Smith even changed his job title to "Chief Big Ass."

The name remains controversial. The Big Ass Fans Facebook page includes a gallery of letters complaining about the company's name. However, sales continued to rise. Smith sold he controlling interest in the company in 2017 to a private equity fund. Big Ass Fans continue to be seen in many of the distilleries operations, warehouses, and tasting rooms throughout Kentucky and Tennessee.

BUZICK

Where a barrel rests in its wooden cradle in a warehouse is called a rick. Whether you call it a rickhouse, a rackhouse, or a warehouse, the Kentucky and Tennessee hills are filled with these giant buildings. And they are fascinating places. Featuring wood interiors, and filled with thousands of 550-pound wooden barrels, they go on for what seems like forever.

When you start asking questions about these unique edifices, one name pops up again and again: Buzick Construction.

When I inquired about the price for a Buzick rickhouse, one distiller told me $5.5 million. That seems like a lot, and yet many of the distilleries are ordering multiple buildings to handle demand. Even some of the newer distilleries need two or three. Is there a volume discount? Nope. You call, you order it, and they will come to build it. It has positioned itself as the only contractor anyone in Kentucky uses. So the price is the price whether you want one or five. Call up and take a number.

Why are distilleries willing to pay such large amounts? Because these unique buildings require an experienced eye and hand. Most rickhouses are seven stories tall. Distillers don't want them much taller. The heat would be too intense, as well as the weight. Shifting of weight is also a problem. And then of course it's managing more floors than seven. Buzick tends to build them all alike, so that the warehouse men know what they are doing regardless of which building they're in.

Buzick Construction is a fourth-generation, family-owned company. It was founded in 1937 by Cliff Buzick (a former distillery equipment salesman) in Bardstown, Kentucky. Buzick saw that the region lacked qualified construction companies familiar with a distillery's unique needs. Thus Buzick was created to service that industry. And it was an immediate success. Years later, Donald Buzick, Cliff's son, expanded the company's mission to include other types of construction. And expansion has continued apace ever since.

Buzick has built for many of the big names in the bourbon business, including Barton Brands, Buffalo Trace, Four Roses, Heaven Hill, Jim Beam, Maker's Mark, and Wild Turkey. According to the company, "Today, due to the boom in the Bourbon Industry, the distillery trade accounts for more than half of our contracts . . . Because the company owns much of the construction equipment required and has many staff positions associated with subcontractors, such as steel pre-fabrication crews and plumbers, Buzick Construction can self-perform 70 percent of the work on any project."

The structure is built from the inside-out. The entire interior, all seven floors of ricks, is complete before the outside beams and the final walls are put up.

THE CLEAR STUFF:
WHITE WHISKEY, CORN WHISKEY, AND SUGAR WASH

The distilling boom in Tennessee also ushered in a new wave of white whiskeys that rivals those made in Kentucky.

WHITE WHISKEY, MOONSHINE, CORN WHISKEY, WHITE LIGHTNING, CORN LIQUOR: WHAT'S THE DIFFERENCE?

There are some major differences. Moonshine is the generic term that was largely ascribed to illegally made hooch, usually made by moonlight in the woods. Thus it was called moonshine.

Today, moonshine is a generic term, like beer, or whiskey, which describes a segment of the market. However, a little while back, the Alcohol and Tobacco Tax and Trade Bureau allowed commercially made, unaged whiskey to be called moonshine—and sales took off. Today, there are many kinds of "moonshine," or unaged whiskeys, on the market, and many of them are misnamed.

Shine or sugar wash, was traditionally made in the 20th century with simple household sugar.

FOUR KINDS OF MOONSHINE

Even though it may say moonshine on the label, it may not be.

Shine or Sugar Wash – 100 percent refined sugar. Super simple and easy to drink. Little to no nose.

Corn & Cane – A mash of corn and some refined sugar. (Technically, if there is more sugar, it would be called Cane & Corn.) Hints of butter and cereal.

Corn Liquor or White Dog – This is a high corn mash bill. Technically it is unaged whiskey, even though it may be labeled moonshine. The good ones have a nose of buttered popcorn and Cream of Wheat or Corn Flakes.

Unaged Rye – Typically, rye is 51 percent or more of the mash bill. A nose full of gingerbread and spice.

entil... confiscated ... the Internal Revenue
...sury Department.

POPCORN SUTTON
A TENNESSEE MOONSHINE LEGEND

Popcorn Sutton captured the imagination of many. He was funny, irascible, and especially quotable, with little bon mots like, "Jesus turned water into wine, I turned it into likker." With an outlook like that, it is no wonder that Sutton's look—overalls, floppy straw hat, unkempt beard—became the image of the moonshiner in America. Few purveyors of wines, beers, or spirits were ever lionized to this degree. Popcorn was an authentic, loveable, hillbilly anti-hero. In short, a classic moonshiner. The last of a breed.

In 2009, Sky Sutton, Popcorn's estranged daughter, wrote a book entitled *Daddy Moonshine: The Story of Marvin "Popcorn" Sutton*. He was so well-known that Hank Williams III wrote and recorded "Moonshiner's Life" on his 2010 album *Rebel Within* and mentioned Popcorn. Sutton also appeared in the 2011–12 season of Discovery Channel's *Moonshiners* television series. He also self-published an authentic guide to moonshining, which also served as an autobiography, entitled *Me & My Likker*. On top of all this, a coffee table book of photographs, *Popcorn Sutton The Making and Marketing of a Hillbilly Hero* was released in 2012.

Sutton was of Scottish-Irish descent, and came from a long line of moonshiners. He acquired the nickname "Popcorn" after he beat a popcorn machine in a local bar with a pool cue. He ran a junk shop in Maggie Valley in the 1990s while living with a woman named Ernestine Upchurch. Sutton spent most of his life in and out of trouble with local authorities. He was caught selling untaxed liquor in 1974, and in 1981, and again in 1985. He was also charged with possession of controlled substances and assault with a deadly weapon. Despite being convicted, he never served prison time, only probation. In 2007, firefighters arrived at Sutton's Parrottsville property. While trying to extinguish the blaze, more than 650 gallons of untaxed hooch were discovered. Again Sutton was tried and convicted, but received only probation.

Slowly he began to become famous, with little star turns in films about Appalachian life by documentarian Neal Hutcheson. Two that were popular included the 2002 documentaries: *Mountain Talk* and the one that made Sutton famous, *This is the Last Dam Run of Likker I'll Ever Make*. He was again the subject of a feature documentary when he appeared in The History Channel's *Hillbilly: The Real Story*. Later recast, edited, and renamed *The Last One*, it was broadcast on PBS and won a Southeast Emmy Award.

In March 2008, Sutton's property was raided by Federal Marshalls and ATF officers. He had nearly 900 gallons of untaxed, illegal moonshine. In 2009, at the time of his trial and sentencing, Sutton discovered that he had cancer. He pled guilty and asked the court for mercy, hoping that his cancer would reduce his punishment to house arrest. But the judge, citing his probation, appearances on television where he instructed people how to make illegal moonshine, and photographs of him surrounded by a multitude of firearms, sentenced Sutton to 18 months. Depressed, ailing with cancer, and unwilling to go to federal prison, Sutton died from carbon monoxide poisoning in his garage. Popcorn's widow, Pam Sutton, said, "He called it his three-jug car because he gave three jugs of liquor for it."

Sutton's traditional gravestone reads: "Marvin Popcorn Sutton / Ex-Moonshiner / October 5, 1946 / March 16, 2009." But Popcorn had prepared to have the last word in death. At the foot of his grave is a marker he had commissioned decades earlier. It read simply: "Popcorn Said Fuck You."

This became more prevalent during the 1920s. The sugar accounted for a certain smoothness. Another variation was "cane and corn" where sugar was combined with some amount of corn.

Corn whiskey is usually made from a recipe that is predominantly corn, though it may contain some other grains. Corn whiskey is the cornerstone of the entire Kentucky and Tennessee distilling region. It is the bedrock of the industry. In short, corn is the standard of the realm, and corn whiskey is the fuel that makes the industry run.

But what is corn whiskey? Corn whiskey is the distillate that comes from the still. It is made from a mash bill that is at least 51 percent corn, and is probably blended with other grains, usually barley and rye. These three components make up the mash bill of 85 to 90 percent of the bourbons and sour mashes made in the region.

Corn whiskey is uniquely American. Whiskeys sold as white whiskey are usually made of at least 80 percent corn. More often than not they are distilled at 160 proof (or 80 percent ABV).

Unaged rye was a new addition to this category, though these versions usually end up in the whiskey section – not the moonshine section. They are 51 percent rye, and are unaged versions of their brethren that are resting in oak. These whiskeys have gained favor, but were originally launched so the distiller could recoup some of their costs while resting aging stocks for release later. As rye is fairly more expensive than corn, and harder to come by, the retail costs of unaged rye usually reflect those in the bottle price.

But there are differences, subtle differences.

In the beginning moonshine was a quick way to make a buck to pay off your still and distillery. But these days, there are some very good moonshines being made. Indeed, for real aficionados of this spirit, eastern Kentucky and eastern Tennessee have become the Napa and Sonoma of moonshine.

A Dozen Popular Moonshines

Moonshine is a popular item in the United States today. Here are ten moonshines made in Kentucky and Tennessee. Ole Smoky and Lucky are among the most ubiquitous moonshine brands from the region. These are very easy drinking brands that can be used for anything from straight drinking to cocktails and punches..

Ole Smoky Tennessee Moonshine	Jakes Creek Tennessee Moonshine
Hook & Ladder Tennessee Moonshine	Boundary Oak Kentucky Moonshine
Short Mountain Shine Tennessee Moonshine	Lucky Kentucky Moonshine
	Kentucky White Pepper Moonshine
Old Glory Moonshine	LBL Moonshine
Doc Collier Moonshine	Donut Shine
Tennessee Legend Moonshine	

Some Great White Whiskeys to Taste

These are the best white whiskeys made with grain mash bills that you can drink straight. They all have the aroma, body, and taste to stand up to their barrel-aged brethren:

George Dickel & Co. White Corn Whiskey

Hartfield & Co. White Whiskey

Buffalo Trace White Dog Wheated Mash

Nelson's Green Brier Distillery Tennessee Handmade White Whiskey

Natchez Trace Tennessee White Whiskey

Fugitives Manifesto Tennessee Nascent Whiskey

Corn whiskey uses a traditional mash process and is usually sold unaged. If a distillery ages this whiskey, the distillate must be aged in uncharred barrels, at 125 proof (62.5 percent ABV). Most are stored in oak for six months or less. Straight corn whiskey is stored in used or uncharred new oak containers for two years or more. Straight corn whiskey that is aged for at least four years may be designated as "bottled in bond."

But is corn whiskey the same as moonshine? Not necessarily. Historically, moonshine was a slang term used to describe illicitly distilled, high-proof spirits. It was called moonshine because the clandestine stills producing it usually operated out of sight and at night, in remote locations far from prying eyes. This practice began in the Scottish Highlands and was later practiced in the American South. In 2010, federal authorities defined moonshine as "clear, unaged whiskey" and it was being soon sold commercially. Moonshine was usually something between sugar wash and some variation of "corn and cane."

In Tennessee, where moonshine and white whiskey are much more popular, there are even rye white whiskeys. Generally speaking, young craft distilleries make these kinds of spirits because they do not have enough aged whiskey to sell. And, of course, it is because white whiskey is more popular than ever. Thus a portion of their run is made for aging, and the other portion is bottled immediately.

But don't let this rush to market dissuade you—there are some very, very flavorful moonshines and white whiskeys out there. Moonshine and white whiskey are great for cocktails, and you can even make a white mint julep to celebrate the Kentucky Derby.

Another popular item is Tennessee moonshine cake! Who doesn't want a slice of that?

BARREL—AGED MOONSHINE

Most whiskey purists turn their nose up at the thought of such a suggestion. Moonshine aged in bourbon barrels, especially used bourbon barrels, is a monstrosity to them, not worth reviewing. On the other hand, they have sold well in the tasting rooms of small craft distillers.

Most distilleries that make white dog or corn liquor, sell a portion of it unaged to pay their bills and keep the lights on until their bourbon matures. Real moonshiners (people who make sugar wash or corn-and-cane) are not in the same place. But several small distillers have been brave enough to age their moonshines in used bourbon barrels to affect a whiskey's flavor.

This idea of aging moonshine has for a very long time been part of the home vatting market. Many moonshine customers have bought these white whiskeys and aged them at home with barrel aging kits bought from home brewing stores, catalogs, and websites. It is a popular holiday gift. One can either buy charred oak chips or sticks to put in a bottle and watch their whiskey mellow, or buy a small oak barrel from 1 liter to 1.25 gallons. Of course, the idea goes back much farther than that. Many a great-great-grandfather who made hooch, barrel-aged some at one point or another. This is just another trick out of the old rucksack.

The bottles that have been super popular include Boundary Oak's Patton Armored Diesel and Casey Jones' Barrel Cut Moonshine. These resulting elixirs are super easy to drink. They are infinitely smooth, and usually lack a lot of the bite imparted by rye, for instance. They are like light whiskeys, though they can still pack a wallop where alcohol is concerned. But there is often not the burn, the Kentucky Hug, that one usually associates with bourbon or rye. These are easy drinking brown spirits that are gaining more and more favor with younger whiskey enthusiasts, and are popular with moonshiners who want entry into the brown whiskey category.

Bourbon

There is not a clear and simple history of bourbon. No single person invented it, not a single town or county. It is, in the best sense, an American mutt. What we know as bourbon was really a combination of trial and error.

There are many contradictory legends as to how bourbon came about. One is that Baptist minister Elijah Craig was the first to age whiskey in barrels. Jacob Spears was said to have been the first to name his whiskey bourbon (as he was located in Bourbon County). All quaint and fun stories to be told on distillery tours. Certainly, these men made bourbon. But are they its pioneers? Hmmmm.

Bourbon was more or less a product that evolved over time, as different makers throughout an agricultural region traded ideas and recipes over generations. In fact, Louisville historian Michael Veach speculated that the whiskey was an homage to New Orleans' famed Bourbon Street. It was there that this unique American spirit first gained popularity and competed with the more expensive brandies and cognacs. In those days, the barrels were stenciled with the words "Old Bourbon."

It has been speculated that Scottish (and other European) immigrants brought the secrets of distilling with them to the Kentucky hills. Bourbon County was originally organized in 1785 (and was considered more Virginia than Kentucky back then) and became part of Kentucky in 1792.

Bourbon was the king of whiskeys, and all American distilling, from the late 1800s to the 1970s. But in the 1980s and 1990s, vodka, gin, and tequila took a sizable chunk out of bourbon's domestic domination. Many Kentucky distilleries either diverted their manufacturing to making other products, or were shuttered.

Initially, there was no codified law in the making of bourbon. Instead, it was a generic name for corn-based whiskeys. It wasn't until 1964 that the United States Congress passed a resolution recognizing bourbon as a "distinctive product of the United States." The law states that bourbon whiskey could only be made in the United States, and that "the appropriate agencies of the United States Government . . . take appropriate action to prohibit importation into the United States of whiskey designated as 'Bourbon Whiskey.'"

According to the law, bourbon must be made with a minimum of 51 percent corn; it must be aged in new charred oak barrels; it must be stored at no higher than 125 proof; and it must be bottled at no less than 80 proof. Fulfilling these requirements allows it to be called bourbon, and being made in Kentucky from start to finish, and aged a minimum of two years in a barrel, gives the producer the right to use the phrase "Kentucky Straight Bourbon Whiskey."

Bourbon has flavors consistent with caramel, burnt sugar, brown sugar, honey, and stone fruits, and can also feature smokiness, hints of spice and gingersnap, and an oatmeal-vanilla finish.

How old is your bourbon?

Single malt scotch is known around the world for being able to age well, and bottles and barrels decades and decades old have been found and shared with glee. But should bourbon be old? There is some debate about that. Off the record, some distillers will say that they think bourbon peaks at around eight or nine years old. Some feel that the signature brown sugar/caramel notes and slight sweetness begin to fade after that.

Dusty Hunters (enthusiasts who scour flea markets, tag sales, estate sales, and dirty/dusty old liquor stores in search of an ancient bottle) have had some success locating individual bottles of old bourbon. As with all antique bottles of unopened whiskey, the provenance is generally suspect, and the care of the bottle may have compromised the contents.

But some have raved about older bourbon. And the bigger, more established distillers have been selectively bottling some of their oldest vintages. Pappy Van Winkle is famous for this. The flavors are still there. They certainly mellow and combine, and yes, some of the sweetness falls away. But older bourbons offer their own advantages, and are highly sought after by whiskey writers, collectors, aficionados, and fans.

Here are a few excellent, older bourbons for those who prefer older spirits:

Wild Turkey Master's Keep 17 YO Bourbon

Elijah Craig 18 YO Single Barrel

Elijah Craig 23 YO Single Barrel

Knob Creek 2001 Limited Edition

Russell's Reserve 1998

I.W. Harper 15YO

Pappy Van Winkle Family Reserve 15YO

Pappy Van Winkle Family Reserve 20YO

Pappy Van Winkle Family Reserve 25YO

My father was a whiskey drinker. Dewar's. Once, when he came over to my house, he asked if I had any whiskey. I shrugged and told him I had some bourbon. He grimaced and said OK. I poured him a glass with some ice. I handed it to him and he took a tentative sip. He then winced as if he was in pain.

"This shit is so sweet," he said, making a face that resembled a pained Lucille Ball. And that's always been the complaint whiskey drinkers have about bourbon. Especially scotch guys. Bourbon is too sweet. A quintessential, American sugar bomb.

That is, until now.

THE INTERNATIONAL STYLE

In architecture, The International Style emerged in the 1920s and 1930s, and emphasized form and aesthetics more than the social aspects of the modern movement. The most common characteristics of International Style buildings are: rectilinear forms, light, taut plane surfaces that have been completely stripped of applied ornamentation and decoration, open interior spaces, and a visually weightless quality engendered by the use of cantilever construction. Glass and steel, in combination with reinforced concrete, are the characteristic materials of construction.

Famous buildings exhibiting The International Style include New York's Seagram Tower, the United Nations, and Lever House; Boston's Prudential Tower; The Willis Tower (formerly The Sears Tower) in Chicago; and Westmount Square in Quebec.

By prioritizing form over function, the belief was that these buildings could fit any skyline, spreading sophistication and elegance all over the world

THE NEW BOURBON INTERNATIONAL STYLE

During a recent trip to Kentucky and Tennessee, I noticed that several phrases and words kept reoccurring when talking to master distillers. Words like brandy, cognac, stone fruit, and French oak.

These new bourbons tend to be finished (after they are first aged in charred, new American white oak barrels) in various toasts of French oak. This new style of bourbon tastes more like whiskey, brandy, or cognac, and eschews, however slightly, the sweeter profile bourbon is famous for. These bourbons play down the sweet caramel, brown sugar notes in popular American bourbon, and provide a dryer, more sophisticated finish.

Others are choosing port barrels to age their whiskeys. These barrels, as well as sherry barrels, also serve to dampen the famed sweetness.

Nino Marchetti, editor-in-chief of *The Whiskey Wash*, highlighted a number of bourbons made by small craft distilleries: Breckenridge Port Cask Finish, Litchfield Batchers Port Cask Finish, Big Bottom Distilling, Traverse City Distilling, and Luxco Blood Oak, to name a few. Jefferson's Reserve Groth Cask Finish is another solid member of this group.

"Wine cask finished whiskeys, as we've explored before, most commonly take the form of sherry cask aging. Beyond sherry, one sees other fortified wine types as barrel choices, including Madeira and port. Regardless of the wine type, however, the barrels chosen for either exclusive or additional maturation retain elements of their former inhabitant, which can then be carried over to the new resident in smell, taste, and color," wrote Marchetti.

That's a nice, quirky trend when it's in the craft distilling business. But what I observed goes far beyond that.

THE GREAT BRASS RING

For many whiskey makers, the great brass ring has always been the single malt whiskies of Scotland, those whiskies that are sought after by deep-pocketed collectors and aficionados. They command huge prices, and their availability is scarce in many cases.

Bourbon's Achilles' heel is that outside of a few major brands, it does not translate in foreign markets. Jack Daniel's, which in truth is a Tennessee whiskey, and Jim Beam are the two most distributed American whiskeys, with a reach of approximately 160 countries. But bourbon is still a curiosity outside the United States, and JD and JB are seen as iconic brands, rather than a category in a portfolio destined for other nations.

Stephen Kaufman wrote in *Dispatches Europe* magazine in 2016, "The United Kingdom, Germany, and Austria were the biggest markets [for bourbon]. France, Spain, and the Netherlands were significant. But, by-and-large, bourbon's stratospheric growth remains an American phenomenon." He later continued, "According to industry research firm IWSR, US sales of super-premium bourbons rose 28.8 percent from 2011 to 2015. Super-premium cognac sales increased only 9.5 percent during that same period. For some perspective, Euromonitor International found 2015 domestic retail bourbon sales were worth $3.8 billion compared to $1.3 billion worth of cognac. Bourbon sales rose 19.1 percent vs. 8.5 percent for cognac year-over-year growth."

So, it would seem that the bourbon gods have it in their heads to create premium bourbons that can make the jump to the international market, manufacturing a product that resembles the great Scottish whiskies

WHAT ARE THE TENETS OF THESE WHISKEYS?

1. They are a super premium expression/label and meant to be the equal of Johnnie Walker Blue, for example.

2. They tend to be older bourbons, aged a minimum of six to eight years.

3. They are not as sweet, possessing a muted caramel/brown sugar palate and a less sweet finish.

4. They feature more wine wood: red wine, port wine, and sherry cask finishing.

5. They exhibit similar characteristics to scotch, brandy, or cognac.

6. They are perfectly positioned for an international market.

7. They feature more sophisticated and internationally appealing packaging.

8. They come from big producers, not small craft ones. Craft doesn't make it out of the country, and, in most cases, is ignored outside of its respective market.

WHAT ARE THE NEW INTERNATIONAL BOURBONS?

Maker's Mark 46, Angel's Envy, and Woodford Reserve Master's Collection are crafted to woo scotch drinkers and reflect a more international palatee.

I am not suggesting that this is a coordinated effort. Nor has this been sudden. But it has gathered a noticeable momentum of its own.

Several of these taste like a cross between good cognac and a Scottish Highlands single malt. They are made to appeal to an export market. And they are intended to stand shoulder-to-shoulder with the highest expressions of single malt and cognac.

In extensive meetings with master distillers Chris Morris of Woodford Reserve and Greg Davis of Maker's Mark, it was clear that the flavor profile of these bourbons was absolutely intentional. Though their designs on the international market were never made explicit, both men emphasized less brown sugar, while playing up the cognac, brandy, and stone fruit notes.

The only reason I include Angel's Envy in this category is that their bourbons were made specifically for this purpose. Legendary master distiller Lincoln Henderson (whose shadow still looms large over the industry) established these criteria as the hallmarks of Angel's Envy when he came out of retirement and created the new brand with his son and grandsons. It may just prove to be his most lasting contribution.

Henderson and Morris worked together for many years at Woodford and experimented with various finishing techniques. Morris slyly hinted at the numerous single malt whiskey-like expressions that will come out of Woodford Reserve in the next two to three years, an insinuation sure to pique the interest of writers and enthusiasts.

There is no question that Woodford and Maker's Mark are the two bourbons best positioned to seize this brass ring. Morris is one of the legends of the bourbon industry, both the grand Southern man of manners (with a general's steely gaze) and someone who presides over what can only be called the Augusta National of the Kentucky bourbon world.

Davis is more like a champion college football coach. He's a big man with a hardy laugh, a firm handshake, and a determined eye. Both men are not to be trifled with, and yet, both are incredibly friendly, as well as shrewd.

The most recent release from Morris's Woodford Reserve Master's Collection was finished in brandy barrels. And, as its own tasting notes reflect, "Finishing fully matured Woodford Reserve in these barrels does not add any new flavors to the whiskey, but instead accentuates Woodford Reserve's rich dried fruit and nut characteristics that come from our grain recipe and long fermentation process."

Maker's Mark 46 is an incredible dram that takes older bourbon and finishes it at cooler temperatures with French oak staves, so the whiskey only picks up the top char and not the notes from deep inside the wood. The barrel selecting program at Maker's Mark is a story for another time, but it's safe to say that Maker's is positioning itself for a big run at the premium shelf.

Gingersnap versus Nilla Wafer

Most bourbon is made with a portion of rye. Many feel that the rye makes bourbon taste more like whiskey and balances out the sweetness of the corn. Others prefer wheated bourbon. It has a softer, smoother finish. When you're shopping or thinking of tasting the different kinds, think of rye as gingersnap and wheat as a Nilla Wafer.

WHEATED BOURBON

The largest portion of Kentucky's bourbon is made with the traditional mash of corn, barley, and rye. The barley acts as a natural enzyme that breaks down the corn and the rye, and lends its own whiskey notes, of course. Rye adds the ginger/ black pepper finish that balances out the sweetness of the corn.

But there is another group known as wheated bourbons. The mash bill in these recipes is not unlike other bourbons. The proportions of corn and barley remain the same. But the rye is replaced with wheat. The wheat adds a softness to the whiskey, and the classic gingersnap finish is replaced with a smooth, vanilla ending. It is similar to the sensation one gets while eating a Nilla Wafer.

The most notable of the wheated bourbons are Pappy Van Winkle, Old Forester, and W.L. Weller. Larceny is another well-known wheated bourbon. Others include 1792 Sweet Wheat, Old Fitzgerald, and Rebel Yell 100. Fans of these whiskeys call these them "wheaters".

Interestingly, Maker's Mark is also a member of this group. Yet Maker's Mark uses a red winter wheat in its mash bill. As a result, the Maker's Mark is not as soft as the Weller. But it also does not have the bite of other bourbons. The red winter wheat allows Maker's Mark to find a middle ground, and separate itself from the pack.

DISTILLER IN THE RYE

Rye whiskey is currently undergoing a very solid revival in the United States. A small segment of the liquor market, it nevertheless is seeing rapid and significant growth. The revival actually started in the Northeast, where young craft distilleries such as Tuthilltown released a few small-batch ryes that were an instant hit with young mixologists and spirits writers. It even brought the classic Manhattan cocktail back into fashion. This new wave was not lost on the folks in Kentucky and Tennessee, where classic ryes had been made for generations. Rye whiskey production began to swell, and demand somehow remained ahead of it.

Rye whiskey traces its roots in America back to Pennsylvania and Maryland, where rye was one of the predominantly grown grains. In the late 1700s and early 1800s Pittsburgh, Pennsylvania, was the largest distiller of rye whiskey in the United States. Even George Washington made rye whiskey on his estate at Mount Vernon.

Rye went out of fashion during Prohibition and became scarce at the end of that period, and drinks like gin and vodka and the martini had become popular. When American production resumed, a new generation of American drinkers fell in love with the only whiskies available – Canadian and Scotch. Rye was made, but was no longer in demand. A few labels hung on for dear life, like Overholt and Pikesville.

Sazerac Rye Whiskey symbolizes the tradition and history of New Orleans and America's obsession with the spirit. Sazerac dates back to the 1800s, around the time when saloons, veiled as coffeehouses, began lining the streets of New Orleans. It was at the Sazerac Coffee House on Royal Street where local patrons were served toddies made with rye whiskey and Peychaud's Bitters. The libation became known as the "Sazerac" and America's first branded cocktail was born.

Traditionally, rye has always been a part of the mash bills of some of Kentucky's and Tennessee's most popular brands. But of late, it's been a rising star on its own. Tennessee and Kentucky distillers cannot seem to keep rye whiskey on the shelves of America's liquor stores—or behind their own tasting bars.

To be labeled rye whiskey, the mash bill must be at least 51 percent rye. Supporting characters normally include corn and malted barley.

Dave Pickerell, former master distiller of Maker's Mark, and one of the best makers of rye in the world, said that there are two styles of rye whiskey: Monongahela and Baltimore. Monongahela-styled rye whiskey is made from a mash bill of 95 percent rye grain. Baltimore-styled rye whiskey is 51 percent rye (minimum) and a blend of other grains. The straight, 95 percent rye is a big, big whiskey with bold flavor and lots of spice. The Baltimore-styled ryes tend to be a bit smoother, but still have that pop of spice and pepper that rye drinkers look for.

Today, rye content is another marker of quality or flavor or both. Some distillers will stress the point that theirs is a high-rye bourbon (usually around 20 to 25 percent, thought Old Dominic in Tennessee has a high-rye bourbon of 40 percent). Or that theirs is a high rye, usually meaning 80-95 percent.

From 2010 to 2015 rye demand grew slowly. However, rye went from zero-to-sixty in about a second flat between 2015 and 2020. And distillers raced to meet the demand. Bourbon drinkers who wanted a less sweet, punchier flavor embraced the gingersnap essence of the whiskey. Another harbinger was the rise of the Manhattan, which also came back into vogue in high-end cocktail lounges across the country. Suddenly, rye was everywhere.

There are several excellent eye-opening expressions that have been exotically finished. Woodford Reserve Barrel Finished Rye has been oaked with new barrels twice (the second being lightly charred and heavily toasted). Angel's Envy finishes their rye in rum casks. Kentucky Peerless did a collaboration project with Copper & Kings, finishing their high rye in C&K's absinthe barrels. Rabbit Hole finishes their rye in PX Sherry Casks. Minor Case Rye Whiskey also produces a Sherry Cask Finish that is notable.

For those that like their expressions pure, Russell's Reserve Single Barrel and Russel's Reserve Small Batch score high with most reviewers, Michter's Single Barrel Rye and Jack Daniel's Single Barrel Rye are also popular. New Riff Kentucky Straight Rye with a mash bill of 95 percent rye is another list topper, as is Willett Estate Cask Stength 3YO.

GREAT RYES FROM KENTUCKY AND TENNESSEE:

Willet Straight Rye Whiskey

Woodford Kentucky Straight Rye Whiskey

Michter's Barrel Strength Rye Whiskey

Kentucky Peerless Small Batch Rye Whiskey

Jack Daniel's Single Barrel Special Reserve Tennessee Rye Whiskey

Davidson Reserve Tennessee Straight Rye Whiskey

Russell's Reserve Kentucky Straight Rye Single Barrel

Thomas H. Handy Sazerac Rye Whiskey

Rabbit Hole Straight Rye Whiskey

Basil Hayden Dark Rye

George Dickel Chill Filtered Rye Whiskey

Leiper's Fork Straight Rye Whiskey

THREE GREAT
WHITE RYE WHISKEYS

LEIPER'S FORK NATCHEZ TRACE WHITE RYE WHISKEY

Leiper's Fork Distillery makes a white rye whiskey. Suspicious at first? No kidding. But wow! Something really, really different! Made from a mash bill of 70 percent rye, 22 percent corn, and 8 percent malted barley, this white whiskey features big notes of white pepper and spice, with a terrific nuttiness, and a hint of anise in its traditional gingersnap ending. This is a white rye to drink neat or with one ice cube. There is a lovely hint of petrol when you add a single ice cube, and the flavor is just so much more lovely. Terrific product!

JACK DANIEL'S UNAGED TENNESSEE RYE WHISKEY

This was a limited-edition whiskey — the first unaged whiskey in Jack Daniel's history, if recent memory is to be trusted. Spirits writer Gregg Jarahian said this on Eat.Drink.Repeat: "Jack Daniel's explains the Unaged Tennessee Rye as Jeff Arnett's exploration into the intriguing flavor drawn from premium rye. It's the first time since before Prohibition the Jack Daniel's Distillery has used a new grain recipe . . . The Unaged Rye grain bill is 70 percent rye, 18 percent corn, and 12 percent barley malt." The result? An incredibly well-rounded dram of unaged whiskey with huge hints of spice, gingersnap, and white pepper, but with that classic Jack Daniel's smoothness. Amazing!

CORSAIR WRY MOON

Corsair Distilling in Nashville is one of the most forward thinking craft distilleries in America. It makes its Wry Moon unaged Kentucky whiskey pot distilled with malted rye. And, of course, it makes it in very small batches. It uses its antique whiskey wash still to do it. This truly handmade whiskey starts off with lovely cereal notes, then features bursts of spice, and finishes with a classic pepper twang. Another incredible whiskey from some of the distilling world's most brilliant minds.

How to Taste Whiskey

You taste all whiskey the same way—bourbon, rye, Tennessee whiskey, moonshine, or just generic whiskey. It makes no difference. You might experience, smell, or taste different things. But the process is the same.

The first thing you need is the proper glass. If you ever see a real whiskey tasting glass, you'll think it has more in common with a champagne flute than the rocks glass you associate with whiskey. That's because to appreciate the nuance in a whiskey, you need a tasting vessel that focuses or funnels the bouquet, or aromas, in a manner that allows them to be appreciated. Is it necessary to have one of these glasses? No. But you might want to try using a smaller wine glass for tasting if you don't have one of these, instead of the lovely rocks glasses you have in your home bar or cupboard.

First, to taste whiskey, you only pour a small amount. It's not a drinking contest. We're savoring. One finger of whiskey—sideways, not downward!—is all you need.

SEE

Why do we look at whiskey? I'll tell you the same thing I tell wine people. Have you ever eaten anything—a hamburger, a steak, or a lobster—without looking at it first? Isn't that an absolutely crucial part of the dining experience? When you are in a restaurant, and the waiter sets down a dish at a neighboring table, haven't you asked, "Hey, what's that?" with envy? How about when you watch your favorite food show on television and you start getting hungry? That's how important sight is when you are eating.

What are you looking for in whiskey? Color, clarity, and legs. Color can range anywhere from pale straw or pale gold to a burnt amber or brown sherry (especially in bourbon). Usually the older the whiskey, the darker the color, but that isn't always true. Bourbons tend to be the darkest. One also

has to remember that caramel coloring is allowed to be added to whiskey to improve desirability. The younger ones usually have that to make them look like their older counterparts.

SWIRL

Adding oxygen to whiskey allows it to reach its full potential, so you'll want to air it out a bit. You do this to accentuate the nose of the whiskey. This means you'll have to give your glass a swirl.

OK, next thing: don't spill the whiskey. If you try to fill the glass, you won't be able to swirl. It's a gentle swirl, not an Olympic event. The best way to learn to swirl is to leave the glass on the table and gently move the base of the glass in a small circular motion. The liquid will swirl easily. Two or three times usually does it. The idea is to coat the sides of the glass with whiskey. This does two things—it aerates the whiskey and it allows you to see the viscosity.

When the whiskey settles back down into the bowl of the glass, the sides of the glass will be coated with liquid. You will notice rivulets descending downward. These are known as legs. Legs are nothing more than a gauge of the whiskey's viscosity. Viscosity usually indicates glycine, sugar, and alcohol. The more pronounced the legs are, the bigger and chewier the whiskey you are about to sample.

SMELL

Ever walk into a house where someone has been cooking a pot roast for about an hour? Or making a big batch of spaghetti sauce (or gravy, whichever term you use)? Or baking brownies? Doesn't it just absolutely make you drool? How about when you walk into a barbecue joint? Or smell a sizzling steak? That's why we smell whiskey. Like any other tasting experience, smell is an important part.

The whiskey glasses of today intensify the sensation of smell by spiraling the aromas of the liquid up to the rim of the glass. What are we hoping to find when we smell? Good and bad things. For example, scents like ripe apples and pears, cereal, grass, wood, florals, smoke, and maple syrup are excellent smells to find in whiskeys. Mushrooms, dank basements, and dirty sweat socks are not good smells in any whiskey.

The vocabulary comes later, but don't be intimidated. It should be fun. It should be enjoyable.

Here's another way to understand how the whiskey glass intensifies smell. Get a nice aromatic cheese and cut a cube. Throw it into an empty whiskey or wine glass. Put one hand over the top of the glass and keep it there while you swirl the glass with the other hand. Shake it up and down. Knock that cube around. Stop. Lift your hand off and smell what's in the glass. It's an amazing sensation. That will help you understand what the proper glass can do. That's the difference it can make.

SIP

When we say "sip," we mean sip. No gulps. The idea is to really try to taste the whiskey. What are we tasting for? There are several characteristics. The foremost among them is whether the whiskey is sweet or dry? Bourbons tend to be on the sweeter side. Single malts tend to be on the drier side. But there's no hard-and-fast rule. Is it harsh or smooth as you roll it around your mouth?

How intense is this whiskey experience? Soft, smooth, hard, harsh? Since whiskey is usually at 80 proof or higher, the finished product is about the alcohol as much as the production and handling of the liquid. Did the distiller coddle the product? Nurture it? Or has it been pushed out the door way too early?

Some people like a bracing shot of whiskey. Others prefer a smoother experience.

What is the mouthfeel you are experiencing? What's the finish like? Is it spicy? Are you getting spices like pepper or fennel or clove or allspice at the end? Are you getting fruitcake or leather? Shortbread cookies or rubber? These are all flavors you might run into.

SAVOR

What do you taste?

Let the experience linger. Don't gulp and get ready for the next swig. Slow down. What are the flavors remaining in your mouth 15 to 30 seconds later? How about after 45 seconds? Does the flavor last? Does it disappear quickly? Is the lingering flavor attractive to you or not?

Just Add Water

Once your tasting experience is complete, now you need to repeat it. But this time you are going to add water. Yes! Just a little bit. This is what will open up the whiskey. It is akin to letting wine breathe, but even more so. With whiskey, we add water. Look, swirl, smell, sip, savor all over again now that there's a little water in it. In some cases it may remain very similar. Sometimes water makes a world of difference. What has it done to yours?

How Master Distiller Dave Pickerell Nosed a Whiskey

I sat trying bourbons and whiskeys from around the world with the late Dave Pickerell, master distiller and industry icon who passed away in 2018. Pickerell was the master distiller at Maker's Mark for 14 years, and skyrocketed to even greater fame with several craft distilleries—most notably Hillrock Estate and Whistle Pig. We were in a tasting room with a small group of people, and Dave had time to explain a great many things.

I watched intensely, to understand how such an accomplished master distiller noses a glass of whiskey.

"Never stick your nose directly into a glass of whiskey. The alcohol will burn your olfactory system," he said. "First, hold the glass slightly away and breathe in through your mouth. You'll be able to pick up a lot more."

The former West Point chemistry professor (and graduate, who played offensive tackle back in the day) has nosed thousands of drams in his time and created some of the world's best whiskeys. Here is how he explains the second crucial part of nosing: "Next, put the glass all the way to one side of your nose, and 'roll' or wave it slowly and completely to the other side of your nose. Slowly. Your olfactory glands are not equal. They work differently, pick up or sense different things. So roll the glass from one side to the other. That way you have the best chance of picking up the nuances of the whiskey."

Secrets of Sipping with Freddie Johnson of Buffalo Trace

There is nothing any whiskey aficionado would like more than to tour the Buffalo Trace Distillery with the distinguished Freddie Johnson. He is easily one of the most famous of the distillery's employees, comes from one of bourbon's most accomplished families, and is tour guide extraordinaire.

To Johnson, bourbon is not just a tug on a bottle of whiskey. He once told whiskey journalist Melissa Alexander, "For every day that we walk this earth, there will always be more barrels of bourbon being made. But friends and family will not always be nearby. So when you bring the bottle out, enjoy the moment, because that's what bourbon is made for."

Johnson explains that there are several secrets to tasting bourbon, especially high-proof, cask-strength bourbon.

"First, make sure you jostle a bottle of cask-strength bourbon before you pour it. There may be some sediment in the bottle. You want your guests to have some of that sediment. It is part of the whiskey, and should be something they experience. It is slight, and hard to see, but," he insists, "it is often there. Especially expensive bourbons, which tend to sit for a long time on people's bars without being touched. Just a gentle turn of the bottle, maybe tilting it sideways gently.

"First, take a very, very small sip of the whiskey. Let it sit on your tongue. Swish it around a touch. Now swallow. When you swallow the whiskey, do not inhale! Calmly exhale. Let all that alcohol out before you breathe in. This does not only reduce the burn of whiskey, especially high-proof whiskey, but allows more air to get at the whiskey so you can taste it better.

"Now, take a small sip of water. Very small. Hold just the slightest bit of water on your tongue for a second. Just a good enough coating on your tongue to know it's still wet. Then take another small sip of whiskey. Let that blend with the water on your tongue and swish it around. Swallow and exhale again.

"Now, you will truly taste the whiskey."

This is how he tastes bourbon at Buffalo Trace.

KENTUCKY CRAFT DISTILLING IN THE SHADOW OF BOURBON

By Richard Thomas

Despite Kentucky's standing as the home of bourbon, "America's native spirit," craft distilling, was not only born elsewhere, it took a long time to set down roots in the Bluegrass. The Barrel House Distillery and Corsair Artisan both started operations in 2008, with Corsair quickly carving out a place for itself with its wide-ranging experiments with smoked grains. Yet Corsair soon shifted most of its operation from Bowling Green to Nashville, Tennessee. In Lexington, The Barrel House went largely unnoticed, even among locals, overshadowed by Kentucky's big distilleries.

Compared to states like Colorado, New York, and Texas, where the pioneering efforts of one or two startups led to plenty of media attention and a statewide explosion of small distilleries, Kentucky's follow-on starts in making spirits came much later. However late in coming, though, the state now has a vibrant craft sector, one in which each distillery has had to find its way in a state dominated by many of the country's largest whiskey makers.

Even today, with well over a thousand craft distilleries in operation in America, a new, small distillery often fires up its equipment in a place where lawmakers, regulators, and taxmen are still trying to figure out how to handle them, and local drinkers and tourists view them as at least a minor novelty. In Kentucky, a new distiller gets started in a setting that has hosted a spirits industry continuously since before Kentucky was a state, operating even during Prohibition. Conditions in the Bluegrass create a unique playing field for the craft sector, with circumstances that help, hinder, and even exploit the business of making liquor in distinctively local ways.

The Dries Shall Tax Your Liquor

One of the peculiar contradictions of life in Kentucky is that it is home to most of America's big whiskey distilleries, an $8.5 billion industry that employs 17,500 people, according to the Kentucky Distillers Association (KDA). Yet it is also a state that is full of people who believe that drinking booze is a sin and a source of yet more sin, and these people have made it a point to exploit the liquor business wherever they can't simply stamp it out.

Although only 20 counties in the Commonwealth are absolutely bone-dry, with old-school Prohibition in full effect, dozens of others have varying degrees of restriction on the sale of alcohol, to say nothing of its production. Even Louisville, the state's largest city and a town long associated with the triple vices of drinking, smoking, and betting on horses, had a dry district right up until January 2017.

Counties that ban or tightly restrict alcohol still benefit from the state taxes raised from their production and sale elsewhere, however, as most of those go into the state's General Fund. And with such a keen, some would say retributive, interest from so many across the state, those taxes are manifold.

If you make whiskey, as almost all craft distilleries in Bourbon Country do, there is the ad valourem tax, assessed on each and every full barrel of aged spirits kept in inventory, year after year. That tax is unique not just in America, but the world. Scotland, Ireland, Japan, and Canada don't have anything like it, nor does Tennessee. Only Kentucky has adopted this peculiar tax, and it makes aging a stock of brown spirits more expensive.

Many craft distilleries, such as Three Boys Farm Distillery outside Frankfort, count on retail sales out their door as a key source of revenue, and Kentucky levies an 11 percent alcohol tax on that, well above the general sales tax. Then there are excise taxes, fees, and all manner of devices designed to pry cash out of those in the business of making and/or selling liquor.

"Kentucky taxes are terrible," says Jay Erisman, an executive at New Riff Distilling in Northern Kentucky and one-time writer for *Whisky Advocate*. "They are the second-highest in the nation. Only Alaska is worse. Alcohol is taxed at every level."

University of Louisville economist Paul Coomes concurs; at least as far as distilled spirits are concerned, ranking Kentucky taxes as the second highest in America. While every small distiller in the nation faces the same federal tax burden, Kentucky craft distillers face a particularly odious situation. At 34.4 cents per dollar of output, the bourbon industry is the most taxed of all 536 officially defined industries in the state, according to the KDA.

After including federal taxes, "nearly 60 percent of every bottle goes to taxes and fees, with seven different taxes on bourbon," says John Pogue, distiller at Old Pogue.

The best contrast is America's other major whiskey state, Tennessee, which has lower taxes than Kentucky. It's an ironic state of affairs when you consider that Tennessee passed statewide Prohibition in 1909, something Kentucky never did, and a decade before Prohibition went national. Yet Darek Bell, founder of Corsair Distillery (which to this day has a foot in both Kentucky and Tennessee), describes his aggregate taxes as slightly below the national average of 54 percent of the value of the bottle.

Fire Safety

In most places, it is a novel experience to have a distillery cranking out high-proof alcohol, let alone put it in oak barrels and store it in a warehouse. Kentucky is one of the few states in the Union where that practice has been the norm for all of living memory. While your typical micro-distillery faces few, or even no, regulatory hurdles for storing its barrels full of brown liquor as it ages, Kentucky has plenty of them.

Fire safety is serious business, of course. One only needs to look at the inferno that consumed much of Heaven Hill's original Bardstown plant in 1996 to understand that. However, that infamous event also highlights what Kentucky's regulations regarding the safe storage of whiskey and other spirits in barrels are designed around: big distillers with hundreds of thousands of barrels stored in several multistory rickhouses on a large piece of property.

Even among those Kentucky craft distilleries making whiskey, not all need to build rickhouses, and those that do are not erecting the seven-floor structures so familiar to the Kentucky landscape. Even so, requirements for fire suppression, spacing between buildings, spillage and run-off control, and a host of other issues are basically the same for one small rickhouse as for a collection of big ones.

Josh Quinn, co-founder of Boone County Distilling Co., regards rickhouse regulations as the single largest barrier to entry he encountered in starting his distillery. "It's all in the name of safety, so we support it 100 percent, but it's just really, really expensive."

Elsewhere in the country, where there hasn't been a distilling industry sitting on top of a million-plus barrels going back decades, there isn't as much regulation. When asked of Texas requirements for warehousing his bourbon, Dan Garrison of Garrison Brothers said, "Those rules all relate to [federal] TTB issues. The state has no regs relating to warehousing."

Shelves And Sign Space
Distribution is a decidedly mixed bag for Kentucky's small distillers. Although some have had positive experiences and gotten their products into big chains and mom-and-pop shops alike, others have not been so fortunate.

"Distribution," says Ross Caldwell of Three Boys Farm Distillery "is a high volume game. If you can't have a tractor-trailer pull up around back and fill it, those guys don't want to talk to you."

"One of the most frustrating challenges is distribution, in and out of state," says Peg Hays of Casey Jones, a western Kentucky legal moonshine distillery. "It should not be so hard to get a distributor."

Distribution is not the only headache for Kentucky micro-distillers, especially those not situated in Louisville, where "urban bourbon" tourism puts visitors on the doorstep. Getting on-site retail sales means drawing in visitors, and a key aid in doing this is having an official sign on a nearby interstate or highway. Getting that signage is a common source of complaint if you aren't a big distiller.

"This process has been interesting, to put it mildly," says Hays. After being told about a Kentucky Transportation Cabinet program to speed up the placement of those brown road signs at a KDA meeting in January, Hays was eager to get started. "We were quickly roadblocked, and then were told that the sign program we were applying for had been discontinued. We are now working on another sign program, wayfinding, that is a completely different and more expensive and difficult project. Kentucky Transportation seems to be consistent in that anytime you deal with them it is long, arduous, and difficult."

This Old Kentucky Home
Even with these difficulties, being a distillery in Kentucky has a big upside, and no small distillery in the state wishes it had started its enterprise somewhere else. After all, Kentucky is synonymous with bourbon.

"If you have a farm in Idaho and want to open a distillery, sell the farm and move to Kentucky. People want Kentucky bourbon," says Erisman.

If the Dries want to squeeze the liquor business of tax dollars and much else is geared for big producers, the presence of those big producers means a lot of necessary infrastructure is already in the state, ready to meet the needs of a craft distillery. The famous Vendome Copper & Brassworks (see page 38) is located in Louisville, and plenty of distilleries great and small have equipment bearing the Vendome plaque on it, testifying to the handiwork of a firm that has been building stills for more than a century. For nano-distilleries and those who want to avoid Vendome's nine-month waiting list, there are Hillbilly Stills and Rockypoint Stills in western Kentucky. The value of having the guys who built your copper pot or column literally down the highway cannot be overstated when it comes to installations and repairs.

Being in Kentucky also means you are in the right place for barrels. Independent Stave Company has one of its major cooperages in Bardstown, Kelvin Cooperage is in Louisville, Speyside Cooperage is in Shepherdsville, and Robinson Stave Company is in East Bernstadt.

While not every distillery gets both its still and its barrels in-state, it's rare for a company to go out of state for both, and copper and wood aren't the end of the local distilling infrastructure. If a custom strain of yeast is required, Ferm Solutions (the elder sister company of Wilderness Trace Distillery) is on hand in Danville. Finally, companies like Big Ass Fans (see page 43) and Sellers Manufacturing (who make boilers) furnish other types of equipment frequently seen in distilleries big and small around the state.

Another aspect of Kentucky's bourbon infrastructure that helps small distillers is the KDA. Although this well-established trade organization was founded by and for the big distillers, the KDA has embraced the craft category in its membership and created a craft subsection for the Kentucky Bourbon Trail.

Through the KDA and on their own, the big distillers also help create a conducive environment for small operators in other ways. When Silver Trail Distillery suffered its tragic still explosion in 2015, it could have been the beginning of a period of overreaction, putting a well-intentioned but ill-informed burden on small distillers. New Riff's Erisman, among others, pointed to the role of the big distillers at that juncture in calming things down at the state capitol. The big guys were protecting their own interests, of course, but in doing so they saved the little guys from potentially worse hurt.

Those trickle-down effects are not universal, or distributed evenly. Small moonshine distillers, like Casey Jones, or Kentucky Mist in eastern Kentucky, are far removed from the heart of "Bourbon Country" in central Kentucky, and thus sometimes don't get the same level of traffic as, say, Peerless Distillery in Louisville or Bluegrass Distillers in Lexington. Even a place like Limestone Branch in Lebanon is better situated, because of its proximity to Maker's Mark. Being in Kentucky does not guarantee steady walk-in traffic.

Hitting The Trail
Perhaps the biggest boon is the impact that the Bourbon Boom has had on interest in whiskey on the population at large. In a direct sense, that translates into more tourism and the aforementioned in-house retail sales, both of bottles and (in most cases) at the bar. While it is true that most people touring the state and visiting its distilleries are there to see how their favorite big brand whiskey is made, there is a genuine interest in craft whiskey, too. That pulls people in through the doors of the small distilleries.

Despite this, the very real interest in craft spirits seems to ensure that everyone in the state catches at least a little of the boom times, even in the remote reaches of the Land Between the Lakes area and coal country. In recent years, over 1,000,000 visitors have come to

Kentucky for bourbon, year in and year out, and of those, hundreds of thousands of people have visited the eleven distilleries that are part of the KDA's craft trail.

The Bourbon Boom has even helped one distillery with the distribution hurdle. "One of the things that has helped us from the start is the idea of bourbon from Bourbon County," says Andrew Buchanan of Hartfield & Co., a nano-distillery in Paris. "It got our white rum and vodka in the door at Liquor Barn."

Sell Me Kentucky Bourbon

A less obvious effect of the Bourbon Boom is how some of Kentucky's larger craft outfits have found a revenue stream in becoming contract distillers. New Riff Distilling contracts out 55 percent of its current production capacity, while Bardstown Bourbon Company (a craft member of the KDA, although admittedly larger than what most people think of when they think "craft distillery") is based in large part on the model of being a contract distiller.

Both Three Boys Farm and Boone County Distilling report having received plenty of contract distilling inquires, and, Quinn added, "I was talking to a guy in New York with a 12-inch column still, but they can't contract out their extra time because no one wants New York bourbon."

Contract distilling has become a common feature for many small distillers in the state, although few who are engaged in it are willing to admit to it openly, and almost none are free to identify a client. Confidentiality has long been a characteristic of contract distilling in Kentucky. But the demand for bourbon that can be identified on the label as being "Made in Kentucky" has created an almost "if you build it, they will come" scenario for the state's craft distillers. As the big distillers have their hands full meeting their own skyrocketing demands, plenty of room exists for others to move into this market.

As America's leading whiskey-making state, Kentucky presents its own particular mix of challenges, benefits, and opportunities for craft distillers. While companies like Jim Beam and Brown-Forman certainly cast long shadows, they don't crowd out the field so much as deny a place in the sun for the little guy. Despite the unique difficulties, stories of small distillers achieving their ten-year business plan in three years or less and working on expansion are not uncommon, as the Bourbon Boom lifts all boats.

LABROT & GRAHAM
DISTILLERY

One of Kentucky's oldest working distilleries was built on Grassy Springs Branch of Glenn's Creek by Elijah Pepper about 1812. His son, Oscar Pepper, later hired Dr. James Crow as master distiller. Crow perfected the art of bourbon making by introducing scientific methods. The Labrot & Graham Distillery succeeded Old Pepper's in 1878.

Presented by Brown - Forman Corp.

BOURBON LIQUEURS AND CREAM

Traditionally in Bourbon Country, bourbon liqueurs were a popular subset. Often brought out for hunting and the holidays, these sweet potions, made with a base of bourbon, and their slightly lower ABV, were the perfect offering of Southern hospitality. But in the last decade, they seem to have come out of grandma's cupboard and found a whole new fan base.

The most commercially famous of all the liqueurs was Southern Comfort. Bartender Martin Wilkes Heron (1850–1920) was working at McCauley's Tavern in the Lower Garden District, not far from the French Quarter in New Orleans, Louisiana, when he created Southern Comfort in 1874. The original name of the cocktail was called Cuffs and Buttons. In 1889, Heron patented his elixir and set up shop in Memphis,

Tennessee. Southern Comfort won the gold medal at the 1904 World's Fair in St. Louis, Missouri.

Spirits historian Chris Morris noted that the original whiskey began with good-quality bourbon that was mixed with "an inch of vanilla bean, about a quarter of a lemon, half of a cinnamon stick, four cloves, a few cherries, and an orange bit or two." Heron let the mixture steep for days. After separating the ingredients he added local honey.

Brown–Forman purchased the brand in 1979. Then in January 2016 the Sazerac Company bought the brand. Over the years neutral spirits had been introduced to the formula.

Also among the most famous and widespread of these liqueurs is craft

producer Pritchard's Sweet Lucy. Sweet Lucy has been flowing up and down the Mississippi flyway for years. This bourbon-based formula is blended with apricot and orange and it has warmed the body and soul of outdoorsmen for years. This is a true southern favorite.

Another such success is from Nelson's Greenbrier Distillery – Louisa's Liqueur. Louisa's Liqueur is named for the woman who single-handedly ran the distillery from 1891 to 1909. This coffee-caramel-pecan liqueur has taken off like a shot for the newly reinvented distillery.

Buffalo Trace Bourbon Cream is the bestselling of the bourbon-based cream liqueurs. Bourbon Cream is a handcrafted pairing of Buffalo Trace Kentucky Straight Bourbon and cream. This liqueur is rich and sweet, with hints of caramel and creamy vanilla. Very much like its Irish cream shelf brethren, but with a slightly more decadent taste. Boone County Bourbon Cream is also very good. Ezra Brooks Bourbon Cream from Heaven Hill is another popular bourbon cream.

Another popular entry is Tennessee Sipping Cream from the Pennington Distilling Company, which is made with classic Tennessee whiskey and real cream. The original is the most popular, but it also comes in a number of flavors, most popular of which are the Mocha and the Pumpkin Spice.

Last but not least, Evan Williams Original Southern Eggnog is the most ubiquitous of the whiskey based eggnogs. Real dairy cream and 7-Year-Old Kentucky Bourbon are blended, producing a thick, sweet liqueur with a nose of créme brúlée and nutmeg, with notes of vanilla and bourbon bread pudding.

Hand Sanitizer

Of course, we don't drink hand sanitizer, but it is an important footnote to this story as the updated edition of this book is being written. Just as many distilleries (breweries and wineries) had to adjust to life during Prohibition – some were able to pivot, many did not or could not — the coronavirus pandemic has caused a multitude of problems for the distilling industry.

The federal government looked on workers in the wine, beer, and spirits industry as "essential workers." That meant workers were obliged to keep reporting for work despite record numbers of illnesses and deaths. But as this issue confronted the industry, different players met the challenge in different ways.

No question, alcohol consumption rose steadily throughout the pandemic. Stores that sold liquor saw serious spikes in purchasing. But that affected only the larger producers. The larger distilleries who profited from third-party retailers kept on making whiskey, albeit, with reduced staffs.

But the smaller craft beverage producers were slammed hard. Those distilleries depended on customer sales through their own registers. With consumers at home, many small craft distillers saw less folks in the tasting room, and dollars became scarce. Distilleries were faced with some stark choices. Many distillers started offering curbside pick-up, still others offered delivery and shipping.

Many of these small distilleries began producing hand sanitizer. Even a few of the big guys joined in, such as Evan Williams and Jim Beam, to help out in the crisis. Sanitizer was in severe shortage, especially at the beginning of the pandemic. Major retailers saw their stocks wiped out in days. In Kentucky and Tennessee many smaller distilleries rose to the challenge. They immediately swapped out their necessary parts and ingredients and began producing hand sanitizer. In many cases, portions, if not all of the initial inventory, were donated to various town organizations. Many of these products were quickly made, and lacked governmental approval. Fast-tracking of sanitizer approval by the government quickly opened the floodgates. Many followed guidelines of the World Health Organization, but also had to follow FDA regulations as well. These distilleries were seen as heroes. Overall, according to the Kentucky Distiller Association, 27 of their members donated more than 125,000 gallons of sanitizer across the commonwealth. That's about 630,000 750 ml whiskey bottles worth of sanitizer.

Kentucky Governor Andy Beshear said, "These companies worked quickly and tirelessly to source the materials and manufacture this essential product for Kentuckians fighting on the front lines of this pandemic. I am grateful and proud to have the KDA and its members on Team Kentucky."

Tennessee distillers also banded together. "We saw a need in our communities, and we are on a mission to make a difference," said Kris Tatum, president of Tennessee Distillers Guild. "It's a great feeling when competitors collectively decide to put profits aside and jointly decide to support the communities that have made us successful in the first place."

"We're trying to help government entities, including fire departments, police stations, physicians offices, and other businesses that are the heartbeat of our state and still on the front lines serving the public and keeping the economy going," said Greg Eidam, head distiller at Sugarlands Distilling Company in Gatlinburg, Tennessee. Many of the craft distilleries in Tennessee answered that same call, donating hand sanitizer to police and fire departments, EMTs, and other frontline workers.

Soon, these small distilleries began to offer their sanitizers for sale. Slowly, the larger commercial manufacturers caught up with the demand, and with distilleries allowed to reopen in summer, with outdoor tastings, the hand sanitizer explosion waned, and the distillers went back to making spirits. But years from now, small bottles of hand sanitizers produced by craft whiskey distillers will be the stuff of legend, much like prescription alcohol and malted beverages from the 1920s.

Two Kentucky Classics

The Mint Julep is the quintessential Kentucky cocktail. The word "julep" derives from the Persian word for a sweet rosewater syrup, gulab. Back in the day, these drinks were issued to help make medicine go down. American mint juleps were mostly medicinal, lightly alcoholic concoctions blended with camphor.

The history of the Julep dates as far back as a mention in Medical Communications, a doctor's firsthand account of administering the drink: "sickness at the stomach, with frequent retching, and, at times, a difficulty of swallowing. I then prescribed her an emetic, some opening powders, and a mint julep."

The first printed cocktail recipe appeared in a book by John Davis published in London in 1803, in which it was described as "a dram of spirituous liquor that has mint steeped in it, taken by Virginians of a morning."

The great popularizer of the drink was the iconic Senator Henry Clay of Kentucky, who introduced the drink to Washington, D.C., at the Round Robin Bar in the famous Willard Hotel in the early half of the 19th century. It eventually made it into the famed 1862 edition of *Bar-Tenders Guide: How to Mix Drinks* or *The Bon-Vivant's Companion* by Jerry Thomas.

The Mint Julep cemented it place in history through its association with the Kentucky Derby, starting in 1938. It is estimated that more than 120,000 juleps are served at Churchill Downs the weekend of the Kentucky Oaks and Kentucky Derby each year.

"While spectators in the stands of the Kentucky Derby sip Mint Juleps, tailgaters in the parking lot gather around 'Kentucky Classics,' a cocktail of Ale-8 and bourbon," wrote Mandy Naglich in VinePairs.com.

If the Mint Julep is the Grand Dame of Kentucky cocktails, her back-porch sister is certainly a Kentucky Mule, more classically, if you're at a BBQ or a tailgate, a bourbon and Ale 8!

Ale 8 (officially named Ale-8-One, but known locally as Ale 8) was created by soda bottler G. L. Wainscott in 1926. Allegedly it was originally named "A Late One" and eventually morphed into "Ale-8-One." It is generally thought to be a blending of ginger ale and citrus flavors. They've been selling the soda ever since. It is an iconic Southern brand. Until 2001 it was only available in Kentucky, but can now be found all over the South and as far west as Texas.

Vodka

Pickers Vodka from SPEAKeasy Distillers (now Pennington Distillery)

Walton's Finest Vodka from SPEAKeasy Distillers (now Pennington Distillery)

Pyramid Vodka

Black Mule Vodka from Tenn South Distillery

Big Machine Vodka from Tenn South Distillery

Old Glory Tennessee Vodka

Old Dominick Memphis Vodka

Corsair Vanilla Bean

Lass & Lions Vodka

Old Forge Vodka

Kore Vodka from PostModern Spirits

Tennessee Legend Vodka

Tennessee Valley Vodka from Knox Whiskey Works

A Side Note on Gin and Vodka

While whiskey, bourbon, and rye tend to be the products most closely associated with Kentucky and Tennessee, there is still a substantial output of vodka and gin in these states. Some of the bigger distilleries have been making these spirits for years.

Gins and vodkas have been produced in the region under such labels as Burnett's, Barton, Heaven Hill, Crystal Palace Gin, Czarina Gin, Fleischmann's Gin, Glenmore Gin, Mr. Boston Gin, and many more.

But the craft distilling boom has brought with it a whole new wave of vodkas and gins. Here are a few to watch out for.

Gin

Corsair Artisan Gin

Corsair Genever

Corsair Barrel Aged Gin

Crane City Gin from Nashville Craft Distillery

Ginferous Gin from Pos Modern Spirits

Jackson Avenue Gin from Knox Whiskey Works

Rum

Prichard's Fine Rum

Prichard's Fine Rum Private Stock

Angry Pecker Rum from Tennessee Hills Distillery

Old Forge Rum

Renegade Rum from Thunder Road Distilling

Barreled Renegade Rum from Thunder Road Distilling

Naked Biscuit from Nashville Craft Distilling

While Nashville Craft Distilling's Naked Biscuit doesn't exactly qualify as a rum (since it's not derived from cane sugar or molasses), it is for all intents and purposes a very good rum! How is that? Well, staying in the true nature of being Southern, Naked Biscuit utilizes one of the region's most popular sugar substitutes—sorghum.

For the generations that survived the Great Depression, and for decades later, sorghum was the South's favorite sweetener. It is made from the sorghum plant and makes a product not unlike dark honey. These days, it's much more popular as a gluten-free flour, but it's flavorful enough for a very fine rum-like product. It makes a mean cocktail. Perfect for daiquiris and piña coladas, or a Naked Biscuit and Coke!

"There's no substitute for time spent in a barrel."

—Lincoln Henderson

LOT NO
LOT NO
RESERVE DISTILLERY
CHINKAPIN
FILL DATE 06-16-16
WOODFORD RESERVE

KENTUCKY

My Old Kentucky Home

There are two things that Kentucky is historically known for—horse racing and bourbon. And both are steeped in tradition.

As a sports historian, I've covered the Kentucky Derby, the Keeneland events, and some of the sport's biggest legends. I've always been entranced with places like Churchill Downs and the Kentucky Three Day Event in Lexington. There is nothing more exhilarating than hanging out on the backstretch of Churchill Downs during the foggy, early morning workouts the week before the Derby, or being around Louisville and Lexington during Derby Week. Men and women from all walks of life, dressed up and down, the crazy hats, track stewards in pinks, strains of "My Old Kentucky Home," and everyone sipping the ubiquitous mint julep.

And now here I am, a dozen years later, covering the same territory, but with a completely different bent—covering that other classic Blue Grass tradition. I've traded the barns and shed rows of the Downs' backstretch for the spirit safes and rickhouses of some of America's most storied distilleries, as well as some of its newest ones.

My most enduring memory of my last visit to the Derby and Kentucky was when I bought a commemorative bottle of Kentucky Derby Woodford Reserve. It was more for memory's sake than the quenching of my thirst or a desire to impress friends and family. But while entertaining one winter night, many years later, several friends caught sight of the dusty bottle, and insisted we break the seal. A tad woozy, I happily indulged them.

It was amazing. The liquid inside was magical. My friends and I all agreed. It was a large bottle, and within a few months, the last of it was drained by the subsequent Derby. And my love affair with bourbon was secured.

HISTORY

"It began in the 1700s with the first settlers of Kentucky. Like most farmers and frontiersmen, they found that getting crops to market over narrow trails and steep mountains was a daunting task," states the Kentucky Bourbon Trail. "They soon learned that converting corn and other grains to whiskey made them easily transportable, prevented the excess grain from simply rotting, and gave them some welcome diversion from the rough life of the frontier."

Of course, the question remains, how did it come to be known as bourbon? Kentucky's Bourbon County was established in 1795 when it was still part of Virginia. Corn and other grains converted to whiskey began making their way to New Orleans down the Mississippi and Ohio Rivers, in barrels stamped Bourbon County. The "bourbon" whiskey soon became popular in the southern port town, and the name stuck. It didn't hurt that the famed street in New Orleans, where most of the whiskey was imbibed, carried the same name.

Bourbon's status as an American drink was cemented in 1964 when Congress declared bourbon a distinctive product that could only be made in the United States. The making of that beverage was codified by federal law.

LEXINGTON VS. LOUISVILLE: A STATE OBSESSION

The one thing you need to know immediately is that there are two main distilling regions in Kentucky: Lexington and Louisville. This is an insurmountable physical and mental fault line in the state. Just as there is Keeneland and Churchill Downs, there is also the rivalry that exists between the University of Kentucky Wildcats and University of Louisville Cardinals. This cross-state rivalry, which goes back to 1913 in basketball, is among the most ferocious of conflicts, as evidenced by the 2012 Final Four meeting between the two in the NCAA Men's Basketball Tournament.

The same kind of state pride is at stake in the distilling business. Friendly chidings and barbs are exchanged regularly. Lexington boasts Buffalo Trace, Woodford Reserve, Wild Turkey, and Four Roses, while Louisville hosts the Evan Williams Experience, Bulleit, the Brown-Forman offices, Stitzel-Weller, Angel's Envy, Heaven Hill, and Jim Beam.

But distilling is an incredibly important industry in Kentucky, employing more than 9,000 people and adding more than $125 million in tax revenues alone. Indeed, the industry has employed some families as far back as seven generations. Few industries have that kind of dynastic feel to them. As with other industries of such an ilk, in a 10- or 15-year career you could move around or stay in one place, and you will probably meet a good portion of the people in that industry. Such is the state of distilling in Kentucky. These are people who are fiercely competitive, but also amazingly compassionate.

In 1996, when Heaven Hill suffered the most devastating distillery fire in modern memory, that indisputable industry compassion kicked into high gear. Rather than ignoring the company's difficult situation, several of the major distillers raided their stores to help Heaven Hill meet its goals and keep running until it was able

to rebuild. That's what makes it a family. As competitive as the industry is, that kind of neighborly camaraderie is a core element of what makes the story of Kentucky bourbon so special.

REBIRTH

Bourbon, and brown spirits in general, has experienced a massive rebirth in the last 10 years. And the sky is the limit. Best-selling wine expert Kevin Zraly of Windows on the World Wine Course once told me that the easiest way to see if a region has arrived is to follow the money. Banks are the least excited about getting stung by a bubble. If money is pouring in from everywhere, it's a safe bet that the region would make it. If that's the case, Kentucky has arrived. Billions of dollars have been invested in refurbishing some of the oldest and largest distilleries in the United States. Likewise, many long-shuttered distilleries, victims of the gin, vodka, and tequila surge over

the last 30 years, have roared back to life. Indeed, these are not the only signs. Massive new distilleries are racing to make enough whiskey to feed the seemingly unquenchable public. The craft distilling movement has made large and small distilleries sprout like mushrooms. Old labels are getting facelifts, being reintroduced, and new ones are being born.

These are exciting times for a state steeped in tradition. It's all happening so fast that both insiders and bourbon-loving observers cannot keep up with the immense growth. Whether it's taking a page from the single malt industry and finishing bourbon with wine, port, or sherry casks, or introducing new mash bills and new wood storage methods, the new expressions being introduced, from bourbon to rye, are all exciting and fascinating.

IS TENNESSEE WHISKEY BOURBON?

By Richard Thomas

One of the classic American bar debates is whether Tennessee whiskey is bourbon. Usually it's "Is Jack Daniel's bourbon?" But George Dickel was part of the category for decades, and it now includes a growing list of Tennessee craft distillers, as well. I didn't hear this discussed often in my native Kentucky, mind you, because at home most folks (or those who weren't dry county teetotalers at any rate) would say respectfully, "We make bourbon, and them folks down in Tennessee do their own thing." I had to move to other parts to really hear about this argument.

If you want to take up this timeless argument yourself sometime, here are some factual talking points that both sides can use:

The Law: Tennessee passed a new whiskey law in 2013, and it overlapped the federal law governing bourbon, with some additional requirements. The main extra requirement is that a whiskey had to use the Lincoln County Process (filtration through sugar maple charcoal prior to aging in new oak barrels) to qualify as Tennessee whiskey. A "grandfather" exception in the Tennessee law was made for Prichard's Distillery, which didn't use the Lincoln County Process (although it was, ironically, located in Lincoln County) and had been calling its stuff Tennessee whiskey for more than a decade. Despite this, nothing prevents a Tennessee whiskey from being called bourbon at the federal level. As Chuck Cowdery has documented on his blog, sometimes the Federal Alcohol and Tobacco Tax and Trade Bureau (TTB) has categorized Jack Daniel's as bourbon in its labeling paperwork, although the approved label itself reads "Tennessee Whiskey." Federal regulations recognize Tennessee whiskey in a loose sense, but do not specifically define it. A whiskey gets to be a Tennessee whiskey by complying with state law and asking the federal government to call it that, but its makers could easily switch and ask to be called bourbon instead.

The Lincoln County Process: As the signature production step of Tennessee whiskey, the Lincoln County Process is central to its definition. Some bourbons are charcoal filtered, too, like Ezra Brooks and Jim Beam Green Label, but this is done after the barrels are dumped and before bottling. Although there are variations of the Lincoln County Process, the important part is that the step is carried out before the newly made whiskey goes into the barrels. Tennessee whiskey sees some impurities removed before aging, whereas the charcoal-filtered bourbons do so after aging, so what is actually removed can be different.

The People Who Make It Say So: Jack Daniel's, George Dickel, Nelson's Green Brier, and others insist that what they do is Tennessee whiskey, not bourbon. Their bourbon-making peers accept that, even in Tennessee. The legal challenges to the 2013 Tennessee Whiskey Law failed to overturn it, so the law will stand for the foreseeable future. No one with the power to attempt to change what the labels say is disputing that there is such a thing as Tennessee whiskey.

Angel's Envy

Set in the middle of downtown Louisville, opposite Louisville Slugger Stadium, nestled among the office buildings of this fine old city, Angel's Envy is certainly the envy of anyone who wants to be in the distilling business. Its stainless steel and copper shine and sparkle like few other places.

The incredibly well-appointed gift shop and education center is the height of sleek and modern industrial glam. The upstairs event space is otherworldly, a combination of beaux arts and the National Park Service, with massive windows cased in steel and brick overlooking the city and the Ohio River. It is nothing short of breathtaking.

But despite the dazzling views and architecture, Angel's Envy is all about genes. It is hard to start a distillery with better genes. Lincoln Henderson and his son Wes Henderson have both spent many years building various whiskey brands.

Lincoln Henderson is one of the most storied master distillers in the history of the region. He created such premium products as Gentleman Jack and Jack Daniel's Single Barrel, and he created Woodford Reserve (with Chris Morris at his side). He also guided much of the distilling program at Brown-Forman for almost two generations.

Wes worked alongside of him. When Woodford was created out of thin air, Wes helped plan the buildings in the distillery we know today. Wes is also a master distiller in his own right. These are two terribly accomplished men.

Lincoln retired in the mid-1990s. And when the new craft distilling boom hit, Wes went to visit his father, on a Sunday morning, with a crazy idea—they should finally start a distillery of their own. Lincoln had never had that kind of backing or control. And so their experiments with mash and finishing began, with Lincoln combing through his legendary black book for ideas.

When the first experimental barrels were ready to taste, Lincoln opened them only to find that the angels had taken a heavy share. Once they tasted the whiskey inside, Lincoln declared that the angels should envy him and Wes. The whiskey left behind was superb. And that's the legend of the distillery's name.

In the beginning the whiskey was made to Lincoln's specific instructions and formula.

The small production run was an immediate hit. While it made bourbon the old-fashioned way, Angel's Envy is a port-finished product, meaning that the bourbon, which had properly rested in charred American white oak, then spent additional time in port casks to acquire a softer, rounder finish that gives it a brandy or cognac feel.

Momentum gathered and demand grew. Today Angel's Envy is the most expensive and lavish bourbon distillery in the Louisville region. It is designed beautifully, simply, and to the teeth. Somewhat resembling the old nave of a church (it is a converted old tool works), it is indeed a modern steampunk temple to distilled spirits—a gem of the distilling world.

The grain for the bourbon is sourced from Doug Langley's farms in Shelby County, Kentucky. And the grain for Angel's Envy Rye comes from Brooks Grain. Its barley comes from Consolidated Grain in Louisville. It uses a char #3 American oak barrel from Kelvin Cooperage.

Sadly, Lincoln has passed on. Despite the many high points of his career, those closest to him still feel that Angel's Envy was his greatest achievement. But that's not true. It might be said that his greatest achievement was his family. The family still runs the distillery, which is now owned by liquor giant Bacardi.

Angel's Envy Port Finished Bourbon is the big product here. It is a sophisticated bourbon, aimed not only at the American market, but positioned perfectly for the European and Asian markets, where it will compete with single malt whiskies from Scotland.

First released in 2015, Angel's Envy Rye Whiskey is a small production rye. It is a six- to seven-year-old whiskey made of 95% rye and 5% malted barley. It is aged for up to 18 months in Caribbean XO rum casks (which had aged cognac before that). It comes from batches of 8 to 12 barrels at a time, twice a year, and the distillery produces approximately 48,000 bottles annually.

B. Bird Distillery

Augusta, Kentucky, is located on a shallow bend in the Ohio River. It is a charming old town, with a number of buildings that are listed on the National Register of Historic Places. Dinah Bird purchased the estate in 2002. It houses a winery, Baker-Bird Winery, and a distillery, B. Bird Distillery.

The original buildings were established by distiller John Baker, a veteran of the American Revolution. John was a distiller in Washington County, Pennsylvania. After the failure of the Whiskey Rebellion John moved to Augusta in 1797. There he founded a new distillery. Abraham Baker, John's son, purchased the land and his son, Abraham Baker, Jr., built the winery and extensive wine cellar in the 1850s.

The Baker-Bird Winery is one of the oldest wineries in America, and is one of only 22 wineries on the National Historic Registry. By the 1870s Bracken County was the country's leading wine-producing county. "At the time, the Ohio River Valley was the place to grow grapes in the US," according to Ms. Bird. "The German immigrants who settled here said the hilly area reminded them of their homeland."

Today, the Baker-Bird Wine Cellar, originally built by Abraham, is the largest, oldest wine cellar in America and the only winery to have survived a Civil War battle. The Baker-Bird Winery is the "Home of Bourbon Barrel Aged Wines" and offers many other internationally acclaimed wines.

The winery partnered with Woodford Reserve Distillery to make their famed Black Barrel wine, which is aged in bourbon barrels. The entire project, including the time the barrels are needed to age whiskey takes up to ten years. The wine is said to offer the classic "Kentucky hug." Doug Padgett is the master distiller, a job he has held since January of 2019.

Historic B. Bird American Revolution Corn Whiskey (100 proof) is a crystal-clear unaged corn whiskey made right there on the premises. This is the same distillate that gets laid down to make their bourbon. Great nose with corn and butter. Incredibly smooth.

Historic Becker & Bird Give Me Liberty Brandy (80 proof) is made from the winery's wines. A total vertical production. The brandy was launched in late 2020.

Historic B. Bird Kentucky Statehood Straight American Whiskey (100 proof) is a bourbon that's been aged for two years in new American charred oak.

THE BARD DISTILLERY

In 2019, Thomas and Kim Bard opened The Bard Distillery in Graham, Kentucky, in Muhlenberg County. The two met each other during their years in NASCAR. They'd visited Maker's Mark in 2006, and had been dreaming of having their own distillery ever since. Then they decided to make it happen. So in 2013, they bought the old Graham School. The school had been closed since 2004. The campus consisted of three historic buildings (60,000 square feet of free space) on 25 acres. The buildings themselves were erected in the 1920s and 1930s and some of the period art deco touches have survived to today.

"One of our reasons for buying this facility was so that we could preserve these buildings. They weren't falling down, but close to falling down," Kim told me in December 2019.

"I went to school here until I was in third grade and we live five minutes from here, so this is our home," added Thomas, who doubles as the distillery's engineer. "The family history has always revolved around Bardstown. I'm the fifth-generation grandson of the founder of Bardstown, William Bard, so the family heritage has always involved bourbon."

"Both of us have given up our day jobs and we're all in at this point," said Kim. "Once we start renovations on it, we'll be able to put a 500- to 750-gallon pot still in that and then a column still at some point so we can run 24 hours a day, 7 days a week." They received their first new American oak charred barrels in July 2019.

Bard Distillery will produce un-aged spirits, whiskey, and high-end bourbon, as well as gin and vodka.

Muhlenberg Silver Muhl Whiskey (124 proof) small batch, new make unaged white whiskey. Crystal clear. Super smooth. Bottled in limited quantities.

Cinder & Smoke Straight Bourbon Whiskey Aged 13 Years (98.6 proof) is made from blended sourced whiskey bottled cask strength. No filtering. Batches are small. Bottlings range from 300 to 500 bottles. Reviews so far have been very positive. This is a new distillery well worth following closely.

Bardstown Bourbon Company

Peter Loftin was the founding member and chairman of the Bardstown Bourbon Company. Before entering the spirits business, Loftin made his mark in the telecommunications industry after the Bell telephone monopoly break up. In 1983, he founded and led Raleigh, North Carolina-based Business Telecom Inc. (BTI). By 1999, BTI had approximately $400 million in annual revenues.

Through a bond issue and a sale of stock to a private equity firm, Loftin essentially liquidated his position and began to cast about for a new venture. Between 2000 and 2013, he bought, restored, and sold Casa Causaurina, the former home of Gianni Versace, turning it into a high-end boutique hotel and club. His next project was among his many loves – bourbon. In 2016, Loftin founded the largest new whiskey distillery in the United States. Bardstown Bourbon is a collaborative whiskey, bourbon, and rye distilling program located in Bardstown, Kentucky. The original intent was to make whiskey for others. Constellation Brands acquired a minority stake in the company in 2016. Loftin passed away in November 2019.

The distillery is currently led by the affable and capable Colonel (Ret.) Mark W. Erwin who now serves as president and CEO. Erwin took command in September 2019. He was an accomplished businessman long before joining Bardstown, having advised major Fortune 500 companies, and having served in the United States Army for 26 years, culminating his military career as the Chief of Staff of the United States Army Special Operations Command. He has a commanding presence, but is always collegial and chatty.

Bardstown is interested in only one thing—making bourbon and rye. Nothing else. However, Bardstown has three distinct programs. First is the manufacture and sale of its own line of excellent bourbon and rye. Second, they produce and package bourbon and rye for other companies under private

labels; for some customers, they handle the extra capacity their partners cannot, for others they are the distillery where all the product is made, and some are special one-off projects or bottlings. Third, they sell bulk bourbon and rye to other companies.

So far it has been an immensely successful endeavor. Running 24 hours per day, 7 days a week, and bulking up on equipment and staff, Bardstown doubled capacity in 2018, and in 2019 yet again. The company has two large column stills and more than 32 fermenters, giving them a current capacity of 100,000 barrels of bourbon per year. They are one of the top ten privately-owned distilleries, by volume, in the country. Some of the partners they have worked with include Jefferson's, High West, Bell Meade, Calumet, and Hirsch. They old hold off about 6 to 8% of their own whiskey for future bottlings under the Bardstown label.

Most amazing about Bardstown is their spectacular welcome center and tasting room. They see themselves as a place where distilling meets the culinary arts and craft cocktails. The massively spacious hall can accommodate diners and has one of the largest whiskey bars in the state, featuring more than 100 Kentucky bourbons. And a few from Tennessee. It's all stunningly presented, including as a tastefully appointed gift shop.

More important is the whiskey. The have four releases under the Bardstown label. The incredibly humble Nally explains that they put more than 52 blends together, and everyone at the company got to try them and comment. He stressed the team aspect of their assemblage. And the unique thing is that the labels are all about transparency. Their "Discovery" and "Fusion" series labels explain the exact blends inside the bottle. For example, the Discovery Series blend is on the label: 45% 13-year-old bourbon from Indiana, 32% Kentucky 13-year-old bourbon, and 23% 16-year-old Kentucky bourbon. The Fusion Series is 40% 13-year-old Kentucky bourbon; 3-year-old 18% Bardstown Wheated; 3-year-old 42% Bardstown High Rye Bourbon. I also liked the collaboration project with Goodwood Brewing where they aged 9-year-old Tennessee Bourbon in Goodwood brewing barrels. They also did a collaboration with

Copper & Kings. The whiskeys have received overwhelming enthusiasm.

"The Prisoner is a collaboration we're doing," McNally revealed. "The Prisoner Wine Company selects several different vintages of their wine, they blend them together percentage-wise to create the Prisoner wine finish. We've got barrels from Prisoner and we're going to age product in those barrels for about 19 months. That product is going to be blended together in the same ratio that Prisoner develops the wines out of. We're excited by that."

Bardstown will start releasing their own whiskeys in individual bottlings when their first whiskeys reach six years of age. Approximately 2022 or 2023. In the meantime, these blends are off the charts fantastic. Super smooth, sophisticated.

CHICKEN COCK WHISKEY RETURNS!

Established in 1856 in Paris, Kentucky, in the heart of Bourbon County, the original Chicken Cock American Whiskey rose to popularity during the 19th century when James A. Miller built a distillery and started making Chicken Cock. It became an instant success, and really thrived during Prohibition, making it an especially iconic brand. Unfortunately, the original distillery where Chicken Cock was made burned down in the 1950s. Grain & Barrel Spirits of West Palm Beach, Florida, have resurrected the brand.

Chicken Cock and Bardstown Bourbon announced that the whiskey would be made at Bardstown as part of Bardstown Bourbon's Collaborative Distilling Program. "Joining the Collaborative Distilling Program at Bardstown completes the exciting resurrection of Chicken Cock, one of the oldest bourbon brands in the country," said CEO Matti Anttila. "The brand is now officially 100 percent back home in Kentucky."

The brand boasts several different bottlings. Most famous is their 90-proof Chicken Cock Straight Bourbon Whiskey. The bourbon is bottled in a replica of the Prohibition-era Chicken Cock bottle. Caramel colored, with notes of dried fruit, caramel, and vanilla; creamy, almost buttery. Butterscotch and toasted vanilla come through. Lovely.

The also offer Beer Barrel Select, 10-Year-Old Bourbon, and Single Barrel 8-Year-Old. They produce two ryes; one of them is a straight rye aged in Goodwood Brewery beer barrels named Ryeteous Blonde.

STEVE NALLY

THE 100 MILLION BOTTLE MAN

Steve Nally was the first person Peter Loftin hired in his new venture. Nally was in Wyoming, having built and established Wyoming Whiskey, that state's first legal distillery. Another notch on the belt of his storied career. The wily industry veteran had been the master distiller at Maker's Mark for more than 15 years, and is a Bourbon Hall of Fame member. It's estimated that he has made more than 100 million bottles of whiskey during his career.

Loftin called Nally and told him he wanted to build a brand. When Nally asked him if he knew anything about the business, Loftin answered honestly that he did not. "That's why I want you," responded Loftin.

"Pete came out here and he had a vision. We looked at several places around Kentucky. When he first started this venture, he wanted to produce a brand to start with," recalled Nally, a big man with twinkling eyes set above his bushy gray mustache. Nally was with Loftin when they purchased the large farm that now serves as Bardstown HQ. "We started construction in 2014. During that time, we started talking to potential clients who are now customers, with the idea of producing for them. And Pete's vision became a reality."

Nally started out at Maker's Mark in 1972. He was born and raised not far down the road from Maker's Mark, and like a number of local kids, he went merely to look for a job. In 17 years he went from janitor and night watchman, to warehouse supervisor, to bottling assistant supervisor, to a mechanic. He became the mater distiller in 1988. He moved to semi-retirement in 2003, after working there for 31 years. In 2007, he went to start Wyoming Whiskey.

"The history of the bourbon industry is that there's always been a lot of secrets about it. Everybody knew about the families that grew it and promoted bourbon but you didn't know a lot about the process itself," Nally explained. "One thing that Bardstown Bourbon is all about is being transparent. No hidden stories and no hidden production practices."

Discussing his "Fusion" series, Nally said, "We're really excited by this. It really shows the art of blending but also shows what our products are coming to be with a very, very good finish. I like to call this finish the Kentucky hug."

Lots more to come from this legendary distiller.

BARREL HOUSE

Barrel House Distilling Company was founded in the winter of 2006 by native Lexingtonians Jeff Wiseman and Pete Wright. They established their new craft distillery in the barreling house of the old Pepper Distillery in historic Lexington. In a short time, Barrel House has garnered a reputation as a small craft house that, even while making moonshine, makes its mark through quality. It released its first product—Pure Blue Vodka—in December 2008.

Its vodka was an immediate hit, and it has since moved on to other spirits. It produces vodka and rum (the aged rum is very nice), as well as moonshine and bourbon. According to the distillers, "In 1877 *The Saturday Evening Post* declared, 'Kentucky is the home of the Moonshiner.' Barrel House has revived this long tradition with the introduction of Devil John Moonshine, named in honor of Kentucky legend Devil John Wright. Devil John was a lawman and moonshiner from eastern Kentucky in the late 19th and early 20th centuries." The recipe is classic 'shine,

a combination of white corn and pure cane sugar. This is actually a lovely, light whiskey, with some nice spice notes and appealing vanilla flavor. And it is great for cocktails.

Its 115-proof RockCastle Kentucky Straight Bourbon Whiskey is "named for the county that is home to our limestone-rich mountain spring water," and is made with local Kentucky corn and wheat. This is a small-batch, wheated craft bourbon—which makes it fairly unique right off the bat. RockCastle is bottled at barrel strength, and features notes of toffee, caramel, burnt sugar, and vanilla. It is a very nice expression; rich and with a nice finish!

THE ELKHORN TAVERN

The Barrel House Distillery features a separate taproom and cocktail lounge. The bar is named after Elkhorn Creek, which runs through town. Here, Wiseman and Wright showcase inventive cocktails made from their products. It also has a local beer list and a nice wine list. The bar features a rustic décor that has a historic touch to it, highlighted by lots of wood and copper. And they have top flight mixologists to boot.

Barton 1792 Distillery

Established in 1879, Barton 1792 Distillery "continues today as the oldest fully-operating distillery in Bardstown, Kentucky. Situated in the heart of bourbon country on 196 acres, the distillery boasts 29 barrel aging warehouses, 22 other buildings, including an impressive still house, and the legendary Tom Moore Spring," according to the company.

Barton produces a full range of bourbons and ryes for the market. Most notable are the 1792 Full Proof Bourbon, 1792 High Rye Bourbon, 1792 Small Batch Bourbon, 1792 Port Finish Bourbon, 1792 Sweet Wheat

Bourbon, and 1792 Single Barrel Bourbon. It also produces Tom Moore Bourbon Whiskey, Kentucky Gentleman Bourbon Whiskey, and Fleischmann's Preferred Blended Whiskey, among others.

The 1792 Barton Small Batch Bourbon is regarded by numerous whiskey writers as the distillery's best. It's made with a mash bill of 75% corn, 15% rye, and 10% barley (same recipe as Very Old Barton 6). There is no age statement, and it is released at 46.85% ABV. According to the distiller's notes, 1792 Small Batch is a "marriage of select barrels carefully chosen by our Master Distiller."

STOVES & CRATES.

TIN WARE.

BLUEGRASS DISTILLERS

Bluegrass Distillers, located in Lexington, opened its doors in 2015. This unique, high-end, small-batch distillery was founded by Nate Brown, Sam Rock, and Matt Montgomery. The aim of Bluegrass Distillers is to craft world-class bourbon in the heart of the Kentucky Bluegrass region. Not only is Bluegrass considered a serious craft distiller, one of its biggest selling points (other than the finished product) is that it attempts to work with local farmers to source its ingredients.

Bluegrass features a 250-gallon copper pot still, working with two mash bills for its bourbons: mash bill #1 is local GMO-free yellow corn and rye; mash bill #2 is the same yellow corn and red wheat. It begins aging all of its bourbons in 53- and 25-gallon barrels. Then it redistributes into its customized program using 5-gallon charred white oak barrels. Bluegrass loves small barrels, saying it "believe[s] the 5-gallon barrel is a very effective way to refine . . . bourbon. This is due to the fact that a smaller barrel has a smaller surface area, which creates an effect

of being aged longer." You may disagree in theory, but the results speak for themselves.

The 90 proof Bluegrass Blue Blue Corn Straight Bourbon Whiskey is an amazing bourbon made from a mash bill of 80% blue corn and 20% wheat. It also makes the 90 proof Bluegrass Kentucky Rye Whiskey 4-Year-Old, which was made in a small batch. It's a dark, spicy rye that you should keep an eye out for. Another special treat is the Bluegrass Wheated Bourbon made from a mash bill of 80% yellow corn, 15% wheat, and 5% malted barley. But the real standout is the Bluegrass Bourbon Whiskey made with a mash bill of 80% corn and 20% rye sourced from a feed store in Woodford County. It is aged in new, 25-gallon, #4 char, white oak barrels. The 25-gallon barrels accelerate aging and produce a big, spicy bourbon that features assertive burnt sugar and oak flavors. A lovely and easy-to-drink bourbon. Loved the cider barrel aged bourbon too, which is only available at the tasting room.

POT STILLED

BLUEGRASS
DISTILLERS™

KENTUCKY STRAIGHT
BOURBON WHISKEY

Single Barrel

DISTILLED AND BOTTLED
BY BLUEGRASS DISTILLERS
IN LEXINGTON, KY

| 117 PROOF/ALC. 58.5% BY VOL. | BARREL 53.0109 |
| MASH BILL 75% Blue Corn 21% Wheat 4% Malted Barley | BOTTLE 12 |

750 ML

5-Year-Old Rye Single Barrel (95% rye, 5% malted barley) and a wheated 6-Year-Old Single Barrel Bourbon (51% corn, 45% wheat, 4% malted barley). The Bourbon Cream is very drinkable and gaining in popularity. The Tanner's Curse Rye Mash and Tanners Curse Bourbon Mash are "New Make" unaged white whiskeys, both of which are very flavorful and distinctive. This is a great example of a small distillery really coming into its own. One to continue to watch.

BOONE COUNTY DISTILLING

The label on each bottle released by Boone County Distilling includes the tagline "Made by Ghosts" as a way for the founders to pay homage to those who came before them. William Snyder, who opened the Petersburg Distillery in Boone County in 1833 is their inspiration. The Distillery was re-established in 2015 at a new location in Independence. The current owners are Jack Wells and Josh Quinnin. "One of the things people don't realize is how big the industry was here in Boone County in the 1800s," said Wells.

Boone County Distilling is a 5,000-square-foot-distillery set on 2.5 acres, with a 500-gallon pot still, four fermenters, and a small bottling line. It can produce 250 barrels of small batch bourbon annually.

The distillery produces a bourbon, rye, and bourbon cream. They also produce a

BOUNDARY OAK DISTILLERY

Boundary Oak Distillery is located in the small hills of central Kentucky, and the Goodins, the family that runs it, have been in this region for more than 200 years. Founder and master distiller Brent Goodin invested nearly $1 million and acquired a license in 2013, making Boundary Oaks the first legal producer of liquor in Hardin County since Prohibition.

Boundary Oak released a number of military-oriented products, including its signature Patton Armored Diesel products through a partnership with the George S. Patton Museum. Goodin also created Blackhorse 1901 in cooperation with the 11th

Armored Cavalry Regiment, known by the nickname Blackhorse. Another successful release was 82nd Airborne, in connection with the unit based at Fort Bragg. Other releases include their single barrel Lincoln Bourbon and their St. Luke's Lavender, whiskey made with lavender, inspired by the distillery's popular mint julep recipe.

Most popular has been their Patton Armed Diesel which has reached pretty wide distribution throughout the south. Diesel is a cane sugar wash finished in used bourbon American oak barrels, and is a lovely slant on traditional whiskey. Quite smooth and easy to drink. Great for sipping at holiday parties or in the backyard.

BOURBON 30 SPIRITS

Jeff Mattingly formed Bourbon 30 Spirits in Georgetown in 2014. It is not a distillery as of yet, but a small, craft blending house. It buys and blends whiskeys, as has long been a tradition in Kentucky. These are all small batch, handcrafted, and hand-bottled. And Jeff can charm any crowd.

One of the cool things Barrel 30 does offer from time to time is an opportunity to bottle your own whiskey directly from the barrel. These are special events, and well worth doing if you are able.

It's most commonly found expressions are the 100 proof Bourbon 30 Small Batch,

90 proof Bourbon 30 Straight Bourbon whiskey, and 98 proof Bourbon 30 Rye Whiskey.

In the last few years, they have released numerous small-batch bottlings in their new blue label J. Mattingly whiskeys. They enjoy names like "Don't Talk About It, Do It," "Another Summer Hayride," "Indian Sumer," "Sugar Lips," "Blondie," "Flap Jack," and the like. These small bottlings are exceptional and smooth, but not inexpensive. That is the beauty of what Barrel 30 does. These elixirs won't be seen again. Super enjoyable tastings in a fun setting. Great staff!

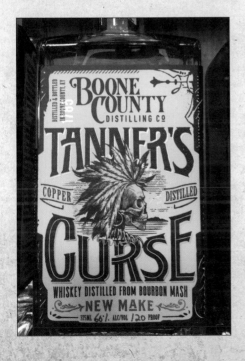

BROUGH BROTHERS DISTILLERY

Brough Brothers Distillery, owned and operated by the Yarbrough brothers — Victor, Chris, and Bryson—became the first African American-owned distillery in Kentucky. This new 850-square-foot craft micro-distillery is on Dixie Highway, in Louisville. Fresh Bourbon, the other African-American led distiller, launched their whiskey earlier, but the distillery's construction was delayed due to COVID-19.

Victor is the CEO, co-founder of Victory Global LLC, and leads the day-to-day operations of Brough Brothers. Bryson is the COO, co-founder of Victory Global LLC, and manages the Brough Brothers manufacturing and production operations. Chris is the CMO and operates the marketing and events programs.

Victor had gotten the idea while living in the UK, exporting hard cider to the US, and importing bourbon to the UK. "When we imported bourbon into the UK and other markets we saw there was a tremendous growth opportunity. We learned a great deal

about the process of distribution and gained an understanding of retailers and pricing," said Victor. "We are the brand, that's the critical distinction," Victor told *Forbes*. "When we were out at trade shows ahead of the launch, people see us and want to talk to us."

"Booze is a good old boy industry. It goes back 150, 200 years in the US, to a time when African Americans weren't free. There was no way we could establish any ownership or legacy, and this is a legacy industry," said Victor. "A fair number of businesses, particularly in the Kentucky spirits industry, started off as family businesses and most of them are still owned by the family. That means that people work with people who look like them. And there aren't many people that look like me in this business. It's very difficult to get in."

Brough Brothers Bourbon Brewery was planned to open in Louisville's West End, where the brothers grew up. They want to be at the center of the neighborhood's revitalization by offering employment and volunteer opportunities to create a driving economic engine. "We are pushing the community forward, " Victor stated. "It's not about us, it's really about the generations behind us, as a lot of blood, sweat, and tears

have been put into the start-up."

Brough Brothers released their first bottling in February 2020, right into the teeth of the global pandemic. "We were fortunate to get it into stores, including Liquor Barn and Total Wine, ahead of the pandemic," Victor said. The good news? It sold out. Keeping the momentum going was the challenge.

Brough Brothers 82 proof Bourbon Whiskey is a medium-bodied whiskey. The mash bill is 75% corn, 21% rye, and 4% malted barley and the grain is sourced from both Indiana and Kentucky. They use a sweet mash, and fermentations can last up to seven days. There is also a filtration process the spirit goes through for a smoother taste. Currently, its whisky is matured in a couple of different locations in Kentucky. Victor called it a "party bourbon," perfect for cocktails, and affordably priced under $30. A golden honey colored whiskey, with floral aromas and notes of green apple and pear, hints of ginger and spice.

Master of Malt, the UK's most recognized purveyor of whiskey called Victor and his plan "brilliant." You can't get much higher praise than that. Looking forward to good things from Brough Brothers.

THE BROWN-FORMAN CORPORATION/DISTILLERY

Brown-Forman is one of the foremost names in the spirits category, and one of the largest distilling operations in the world.

George Garvin Brown founded the company in 1870 with his half-brother, and they started selling JTS Brown Bourbon by the bottle instead of the barrel, the first to do so. Today, Brown-Forman owns such brands as Jack Daniel's, Woodford Reserve, Early Times, and Old Forester. It also owns such world-renowned brands as Canadian Mist, GlenDronach, BenRiach, Glenglassaugh, Finlandia, Herradura, Korbel, and Chambord. In 2016, the company's reported sales had reached $3.08 billion annually.

The company's world headquarters, which resembles the campus of a small liberal arts college, is located in Louisville, although no longer in downtown. While several of its major brands, like Woodford and Jack Daniel's, have their own distilleries, the company's massive Shively plant is the engine that drives the Brown-Forman machine. Early Times and Old Forester have been made there for years, as have the components for other brands.

OLD FORESTER

Old Forester is the oldest and longest running bottled whiskey in America, and has been sold for 150 years. From 1920 to 1933, Old Forester was one of only 10 whiskey brands authorized for medicinal purposes, which is why it survived Prohibition.

Chris Morris, of Woodford fame, has been Brown-Forman's master distiller since 2006. Old Forester and Woodford Reserve are both made from a mash bill of 72% corn, 18% rye, and 10% malted barley, and this relatively high rye component provides a spicier ending.

Brown-Forman produces several expressions including Old Forester Classic (86 proof); the Whiskey Row series, which includes 1870 Original Batch, 1897 Bottled in Bond, 1920 Prohibition Style, and Birthday Bourbon; Old Forester Signature (100 proof), Old Forester 1920 Prohibition Style (115 proof), and Old Forester Birthday Bourbon (94–97 proof). These last two are personal favorites.

The Old Forester Signature is an exceptional buy! This is a big, rich whiskey with immense flavor to go along with the ABV. There is no age statement, which is disconcerting, until you nose the glass and taste the whiskey. Whatever Chris Morris and his team did, they did it right. Big caramel and brown sugar notes precede a gingersnap ending.

Old Forester 1920 Prohibition Style, a nod to the distillery's former shepherd Owsley Brown, is the third release in the Old Forester Whiskey Row series. This has lots of big bold flavor, with a nose and finish to match. There are lots of chocolatey notes in this one.

The biggest, and best, of the line is the Old Forester Birthday Bourbon, which is released annually. The 2017 release marked the 17th issuing of this legendary bourbon. According to the distiller's notes, "The 2017 Birthday Bourbon barrel selection was drawn from 12-year-old barrels from different warehouses and floors on May 27, 2005. Ninety-three barrels matured together on the 4th floor of G warehouse, yielding an extremely spice-forward expression. The remaining 27 barrels matured together on the fifth floor of K warehouse, contributing a rounding sweetness to the blend. Several barrels from both lots basked in the sun, highlighting the effects of maturation along an external wall in Old Forester's heat-cycled warehouses."

The proof has also varied, per Brown-Forman: "The 2017 Old Forester Birthday Bourbon will be on shelves with a suggested retail price of $79.99. Florida and Georgia will receive the 95.4 proof expression and remaining states will receive the 96 proof expression. Kentucky is the only state which will receive both expressions with the 96 proof expression shipping first."

This is an amazing whiskey, with lots of dark caramel flavor and a big spicy ending that does not overpower the whiskey. An exceptional, incredible whiskey, with an incredibly beautiful nose and palate. If you're looking for a bourbon to impress your friends and family over the holidays, this is it.

THE MASTER TASTER OF OLD FORESTER

Jackie Zykan went to college in St. Louis where she majored in biology, and had every intention of going to medical school. To make money during her undergrad days, she held down bartending jobs. Tearing through Nashville and St. Louis, and dubbed a "rock star" by one journalist, she now thinks of herself in those days as a "shaker for hire," doing freelance bartending jobs from numerous brands. Then she became beverage director for a local hospitality company. Then she became the brand ambassador for Brown-Forman.

She started as master bourbon specialist, then took on a hybrid role combining the talents of a brand ambassador and mixologist. What was it like to go from a master specialist to master taster? "The main difference between the two is just a little bit more production training. I still do all of the job requirements of the first one, I just added more onto my plate."

By 2020, Zykan been with Brown-Forman for more than five years, and held what is certainly one of the most coveted jobs in the entire industry. Has it been difficult as a woman working for one of the oldest names in bourbon? "It's going to be as hard as you want it to be for yourself being a female in a male dominated industry. You can either focus on it or you can just lean in and focus on doing your job and rise above it and just carry on," Zykan said. "I don't ever think of it as oh I'm young for this role or I'm a woman in this role, I just go to work."

Zykan was also instrumental in the highly acclaimed Whiskey Row Series from Old Forester. "Whiskey Row is a little bit more elevated craft, a little bit smaller batch, definitely a lot more labor intensive and filtered quite a bit less." This was the introduction of the numerous more craft like expressions of Old Forester. Zykan also collaborated with Bourbon Barrel

Foods to produce a line of Old Forester Cocktail Provisions, a collection of bitters and syrups.

In 2020, Brown-Forman celebrated its 150th Anniversary, and Zykan was charged with debuting Old Forester Birthday Bourbon, an annual release honoring company founder George Garvin Brown. She has worked on a number of those releases with master distiller Chris Morris. It is one of the high points of the Brown-Forman calendar. "It's more about this concept of blending practice than it is the exact flavor profile definition," Zykan explained.

The Old Forester Birthday Bourbon 2020 (98 proof) was released in September 2020. On June 5 of that year 95 barrels of the whiskey were barreled. This release was the third Birthday Bourbon to be bottled at the Old Forester Distilling Co.

"I think we could not have done a better job picking a lot that was going to be a bottle of escapism in the craziness of the world that's going on right," Zykan said of the 2020 release. "And it's fantastic. There's so much tropical fruit. There's some nice macadamia nut qualities to it. It's incredibly well-rounded.

EARLY TIMES

Early Times was first established in 1860, created in Early Times Station, Kentucky, and centered on a spring that was filtered by local limestone. The Early Times line remained quiet for many years, and was bought for strategic purposes by Brown-Forman in 1923, as a preparation against the Volstead Act (also known as Prohibition). After Prohibition was rescinded, Early Times became the bestselling whiskey in the United States, and remained in the top spot for many years.

Today, Early Times is marketed and sold in more than 40 countries around the world. While not as popular at home, it is one of the top-selling Kentucky bourbons in the world, and is the bestselling one in Japan.

In 1983, Brown-Forman, following an industry trend (Four Roses was another example), started selling Early Times in two tiers: the best quality Kentucky bourbons made by the company were sold internationally. While Early Times' reputation soared abroad, it fell off the face of the earth in the United States, where it was judged to be inferior whiskey. In 2011, with interest in bourbons on the rise, Brown-Forman started making higher quality bourbon for the US market. Since then, the brand's reputation has been recovering domestically.

It is important to note that Early Times Mint Juleps have been the "official drink" of the Kentucky Derby for more than 40 years! More than 100,000 of these cocktails are imbibed during Derby Week annually!

COOPERS' CRAFT

Coopers' Craft Kentucky Straight Bourbon Whiskey, Brown-Forman's first new bourbon brand since the introduction of Woodford Reserve, is a blend of a number of Brown-Forman bourbons. First, the bourbon is properly matured for four to six years. The whiskey is then passed through a charcoal made from beech and birch wood. The idea, according to the company, is to add extra smoothness and extra oak to the whiskey to produce a lighter, softer bourbon.

BROWN-FORMAN COOPERAGE

In 2009, Brown-Forman opened the doors to the Brown-Forman Cooperage. Originally named the Blue Grass Cooperage, the name was changed to honor the company for which it makes barrels. The Brown-Forman Cooperage is where barrels are handcrafted for the aging of spirits such as Jack Daniel's, Woodford Reserve, Old Forester, Early Times, Canadian Mist, El Jimador, and Herradura. Brown-Forman is the only spirits company in the world to make its own barrels. They are made from American white oak. The plant currently produces more than 2,500 barrels a day.

Public tours include the lumberyard, a view of how the staves are selected, and insight into how barrels are assembled. The tour also provides a look at the charring and finishing process.

"The aromatic smells are the best part of the tour," Brown-Forman master distiller Chris Morris told the press. "By toasting and charring these barrels, we activate natural flavors and aromas in the wood which give our spirits such distinct tastes. We know oak barrels were introduced to the world by the Romans more than 2,000 years ago. The Romans obviously didn't have the technology we have available today, but we are still following the same processes they followed back then."

Buffalo Trace

When you first get to Buffalo Trace, you are instantly overwhelmed by the size of the place. It almost resembles a steel mill more than it resembles a distillery. It is one of the largest distilleries in the region. It is also the oldest continually operating distillery in the United States.

There is something steampunk about Buffalo Trace. To walk around its distillery is to step back in time. All the stairs are well worn. All the walls are smooth from wear. Portions of the operation have the look of 19th century industry. But here it's not marketing. It is authentic.

To give you a sense of the enormity of the place, Buffalo Trace has twelve 39,000-gallon fermenters. That's almost half-a-million gallons of distiller's beer! It has a continuous still that runs 24/7. The feed grain that exits

the process is warehoused in a tank the size of an eight-story building. Its production line fills its 17 rickhouses with 400,000 barrels of spirits every year!

Located in Frankfort, Kentucky, the distillery is believed to have been founded on the banks of the Kentucky River, in Franklin County, at the site of a centuries-old buffalo crossing. Another name for where American bison trails cross is a trace, giving the distillery its distinctive name. However, the distillery has operated under many names, including the George T. Stagg Distillery and the O.F.C. Distillery. The distillery and grounds were officially listed on the National Register of Historic Places on May 2, 2001, and designated as a National Historic Landmark two years later.

Records show that Hancock Lee and his brother Willis Lee began distilling on this spot in 1775. Commodore Richard Taylor constructed the first building on the site in 1792, Riverside House, which still stands today. Harrison Blanton built the first full distillery in 1812, and Edmund H. Taylor bought the distillery in 1870. Taylor named the distillery the Old Fashioned Copper (O.F.C.) Distillery. George T. Stagg bought the distillery, along with the Old Oscar Pepper Distillery, eight years later. Stagg built the first steam-fitted, climate-controlled warehouse for whiskey aging in the United States.

Today, Buffalo Trace's 17 rickhouses are chock full with barrels, and the company believes that each floor has its own terroir, its own unique climate. A small-batch whiskey at Buffalo Trace is somewhere around 1,000 barrels. A large run could reach up to 50,000 barrels. But a single barrel is still a single barrel.

Sazerac Company, based in New Orleans, Louisiana, bought the distillery in 1992. It is hard to believe that one of the oldest and largest distilleries in the nation will undergo a complete renovation and expansion, totaling $200 million in costs, but that is what the distillery announced in 2016. Harlen Wheatley is currently the master distiller, taking over the reins in 2005 from Gary Grayheart, who had been with the company since 1972.

Buffalo Trace produces numerous bourbons and whiskeys, including such brands as Buffalo Trace, E. H. Taylor, W. L. Weller, Sazerac, Pappy Van Winkle, Rare Eagle, and George T. Stagg.

BUFFALO TRACE ANTIQUE COLLECTION

Each fall, Buffalo Trace Distillery releases its Antique Collection of whiskeys. The Antique Collection was introduced in 2000, and has become a cult favorite among whiskey connoisseurs. These whiskeys are eagerly anticipated, and have received scads of medals, high ratings, and praise from around the world. The highly regarded collection features five limited-release whiskeys of various ages, recipes, and proofs. The George T. Stagg whiskeys (approx. 120-130 proof) are usually around 15 years old and present cinnamon, caramel, and cherries on the nose, and a creamy vanilla, dark cherry, and spicy palate. The 2020 release of William Larue Weller Wheated Whiskey (approx. 130 proof) was around 12 years old, and displayed soft caramel chew and spices. The Thomas H. Handy Sazerac Rye (129 proof) was a 16-year-old uncut and unfiltered straight rye whiskey. It exhibited notes of cinnamon, anise, and honey. The Eagle Rare 17-Year-Old (101 proof) had a nose of ripe cherries, vanilla cream, and oak, finishing with caramel, coffee, and pepper. The Sazerac Rye 18-Year-Old (90 proof) had notes of oak, caramel, and dark chocolate, with a finish of coffee, black pepper, and cherries.

O.F.C. VINTAGES

Colonel E.H. Taylor Jr. christened the Old Fire Copper (O.F.C.) Distillery in 1870. Each year, honoring the heritage of the O.F.C. Distillery, Buffalo Trace releases a very rare and collectable bourbon. Each hand-cut crystal bottle is vintage dated according to the specific year in which the bourbon was distilled.

O.F.C. Vintage whiskeys are packaged in a wooden display box containing a provenance card. Nestled inside the wooden box is a crystal bottle with real copper lettering in-laid in the bottle and a paper label applied by hand. The label on the back of the bottle as well as the provenance card note the milestones for that expression.

The first release in 2016 was a whiskey laid down in 1980 (100 bottles); a whiskey laid down in 1982 (50 bottles); and one laid down in 1983 (50 bottles). Releases two and three (April and December) weren't until 2018 when they released one whiskey laid down in 1985 (61 bottles), one from 1989 (18 bottles), one from 1990 (63 bottles), and a 1993 (882 bottles). The fourth release in 2019 saw a whiskey from 1994 (1,095 bottles). The 2020 release saw a whiskey laid down in 1995 (1,500 bottles).

THE JOHNSON FAMILY

One of the biggest secrets about Buffalo Trace is its employees, a surprising number of whom are second- or even third-generation. If you are lucky enough, you will be given the tour by bourbon industry legend Freddie Johnson, whose grandfather and father were invaluable employees at Buffalo Trace during the 20th century. Freddie's grandfather, James B. "Jimmy" Johnson Sr., was the first Black foreman in Kentucky and stayed with the distillery until 1964.

Jimmy Johnson

Jimmy Johnson Jr.

In 1936, James B. "Jimmy" Johnson Jr. joined the distillery, following in his father's footsteps. Jimmy Jr. was as adept at the distilling business as his father, and was soon inspecting warehouses across the industry. He was a master barrel repairer, able to fix them while keeping the whiskey inside, a rare skill. He also had an uncanny knack for finding "honey barrels," those special barrels that are good enough to be used for select bourbons or single barrel bottlings. He became the first Black warehouse supervisor in Kentucky. After 40 years at Buffalo Trace, Jimmy Jr. retired in 1978, but remained active with the distillery until his passing in 2011.

Jimmy Jr. was a decorated veteran. He served a five-year tour with the Army Air Corps during World War II, and was stationed in Guam. It was the only time he was away from the distillery for any extended period.

One of the things Jimmy Jr. was most proud of was "his participation in loading the barrels into Warehouse V—the world's smallest bonded warehouse—holding only one barrel of bourbon. Warehouse V was built in 1952 to house the two millionth barrel of bourbon produced after Prohibition, and has housed every millionth barrel since," the company proudly proclaims. Jimmy Jr. helped load all of these barrels—six in total—into Warehouse V, including the six millionth barrel in 2009.

"I'm thrilled to be able to come back to the distillery and help with the six millionth barrel," said Johnson. "This is history and I'm honored to be a part of it."

Johnson was so well-loved and so highly respected that the distillery threw a lavish party for his 90th birthday. He commented, "To be able to celebrate my 90th birthday here with my family and friends is just icing on the cake."

Today Freddie Johnson, who grew up playing in the stockyards of the distillery, and who later became an engineer at AT&T, is easily one of the most recognizable figures roaming among the many buildings on this huge campus.

"It is very special for me to be able to continue the Johnson family legacy at Buffalo Trace," said Freddie. "I'm very proud of my family and their accomplishments." At one point during our tour with Freddie, we watched the cooper mending barrels. The cooper was also second generation. The cooper's father and Freddie's grandfather had worked there together, just like these two were working together now. That is Buffalo Trace's secret weapon.

Freddie Johnson

BUFFALO TRACE EXPERIMENTAL

Buffalo Trace has more than 5,000 experimental barrels of whiskey now aging in its warehouses. According to the distillery: "Each of the barrels has unique characteristics and experimental changes in the mash bill, types of wood, barrel toasts, and more. Periodically, an experimental whiskey is bottled and sold on a limited basis." The first expressions of these whiskeys were released in 2006. It has been a well-received series, both critically

and commercially. Barrel experiments have included French oak, American oak, twice-barreled, Chardonnay, Zinfandel, Cabernet Franc, rum, fine- and coarse-grained oak, rice bourbon, oat bourbon, 19- and 21-year-old releases, wheated bourbons, rye bourbon, aged wheated expressions, and an organic six-grain whiskey, among others. The keeper? The 12-Year-Old Wheated Bourbon (any one of the three expressions).

BUFFALO TRACE:
FREDDIE JOHNSON AND THE 7 MILLIONTH BARREL

In April 2018, Buffalo Trace No. 43 "V" – the world's smallest bonded warehouse – rolled away its 6 millionth barrel to make room for its 7 millionth barrel. Warehouse No. 43 "V" sits on the banks of the Kentucky River in Frankfort. This single rick barrel warehouse was built in 1952 to house the company's two millionth barrel of bourbon whiskey and has held every millionth barrel produced at the distillery ever since.

"These special barrels have raised over $2 million for charities," said Distillery President and CEO Mark Brown. "The 6 millionth barrel, which was in this warehouse, has been put away to age a little bit longer and it will be released for charity as will the 7 millionth barrel. The irony of the millionth barrel celebration is getting to be quite amusing. It took us forever to get from 5 million to 6 million. It's taken us eight years to get from 6 to 7. We will get to 8 in four years. We will get to 9 in two years and eventually we will be doing them every year and a half."

Freddie Johnson is a third-generation Buffalo Trace employee and well-known tour guide at the distillery. Freddie and his grandson, Osiris Johnson, took part in the millionth barrel celebration by carrying on a family tradition started by his father Jimmy.

"This tradition started with the first 1 millionth barrel that was made after Prohibition and that barrel was rolled away by Jimmy Johnson," said Mark Brown. "He then rolled away the 2nd million one and the 3rd and the 4th and the 5th. And I met him somewhere around 5.1 million barrels. And I said to Jimmy, well, you've got to carry on the family tradition. And he said, 'What do you mean?' I said you've got to roll away the 6th millionth barrel. And he said, 'When do you think you are going to do that?' I said about nine years from now. He said, 'But I'm 83.' I said I don't care, you're just going to have to figure out how to make it. Thrillingly, Jimmy, his son Freddie, and I, eight years ago, nine years ago now, stood here and rolled away that 6th millionth barrel. Unfortunately, Jimmy refused to do the 7 millionth barrel.

"So, in the spirit of honoring tradition and embracing change, today marks the day when Freddie takes over that mantel. And originally, Freddie had signed up for 7, 8, 9 and 10. However, at the pace we're going, we've redone those numbers and he's now on the hook all the way up to number 20. Freddie is the 3rd generation of his family, and there are many 2nd and 3rd generation folks that work for us. It's one of the things that we are very thankful for which is to have a family company with family members working in it through the generations. I think that's a very nice part of who we are and what we do. And I'm particularly proud to have Osiris Johnson, the fifth generation, to participate in this. And I'm figuring that Osiris should be able to carry the Johnson name all the way to the 50 millionth barrel."

WAREHOUSE X

For years, Buffalo Trace Distillery has been conducting whiskey experiments by exploring such variables as unique mash bills, barrel char levels, and types of wood. "We push the envelope here at Buffalo Trace. We have crazy ideas and aren't afraid to try them. The possibilities for bourbon here are endless," said Harlen Wheatley, master distiller.

One example is how Buffalo Trace constructed a one-of-a-kind experimental warehouse, called Warehouse X. It was custom built with four distinct chambers. The distillery has planned numerous experiments over the next 20 years. Barrels are wired with temperature gauges, they are studying the effects of light, temperature effects due to location, air flow, barometric pressure, humidity, you name it. Several of these studies will be multi-year, while others should produce results in one year's time.

The study started in 2014, and yielded in a short time more than 3.5 million data points. By 2020 their experiments and studies had pushed those results to more than 6 million data points.

"I admire the willingness of Sazerac/Buffalo Trace to invest real money in experiments that won't yield any useful results for decades, and maybe not even then," wrote industry journalist Chuck Cowdrey. "That's what companies do when 'long-term thinking' is more than just a commercially-attractive catch phrase." High praise indeed. And former *Whisky*

Advocate editor and whiskey legend Lew Bryson wrote at the time: "Distillery president Mark Brown has likened the multi-decade experimental project to a car company's Formula 1 racing program: technical innovation to improve the general process and product."

COLONEL E. H. TAYLOR

Buffalo Trace first introduced this line of fine bourbons in 2011. Colonel Edmund Haynes Taylor Jr. was the descendant of two American presidents: James Madison and Zachary Taylor. In his lifetime he served as a mayor, a state representative, and a senator. He was first introduced to the bourbon industry as a banker, but by 1870 he purchased a small Leestown distillery that he named Old Fashioned Copper, or O.F.C. He was among the first to modernize whiskey distilleries in the America, and is credited for such innovations as copper fermentation tanks, state-of-the-art grain equipment, column stills, a more efficient sour mash technique, and a first-of-its-kind steam heating system that is still used in the warehouses today. He also pushed for the Bottled-in-Bond Act of 1897.

Colonel E.H. Taylor Single Barrel and Colonel E.H. Taylor Four Grain Bourbon are two exceptional offerings from a long line of Taylor whiskeys. They are special indeed. The Single Barrel is one of the most highly rated, and the Four Grain was among the first-such releases from a distillery in Kentucky.

EXPANSION LEADS TO HISTORY

When Buffalo Trace underwent an extensive expansion, construction crews started digging up the floors and foundation in the oldest part of the distillery, the section closest to the river, and found a massive cement works underneath.

They had discovered the original works of Colonel E. H. Taylor's Old Fashion Copper distillery. Deep wells, which were used to house the bottom of copper stills, were used as large cement pool fermenters for the sour mash.

BLANTON'S

Albert B. Blanton joined the George T. Stagg Distillery as an office boy in 1897, at the age of 16. In 1921, Col. Blanton was promoted to president of the distillery. He was with the distillery for a total of 55 years when he retired in 1952. According to the distillery: "Under Col. Blanton's direction, the Distillery survived and even thrived through Prohibition, the Great Depression, a devastating flood, and numerous other challenges throughout the early 20th century. Col. Blanton kept the distillery alive through Prohibition, obtaining a special government license to produce 'medicinal whiskey.' It was one of only four distilleries in the country to obtain this special permission."

According to whiskey authority Clay Risen, "In a way, the bourbon renaissance began with Blanton's." Introduced in 1984, Blanton's was the world's first single barrel bourbon, a concept that Blanton himself originally utilized for his own private stock. This is an exceptional bourbon, with rich deep flavors and a long-lasting aftertaste.

W. L. WELLER

W. L. WELLER SPECIAL RESERVE

Born in 1825, William Larue Weller opened his Louisville wholesale liquor business in the 1840s and invented the first commercially sold bourbon to feature wheat instead of rye in the mash bill.

This orange-colored elixir is bottled at 90 proof and remains one of the best buys among all bourbons. Affordable and incredibly smooth, it is a treasured whiskey, and often a favorite among the whiskey cognoscenti.

SAZERAC RYE

In 1869, Thomas H. Handy founded a bar known as the Sazerac Coffee House in New Orleans. The bar had been named after the drink created in 1838 by a Creole immigrant named Antoine Amédée Peychaud, who owned a pharmacy on Royal Street in the French Quarter. According to the distillery: "Local patrons were served toddies made with Rye Whiskey and Peychaud's Bitters. The libation became known as the 'Sazerac' and America's first branded cocktail was born." Handy and his company began to acquire and market brands of liquor—today they own and distribute more than 30.

Sazerac Rye Straight Rye Whiskey is one of the most iconic ryes made in North America. The whiskey has been lauded by Jim Murray, Malt Advocate, Wine Enthusiast, and numerous writers for more than a century. This is a 6-year-old whiskey that is not as spicy as many other ryes, and is noticeably sweeter and smoother, with lots of caramel, cinnamon, and pepper. "Baby Saz" (as insiders call it) is a standard at any bar, and a great buy. In addition, Buffalo Trace Antique Collection's 18-year-old Sazerac has been released in limited amounts annually since 2014.

—STRAIGHT—
RYE WHISKEY

VAN WINKLE

Julian P. "Pappy" Van Winkle Sr. was quoted as saying: "We make fine bourbon at a profit if we can, at a loss if we must, but always fine bourbon." The highly collectible, long-aged bourbon that bears his name is among the most hotly acquired spirits in the United States.

Pappy started out as a traveling salesman for W. L. Weller and Sons in 1893. According to Buffalo Trace: "He and a friend, Alex Farnsley, eventually purchased the A. Ph. Stitzel Distillery, which produced bourbon for Weller. The two companies merged to form the Stitzel-Weller Distillery. Opened on Derby Day in 1935, Stitzel-Weller quickly became known for its wheated bourbon

recipe, which used wheat instead of rye in the mash for a softer, smoother taste. Pappy remained highly involved with the distillery up until his death in 1965, at the age of 91."

Since 1935, four generations have continued his legacy, producing aged, wheated bourbons. The easiest one to get ahold of is the Old Rip Van Winkle 10-Year-Old. Then there is the Van Winkle Family Reserve series. The most coveted is the Pappy Van Winkle series, with age statements that run 10, 12, 15, 20, 23, and 25 years. There is also a Van Winkle Family Reserve Rye.

While every offering from this distillery is stellar, the Pappy Van Winkle 23-Year-Old is the granddaddy of all bourbon.

Bulliett Distillng Co.

According to Tom Bulleit, his great-great-grandfather, the tavern keeper Augustus Bulleit, developed the first batch of Bulleit Bourbon around 1830. Augustus made and sold it up until 1860, when he died. The original Bulleit recipe was two-thirds rye and one-third corn in its mash bill (technically making it a rye by today's standards).

Tom Bulleit began distilling in 1987, making a high-rye version with a decent amount of aging. Seagram bought Bulleit in 1997 and moved the distilling operations to Lawrenceburg, Kentucky, where the whiskey was being produced at Kirin Brewing's Four Roses distillery. After a successful rebranding, the whiskey sky rocketed to popularity in the early 2000s.

On March 14, 2017, Diageo opened a new Bulleit distillery in Shelbyville, Kentucky. The 300-acre, $115 million facility is designed to eventually operate at a peak capacity of 1.8 million proof gallons annually.

In June 2019, Bulleit opened its visitors' center at the Shelbyville distillery, which features guided tours, tasting classes, a cocktail bar, and an opportunity for adult visitors to design a customized Bulleit label to apply to their own bottles.

Bulleit Bourbon maintains a consistent mash bill of roughly 68% corn, 28% rye, and 4% malted barley. Bulleit Rye (a sourced rye) is a high-rye with a mash bill of 95% rye and 5% malted barley. Both are very drinkable. The Bulliet 10-Year-Old and the Barrel Strength are imminently drinkable.

HOW MAD MEN CREATED
BULLEIT WHISKEY

According to Bulleit, it was Fran Taylor, at Meridian Communications, who suggested the family name. "Bulleit was a great name—why not go with Bulleit," said Taylor. "And every time I see him, if he's with a bunch of people, he'll introduce me as the person who talked him into Bulleit Bourbon—to changing the name." At the time, the whiskey was sold in a square brown bottle with a horse lightly sketched in the background.

In 1997, Bulleit sold his company to Seagram. According to Bulleit Seagram paid him a royalty on all products sold, and he maintained a consulting arrangement. It was then that the ad men stepped in. Seagram hired Jack Mariucci and Bob Mackall, at Doyle, Dane, and Bernbach. DDB was seen in many circles as the inspiration for the show Mad Men.

"They were the quintessential Madison Avenue advertising firm," said Bulleit. Ultimately, DDB hired Steve Sandstrom, of Sandstrom Designs out of Portland, Oregon, to spearhead the project. Sandstrom worked with Bulleit and the Seagram team to invent the new bottle and the new look for the whiskey.

Seemingly, intentionally or not, Sandstrom took a page out of an old Madison Avenue playbook. Marlboro cigarettes were initially named for the street Philip Morris Company was located on, and marketed as a cigarette for women with the slogan "Mild as May." The filter had a printed red band around it to hide lipstick stains, calling it "Beauty Tips to Keep the Paper from Your Lips". But the brand went bust.

Philip Morris went to Leo Burnett Worldwide. And in 1954 Burnett introduced the Marlboro Man and Marlboro Country, completely rebranding the cigarette toward men. The campaign centered around cowboys and ranch hands, positioning the cigarettes as masculine and rugged.

Bulleit received the same treatment as Sandstrom and his team created Wild West frontier marketing. Sandstrom's team invented the bottle and the label pretty much as we know them today. Little more than 40 years later, the old trick had been reinvented and still worked like a charm. Bulleit Bourbon and Bulleit Rye were a sensation.

CASEY JONES DISTILLERY

It's hard not to like Casey Jones Distillery. This place is authentic.

In 1987, Tom Bulleit founded the Bulleit Distilling Company. In 1989, he launched a new line with a product called Thoroughbred. In 1992, after much consultation and thought, he rebranded it to Bulleit Bourbon.

"In Golden Pond, Kentucky, Casey Jones was a legend. In a time when it was a risk to be this kind of legend, Casey Jones built an estimated 150 stills from the 1930s to the late 1960s," wrote local historian and moonshine expert Albert T. Joyce. Jones called his stills "outfits" or "docks," and set them up in "just about every hollow between Grand Rivers and Dover, Tennessee." He was brazen enough to build one in Lyon County, on a bank of the Cumberland River opposite from Eddyville Penitentiary. Even Jones admitted that this was "a little too close to the law for comfort."

Master distiller and Casey Jones's grandson, Arlon Casey "AJ" Jones, has gone back into the family business, albeit legally, and is paying homage to his infamous grandfather. Pictures of the old moonshiner are pasted everywhere in the distillery, where AJ produces a line of small batch moonshines and flavored moonshines.

Still Proof (118 proof) is made from a mash bill of 50% corn and 50% cane. It's got a little butter on the nose, and goes down super smooth. Despite the high proof, it doesn't drink like it. Casey Jones Kentucky Bourbon (118.9 proof) is a big cut of bourbon whiskey aged for 20 months in new oak, making this sweet and smoky, with some nice heat and a smooth caramel finish. Then there's the Barrel Cut Moonshine (102.7 proof), which is cane and corn whiskey aged in bourbon barrels. Hints of corn, caramel, and toasty oak, for an easy dram.

Castle & Key Distillery

Castle & Key Distillery is one of the most notable distilleries in Kentucky. It is located on the historic site of the iconic Old Taylor Distillery built by Colonel E. H. Taylor in 1887. Castle & Key was founded by owners Will Arvin and Wes Murry (and Brook Smith, who joined later). The Old Taylor Distillery, which produced the famous Old Taylor Bourbon, better known today as E. H. Taylor (which is now produced by Buffalo Trace), is situated by Glenns Creek, near Frankfort. It was created to look like a medieval castle, and has attracted tourists and picnickers for generations.

Work restoring the neglected citadel and accompanying buildings began in 2014. Vendome Copper & Brass Works installed a new still in October 2015. Original capacity was 12,000 barrels annually, which was upped to 45,000 barrels by 2020. The goal of the distillery is to work with local farmers for grains and botanicals. The goal of the new distillery is to produce bourbon, rye whiskey, single malt whiskey, vodka, and gin. But the concentration is on bourbon and whiskey. Production began in the summer of 2016.

Under its own label, Castle & Key hasn't released any whiskey yet. But they have released several clear spirits, including gin and vodka. They have released London Dry Gin Spring Recipe and London Dry Gin Autumn Recipe. The Spring Recipe features lighter, more citrus-based notes, while the Autumn Recipe is spicier, bolder. The Restoration Gin is made using a rye base and is super aromatic. The Restoration Vodka is made from a whiskey, and is extremely fine and drinkable.

Castle & Key has made whiskey for other labels, most notably Pinhook.

In December 2020, Restoration Kentucky Rye Whiskey was released as a tribute to the restoration of the historic property originally built over a century ago. "We are more than excited to release our Restoration Rye, a spirit that is thoughtful in every detail, from grain to glass, and is a true representation of the team's hard work and attention to detail over the past five years," said Castle & Key quality manager Jon Brown.

The whiskey was four years in the making and features two batches, both with unique flavor profiles. Batch #1 is created from a blend of 60 barrels, and Batch #2 is comprised of 57 barrels. During the blending process, barrels were grouped into pods with specific sensory profiles. Those pods were then blended together to achieve the unique, high-quality flavor profiles.

Restoration Rye Batch #1 (103 proof) has a mash bill of 63% rye, 17% yellow corn, 20% malted barley, with aromas of brown sugar, dried figs, tobacco, cocoa, and orange zest. Notes of baking spice, caramel, dried currants, with long lasting notes of maple syrup and dark honey.

Restoration Rye Batch #2 (99 proof) has a mash bill of 63% rye, 17% yellow corn, 20% malted barley with aromatic notes of lemon zest, apricot, and a lovely floral background. Graham cracker, honey, and stone fruits come across the palate, and it finishes with a lovely dry pop of white and black pepper.

CASTLE & KEY

PRODUCT TYPE

VODKA

BATCH/BOTTLE
9/15/15

MASHBILL
☐ 73% White Corn, 10% Rye, 17% Malted Barley
☐ 73% White Corn, 10% Wheat, 17% Malted Barley
☐ 17% Yellow Corn, 63% Rye, 20% Malted Barley

| PROOF 80 | ALC/VOL 40% | RESTORATION RELEASE |

DISTILLED FROM GRAIN

Product of Kentucky   750 ml

JIM RUTLEDGE
RETIRED?
WHO'S RETIRED?

Hall of Fame Master Distiller Jim Rutledge retired from Four Roses in 2015. He'd been working in the whiskey business for almost 50 years then, and had been a master distiller for 20 years. He'd already earned a Lifetime Achievement Award from *Malt Advocate* in 2007, and in 2008 *Whisky Magazine* honored him as Whisky Ambassador of the Year – American Whiskies. And in 2012, *Whisky Magazine* inducted him into its Icons of Whisky Hall of Fame.

"It took me about a week of retirement to realize a retirement week consisted of six Saturdays and one Sunday," he chuckled.

He started working on plans to create his own distillery, J W Rutledge, with his business partners, Jon Mowry, Will Conniff, and Stephen Camisa (all accomplished industry insiders). In late 2018, Rutledge unveiled plans for a new $25 million, environmentally sustainable 69,000-square-foot distillery. Plans were for a site in Oldham County, east of Louisville.

"COVID-19 has put everything at a standstill, and quite a few investors needed their money back," said Rutledge in October 2020. "I've been approached by several other groups but made no commitments yet."

Then Peter Brook Smith of Castle & Key called him up. "Brook contacted me earlier last year and told me about his ideas for Reclamation Rye. The idea was reclaiming the lands of Eastern Kentucky for the people, which was so desolate after the coal mines had left the area," said Rutledge.

That began his run of making spirits at Castle & Key, first for his own brands Cream of Kentucky Bourbon and High Plains Whiskey, as well as contract distilling for clients like Blue Run Bourbon. He has several other projects as well. We're glad he's slowed down.

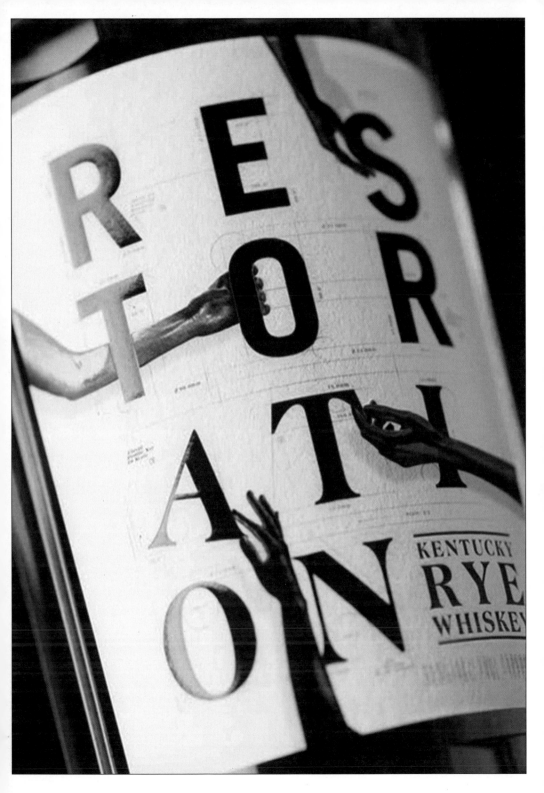

CREAM OF KENTUCKY

In 1888, I. Tragers & Co. in Cincinnati, Ohio, released for the first time The Cream of Kentucky Bourbon. The brand survived Prohibition, and soon found success in the 1930s and 1940s with the help of advertisements illustrated by Norman Rockwell.

The brand is now owned by Jim Rutledge, who was master distiller at Four Roses for 21 years, before branching off to found his own distillery, J.W. Rutledge Distillery. Cream of Kentucky is Rutledge's first release.

"It's one industry that has survived the great recession, and it's done well through COVID-19," Rutledge told the *Bourbon Review* in 2019, addressing the loss of financial backing for his own plans to build a distillery. He insisted the growth would continue through the next decade and a half. "We're still at the point where we're just catching up from where the bourbon industry was in the late 1960s. The number of barrels ageing in 1968 reached the peak then it started dropping for about 20 years and levelled out."

Rutledge pointed out that back in the 1960s, 10% of the barrels were marked for export. "Today it's 40%. We've got a long, long way to go before we reach the peak and level out. I have no concerns about that. The future looks very bright for the industry."

Rutledge worked with the folks at Castle & Key to make his first whiskey. Cream of Kentucky Straight Bourbon Whiskey (approx.102 proof) has come out in several batches. Each has been unique. One bottling was 11 years. Another bottling was 13 years. However, in the hand of Rutledge, the whiskeys have been elegant and smooth, and Cream of Kentucky has accomplished what Routledge has set out to do. Most of his whiskeys were sold out before they were bottled. Cream of Kentucky has established J W Routledge Distilling as a small house with a big reputation.

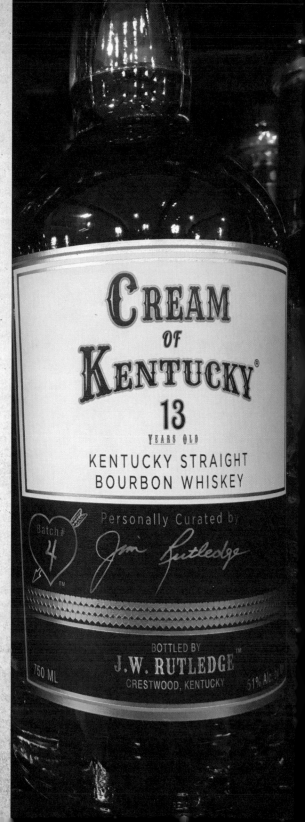

PINHOOK

Pinhook is possibly some of the most coveted boutique whiskey coming out of Kentucky today. However, it is at the same time an anomaly. Each year, Pinhook releases a new vintage of bourbons and ryes. They are master blenders. Through a combination of careful barrel selection, blending in small batches, and meticulous proofing, each Pinhook vintage has its own personality. And each bottle is named for a famous thoroughbred.

Pinhook was founded by Sean Josephs, along with Jay Peterson and Charles P. Fulford III. Josephs worked at such high-end restaurants as Chanterelle and Per Se in New York City. He then opened three American whiskey bars and restaurants: Char No. 4 and Maysville in New York and Kenton's in New Orleans. Pinhook Bourbon was started in 2010. Josephs wanted "to bring the concept of vintages to bourbon and celebrate the tradition of Kentucky horse racing." The brand name comes from the thoroughbred industry term, "pinhooking." Investors back a young horse and build its reputation, but generally sell for as much as possible before it turns three and is considered ready for racing.

The original whiskeys were sourced from MPG and were incredibly smooth and delicious. Josephs quickly developed a reputation for master blending. Starting in 2020 the bottlings of Pinhook have been produced by Castle & Key. Josephs's vintage bourbon approach has now come full circle. The first two releases were Pinhook 2020 Bohemian with a mash bill of 75% corn, 10% rye, and 15% malted barley. This 34-month bourbon (114.5 proof) was bottled from 100 barrels. The other was Pinhook 2020 Rye'd On (97 proof) with a mash bill of 60% rye, 20% corn, and 20% malt.

"Beginning three years ago, we've made our home at Castle & Key Distillery," said Josephs. "The very first Pinhook barrels we've distilled there are now mature."

These whiskeys have garnered incredible reviews, and are well worth searching out. The relationship between Castle & Key and Pinhook is one to watch.

Blue Run Spirits

Blue Run Spirits is a new spirits company, started in 2019 by a group of friends and bourbon lovers – a Nike designer, Facebook's first director-level employee, a hospitality executive, a political advisor, and a philanthropist. The Blue Run name is a nod to one of the founders being from Georgetown, the birthplace of bourbon in the Bluegrass State. It's an interesting group, but only just that until you add the last ingredient: Jim Rutledge, who serves as the brand's liquid advisor.

Their first whiskey was Blue Run Kentucky Straight Bourbon Whiskey Aged 13 Years (113 proof), a small-batch expression handcrafted by Rutledge. He carefully selects and distills every drop of liquid that goes into Blue Run Bourbons. Only 2,600 bottled were released in October 2020. On the nose, crisp vanilla and hints of herbs. Brown sugar and brown butter sauce on the palate give way to apricot and golden raisins.

"Blue Run is bottled at a higher proof than most extra-aged bourbons, providing more flavor because less water is added to reduce proof," said Rutledge. "While the proof is almost as high as a barrel-strength bourbon, its smoothness could be compared to bourbons with proofs 10 to 20 points lower."

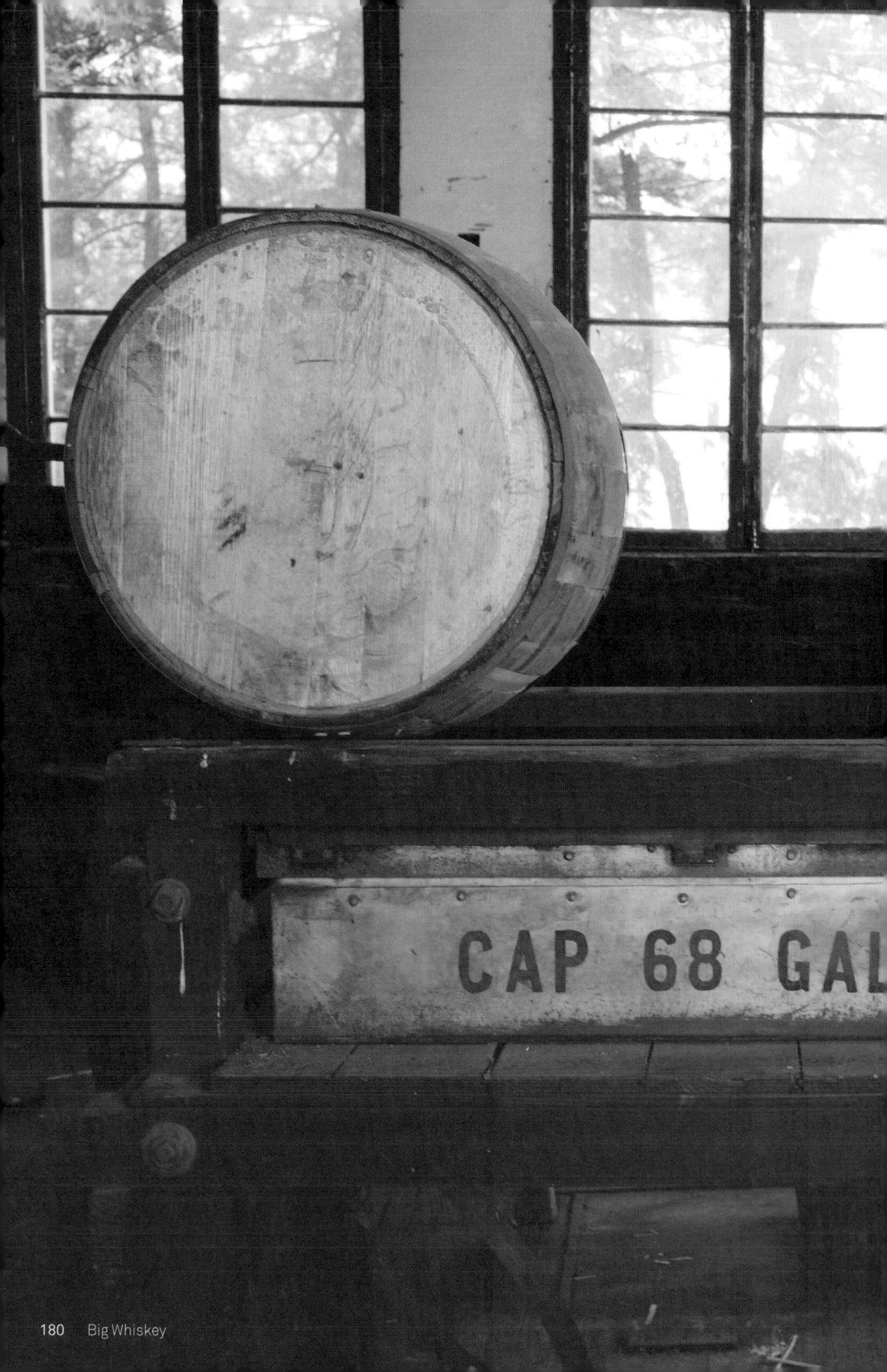
CAP 68 GAL

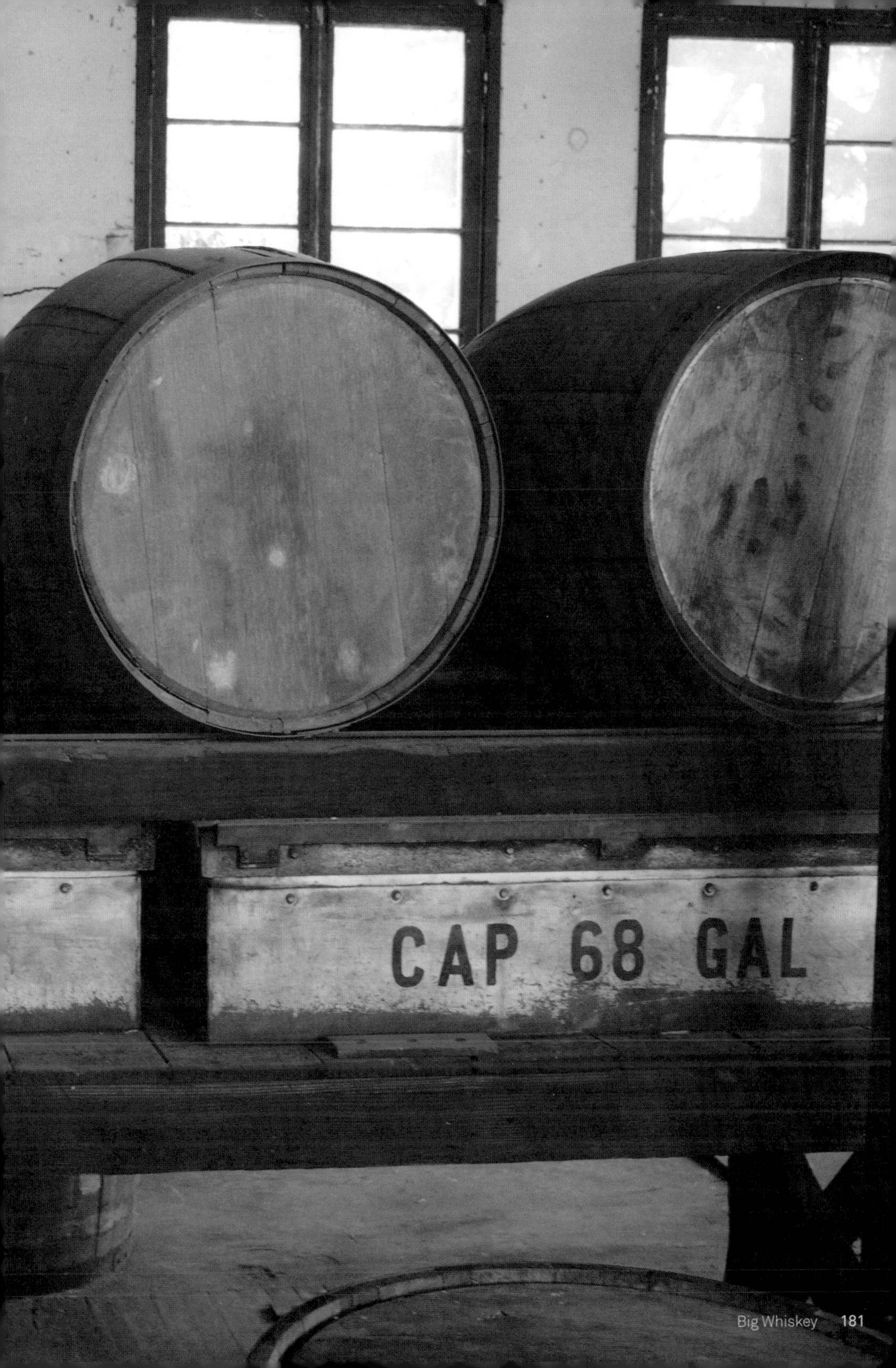
CAP 68 GAL

CHARLES MEDLEY DISTILLERY

Charles Medley Distillery is a throwback to the old Medley Distilling Company, which was first established in 1937 in Owensboro, Kentucky, by five brothers. The brothers sold the distillery in 1958, but stayed involved in the day-to-day operations until the 1970s. The last living member of the Medley family involved with the operation was Charles Medley, who also happened to be the last master distiller at the facility, which was shuttered in the 1990s.

With the rebirth of bourbon, Charles was able to purchase the rights to the moribund label and brand. Along with his son Sam, he has renewed both the family name and the old label. Charles Medley Distillery does not produce anything. Instead, Charles has all the bourbon contract-made (probably by Heaven Hill) to his specifications, including his mash bill of 77% corn, 10% rye, and 13% malted barley. Note the unusual high-barley, low-rye recipe.

In 1996 Charles Medley Distillery released Wathen's Kentucky Bourbon Single Barrel Eight Generations 8-Year-Old (94 proof), which was aged in charred American oak. Several reviewers insist that a splash of water is necessary to enhance the caramel and grain on this whiskey, and I quite agree. A few drops open up the bourbon beautifully.

Medley released a limited, small-batch run of Medley Family Private Selection Kentucky Straight Bourbon Whiskey, part of an 11-barrel release (268 cases) coordinated by Sam Medley to celebrate his father's 75th birthday. There is no age statement on the bottle, so the resulting whiskey is more than two years old, but probably less than six.

The other popular release from this distillery is Medley Bros. Kentucky Straight Bourbon Whiskey (102 proof). It has the same high-barley recipe as Wathen's and is a straightforward bourbon with no fancy gimmicks. It's easy to drink or mix. The distillery also released an Old Medley 12-year-old (86.8 proof) that has received some nice attention.

Plenty of solid offerings from this brand, but the keeper is the Eight Generations.

COPPER & KINGS
AMERICAN BRANDY COMPANY

Without exaggeration, outside of the bourbon and whiskey business, there is no more respected distiller than Copper & Kings. While many of the region's distilleries are concentrating on whiskey, Copper & Kings Distillery is attempting to become the nation's premiere craft spirits and brandy producer. And so far the plan is being executed flawlessly.

The Copper & Kings distillery is located in Louisville's Butchertown section, and was founded in 2014 by famed beverage entrepreneurs Joe and Lesley Heron. The Herons created Nutrisoda (they sold it to PepsiAmericas in 2006) and the Crispin Hard Cider Company (sold to MillerCoors in 2012). Copper & Kings is their latest project.

Thus far, it has created a line of fine, high-end small-batch brandies, absinthe, and liqueurs that are available in more than 31 states.

"I'm from the South, the far South—South Africa," joked Joe with Saveur magazine. "There was no $35 brandy. More importantly, we wanted to create an American brandy that defines the American spirit culturally and physically."

The distillery is segmented into four parts: the basement is a maturation cellar; the first floor is the distillery/production space; the second floor contains an art gallery and office space; and the top floor holds the tasting room and event space, providing incredible views of downtown Louisville. Most notable are the stacks of iconic orange-and-black shipping containers that form the distillery's shop. Outside the shop is a butterfly garden and habitat certified as a registered Monarch Waystation.

According to its website, Copper & Kings uses "traditional copper pot-distillation to forge untraditional craft-distilled, natural, pure pot-still brandies. We make definitive American brandy influenced by American whiskey and American music. We do not make derivative brandy styled upon a European sensibility. Our brandies are batch distilled exclusively in copper pot-stills, and are non-chill filtered, with no added sugar, boisé (powdered oak, shavings or infusion), other flavors, synthetic chemicals, or caramel colorants for an uncorrupted, authentic, natural flavor, nose, and color."

The company makes an apple brandy using Michigan apples; two different absinthes (Ansinthe Alembic Blanche and Absinthe Alembic Barrel Finished); five gins (American Dry, American Old Tom, The Moons of Juniper, Distilled Gin Finished in Orange Curacao Barrels, and Distilled Gin With Rose Hibiscus, Strawberry, and Honey). It also features several interesting liqueurs in its Destillaré series, including an Orange Curaçao, Café Liqueur, Chocolate Liqueur, and Pomegranate, as well as the CR&FTWERK series of brandies, each of which rests in craft beer barrels for no less than 12 months.

The company's two standouts are the Copper & Kings American Brandy (62% ABV), which is a solera method brandy. Combining sourced, aged pot-stilled brandy from local distilleries with Copper & Kings own brandies, and aged in Kentucky bourbon barrels and American white oak, creates a lovely brandy with rich notes of caramel, fig, and stone fruits. The other is the outstanding Copper & Kings Butchertown Reserve Casks Brandy (62% ABV), which is a small-batch brandy aged for 75% of the time in Kentucky bourbon barrels and 25% in new American oak. The result is deep and rich, with an incredibly long-lasting finish. This is a brandy that whiskey lovers can really appreciate!

DISTILLED SPIRITS EPICENTER

The brainchild of Scott Weddle, Distilled Spirits Epicenter is a fascinating place. It is not a distillery, but rather a learning center, custom distilling house, and bottler. It is comprised of three sections: Moonshine University, a learning center that teaches distilling as well as the business of how to run a distillery; Greasemonkey Distillery, which is a custom distillery where it develops mash bills, creates prototype batches, and experiments with processing for full-run productions; and Challenge Bottling, a flexible bottling line for small producers that are either quickly outgrowing their own bottling capacity, or want to outsource their packaging. It's a fascinating and much needed addition to the craft distilling scene.

Dueling Barrels Brewery & Distillery

Pearse and Deirdre Lyons founded Dueling Barrels Brewery & Distillery in Pikeville, Kentucky. After immigrating to Appalachia from Ireland, Pearse and Diedre fell in love with the region because of the many ways it reminded them of home. Pikeville is close to the area of the legendary rivalry of the Hatfields and McCoys, the dawn of Bluegrass music.

Deirdre and Pearce co-founded Alltech in 1980 to help farmers feed the world, raise healthy animals, and protect the environment through natural, nutritional innovation. Today, Alltech is a $2 billion company with more than 5,000 employees supporting its business presence in over 120 countries. Alltech also owns Town Branch in Lexington and Pearse Lyons Distillery in Dublin, Ireland.

The brewery offers more than a half dozen beers year-round, as well as seasonal brews throughout the year. The distillery also offers Dueling Barrels Kentucky Mountain Flower Moonshine, Original Moonshine, Apple Orach Moonshine, and Bonfire Moonshine. Original is corn liquor, suitable for aging as bourbon. It is bottled at 100 proof, with a blend of corn, malted barley, and a pinch of rye for a hint of spice. Smooth and with a slightly sweet finish. Mountain Flower is infused with elderberry at 80 proof. Bonfire is infused with cinnamon, and Apple Orchard has notes of apple, caramel, and vanilla. The Original is for aficionados, and is a good harbinger of aged whiskeys to come.

DUELING GROUNDS DISTILLERY

Franklin's Dueling Grounds Distillery is named for its local legendary historical site turned thoroughbred race park. In its heyday, The Dueling Grounds of Franklin saw more than 40 duels, the most famous of which took place on September 22, 1826, pitting Tennessee Representative Sam Houston against General William A. White over one of Andrew Jackson's political appointments. Jackson advised the younger Houston to bite down on a bullet during the duel to improve his concentration and aim. The trick worked, as Houston hit White in the leg. Both men survived.

Dueling Grounds Distillery is owned by Marc Dottore, who also serves as master distiller. He claims that the distillery aims to produce "very small-batch ultra-premium bourbon using the best local ingredients. That means Estate Grown Grains from Walnut Grove Farm, all non-GMO, grown on one farm—by one farmer—in one season. I make a few thousand gallons a year from local ingredients to sell to local people and a few lucky ones who come through."

The distillery currently offers numerous products: Kentucky Clear is their white whiskey, which is quite good, and a quality Kentucky Apple Pie. They also offer a solid gin, and an excellent line of fruit liqueurs. Kentucky Clear is a quality white whiskey made from locally grown and milled Kentucky corn and wheat. Featuring notes of cornmeal, porridge, cornbread, and florals, with hints of butter. A quality dram.

The uniquely handcrafted batches of Dueling Grounds, Linkumpinch Bourbon, are double-pot distilled, aged for four years in charred oak barrels, and embody grains of the region. Dueling Grounds have named their bourbon Linkumpinch for Linkumpinch Farm, where legendary duels took place. There is a Linkumpinch 4-Year-Old Single Barrel Cask (proof varies). This whiskey was aged for four years in char 3 new oak barrels. There's also the Linkumpinch Small Batch (100 proof) also aged in char 3 new oak barrels. Both whiskeys are nutty, with notes of pepper, vanilla, orange zest, caramel, cereal corn, and hints of tobacco, with a caramel and corn flavor that lingers nicely. Great quality products.

Four Gate Whiskey Company

Four Gate Whiskey Company is a small blending house located in Louisville. They started releasing whiskeys in 2019 in very limited, small batches. So much so, that their first two whiskeys never made it out of Kentucky before it was all sold. The company is co-owned by Bill Straub and Bob D'Antoni, and they release micro-batch bottlings.

Four Gates first 10 releases were all numbered, i.e. Release 1. The Kelvin Collaboration Batch 1; Release 2, Outer Loop Orbit; Release 3, Foundation, etc. They are wonderful blenders. They also do a fair amount of finishing, working very closely with Kelvin Cooperage.

According to the owners: "All of our releases, no matter the barrel finish we choose, must start with excellent whiskey. That's our #1 rule, and we won't compromise. It's the foundation of what we do."

In September 2020, they released Four Gate Rye Batch 7 River Kelvin Rye (113.2 proof), which was bottled using MGP-sourced straight rye. This was a high-rye rye, with a mash bill of 95% rye and 5% malted barley. The whiskey was 7 years old. Approximately 1,480 bottles were released.

There was also Tennessee Foundation Tennessee Straight Bourbon Whiskey (112.2 proof) with a mash bill of 84% corn, 8% rye, and 8% malted barley. Straub and D'Antoni chose five barrels of the 10-year-old Tennessee Straight Bourbon. Only 800 bottles were released. "We knew when we released Batch 5 [Foundation] that there were so few bottles, our customers in Tennessee would likely miss out," said D'Antoni. "Our distributor in Tennessee asked us if we could do something else for markets outside of Kentucky, so we answered the call."

Macadamia nuts, chocolate, coffee, and rich leather on the nose. On the palate peanuts, oak, hints of cinnamon, and earthy tobacco. The nutty and earthy characteristics linger to a pleasant close.

Four Gate is getting lots of praise for such a little operation.

Four Roses is one of the hottest brands in Kentucky bourbon. But the history of the label is complicated. Throughout the 1930s, '40s, and '50s, Four Roses Kentucky Straight Bourbon was the bestselling of its kind in the United States. However, the label then all but disappeared from the domestic market for decades, while continuing to sell very well in Asian and other foreign markets. Happily, Four Roses has made a huge comeback in the United States, and is headed back to its rightful place among the country's top whiskeys.

It is said that when Paul Jones Jr., the founder of Four Roses, wrote to propose to his future wife, she replied that if her answer was "yes," she would wear a corsage of roses on her gown to the ball. Lo and behold, she did, and in doing so inspired the name of Four Roses Bourbon. Jones, a seasoned distiller, registered the name in 1888, and the Spanish Mission-style distillery in Lawrenceburg was erected between 1908 and 1910. It is listed on the National Register of Historic Places.

In the 1940s, Seagram bought the brand, and by the late 1950s had decided to discontinue sale of Four Roses Kentucky Straight Bourbon in the United States, choosing to use the label to push an inferior blended whiskey domestically. The real bourbon the distillery made was exported to Europe, Asia, and other international markets.

Four Roses Kentucky Bourbon was not available in the United States for more than two generations. That all changed in 2002 when Diageo purchased the brand, and then sold it to Kirin, Four Roses' Japanese distributor. Thanks to the lobbying of former master distiller Jim Rutledge, Kirin quickly cut the sale of blended whiskey in order to concentrate on producing quality bourbon, and returned the brand's Kentucky Straight Bourbon to the US market.

In September 2020, Four Roses offered a Limited Edition Small Batch. Non-chill filtered and bottled at a 111.4 proof, it featured four different hand-selected batches aged 12 to 19 years. These batches represent four of the distillery's ten distinct Bourbon recipes – a 12-year-old Bourbon from the OBSV recipe, a 12-year-old OESV, a 16-year-old OESK, and a 19-year-old OBSK.

"Each batch in this year's limited-edition bottling is an exceptional whiskey that could have stood on its own as a single barrel offering," Elliott said. "But in this case the sum is even greater than the parts. Together, these bring a perfect balance of bright, vibrant flavors and aromas from the 12- and 16-year-old barrels combined with the oak tones and aged expressions from the 19-year-old batch."

Four Roses special releases are always an event, and this one did not disappoint. Fantastic!

Today, the distillery is receiving major accolades, thanks to the releases from former master distiller Jim Rutledge. The distillery is not only getting a complete and total upgrade and rebuild, the brand is also being polished. Old antique bottles from the glory days of the '40s and '50s are being reintroduced in retro packaging, and new high-end expressions are a huge hit with the press.

To celebrate Jim Rutledge's 40th Anniversary as master distiller, the brand released a limited unfiltered/uncut edition of bourbon in September 2007(1,442 bottles). It was an instant success. A 120th anniversary brand edition was released a year later to still more raves and insane demand. This was followed by the 2008 release of the Four Roses Marriage Collection. These small releases instantly re-established Four Roses' prominence.

Four Roses master distiller Brent Elliott uses two mash bills that are mixed and matched with five yeast strains to produce their Kentucky bourbon. That makes for ten different bourbons. The standard Yellow Label is made from an even blend of all ten. It's aged for six to seven-and-a-half years, is bottled at 80 proof, and is a light, smooth, easily drinkable bourbon. The Four Roses Small Batch contains only four of the recipes (Obsk, Oesk, Obso, and Oeso) and is bottled at 90 proof. It's a bigger, richer, and darker whiskey than the Yellow and offers what locals call the "Kentucky Hug," a distinctive, overwhelming sensation of flavor and warmth. The Four Roses Single Barrel uses only one recipe (Obsv) and is aged eight-and-a-half to nine years in oak. It's bottled at 100 proof. Elliott Select Single Barrel uses one recipe (Oesk) and spends 14 years in oak. It's bottled at 113 proof, and is approximately cask strength. The Single Barrel is a big, big whiskey with lots to offer. Be aware, cask-strength fans—this is most definitely a whiskey worth seeking out.

Elliott is probably one of the most promising master distillers in the entire region. He is taking on a project few distillers ever get the chance to, and using this opportunity to create some spectacular bourbons. His single barrel releases and his meticulous attention to recipes and pairings reveal the promise to become one of the great distillers of all-time. In other words, Four Roses is back.

Four Roses.

SMALL BATCH SELECT

Kentucky Straight Bourbon Whiskey
Crafted from Six Unique Bourbons
52% ALC./VOL. (104 proof) 750 ML

BRENT ELLIOTT
BOURBON'S NEWEST STAR!

Brent Elliott has got to be one of the most confident people you will ever meet. Four Roses Distillery is one of the mythical names in the bourbon business, and Elliott was named master distiller in September 2015. He succeeded Bourbon Hall of Fame member and legendary distiller Jim Rutledge, and is also the spokesperson for the brand in the wake of brand ambassador Al Young's semi-retirement. Following that duo is an incredible task. And Elliott was also tapped to lead Four Roses on a massive $65 million expansion at a time when bourbon has never been hotter.

No pressure whatsoever.

But he can handle it. Elliott, one of the newest and hottest master distillers in Kentucky, is without a doubt the driving force behind the Four Roses renaissance. And it's not just this author's opinion. It's the industry's. His new whiskeys received the coveted "America's Best Kentucky Bourbon" award from Whisky Magazine's World Whiskies Awards.

Since Elliott took over, the accolades have not stopped. And sales for the recent releases of its high-end expressions have been through the roof. A special release day in July 2017 attracted a line almost a half-mile long, filled with people eager to buy a bottle. Vehicles parked along the sides of the road ranged from rusted-out old pickup trucks to Cadillacs, BMWs, and Mercedes-Benz. And even at $150 per bottle, there were enthusiasts and collectors walking out with half-cases, or more.

Elliott earned a degree in chemistry from the University of Kentucky, and early on, his only understanding of bourbon came from imbibing too much. But in 2005, an opportunity to work for the distillery as a chemist opened the door for this brash young superstar. As the industry boomed, his opportunities just kept growing.

"We grew rapidly," Elliott told industry insider Tim Knittel. "So there were always opportunities to go out and learn new aspects of everything from production to pitching in with events, or marketing, or whatever it might be."

Elliott also had a chance to work side-by-side with Jim Rutledge, which he recognizes as a great learning experience. "When I see Jim interact with the public, I immediately recognize the magic that endears him to people. He takes the time to listen and talk to anyone, anytime . . . As master distiller, Jim has always been eager to share his valuable knowledge." And there are some fun memories, as well. "Jim and I have a nice history of karaoke duets of Johnny Cash songs at Four Roses Christmas parties. Jim is really good at hitting the low notes. I'm not sure about me," Elliot said.

In 2020, Elliott was awarded Master Distiller of the Year by *Whisky Magazine*.

Fresh Bourbon Distilling Co.

Fresh Bourbon Distilling is one of the newest and most exciting stories in Kentucky whiskey. Founded by Lexington natives Sean and Tia Edwards, Fresh Bourbon Distilling Co. was registered in 2017 with the aim of creating a "premier, African American-owned Bourbon brand." The company released its first whiskey in 2020, and has plans to open their new distillery in 2021 in downtown Lexington, despite construction delays brought on by COVID-19.

The 35,000-square-foot site will be located near the Distillery District. The plant will produce several bourbons and other whiskies. It will feature an event space, tours, and guided tastings. The production facility will also create approximately twenty-five jobs. In December 2019 the Kentucky Economic Development Finance Authority (KEDFA) approved a 10-year performance-based deal with Fresh Bourbon Distilling through the Kentucky Business Investment Program. The plant has an estimated cost of $5.4 million.

"Bourbon is a mainstay of Kentucky's economy, and I am thrilled to see this step toward greater inclusivity in this iconic industry," Kentucky Gov. Andy Beshear announced. "Creating opportunities for all Kentuckians is essential."

"Our aspirations and dreams are to be a world-recognized brand," said Sean. "The ideal for us is to be one of the top bourbon brands produced." Sean is the president of S & D Construction Management of Lexington, which specializes in commercial and industrial construction.

Fresh Bourbon Distilling Co. is the first Black-owned bourbon distillery in Central Kentucky. The first bottlings were produced from the Edwards' own custom recipe under a contract with Hartfield & Co. in Paris, Kentucky. Hartfield & Co, is one of the hottest small boutique bourbon producers in the country.

"For nearly three years, we have been diligently developing an authentic and unique bourbon and spirits line. We chose not to buy bourbon from someone else and just place our name on a bottle. We have been very intentional and deliberate in crafting our spirits, from the mash bills up," stated Sean.

The second batch will arrive on store shelves in 2021. Fresh Bourbon Distilling Co. has secured distribution, and will initially launch in five states.

"The story sells the first bottle, but what's in it will sell the second bottle," said Sean.

"And the one after that," added Tia. "This is history in a bottle."

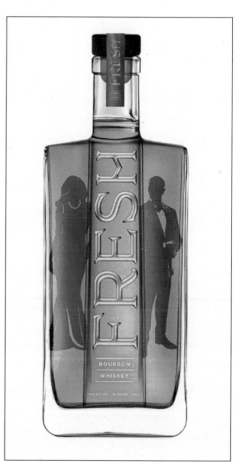

GLENNS CREEK DISTILLING

In December 2013, Neil Craig and David Meier bought the remains of the Old Crow Distillery, which had been abandoned for more than 30 years. They plan to slowly, step-by-loving-step, refurbish the old distillery.

According to the owners, "The road ahead to restore and preserve these great buildings is a long one, but one that everybody at the distillery is willing to undertake. We reuse and repurpose items salvaged from the old buildings, and almost all of the work done to clean up the distilling building has been done by us. We have also designed and built nearly all the equipment we use during the cooking of the mash, fermentation, and distillation process. To make a truly hand-crafted bourbon we wanted to make the entire process hand-crafted and custom to our distillery."

The distillery sells a number of products: OCD #5 Bourbon, Prohibition Kentucky Rum, Ryskey Rye Whiskey, and Stave + Barrel. Ryskey Rye Whiskey is a very good sourced rye whiskey that is 95% rye, and packs plenty of spice and flavor. The Stave + Barrel is also sourced, and is another solid, high-rye bourbon.

Hamilton's Spirit is an unaged corn and cane spirit. Hamilton Dark is made from grain spirit and cane sugar. A lighter style of bourbon with a slightly sweeter, more mild finish. Millville Malt is a peated whiskey. Café Ole is a bourbon made with the same

mash bill as their OCD #5 bourbon with an addition of a heavily toasted barley malt. It boasts notes of chocolate and mocha. The Prohibition Kentucky Rum (58.5% ABV) is made the old-fashioned way, from fermented molasses, and is distilled on site. It's got some lovely hints of burnt sugar and caramel, as well as cotton candy.

But the most important label in the portfolio is Glenns Creek Distilling OCD #5 Bourbon (53.8% ABV). This pot-still bourbon, which is made onsite in small quantities, has a unique story behind it. While rummaging through the wreckage of the old plant, it turned out that Old Crow fermenter #5 had been sealed all these years. When Craig and Meier discovered this, they took samples and grew a cultured yeast that might harken back to the original yeasts the distillery used more than a century ago. Whether it was in fact an older yeast or a wild yeast, the point was that it was site-specific.

OCD #5 (which stands for Old Crow Distilling fermenter #5) is made and aged onsite in 53-gallon new charred American oak barrels that feature three different oaks and have extra staves inserted in them. The most recent expressions released were aged for approximately six months or longer. The bourbon is sold at full-barrel strength from a single barrel, and is definitely worth seeking out!

Their newest bourbon release is ¡Cuervito Vivo! This is a single barrel nano batch bourbon. Glenns Creek's vision for this expression was to recreate the top shelf bourbon once produced on the grounds where they operate today. They had the benefit of the insight of the last supervisor to manage this distillery. Glenn's Creek is inching closer to gaining a much bigger, well deserved reputation.

GOODWOOD BREWERY

Ted Mitzlaff is the CEO of Goodwood Brewery. The group behind the brewery comprises some of Louisville's longest-serving brewing veterans, running production breweries there since 2001. The philosophy of Goodwood is in barrel aged beers. "At Goodwood, we've come to believe that what's good for bourbon is even better for beer. Our extra steps are an homage to this region's distilling legacy and to those old barrels out there that still have so much flavor left to give." All Goodwood beers are wood-seasoned on poplar, oak, ash, and other woods, or in reclaimed oak casks once used to house wine, brandy, and local bourbon.

The brewery has proved immensely popular. They have two locations in Kentucky, one in Louisville and the other in Frankfort. You will also see the Goodwood name on many whiskey shelves, as they believe in collaboration projects with different distilleries. And them there are three whiskeys that bear their name.

Goodwood Stout Barrel Finish Kentucky Straight Bourbon Whiskey (90 proof) was aged in charred white oak American barrels for 12 years, before a three-month catnap in Goodwood's award-winning Bourbon Barrel Stout barrels. The whiskey is available in both 5- and 12-year-old expressions.

Goodwood Honey Ale Barrel Finish Kentucky Straight Bourbon Whiskey (90 proof) is aged 5 years in charred American white oak barrels, then finished in Goodwood's award-winning honey ale brandy barrels.

There is also is a collaboration between Bardstown and Goodwood, as part of the distiller's Collaborative Series. A limited release, Bardstown Bourbon Company Goodwood Brewing Company Walnut Brown Ale is an exceptional high-proof 9-year-old Tennessee straight bourbon whiskey aged in Goodwood walnut brown ale casks for 18 months. "This spirit is very complex, with a layered pairing of walnut, toffee, oak, biscuit and malt notes," said Bardstown's Nick Smith. "The subtle finish of ale really enhances this one-of-a-kind pour."

All of these bourbons have received critical praise, and Goodwood remains an innovative collaborator to be reckoned with in the distilling world.

Green River Distilling

J. W. McCulloch began making Green River whiskey in 1885. Advertising for the brand included the slogan "Green River – The Whiskey Without A Headache." Green River Whiskey was presented with a grand prize at the Leige Exposition in Belgium in 1905. However, in 1918, a fire ignited after hours and burned through the distillery. All the whiskey, and almost all of the buildings, were completely lost. The fire ultimately proved to be the fatal blow to the Green River Distillery.

In 1936, the property was sold to the Kentucky Sour Mash Distilling Company. The company went bankrupt shortly after rebuilding the facility. Three years later, the Medley family purchased the facility and formed Medley Distilling Company. Over the next 70 years the distillery changed hands a few more times, but Medley family members remained in various management roles.

In 2014, the Terressentia Corporation, led by Simon Burch, purchased the distillery and began renovations. Ron Call, a master distiller with 40 years of experience at Jim Beam Brands and Florida Caribbean Distillers, was tapped to consult on the project. Ron's son, Jacob Call, was brought in to oversee the extensive renovation and, ultimately, manage distillery operations under the O. Z. Tyler name. The distillery opened for production in 2016 and began laying down whiskey for barrel aging. Ron passed the master distiller torch to Jacob, and in 2018 the distillery was declared a heritage member of the official Kentucky Bourbon Trail and its western most point, reviving the historic distilling history of Owensboro. Finally, in 2020, with the support of J. W. McCulloch's great-grandson, the distillery was restored to its original name, Green River Distilling Co.

Green River is currently one of the top-ten largest privately owned distillers, providing contract brewing and bulk spirits while also producing their own line of whiskeys. Green River now produces close to 100,000 barrels of bourbon yearly. Green River actually ships bulk bourbon all around the world as part of their wholesale business. Many popular brands are produced at Green River. Their own Green River Bourbon will be released in 2021.

JOHN & RON & JACOB CALL
A LEGACY

John Call made his name with the Jim Beam brands back in the day. His son Ron Call is a legendary figure in the distilling world. In Ron's 42-year career in distilled spirits, he helped develop Jim Beam Black Label with his mentor the late Booker Noe. He left Beam after 16 years, and moved to Florida Caribbean Distillers where he was instrumental in developing the Cruzan Rum line and other lines as master blender and, later, master distiller. Ron was instrumental—along with his son Jacob—in developing the renovation and operating plan for the Green River Distillery.

A third-generation master distiller, Jacob knows something about the business. Jacob is a seventh-generation Kentuckian (born and raised in Bardstown). He graduated from Murray State University with a degree in business administration. He started his career in banking, rising in the ranks to COO before eventually succumbing to fate and legacy.

Jacob cut his teeth at Florida Caribbean Distillers, which he joined in 2007. He held various senior management positions in purchasing, bulk sales, and distillery operations. Jacob joined Terressentia (Green River's parent company) in late 2014 to oversee the renovations. As master distiller, he oversees all aspects of whiskey production and warehousing for the facility. His whiskeys are gaining in reputation and popularity. The Call family tradition lives on. But with his recent successes, it certainly seems like it's Jacob's star turn!

BRADSHAW

Drafted number one overall in the NFL 1970 draft, Terry Bradshaw had one of the most iconic and prolific careers in the history of the league, resulting in four Super Bowl championships. Today, Bradshaw is one of the iconic football analysts on television. Bradshaw also focuses his resources on philanthropic tasks such as funding projects to bring solar powered wells to struggling communities in East Africa. "There is something quintessentially American about bourbon," said Bradshaw. "There's just nothing better than a fireplace, two fingers of bourbon, a great cigar, and Pavarotti playing in the background. I've always appreciated a good bourbon, and now I'll be enjoying my own!"

The whiskey is a collaboration between Green River Distilling and Silver Screen Bottling Company. Bradshaw Kentucky Straight Bourbon Whiskey 103.8 proof has a mash bill of 70% corn, 21% rye, and 9% malted barley. The whiskey has garnered excellent reviews in the press.

QUARTER HORSE

Quarter Horse Kentucky Bourbon Whiskey (92 proof) is a brand produced at Green River Distilling. It is designed to be an easy drinking bourbon, with interesting notes of strawberry, gingerbread, honey, caramel, orange zest, and cereal. Ginger and black pepper on the back. Quarter Horse is aged using O.Z. Tyler's patented TerraPURE machinery. Oak staves are secured inside the machine, in an effort to help create traditional bourbon flavor. The machinery is designed to reduce the barrel aging process. The claim is that in 12 hours the ultrasonic exposure simulates four years in the barrel. A unique product.

DUKE

John Wayne, also known as The Duke, was a Hollywood legend. A famous actor, he was also an avid fisherman, horseman, hunter, and adventurer. He was also a fan of American and Scotch whiskies. He was often quoted as saying that if he was going to have a drink, "It had better be a good one."

The Wayne family has carried over his love of fine brown spirits to a line of excellent bourbons made in Kentucky. A collaboration between Founder Chris Radomski and Green River Distilling, they have released three whiskies.

Duke Kentucky Straight Bourbon (88 proof) is the flagship expression. The idea is that this whiskey honors the tasting notes and profile preferred by John Wayne himself, using his extensive, original tasting notes from 1962 and his private collection as the inspiration for flavor and aromatics. The mash bill is 75% American dent corn, 13% rye, and 12% sixth-row barley. Distilled and aged in small batches in Kentucky, it's aged five years in heavily charred new American Oak barrels. Caramel, cherry, toasted nuts, and spice. It's very smooth and drinkable.

Duke Grand Cru Kentucky Reserve Bourbon is a 9-year-old Kentucky Straight Bourbon finished in used wine oak casks. Classic French oak barrels that housed big red wines from Napa Valley wines like St. Helena, Howell Mountain, and Rutherford. A much higher expression spirit, aimed at connoisseurs. A much more bourbon as cognac experience. Lots of stone fruit, hints of orange zest, honey, and caramel. Duke Grand Cru Double Barrel Rye is a formidable entry into the fast rising rye market. This rye marries the classic and powerful flavors of aged Kentucky rye with French Oak Grand Cru wine barrels. This is a big rye, with a mash bill of 95% rye and 5% malted barley. After aging in new French oak, it is then moved to rest in a second French oak wine barrel that has rested both world-class wines and the Duke Grand Cru. This secondary finish absolutely rounds out the whiskey, giving it a velvety finish.

YELLOW BANKS

Yellow Banks is a collaboration between Green River Distilling and the Kentucky Corn Growers Association (KyCorn). This grassroots organization, founded in 1982, represents the interests of more than 6,000 corn farmers in the Commonwealth by improving markets and demand, strengthening consumer trust for products and practices, investing in research for economically and environmentally sustainable production, and advancing leadership and membership to provide a voice for Kentucky Corn Grower. KyCorn is an official state affiliate of the National Corn Growers Association. Their logo is on the label. A portion of the profits go toward corn research. It is a Kentucky Proud product. The distillery uses 800,000 bushels of Kentucky corn each year in its whiskey. "It has a very smooth, sweet flavor," Call said. The whiskey was released in November 2020.

WINCHESTER

Another Green River collaboration, Winchester Bourbon Winchester Straight Bourbon is aged in new charred American oak barrels the "old fashioned" way for at least two years. The Winchester brand also sells an Extra Smooth Bourbon and a Rye Whiskey. Sold in select stores.

Hartfield & Co.: Bringing Bourbon Back to Bourbon County

It's almost impossible not to fall in love with Hartfield. Maybe it's the cool yet unpresuming location? Maybe it's its sense of nostalgia and design? Maybe because history is in its corner? Or maybe it's just the really great whiskey!

First off, Hartfield is located in Paris, Kentucky. Now, that alone makes them not only quirky, but cool. But then you need to know that Paris is in Bourbon County. And what you also need to know is that it is the only distiller of bourbon in Bourbon County. That's right. With all the bourbon being made in Kentucky, none of it has been made in Bourbon County since 1911. Hartfield brought bourbon distilling back to Bourbon County.

Formerly known as the Gentleman (it had to give up that name in a spurious legal dispute), Hartfield is named for one of the owners' ancestors, who also distilled bourbon in Bourbon County before Prohibition wiped out the industry. "Hartfield & Co. is named after a branch of Andrew [Buchanan's] family that stretches all the way back to 1700s Germany," the distillery claims. "The Hartfield family left the motherland and settled into modern day Pennsylvania and Ohio with a very pioneering portion making its way to Green County, Kentucky. There they founded a distillery which ran for 20 to 25 years upon which it ended in an unfortunate fire."

Hartfield was founded by Andrew Buchanan and his wife Larissa in 2014. Both were design and marketing professionals before being drawn into the craft distilling world. They are assisted by Jeremy Coffey. Their distillery is located in an old, turn-of-the-century feed building from 1911 that was a Chevrolet dealership in the 1920s and later an antiques warehouse. The tasting room is studded with old, late 19th-century pharmacy counters, display cabinets, and a counter. The whiskey is packaged in old-fashioned apothecary bottles with labels that look like something from an ancient pharmacy.

The one thing you instantly like about the Buchanans and Coffey is that they let the beer ferment longer than most. They are striving to bring out the brandy, cognac, apple, and pear notes in their product. Formerly made in 26- or 100-gallon stills, and now in a 500-gallon one, the sweet nectar is worth searching out. Their goal is

HARTFIELD & CO.
A BOURBON COUNTY DISTILLERY
bourbon whiskey
50% alcohol by volume / 100 proof
distilled from corn, rye and barley
750 ml
MADE IN BOURBON COUNTY, KY

not to let the wood overpower their product, but rather have the wood complement it. While other distillers would either argue with this or give lip service to it, this trio is a slave to it. Each small batch is aged in small, 5-gallon American oak barrels. They use Minnesota oak, which Andrew will tell you is sugar rich.

Like most small distilleries, small barrels allow more liquid-to-wood contact. Whiskey can thus be pushed out faster. But here is where Hartfield differs from the world. It doesn't want its whiskey to be in the wood too long. It all sounds a bit screwy, but the proof of its philosophy is in the glass.

Since their founding, they've continued to grow carefully. They are now even contract distilling for a few small fellow artisan distillers. They've worked with Second Sight Distilling and, most notably, Fresh Bourbon Distilling Co., among others.

Hartfield was included in the revolutionary and fascinating bottling of Corn Trooper 2020 United Craft Bourbon, which blended bourbon whiskeys from seven small craft distillers into one bourbon. Hartfield was one of those distillers paired alongside such nationally known crafters as Balcones, Kings County, Breckenridge, and OOLA. Pretty heady company.

Even bigger news? Their bottles have started to pop up in liquor stores throughout the region. In small quantities they are in some of the largest distributors in Kentucky, and can be found in a dozen states. Couldn't be happier for these folks, who are making some of the best small, boutique craft spirits in the region.

The impressive Hartfield White Whiskey is made from the same mash bill as its bourbon, but it has an incredibly large flavor! One could easily close their eyes and think they were drinking a more mature whiskey. It truly is amazing. One of the two or three best white whiskeys in America.

The Hartfield Bourbon has a mash bill of 62% corn, 19% rye, and 19% barley. It's aged for 5½ months in small, 5-gallon charred barrels of new Minnesota white oak. The whiskey has the qualities of Highlands scotch, featuring pears and apples, but also has lovely notes of caramel. This is a big craft bourbon. Chocolatey and impressive.

Hartfield Wheated Bourbon is 80% corn and 20% malted wheat, and has a big nose of butter toffee and caramel. The Single Malt is 100% barley and very impressive. It was aged in a used bourbon barrel, like all good single malts are, for six months, and displays an unmistakable nose of chocolate, brown sugar, and caramel, but also contains fig, pear, and apple notes, with a hint of smoke.

The Hartfield American Whiskey is 62% corn, 28% rye, and 10% barley. It also does two rums, an aged and a non-aged version. The non-aged was incredible (not what you might expect to hear from me—the browner, the better). Kettle corn in a glass,

with sugar, molasses, and impressive butter notes. The aged rum was just as good, aged for three months in used rum barrels.

Hartfield released its first single malt whiskey in 2020. Hartfield & Co. American Single Malt Whiskey (122.7 proof) is distilled from 100% malted barley. As single malt laws declare in Scotland, the whiskey was aged in ex-bourbon barrels (from the same distillery) before ultimately being bottled. It is barrel strength and was received very well.

Hartfield & Co. is as pretty in the bottle as it is in your glass. This is small-batch craft distilling at its best. Hartfield is the real thing. Given the quality of the hooch, the beauty of the design, and the upstart sentiment, it is hard not to root for this company. Other local spirit professionals are watching Hartfield intensely, and it is sure to experience a wild ride. If it can hold on, this new iteration of Hartfield should be around for more than 25 years.

Big Whiskey

Heaven Hill Distilleries

Heaven Hill Distilleries is located in Bardstown, Kentucky. It has its own remarkable story, as well as being home to some of the most impressive names in the whiskey business. Among the general public, even those who drink whiskey, it is perhaps the least known and best-selling distillery in the state. But to insiders, it is an American treasure.

To give you just a measure of how amazing this place is, you need to understand that Heaven Hill is the seventh-largest seller of spirits in America. Heaven Hill also warehouses the second-largest cache of bourbon whiskey in the world. The distillery has 54 rickhouses in all. Heaven Hill is also the largest independent family-owned-and-operated distiller and seller of spirits in the United States. And to top it off, of all the liquor giants, it is the only large, completely family-owned distillery headquartered in Kentucky.

Heaven Hill was established in 1935 by a group of investors that included famed distiller Joseph L. Beam (first cousin of Jim Beam), a member of the Shapira family, and several others. Over the intervening years, the Shapira brothers slowly bought out the other investors. The five brothers – Ed, Gary, George, David, and Mose – were a tight-knit group who gathered every Sunday at their mother's house with their families. As the children played, the men reviewed the previous week's events, and planned out the next week. Since then, the Shapiras have always owned Heaven Hill, and a

Beam was the master distiller until just recently.

The first master distiller was Joseph L. Beam. His son Harry succeeded him. Earl Beam (son of Park Beam, brother of Jim) then took over the distilling responsibilities. Earl was followed by master distillers Parker Beam and his son, Craig Beam.

Another key to the distillery's success was traveling salesman Harry Homel, who signed up distributors and created relationships that far outlasted his tenure with the company. His deals and agreements made Heaven Hill a national powerhouse.

Originally named the "Old Heavenhill Springs" distillery, the organization was focused around bourbon, and established such classic brands as Evan Williams and Elijah Craig. During the downturn in the sale of brown spirits, the company expanded by purchasing other brands, and built a list of gins, malt whiskey, vodkas, and other drinks.

The column still at Heaven Hill is approximately six storeys high. Even with all the whiskeys being double distilled, this behemoth allows Heaven Hill to produce 20,000 gallons a day.

Heaven Hill uses two barrel manufacturers to supply 90% of its needs—McGinnis Wood Products Co. Inc. in Cuba, Missouri, and Independent Stave Company in Lebanon, Missouri. It also buys from Kentucky Cooperage in Lebanon, Missouri.

"I have never in my life seen a Kentuckian who didn't have a gun, a pack of cards, and a jug of whiskey."

—Andrew Jackson

In 2020 Heaven Hill celebrated 85 years of distilling with the release of the limited edition Heaven Hill 85th Anniversary 13-Year-Old Single Barrel Kentucky Straight Bourbon Whiskey (107 proof), which was barrel filled on December 13, 2006, and bottled on December 13, 2019, as a nod to the December 13 date that the distillery filled their first barrel of bourbon in 1935. The bourbon was aged 13 years in Rickhouse G and bottled without chill filtration at 107 proof to commemorate Heaven Hill's original barrel entry proof.

"Perseverance is a hallmark of Heaven Hill's history, and a value resonating across the industry this year," said President Max L. Shapira. "Our steadfast commitment to quality and an enduring legacy continues to guide Heaven Hill's path forward. We look forward to lifting America's spirit for the next 85 years, as we have since 1935."

BOURBON HERITAGE CENTER

Heaven Hill built a new, lavish welcome center at its Bardstown location: a gleaming glass, steel, and oak building. At the new center, an immensely informative (even for the moderately knowledgeable) self-guided tour not only tells you about Heaven Hill, Elijah Craig, Evan Williams, and others, but also about bourbon in general. The center also offers two distinct experiences. The Mash Bill Tour takes visitors through Warehouse Y, explains how bourbon is made, and ends with a tasting of three whiskeys. The Connoisseur Tour is a more in-depth tasting experience, shepherding visitors across four whiskeys, where the intricacies of tasting bourbon are explored.

Several times a year the center offers special events, tastings of new releases, book signings, and talks. So be sure to keep tabs on them.

Fire!

On November 7, 1996, a fire started in one of the aging warehouses at Heaven Hill and eventually spread to a second warehouse and the manufacturing facility. More than 90,000 barrels burst into flames, and a river of flammable, volatile bourbon wound its way through the various lots, destroying the buildings and vehicles in its path.

The Bardstown Fire Department's First Assistant Fire Chief Anthony Mattingly said, "When the metal siding on Warehouse I disintegrated, it sent an 80-foot wall of flames into the air . . . high winds pushed much of the fire shooting toward Warehouse J low to the ground. Firefighters were forced to abandon the second warehouse when the tar roof ignited and, inside, fire began spreading beneath the single wooden staircase that gave firefighters access to the upper floors. The warehouse went from 10 percent involvement to 90 percent involvement in less than three minutes. When that fire started laying down on the ground, it was really a run-for-your-life situation.

"The combined heat from the two burning warehouses made it impossible to save the next closest warehouse downwind, Warehouse K. Firefighters pulled back to protect the other hilltop warehouses nearby. As Warehouse I collapsed, crushed barrels inside sent burning alcohol flowing downhill, spreading fire to Warehouses C and D below it."

The first warehouse was gone in 15 minutes once the whiskey itself caught fire. It took 150 firefighters from 25 fire companies to tame the massive blaze. Seven warehouses were lost in four hours, as well as the distillery. More than 90,000 barrels of bourbon were lost, approximately 2% of the world's bourbon stores.

The subsequent explosions could be felt and seen for miles. According to witnesses, "Flames leapt hundreds of feet into the air and lit the sky throughout the night. Witnesses reported seeing whiskey barrels explode and rocket across the sky like shooting stars . . . a two-mile long stretch of the creek that supplied process water to the distillery was set ablaze for a brief time."

Buoyed by distilling neighbors Jim Beam and Brown-Forman, Heaven Hill was able to honor its contracts and keep its supply chain going until it could get its new Bernheim distillery in Louisville up to speed. Fermenting, mashing, and distilling now takes place at the new distillery, while aging, bottling, and shipping still occur in Bardstown.

It was the worst American distillery fire in modern memory.

BERNIE LUBBERS

THE "WHISKEY PROFESSOR,"
HEAVEN HILL'S AMERICAN BRAND AMBASSADOR

There are few people in any industry who will make you feel more comfortable, more quickly, than Bernie Lubbers. A former singer and comedian, Lubbers is confident and sure. His sense of humor and easy demeanor are disarming, but don't let the cocksure act fool you. Originally from Louisville, Lubbers graduated with a B.A. in business from the University of Kentucky. Lubbers knows a lot about bourbon and the bourbon industry. He also knows everyone. And everyone claims to know him. Lubbers is a past winner of the "Global Ambassador of the Year" award in *Whisky Magazine's* "Icons of Whisky" presentation, is cited in numerous trade publications, and has served as judge at whiskey competitions.

On average, Lubbers has been known to travel more than 100,000 miles a year preaching the gospel of bourbon and American whiskey. Affectionately known as "The Whiskey Professor," Lubbers authored the 2011 book Bourbon Whiskey–Our Native Spirit, which has now seen three editions, and received endorsements from people as well-known in the industry as Jim Meehan, the popular mixologist and creator of PDT. Before being named brand ambassador for Heaven Hill, Lubbers spent seven years in the supplier tier, implementing special training and educational programs with consumers and the trade. Before working for Heaven Hill he worked for Beam/Suntory.

Steve Feller, vice president of North American sales for Heaven Hill Distilleries, said of Lubbers, "Having someone of his knowledge and reputation in the market to educate consumers and engage both on- and off-premise trade will be a great asset as we continue to grow our portfolio of world-renowned American whiskeys."

During our tour, Lubbers took us to Warehouse Y for a tasting of 18-year-old bourbon. Filled with charming stories and funny gags, Lubbers also dispensed a ton of knowledge. One gets the impression that Lubbers could keep conversation from lagging at any sort of event, and would have some tidbit of knowledge that no one else at the table knew.

My favorite fact from our tour was an introduction to the word "kreel." These are strategically placed all around a rickhouse, and dropped through holes drilled into all seven floors. When a rickhouse starts to lean, the kreel begins to touch one of the sides of the drilled hole. If this happens, then the whole rickhouse is improperly balanced and may be in danger of collapsing from the unevenly distributed weight.

Another fun fact provided by Lubbers was the "money end" of a barrel. This is the side that all the information is written on, including the date of filling and the initials that mark the mash bill.

EVAN WILLIAMS

Of all the brands in the Heaven Hill portfolio, none is bigger than Evan Williams. It is one of the world's best-selling bourbons. This bourbon is named after Welsh immigrant Evan Williams; in 1783, after crossing the Atlantic, he settled in an area now known as Louisville. He founded Kentucky's first commercial distillery, an achievement now commemorated with a plaque. Several whiskey historians have challenged the veracity of these claims, but nothing concrete has ever been produced to name another claimant.

Evan Williams is the second best-selling brand of Kentucky straight bourbon in the world, only behind Jim Beam. It comes in a number of variants, including white label, black label, single barrel, and 23-year-old expressions. The best one of these is without a doubt the nine-year-old Evan Williams Single Barrel Vintage Bourbon sealed with black wax. Not only is it a great value, it is among one of the best single barrel offerings in the industry. This is a bottle to keep around for special occasions to share with friends and family. Once, when I was at a whiskey event with several famous whiskey writers, we sat around expressing our wonder at how well this bourbon compared with everything else we were tasting. A must-have for any collection.

THE EVAN WILLIAMS EXPERIENCE LOUISVILLE

Located in downtown Louisville's historic Whiskey Row is the fantastic multi-storied tasting room, educational center, and entertainment space named The Evan Williams Experience.

It offers traditional tours and tastings, but there's so much more. The Experience also has events throughout the year, including bourbon and cigar nights, food pairing dinners, Derby Day and Mint Julep parties, and special releases. There is also the Speakeasy Experience, where it offers craft cocktails using its numerous brands. It also features its Sweet & Neat experience—a bourbon and chocolate tasting. It even has rooms to rent—its Warehouse J Loft for large events, the Speakeasy Lounge, and the Black Label Room for business meetings and tastings.

And, of course, there's a shop that offers merchandise as well as unique bottlings and labels. It's a fantastic place to visit if you ever find yourself in downtown Louisville.

ELIJAH CRAIG

Elijah Craig Kentucky Straight Bourbon Whiskey was named for the Reverend Elijah Craig, a Baptist preacher and educator from a part of Virginia that later became Kentucky. Around 1789 the minister established a distillery in Fayette County. Whiskey experts doubt the claim that Elijah invented bourbon, but acknowledge he was a verifiable character. They say that he may have been making whiskey, but it was probably not bourbon. Regardless, Elijah Craig has been a solid, long-established premium brand whose stature continues to improve.

Elijah Craig Kentucky Straight Bourbon Whiskey is only released in either "Small Batch" or age statement "Single Barrel" bottlings. The Small Batch bottling is a blending of 8- and 12-year-old bourbons (although if you find a bottle predating 2016, the age statement will be 12-years-old). The Small Batch is released in a 94-proof bottling. The Single Barrel is an uncut whiskey that ranges from 128 to 142 proof. Elijah Craig regularly releases a 12-year-old, 18-year-old, and a 23-year-old expression.

According to Heaven Hill: "From an aging inventory of 1.1 million barrels, the second largest American Whiskey holdings in the world, master distillers Craig Beam and Denny Potter select only barrels that have rested at low storage, and then further choose only those that meet their strict nosing and taste criteria. While taste nuances will vary slightly from one barrel to the other, as they should in a single barrel offering, in general they have been selected for complex, multi-layered taste profiles that balance the 18 years in new charred oak with sweet and spicy grain notes."

Interestingly, Elijah Craig bourbon barrels are used by Goose Island Brewery to make its famous Bourbon County Imperial Stout.

The consensus about Elijah Craig among whiskey writers is crystal clear. The 18-year-old and 23-year-old expressions are the go-to bottles. They display the classic notes of caramel, toffee, vanilla, and raisin, as well as ethereal notes of stone fruit with baked apple and pear and fig, all of which are layered with a slight sweetness and a hint of spice.

In 2020 Elijah Craig Beer Barrel Finish was released in partnership with Goose Island Beer Company. The whiskey was aged in barrels that stored both bourbon and beer, and was a collaboration project between Heaven Hill Distillery master distiller Conor O'Driscoll, Goose Island brewmaster Keith Gabbett, Goose Island Research & Development Brewing Manager Mike Siegel, and Mike Smith, Goose Island Senior Brand Manager.

Only three barrels were used to finish this bourbon, originally beginning their life as a new, #3 charred oak aging Heaven Hill's traditional bourbon mash bill. The freshly emptied barrels then traveled to Chicago to eventually age the award-winning Goose Island Bourbon County Stout released on Black Friday 2018. The barrels then returned to Kentucky for a third life to finish for 10 months to become fully matured Elijah Craig Small Batch.

A unique experience, and a collaboration worth watching.

OLD FITZGERALD

Originally produced in 1870 for rail and steamship lines and private clubs, Old Fitzgerald was eventually released commercially around 1900. Pappy Van Winkle eventually bought the brand for $10,000, and introduced wheat into its mash bill after Prohibition. Heaven Hill purchased the distillery and the brand in 1992.

Old Fitzgerald is one of those storied brands. Many a whiskey writer has shrugged his or her shoulders at the mention of it, but no writer I have ever known has walked away from a vertical tasting of old and new Old Fitzgerald without being in absolute awe.

There are four current bottlings of Old Fitzgerald: Prime, Bottled-in-Bond, 1849, and Very Special Old Fitzgerald 12 Years Old. Steven Ury once attended a Los Angeles Whisky Tasting Society vertical

tasting of seven different, and dusty, very, very old Old Fitzgerald. The oldest bottle was dated 1951. The usually skeptical Ury has been unable to let go of his memory of that tasting, saying, "And so it was, almost undoubtedly the greatest bourbon tasting I'll ever have the pleasure to attend."

No question the Very Special Old Fitzgerald 12 Years Old is the go-to bottle of this label—if you can find it.

In September 2020, Heaven Hill Distillery announced the release of the Fall 2020 edition of Old Fitzgerald Bottled-in-Bond Kentucky Straight Bourbon Whiskey at 14-years-old. Comprised of barrels produced in 2005 and bottled in 2020, it was bottled in an ornate decanter. This edition's tax strip disclosed when the liquid was produced and bottled. This 2020 edition of Old Fitzgerald Bottled-in-Bond Kentucky Straight Bourbon Whiskey is the first 14-year-old of the nationally released series and features bourbon pulled from different rickhouses, at different floors, and on different production dates.

LARCENY

This brand was also named after John E. Fitzgerald. Fitzgerald was actually not a distiller, as Pappy Van Winkle's autobiography later revealed. Fitzgerald was a bonded treasury agent. In the old days, just like in Scotland, treasury agents were the only ones with keys to bourbon warehouses and spirit safes.

According to Heaven Hill, Fitzgerald had a very select palate that demanded fine, long-aged bourbon. On days when no one was around, Fitzgerald would find "honey barrels" and slowly drain them. These were jokingly called "Fitzgerald Barrels." The Larceny brand was named for this act of theft.

Larceny Kentucky Straight Bourbon Whiskey is aged six years in new American oak, and is a wheated bourbon that contains 68% corn, 20% wheat, and 12% malted barley. This high-corn, high-wheat recipe offers both softness and sweetness, and produces wonderful, highly coveted bourbon.

MELLOW CORN

Mellow Corn Kentucky Straight Corn Whiskey is one of the few official corn whiskeys on the market. To qualify as a straight corn whiskey, the mash bill needs to be at least 81% corn and aged in new charred American white oak barrels.

Acclaimed whiskey authority Jim Murray wrote of corn whiskey: "If you are a true student of whiskey, your education is a long way from being complete until you have mastered this particularly charming form." Corn whiskey was the popular spirit that formed the later backbone of bourbon. Mellow Corn is an easy drinking spirit, smooth and light, with lots of vanilla, baked apple, and yellow cake. A lovely, easy, simple dram.

PIKESVILLE

Pikesville Straight Rye Whiskey (110 proof) was first distilled in 1895. But it was originally made in Maryland as part of that state's once-booming rye industry. The brand was lost after Prohibition. A lighter, less expensive version—The White Label—was taken off the market in 2016. But dusties can still be found. This 110-proof expression with a retro label is a classic Baltimore rye (37% corn, 51% rye, 12% malted barley) aged for six years in new #3 char American oak. Pikesville is now made in Kentucky, but the location doesn't seem to matter—this continues to be a go-to rye.

RITTENHOUSE

Though Heaven Hill has kept the old Philadelphia brand alive (the liquor was named for the city's famed Rittenhouse Square), the whiskey inside is actually a Baltimore rye (meaning more of a blend, allowing for more corn). Rittenhouse has the same mash bill as Pikesville, but the whiskey is not aged as long. It is one of only two bottled-in-bond ryes in the United States, meaning it was made at the same distillery, in the same season, aged at least four years, and bottled at 100 proof (50% ABV). Like Pikesville, this is a softer, sweeter rye, but it is lighter on wood and alcohol than Pikesville. And, oh, yeah—it's quite a lovely dram!

BERNHEIM ORIGINAL

Bernheim Original Kentucky Straight Wheat Whiskey Small Batch (90 proof) is a wheat whiskey named for Isaac Wolfe Bernheim, a German immigrant who worked as a traveling salesman. By 1888 Bernheim had moved to Louisville and was the founder of I. W. Harper brand of bourbon whiskey. Bernheim's distillery and distribution business was so successful that he helped coalesce the distilling industry in Louisville. Bernheim was also very involved in the community life of the city, and he established a 14,000-acre arboretum in Bullitt County. Bernheim sold the business after Prohibition (it had been one of only 10 liquor licenses to retain the right to make whiskey for medicinal purposes during the Great Experiment).

Introduced in 2005, Bernheim has been incorrectly called a wheated bourbon by many food and spirits writers. It is not a bourbon. It is a wheat whiskey with a mash

bill of 37% corn, 51% wheat, and 12% malted barley, and it is aged seven years in new #3 char American white oak barrels. The bottled small batches are from dumps of 100 or less select barrels. Bernheim Straight Wheat Whiskey was named Pioneer Whiskey of the Year by *Whisky Advocate* the year it was released, and has gone on to win countless awards since then.

GEORGIA MOON CORN WHISKEY

Shine On Georgia Moon Corn Whiskey is the best-selling corn whiskey in the United States. Georgia Moon is authentic American corn whiskey, with a mash bill of at least 81% corn, and is rested in new American oak barrels—both uncharred and used charred. The company also introduced two new flavored moonshines—peach and lemonade.

HENRY MCKENNA

Henry McKenna Single Barrel Bottled-in-Bond 10-Year-Old Kentucky Straight Bourbon Whiskey was named for distilling pioneer Henry McKenna, who was born in Ireland and came to America at the age of 19. By 1855 he had taken a share in a partnership to mill flour in Fairfield, Kentucky, and quickly became appalled by the waste of milling. He set up a still behind the mill and soon founded a distillery. He claimed that all his whiskey was aged no less than three years. Business was so good that the company moved its offices to Louisville in 1880. McKenna died in 1893, and one of his sons carried on the business until 1940, when the family sold lock, stock, and barrel to Seagram.

Henry McKenna carries the standard Heaven Hill mash bill of 78% corn, 10% rye, and 12% malted barley, and is aged 10 years in new #3 and #4 char American white oak barrels. This single barrel release is bottled-in-bond.

> # "I've got a whole lot to live up to with my father and grandfather. I've got a lot of weight on my shoulders."

PARKER'S HERITAGE

Parker's Heritage collection is a series of rare, limited-edition whiskey selected by master distiller Parker Beam. The first was a cask strength bourbon released in 2007. In 2008, it released a 27-year-old bourbon, and other editions have been a wheated bourbon, a cognac-finished expression, a malt whiskey, a 24-year-old bourbon bottled-in-bond, and an 11-year-old, single barrel bourbon.

Many of these offerings were selected by a man who spent more than 50 years in the distilling business. Parker Beam began working at Heaven Hill in 1950, and oversaw one of the largest stocks of bourbon in the world. "Beam's pedigree as a bourbon maker was impeccable. As a grandnephew of Jim Beam, Parker Beam was born into a family that traces its whiskey-making roots in Kentucky to 1795, when Jacob Beam set up his first still. Park Beam, Parker's grandfather and namesake, was Jim Beam's brother," reported the Associated Press in 2017.

"If you were a Beam, you sort of were destined to follow in the footsteps of either your father, grandfathers, cousins, or uncles," Parker Beam said in an earlier interview with The Associated Press. "I've got a whole lot to live up to with my father and grandfather. I've got a lot of weight on my shoulders."

"In his case, he lived up to and exceeded the burden of having the most famous name in bourbon," said Bill Samuels Jr., the retired master distiller of Maker's Mark, who referred to his friend as "one of the good guys."

Parker died in January 2017, at the age of 75, after losing his fight with ALS. Parker Beam had the title of Master Distiller Emeritus at Heaven Hill at the time of his death. His son Craig was master distiller, but took time off, moving to a consultancy role in 2014, in order to spend more time with his father and family in the face of the illness.

Parker was known for his wry sense of humor and down-to-earth demeanor. When one whiskey writer described some very exotic flavors in one of the whiskeys he had bottled, Parker shrugged, smiled, and said, "I didn't put any of the shit in there."

The 11th edition of Parker's Heritage was released in 2017. It was an 11-year-old, single barrel bourbon (122 proof). And in honor of Parker, Heaven Hill now donates a portion of the proceeds from each bottle sold to ALS charities.

JEPTHA CREED

Jeptha Creed is a family-run business. It is owned and run by Joyce, Bruce, Hunter, and Autumn Nethery. Joyce, the matriarch, has two degrees in chemical engineering from the University of Louisville, and worked for 15 years as a process engineer. Her husband Bruce is a farmer with an entrepreneurial bent, having long operated a dairy farm in Shelby County. Autumn, Joyce and Bruce's daughter, spent a school year in Edinburgh, Scotland, learning brewing and distilling at Heriot-Watt University, while Joyce took a refresher course at Distilling Epicenter. Son Hunter is still a student who does blacksmithing and a little bit of everything else. They founded their distillery in 2016.

"Creed is more of a value statement," Joyce told the *Louisville Insider*. "We're going to stand by the heritage statement and authenticity in our product. Our creed is we use old-fashioned methods to meet modern tastes, and we are honest and authentic about everything that'll go into our spirits."

According to the Insider, "Perhaps what most sets Jeptha Creed apart from the others will be their use of open-pollinated, non-GMO heirloom Bloody Butcher corn the family has been growing since 1845. When dry, the corn has a deep red color and is often used as decorations in the fall."

Jeptha Creek makes a moonshine with a grain bill that is built on a four-grain barley mash, and features the family's unique corn. It also makes flavored versions—blackberry, apple pie, and Louisville lemonade. Jeptha Creek Vodka is heirloom Bloody Butcher corn used in a classic bourbon mash and made using vodka yeast that supplies hints of apple and cake batter. Jeptha Creed also released an Unaged Corn Whiskey (80 proof) that was exceptional. Everything this distillery does is great, but the hype machine was cranked up for Jeptha Creed Bloody Butcher's Creed Bourbon (100 proof). A small, limited run was released in 2019.

Jim Beam

If there is a first family of bourbon, it is the Beam family. There are no less than three or four distilleries that boast a Beam family connection. The name and the family have been synonymous with bourbon for more than 200 years.

"The first Boehm in Kentucky was Johannes Jacob Boehm, who arrived in Kentucky in 1787 or 1788. He preferred to be called Jacob Boehm and later Jacob Beam," wrote Frank Prial in the New York Times. Jacob had been a farmer, and sold his first barrels of corn whiskey sometime around 1795. The whiskey more or less resembled the bourbon we drink today. His distillery came to be known as Old Tub, and the whiskey came to be known as Old Jake Beam Sour Mash.

When Jacob turned 60, or thereabouts, David Beam took over the day-to-day operation of the family business—at the age of only 18. He magnified the business substantially, expanding its distribution by leaps and bounds. In 1854, the year of his father's death, David M. Beam relocated the

distillery to Nelson County. With increased access to railroads, the brand became bigger than ever before. James Beauregard Beam guided the business just before and long after Prohibition. In 1933, he rebuilt the distillery close to his Bardstown home in Clermont.

In 1935, with Harry L. Homel, Oliver Jacobson, H. Blum, and Jeremiah Beam, the James B. Beam Distilling Company was established. The brand was now "Jim Beam Bourbon" bearing the slogan "None Genuine Without My Signature," and Jim's scrawl. T. Jeremiah Beam, who had begun his apprenticeship in 1913, later ascended to master distiller at the Clermont distillery.

The grandson of Jim Beam, Frederick Booker Noe II, known simply as Booker Noe, was master distiller at the Jim Beam Distillery for more than 40 years.

"Mr. Noe, who attended the University of Kentucky, joined the company in 1950 as an assistant distiller, though he had helped out around the distillery since he was a teenager," wrote Prial. "At 6-foot-

4, Mr. Noe was a commanding figure. He retired in 1992 and spent the rest of his life traveling and fishing around the world and acting as an ambassador for Jim Beam, playing host at bourbon tastings and entertaining audiences with reminiscences and anecdotes. At home in Kentucky, he was the host of parties and dinners featuring his own bourbon, of course, and Kentucky hams, which he cured in a backyard smokehouse."

Booker was among a handful of people who helped revive interest in bourbon during the heyday of gin and vodka. In 1987, after Blanton's had been a success, Noe released Booker's, Beam's first uncut, straight-from-the-barrel bourbon. It was the first of the whiskeys released in a portfolio now known as its "Small Batch Bourbon Collection."

In 2007, Booker's son, Frederick Booker Noe, became the seventh master distiller at Jim Beam.

"None Genuine Without My Signature"

FIRE!

In 2003, 19,000 barrels of Jim Beam bourbon were destroyed when a Jim Beam rickhouse caught fire. As the fire consumed the warehouse the bourbon flames rose more than 100 feet into the air. Bourbon, flaming like lava as it sought lower ground, eventually washed into a nearby creek, killing an estimated 19,000 fish.

Jim Beam has been sold around the world for many generations. Jim Beam and Suntory, the major Japanese whiskey producer, enjoyed a reciprocal relationship, whereby they distributed whiskey for each other in their respective markets. This symbiotic relationship culminated in a 2016 merger, wherein Suntory bought Beam.

Beam reached 14 million barrels in 2016. It produces approximately 300,000 barrels per year. Most of the barrels are new #4 char, also known as "alligator skin," American white oak. The distillery has 22 fermenters that produce 45,000 gallons each of distiller's beer, and the column still is six storeys high. Warehouse D, the oldest rickhouse at the distillery, holds approximately 20,000 barrels. But as it has grown, so have the sizes of its warehouses, with most of its rickhouses holding about 50,000 barrels each, and the newest ones holding approximately 60,000 barrels each. Almost all of Jim Beam's bourbons have a similar mash bill: 75% corn, 13% rye, and 12% malted barley.

It has two bottling lines, and can expect as much as 9,000 cases a day from its best line, which can reach speeds of up to 300 bottles per minute! Jim Beam is not only sold in all 50 states, it is currently sold in more than 125 countries around the world.

Highlights from the extensive Jim Beam lineup are difficult to parse out. It has a series of flavored and spiced bourbons that have been a huge hit. But a narrower interpretation keeps us toward the classics. Simply put, one of the best whiskeys it produces is the Jim Beam Single Barrel. While it has no age statement on the bottle, we know the whiskey is aged between four and seven years, is chill-filtered, and weighs in at 95 proof. The next star in the Jim Beam portfolio is the Jim Beam Double Oak, which is first aged in charred American white oak barrels, and then poured out and re-casked in #4 char new American oak barrels for additional aging. This second go-round produces a big, intense, bold whiskey that is aged four years sold and sold at 86 proof. Jim Beam Black is sold at 86 proof. It used to be aged for eight years (aged six years for export markets), and though it no longer carries an age statement, it's still a very, very solid whiskey.

Two specialty items from the Beam lineup include Jim Beam Signature Craft whiskey, which is finished in rare Spanish brandy casks. This 12-year-old bourbon is bottled at 86 proof.

The other is Jim Beam Distiller's Masterpiece, which, according to the company, "is Fred Noe's magnum opus. After hand-selecting extra-aged bourbons that were aging in the optimal positions of his rickhouse, Noe finished the bourbon in Pedro Ximénez sherry casks."

"This bourbon expression from Jim Beam is the most exclusive, highest quality offering within the family," says no less an authority than Noe himself. Take his word for it—this is a rich, opulent, decadent bourbon.

Jim Beam Straight Rye Whiskey is the company's entry into the rye market. This is definitely a Baltimore-styled rye (55% rye, 35% corn, 10% malt), with big notes of spice and caramel, and a sweetness that offers a softer, smoother experience. This iconic green label rye is aged four years in oak and is sold at 90 proof.

Jim Beam also released the Alberta Rye Dark Batch 90 Proof (45% ABV), which is a blend of Canadian rye, bourbon, and sherry. Another "dark rye" entry in the industry, this is a caramel bomb with a complex flavor and spiciness all its own. It's a winner.

The Small Batch Bourbon Collection is a portfolio of Beam's premium craft-styled bourbons. This group includes such prestigious, limited-edition brands as Knob Creek, Booker's, Basil Hayden's, and Baker's. This is a very special group.

BAKER'S

Introduced in the early 1990s, this fine bourbon was named for Baker Beam, grandnephew of the legendary Jim Beam. Baker's is distilled at a lower proof and barrel-aged in small batches, allowing the bourbon to pull more flavor from the barrel. According to the company, this bourbon is "aged seven years and bottled at 107 proof; utilizes a special strain of jug yeast, which results in a silky-smooth texture and consistent taste from batch to batch."

"We pull barrels from throughout the warehouses where they are aged—including the top floors—to create a well-balanced bourbon with robust flavors and that signature silky-smooth finish that Baker's is known for," Baker Beam told the *Bourbonr* blog. "Baker's Bourbon is inspired by my personal preference."

BASIL HAYDEN'S

Also introduced in the early 1990s, Meredith Basil Hayden Sr. Bourbon was named for the distiller whose family eventually bottled the iconic brand Old Grand-dad. This high-rye bourbon has incredible spice, and is also the lowest alcohol of the four classic bourbons in the Beam Small Batch Collection. Unlike many of the other bourbons in its lineup, Basil Hayden's mash bill is unique: 63% corn, 27% rye, and 10% malted barley.

Basil Hayden's Dark Rye 80 Proof (40% ABV) is a new, big, complex, rich, intense, high-rye blend of Kentucky straight-rye whiskey mixed with Canadian rye whiskey and port. It was first released in 2017 and is an absolute must-have, one-of-a-kind experience.

BOOKER'S

Booker's, named after famed master distiller Booker Noe, is a barrel-strength bourbon. It was said that Booker originally bottled his own personal whiskeys at cask strength, and gave these small bottlings to friends and family. The first release to the public was 1,000 cases in 1988. Booker personally selected every barrel. According to Noe, the sweet spot for this favorite cut was the center of the rickhouse. It was his feeling that the temperature and humidity at this location are perfect for exceptional bourbons. It looks like he was onto something, because the company still does it this way. Booker's is matured in a cask for six to eight years. The final aged spirit is bottled un-cut and features no chill filtering, and the average proof is somewhere between 121 and 130.6 (60.5% and 65.3% ABV). While many cask-strength drinkers like their whiskey neat, Noe himself preferred a splash of distilled water to release the whiskey's various flavors.

KNOB CREEK

Like several of its small-batch brethren, Knob Creek was first released in the 1990s—1992 to be precise. The bourbon is distilled at the Jim Beam Distillery in Clermont, and is "named for the creek that ran behind Abraham Lincoln's childhood Kentucky home. The late Booker Noe, Jim Beam's sixth-generation master distiller, chose the name because he thought it reflected his values in making whiskey," wrote journalist Claire McCafferty in *Mental Floss*. While there are several different expressions of Knob Creek, but a few of them deserve special attention:

The original Knob Creek released in 1992 was aged nine years and bottled at 100 proof (50% ABV). It was a big, rich, robust bourbon.

Knob Creek Single Barrel Reserve was first offered in 2010. This whiskey is aged nine years, and the barrels are hand-selected. It is bottled at 120 proof.

Released in 2012, Knob Creek Rye is a big rye with hints of sweetness. Bottled at 100 proof, this mature whiskey features a mash bill of 55% rye, 35% corn, and 10% malt. This combination produces a rye that is very popular among both mixologists and collectors.

KNOB CREEK

SINGLE BARREL RESERVE 9

KENTUCKY STRAIGHT BOURBON WHISKEY

KY·US

KNOB
CLER
DIST.
COM

CLERMONT, KENTUCKY

120 PROOF
60% ALC./VOL.

CRAFTED FOR SUPERIOR
TASTE & SMOOTHNESS

120 PROOF

SINCE
1992

110-KCS0111

L0073CLA
353991211

750

LEGENT

Legent (94 proof) is a collaboration between two whiskey legends, Fred Noe, Jim Beams seventh-generation master distiller, and Shinji Fukuyo, Suntory's fifth-ever chief blender. The whiskey begins its journey as a Kentucky Straight Bourbon created by Noe. Noe in turn worked with Fukuyo to create the final blend of casks that would become Legent. Some of

these casks were bourbons finished in used wine and sherry casks. The mash bill is 75% corn, 13% rye, and 12% malted barley.

"Legent is really something special. As a bourbon distiller, I enjoy breaking rules and creating new traditions. It was a real honor collaborating with Shinji Fukuyo on what I think is different from anything out there in the bourbon world," said Noe. "Blended whiskey was kind of a dreaded term when we were growing up, but Shinji's style is completely different."

"I'm not familiar with the bourbon climate," says Fukuyo. "Bourbon whiskey reaches my nose much quicker than Japanese whisky. We don't have the mash bills concept, and bourbon is made in a continuous still, so it's totally different. I was surprised by the great flavor from the bourbon casks with sherry," said Fukuyo. "But too much sherry masks the wine. We had a lot of discussion on the sherry finish.

"For me it was baby steps with this. There was a whole lot of levers to be pulled that I've never pulled before, and it goes places that normal bourbon made in Kentucky doesn't go. This was all new territory for us."

The final result is a blend of three bourbons that issues a big, luxurious statement. Big notes of stone fruit, cocoa, caramel, honey, and baking spices. Lovely!

LINEAGE

In the fall of 2020, Jim Beam Bourbon released a special premium version that only overseas travelers can buy. Called Lineage, it is the first bourbon collaboration between master distiller Fred Noe and his son, Freddie.

"Lineage represents a significant moment in the history of Jim Beam. Not only is it a collaboration between the seventh and eighth generation of distillers in our family,

but it's a blend of the past, the present and the future," said Fred.

"Having spent a lot of time exploring travel retail outlets in my time, it was important to me to offer something special to travelers – especially during these trying times. Launching a product exclusively to travel retail is not something we often do, so we are excited to bring such a unique expression to our friends in airports across the world."

This is the first bourbon in the Beam portfolio with Freddie's name on it, and comes at a time when Bean is trying to insert itself in the race toward more elegant whiskey expressions to compete in the world market at the super premium level.

OLD TUB

The Old Tub brand was released in 1880. Back in the day, before the introduction of uniformed, corked bottles, and fancy packaging, customers simply came to the distillery and submerged their jugs in a tub full of whiskey to fill them. By the late 1800s bottled Old Tub was a popular brand. This is how the Beam family sold their whiskey until 1943, when they changed the name to Jim Beam. Old Tub was re-introduced in 2020.

Old Tub Kentucky Straight Bourbon Whiskey (100 proof) is a 4-year-old bottled in bond, non-filtered bourbon. Notes include warm cereal, caramel, golden citrus, honey, fried fruit, and vanilla, Very pretty.

KENTUCKY ARTISAN DISTILLERY

The Kentucky Artisan Distillery (KAD) is a unique place in the craft distilling world. Managing director Steve Thompson says that KAD produces its own brands and also offers contract production, bottling, barrel storage, and more. "Opening a distillery is a lengthy and expensive process," said Thompson, a former Brown-Forman executive. "We can help prospective distillers get started and get their products on the shelves, while they're concentrating on set-up, sales, and marketing."

Established in 2012, KAD renovated and retrofitted a 15,000-square-foot former ice cream plant into a distillery featuring four stills capable of producing vodka, gin, brandy, rum, and whiskey, as well as an automated bottling line and test laboratory.

"Our dream is to create opportunities," Thompson said. "We're truly offering everything for people to distill their own unique spirit without great expense. We're thankful to the KAD and their members for all their support and all they do for our signature industry."

KAD's house brand is Whiskey Row Bourbon, a pre-Prohibition styled bourbon that is only for sale in Kentucky. It also contract-makes Highspire Whiskey, a 100% rye aged for Hope Family Wines in Napa. But its best-known product is Jefferson's Reserve Bourbon.

Jefferson's was established in 1997 by Trey Zoeller and his father Chet, a famed bourbon historian. The Zoellers used Thomas Jefferson as an inspiration for their brand because he was known for "his curiosity and experimental spirit." All the bourbon is sourced for these whiskeys. "Jefferson's claims its competitive edge as a blender, not a distiller," wrote whiskey expert Clay Risen. "Every bottle is a winner."

In June 2015, Jefferson's acquired KAD. Slowly but surely, KAD is producing more of the bourbon for Jefferson's. Some 25% percent of the barrels warehoused for aging in 2017 was made at KAD. The other 75% was sourced from other Kentucky distilleries.

KAD also produces 10 to 12 small, limited bottlings per year. Each small batch release is only 8 to 12 barrels per batch. This is craft distilling at its finest. The Jefferson's Reserve and Jefferson's Very Small Batch include four different recipes that are aged up to 18 and 12 years, respectively.

Most notable among these offerings are Jefferson's Ocean and Jefferson's Ocean Cask Strength, which are both aged at sea. The bourbon spends the last six months in barrel aboard a ship that travels to five continents and crosses the equator multiple times. The belief is that the rocking motion and change in temperatures agitate the whiskey and push the liquid in and out of the wood.

KENTUCKY PEERLESS
DISTILLING

In the 1880s, Peerless whiskey was a powerful brand and a regional powerhouse. In 1917, Peerless was knocking out 200 barrels of whiskey a day and approximately 23,000 barrels annually. The label was laid low via Prohibition and stayed there until just recently. But in 2009, after 98 years, Corky Taylor, a veteran of the financial services industry, insisted on reestablishing this forgotten brand that his great-grandfather owned from 1896 to 1917. Carson Taylor, Corky's son, has overseen the construction of the buildings, the installation of the stills, and the production of the whiskey. The head distiller is Caleb Kilburn, who is backed by a sizable team of professionals bent on returning Peerless to prominence.

They have a very particular view on their production. They get their grains from Consolidated Grain and Barge in downtown Louisville. They use Kelvin Cooperage. And they barrel their whiskey at the same proof

they bottle it. "If you barrel at 125 proof and then dilute to 80-proof bourbon, 36% of your final bottle is going to be water," Kilburn said. "Choosing to go in at lower proof costs us 17% more in barrels, which is one of the most expensive links in the chain of making whiskey. So we're not going to be the most financially efficient, we're not going to be the biggest." As they see it, you get the whiskey at barrel proof and at its maximum flavor, with grain and wood. Their goal isn't to make the most, but to make the best and most unique. The label says: "Non-chill filtered. Strictly sweet mash. Barrel proof. No water added." That said, currently the distiller's rye is in

42 states and their bourbon can be found in 18 states.

Kentucky Peerless Small Batch Bourbon (approximately 108 proof) has a mash bill that is a majority corn, approximately 65%, with 10 to 20% rye (still a sizable rye content), and 9 to 15% malted barley. Their goal is a rich, earthy, and textured whiskey. And boy are they successful! It's a big caramel bomb that starts off with notes of citrus, cherry, cocoa, and brown sugar, but it's got a healthy dose of rye to make it a clean ending. Rich and flavor forward.

Kentucky Peerless Single Barrel Bourbon (approximately 112 proof) is a single barrel

selection that carries additional labeling, like "Farmer's Market – with notes of Spicy Florals, Honeysuckle & Leather," or "Havana Nights with Notes of Citrus, Humidor, Cocoa." This bourbon is aromatic, with more intense highlights. Chocolate, cherry, wintergreen, with the same hit of gingerbread at the end. Exceptional.

While their bourbon is delicious and well worth searching out, their rye is spectacular. Kentucky Peerless Small Batch Rye (approximately 108 proof) is a high-rye spirit (approximately 61% or more corn and about 8% malted barley). It's a 3-year old whiskey. Maple, brown sugar, cranberry,

cherry, orange zest, vanilla, and pine. Spicey and impressive. One of the best ryes on the market.

Kentucky Peerless Single Barrel Rye (approximately 108 proof) is a barrel that most appeals to Kilburn. Single barrel bottles usually have specific tasting notes, like "Toasted Cedar – Molasses and Warm Cider," or "Charred Citrus – with notes of Orange Zest and Burnt Sugar." Kilburn likes to accentuate the most outrageous flavors, with notes of big citrus, spice, pine, and cherry. Super expressive.

Kentucky Peerless Double Barrel Rye (approximately 108 proof) is not whiskey

that has been re-barreled, it is instead two barrels wherein Kilburn feels the whiskeys most match one another expressively, so that a unique whiskey is bottled. The big boys can't even think like that. Amazing.

Easily, the most impressive Peerless was the Small Batch Rye Aged in Copper & Kings Alembic Absinthe Barrels (approximately 110 proof). "Early on, we took the stance that Peerless would never say never in regard to doing barrel finishes, but we also recognized that it would require time and the perfect partner to [pique] our interests," said Kilburn. "We knew that as a young company we had to grow and walk before we could run. We took our time, established our bourbon and rye as respected top-shelf products, and finally reached a point where we could discuss different product innovations. This is when the opportunity to work with Copper and Kings presented itself and we couldn't have found a better fit." It's a match made in heaven. The nose is a giant pop of anise and licorice. Lots of botanicals, spices, honey, dried apricot, pine, and citrus. Something so unique, so different, that it still sits with me. Absolutely

loved it. One of the most unique bottles in all of Kentucky or Tennessee. Amazing. It blew me away.

CALEB KILBURN
WHISKEY PRODIGY

After tasting Kentucky Peerless, meeting its maker, master distiller Caleb Kliburn, is a bit of a shock. You're not exactly sure if you're being punked. He is incredibly young. He is clean cut and impressively respectful. He's unapologetically enthusiastic. And he is incredibly humble, though confident about what he is saying. But the more time you spend with him, the more you understand what the word "prodigy" means.

Kilburn was raised in Salt Lick, Kentucky, on his family's dairy farm. He's not a stranger to hard work, and he knows his way around stainless-steel fittings, hoses, clamps, tanks, and pumps. "Dairy farming isn't a 40-hour a week job. It is a way of life and you had better love it. There are no sick days, no vacations or days off," said Kilburn. "It is a full day of work every day of the year, and that really defined work ethic for me."

He graduated valedictorian of his high school, and then attended Morehead State University, where he excelled at biology, chemistry, physics, engineering, and math. While there he became fascinated by distillation, which was a confluence of his interests.

Kilburn attended courses at the Distilled Spirits Epicenter. There he befriended instructors who would later become his mentors: Rob Sherman, vice president of Vendome Copper and Brass Works in Louisville; Pete Kamer, the retired head engineer of Barton Brands in Bardstown; and Randy Allender, distillery consultant.

"I met Caleb on the first day of the Epicenter six-day class. Before the class even started, he was already asking questions about the equipment and how it worked," recalled Kamer. "On the still there was a mistake in how it was piped. About the second day of class, Caleb found the mistake and asked why it was piped the way it was. I could tell that he would make a great distiller someday soon."

"When the Taylors asked me if I knew anyone they could hire to help oversee the distillery construction, and possibly be their distiller, Caleb was the first person who came to mind," said Sherman.

Kilburn took to the distillery like a fish to water. He started out as a grunt, moving construction debris and carting building materials. But it soon became apparent that his backlog on practical knowledge, and his experience at the Epicenter, made him an incredible candidate for bigger and better opportunities at Kentucky Peerless. He knew how to assemble the equipment, where to place it and why, how to work the pumps and machinery. Many times, people stood

back, and let the enthusiastic youngster work his magic. "It was sort of fortuitous how all that tinkering as a kid turned into a career," said Kilburn.

Before long, as construction continued, Kilburn was taking his finals. "But I made sure to let my professors know, distilling was my only priority." He soon found himself fielding contractors' questions in the middle of his finals. He was 22 years old.

It was clear to the Taylors that they would let Kilburn craft the inaugural rye whiskey for Peerless. By the end of that summer, Kilburn was promoted to head distiller. On March 4, 2015, he distilled Peerless's first barrel of whiskey in 98 years. In Fall 2017, Peerless Straight Rye was named one of the top 15 in the world by Whisky Advocate.

When chatting with Kilburn it's easy to understand his appeal. His incredible humility, his neat appearance, his gracious and enthusiastic demeanor – they all make him undeniably likable. But he can talk whiskey. His has views on sweet vs sour mash, and he's as happy to get into the weeds of it. He is a staunch believer in sweet mash. He has his ideas on barrel selection, and likes picking barrels that taste alike, so that he can offer two expressions that are completely different. Some might be smooth and caramel dominant, other might be more spice oriented. Why blend them, he might ask. He doesn't want to blend away their high points, he wants to accentuate them. It's all done by hand, and by the distiller's whim. He is as much chef and artist as he is distiller. He is out to make stand-out artisanal spirits. And he believes in his cause. Politely.

"Caleb Kilburn is on his way to be one of the great master distillers in Kentucky," said Bill Thomas, of the famed whiskey mecca, Jack Rose, in Washington, DC. "His understanding of, and reverence for, the distilling history of Kentucky and his technical skills ensure Kentucky traditions and innovations will be carried on into a new generation."

Sherman added, "He's got an incredible career ahead of him." With great praise, comes great expectations. So far, Caleb Kilburn has exceeded them all.

LIMESTONE BRANCH DISTILLERY

Limestone Branch Distilling is owned by brothers Steve and Paul Beam. Yes, they are members of that great distilling family. In 1871, M.C. Beam began his distilling career under the supervision of his Uncle Jack Beam. By 1883, he was a partner at his own operation, where he brought his son Guy (Steve and Paul Beam's grandfather) into the business.

"I always felt like it was an unfinished chapter for my family," said Steve, regarding the 200 years of family history. "In 2010, I made the commitment to do it, put my side of the family back in the distilling business. It was something I always wanted to do. I began researching and apprenticing, and formed Limestone Branch Distillers, Inc. in October 2010."

According to the company's website: "Using recipes—some of them plucked from their grandfather Guy's notebook—and family knowledge gleaned from the previous generations of master distillers that came before them," they began making new products. Jimmy Beam, with Steve and Paul standing alongside, cut the ceremonial ribbon on February 12, 2012.

A fascinating new addition to the Limestone Branch family is the Bowling & Burch New World Gin (96 proof). This elegant botanical gin is a combination of distilling know-how and local agriculture. This small-batch gin is crafted with 17 botanicals, some of which are grown right there on the property. It is infused with flavors such as honeysuckle and lemon verbena. Super floral and aromatic. Rosemary, thyme, and citrus on the nose. Orange tangerine, honeysuckle, lemon, and spice across the palate, and ending with a lovely spice note. Elegant. A gin hunter's dream.

"In 1910 my father's grandfather, Minor Case Beam, sold his Old Trump Distillery to Joseph Bernard Dant, pioneer distiller and relative to my mother, and began producing Yellowstone at the distillery. I am proud to welcome the Yellowstone brand back to our family 105 years later," said Steve.

Yellowstone Kentucky Straight Bourbon

Whiskey (93 proof), which is made with sourced whiskey, is a small-batch blend of handpicked 4- and 7-year old whiskeys. Leather, cherries, honey, smoked caramel, and lingering brown sugar. An excellent, incredibly well-branded, and well-presented whiskey. Wonderful!

Each year, Limestone Branch releases their Yellowstone Limited Edition. So far, the annual bottlings have included as many as three bourbons used in a blend and bourbon aged in wine casks, in re-charred wine casks, and even wine casks charred three different times. The 2020 edition of Yellowstone Limited Edition Kentucky Straight Bourbon Whiskey (101 proof) is a blend of 7-year-old bourbon finished in Armagnac barrels. It came packaged in a stunning new bottle. Leather, honey, caramel, vanilla, burnt orange and dried plum. Super impressive.

A longtime favorite is the Limestone Branch Minor Case Straight Rye Whiskey Sherry Cask Finished, which is bottled at 90 proof. Inspired by Minor Case Beam, Steve and Paul's great-grandfather, this is an incredible spicy and smooth 2-year-old rye whiskey that is then sherry cask finished at Limestone Branch. Notes of sherry, butterscotch, and dried fruits. This finishing touch makes it one of the best ryes on the market, bar none. Love this whiskey.

Lux Row Distillery in Bardstown, Kentucky, broke ground on May 2, 2016, with Luxco's chairman and CEO, Donn Lux, and president and COO, David Bratcher, joined by Governor Matt Bevin and other local elected officials.

The 90-acre site includes an 18th-century stone house (a registered National Historic Place) that is part of the 18,000-square-foot distillery, which features six barrel warehouses, a visitor center, and a tasting room and event space.

Speaking to Modern Thirst website about his new distillery, Lux said, "This has really been transformational for Luxco. Because we're going from just another bottler or processor who owns some valuable brands to someone who is actually distilling. It's very important to today's consumer. We think it's part of the authentic story. While it's more money than we've ever spent on any capital project, it feels really cool and really authentic, and we're super excited."

The distillery is one of the jewels of the region. The front of the house, the grand tasting room, was designed and styled by Michelle Lux, who is also the distillery's creative director. Her efforts were spectacular. Most impressive was a visit to the barrel house No. 1, which is a photo op dream of a barrel warehouse. Stunning. Six stories of nothing by barrels as high up as the eye can see. A terrific experience.

Luxco currently makes Rebel Yell, Ezra Brooks, Blood Oath, Daviess County, and David Nicholson. And they released their Lux Row Limited Edition.

In January 2021, Lux Row Distillery was bought by MPG Ingredients of Indiana, giving the Midwest spirits giant a foothold in Kentucky proper. It is a purchase of historic import.

"Luxco presents a unique opportunity to take a material step toward realizing our long-term strategy. It significantly expands our product line in the higher-value branded-spirits sector and increases our sales and distribution capabilities across all 50 states," said David Colo, president and CEO of MGP Ingredients, Inc. "We have enormous respect for the platform Luxco has built."

"There is a clear strategic fit between Luxco and MGP and I believe this transaction represents a great outcome for Luxco employees and customers," said Donn Lux, chairman and CEO of Luxco. "I'm excited to continue my involvement with this blend of two well-positioned companies whose strong records of performance and commitment to excellence provide an attractive platform for continued growth.

BLOOD OATH

John E. Rempe is the man behind Blood Oath. He travels around Kentucky sampling barrels of bourbon to select for this small-batch offering. According to the distillery, "Rempe, a Certified Food Scientist, received his bachelor's degree in biology from Saint Louis University. He then spent some time developing carbonated soft drinks and fruit drinks and creating new beverages before moving on to Luxco." He has been at Luxco for more than 17 years, and Blood Oath's small-batch bourbons are of the highest caliber. Some bottlings are as small as three barrels. Each one is labeled by number Pact 1, Pact 2, Pact 3, etc. "As long as there's still that demand for Blood Oath, we'll keep going. I won't repeat anything, and that's going to be the challenge.

Rempe makes sure that all of the blending notes are included in the very luscious and deluxe package. As all three of Blood Oath's whiskeys have been extremely well received, this imprint is a must-have for collectors!

"That's my signature. That's my baby. I come out with a new one every year. I kinda do something different with it every year.

We always release it in April." Rempe has experimented with all kinds of finishes. He's already hard at work on the releases scheduled years out. "Always trying to find the next Pact," he said. "I love being creative and thinking of new expressions and innovative ideas we can develop."

REBEL YELL

Charles R. Farnsley, a former mayor of Louisville, was said to have created the brand "Rebel Yell" for Stitzel-Weller in the mid-1900s. Originally produced in small quantities, it was only distributed in the southern United States. The brand was later purchased by David Sherman after the breakup of Stitzel-Weller.

Rebel Yell, after its current rebirth, offers a number of different bottlings, including the classic Rebel Yell Kentucky Straight Bourbon Whiskey, Rebel Yell American Whiskey, Rebel Yell, Rebel Yell Small Batch Rye, and Rebel Yell Small Batch Kentucky Straight Bourbon Whiskey, as well as ginger and root beer-infused editions.

The classic Rebel Yell Kentucky Straight Bourbon was distributed around the country starting in 1984. Rebell Yell is sourced from Heaven Hill and features a mash bill of 68% corn, 20% wheat, and 12% barley, allowing it to fit in with the earlier Weller portfolio. It is a well-rounded bourbon with a hint of spice and a nice easy finish.

Lux Row has also produced two new releases of Rebel Yell Bourbon: Rebel Yell 100 Proof and the Rebel Yell Single Barrel, along with newly updated packaging for the whole line. The 100 is something special for those who like high-proof whiskeys.

There are innovations taking place with Rebel Yell. John Rempe explained that they started to experiment with French oak Bordeaux barrels A special version of Rebel Yell aged in these was released in the UK. Going forward Rempe will be looking at different char levels and different barrel entry proofs.

EZRA BROOKS

The Ezra Brooks Bourbon Whiskey Kentucky Sour Mash is primarily bottled at 80 proof. Ezra Brooks is distilled, aged, and bottled in Kentucky by Heaven Hill Distilleries using a mash bill of 78% corn, 10% rye, and 12% barley. Starting out like any other bourbon, Ezra Brooks undergoes one more step: a charcoal mellowing process like a Tennessee whiskey. Another whiskey from Ezra Brooks, Old Ezra Kentucky Straight Bourbon Whiskey 7-Year-Old, is bottled at 101 proof and is absolutely worth trying. It was recently named Best American Whiskey by *Forbes* magazine!

LUX ROW LIMITED EDITION WHISKEY

Lux Row Limited Edition Whiskey is a limited-release ryed bourbon. "Even the proof, 118.4, commemorates the distillery's grand opening in April 2018," said John Rempe, head distiller and master blender for Lux Row Distillers.

Lux Row Distillers Limited Edition is a straight bourbon whiskey and is a double barrel release, having been aged in two different barrels — for 12 years each. The goal was an extra-aged expression.

"Normally it's taken out of the primary barrel and then finished in something else. With this one, I tasted through a bunch of different 12-year-old barrels, made real meticulous tasting notes on it, and then paired two barrels, and two barrels, etc. So it's basically the smallest small batch you can have," said Rempe. "I paired barrels that complemented each other." One might be stronger on the nose, where another might have a longer finish. "And I mingled them for an exceptional offering."

He thinks the bourbon "is best neat, or maybe with just a drop or two of water." This is a big, rich bourbon with caramel, vanilla, oak, and tobacco, with hints of cherry and honey. Impressive.

40004

LUX ROW
DISTILLERS

DOUBLE BARREL
CASK STRENGTH
BARDSTOWN 40004
NELSON CO. KENTUCKY

LIMITED EDITION
WHISKEY
BARDSTOWN, KENTUCKY

· KENTUCKY STRAIGHT BOURBON WHISKEY ·

DOUBLE BARREL AGED **12** YEARS

| BARREL NO. | 5154523 | AGED SINCE | 5/4/07 |
| BARREL NO. | 5154524 | AGED SINCE | 5/4/07 |

750ML · 118.4 PROOF · *Cask Strength* · 59.2% ALC/VOL

DAVIESS COUNTY BOURBON

Daviess County Distilling Company dates back to 1874, and was one of the first great bourbon distilleries of Kentucky. Daviess (it's pronounced "Davis") County Distilling also paved the way for more than a dozen other distilleries that opened in Daviess County before Prohibition. It was acquired by the Medley Distilling Company in 1901 and survived through Prohibition. The label was eventually let go by its eventual parent Diageo back in 1992. Lux Row acquired the name in 1993.

Lux Row has released three labels: Daviess County Kentucky Straight Bourbon (96 proof), Daviess County Kentucky Straight Bourbon – Cabernet Sauvignon Finish (96 proof), and Daviess County Kentucky Straight Bourbon – French Oak Finish (96 proof).

The Cabernet Finish is rested for six months in cabernet sauvignon barrels from California's Napa region. The French Oak Finish is rested in French oak barrels for six months.

"The combination of mash bills really sets this bourbon apart – the smooth wheated mash bill and the traditional spicy ryed mash bill come together for a balanced taste profile," said Rempe. "The secondary aging in the cabernet sauvignon and French oak barrels adds a nice extra layer of flavor with a slight sweet fruitiness and oaky caramel undertones.".

JOHN REMPE

"Usually, the first thing I do in the morning is check with the distillery operators at the cookers and fermenters and see how the still is running before heading to my office to check emails," said John Rempe, head distiller at Lux Row.

Rempe also spends time in the lab. Quality control is an important part of his job. "What's great about our lab techs is that they are University of Louisville chemical engineering students working here for college credit and they are eager to learn," he explained. Rempe is constantly checking the mash from the cookers, the grains, the yeast, the distillate, and many other components.

Rempe is St. Louis born and bred. He graduated from St. Louis University and is a certified food scientist. His first job was in quality control at Cott Corporation, a major beverage manufacturer of sodas and seltzers, as well as coffees, teas, and bottled water. He then became a production manager, R&D manager, and quality control manager at Citrus Springs, a producer of juices, cocktail mixers, and other beverages.

In 1998 Rempe joined Lux Row. He was director of R&D, and eventually worked his way to master blender. Lux Row was known for sourced blends. But Lux Row doubled down on the bourbon trend, and today, 22 years after joining, Rempe is head distiller at a new, state-of-the-art distillery that has become one of the major attractions in Bardstown, Kentucky.

And, he has, with the marketing and sales groups, created whole new lines of bourbons and whiskeys, as well as revived old labels such as Rebel Yell and Daviess County.

Rempe had an industry reputation for having an incredibly deft blending palate. He worked closely with a number of Lux Row partners, always involved in the process, the mash bills, the aging. He was living with the creation of the distillery. Construction started in 2016. He distilled the first barrels in January 2018. The distillery can currently produce 22-25,000 barrels per year. And they have no plans to do anything other than whiskey. Everything they make there is for them. And they are up to five warehouses.

One of the biggest changes for Rempe was the move from St. Louis to Kentucky. In fact, he lives in a small house on the distillery grounds (the distillery is set on a 90-acre farm), where he keeps chickens and peacocks. "We inherited them when we bought the property. It's one of the things we had to agree on when we took it over," hje said with a laugh. He's even grown his own non-GMO corn for some experimental batches.

"I'm actually just now starting to be able to experiment and use my creativity. Now I'm getting to use some different barrels, and different mash bills." For example, he's been experimenting with high-wheat mash bills and heirloom corn to create a Lux Row "estate" wheated bourbon. He's also looking at growing a different grain every year to create variety for limited-edition whiskeys.

"I've always loved what I do," said Rempe. "It's nice to wake up every morning and smell that mash cooking. I always joke about my commute to work. It's a 200-yard walk. My traffic jams are my peacocks. I just have to wait for them to cross. They're up in my trees. During mating season, they're very vocal."

Maker's Mark

Where does one begin with Maker's Mark? To visit this distillery is like visiting Anheuser-Busch in St. Louis. It is a blend of old and new, of high-tech and incredibly antique means. And it is beautifully and lovingly maintained, like a cherished vintage car. The copper at Maker's Mark always glistens as if it was just polished yesterday (and it probably was). There is fresh paint everywhere. The place sparkles and shines, and is neat as a pin. It is hard to believe that anything gets made here. But it does—does it ever.

The grounds are also beautifully manicured, like a country club. There are few places like it in the industry. But there is a different feeling here. The campus is dotted with black, brown, and red buildings. There is attention to every detail.

On December 31, 1974, the distillery was listed on the National Register of Historic Places, and in 1980 was designated as a National Historic Landmark. Maker's was the first distillery in the United States to achieve this status while the buildings themselves were still in active production.

Master distiller Greg Davis is the brand's best ambassador. A big man with a laugh to match, he preaches the gospel of Maker's Mark with a smile on his face. Davis is someone who seems to work well with everyone, from lab technicians to the maintenance crew.

The Maker's Mark brand was born in 1958. T. William "Bill" Samuels Sr. bought Burks' Distillery, which was built in 1889, five years earlier. The whiskey was sold in a squarish-bottle. And the unique, trademarked red wax seal was the idea of Marjorie "Margie" Samuels, Bill Sr.'s wife, who also named the whiskey.

Another thing that made Maker's unique is that it is among only a handful of American producers that use the traditional English spelling "whisky" on its labels. And it letterpresses every label in-house, on an antique press. And yes, each one of those bottles is hand-dipped on the bottling line by a quartet of women.

Another unique thing about Maker's Mark is that it uses no rye in its mash bill. Maker's Mark uses winter red wheat instead.

is produced/distilled in small quantities of approximately 1,000 gallons or less (20 barrels) from a mash bill of around 200 bushels of grain."

There is no question that the level of detail put into the whiskey is nothing shy of intense. There are four major labels for Maker's Mark: The Red Top; the Mint Julep with green wax, which is released seasonally in limited amounts around Kentucky Derby time; 46, which is bourbon aged for an extended amount of time and finished with French oak; and Maker's Mark Cask Strength Bourbon, which was released in limited quantities in 2014, and has since been released globally.

The blend is 70% corn, 14% malted barley, and 16% soft red winter wheat. Legend has it that Samuels judged the final grain bill by baking bread composed of the candidates for the final recipe. But Samuels was also a friend and acolyte of Pappy Van Winkle, who made famous wheated bourbons such as Pappy Van Winkle, Old Forrester, and W. L. Weller & Sons.

Maker's Mark stays in the barrel six years. It uses a #3 char, and the whiskey goes into the barrels at 110 proof. The barrels in the rickhouses get rotated. They stay in the first spot for three years. Then those stored on the seventh floor (the hottest) are moved to the first floor (the coolest). Those on the sixth floor are moved to the second floor. Those on the fifth floor move to the third. Those on the fourth floor stay put.

Maker's Mark positions itself as a small batch bourbon, claiming, "A bourbon that

GREG DAVIS
THE HEAD COACH
OF MAKER'S MARK

If Chris Morris of Woodford Reserve seems the embodiment of an older Southern gentleman, Greg Davis is almost his exact opposite. A big, virile man with broad shoulders, giant hands, and a booming voice, Davis is an explosion of enthusiasm and determination. In his red-and-white shirt, he shakes your hand with a bear-paw grip and flashes a smile as wide as a billboard. One gets the impression that if Davis wasn't the master distiller at Maker's Mark, he would be the head football coach of the Louisville Cardinals or Tennessee Volunteers. It's easy to see him barking orders at linebackers and schmoozing with boosters.

But behind the big smile and the booming laugh is a man with a serious passion for bourbon. Davis has been in the wine and spirits business in one form or another since 1990. He had studied brewing science, and worked in the research and development department at Brown-Forman. Once a master brewer at Bohanan Brewery, he later moved to Tom Moore Distillery, where he created new best practices and pushed the envelope of innovation.

Davis loves to recall how Maker's Mark had tried to woo him, and he resisted. But the Maker's Mark executives were determined to get their man. After a year, they did. And there were big shoes to fill, both literally and figuratively. Dave Pickerell, a former offensive tackle for West Point, had been the master distiller at Maker's from 1994 to 2008. In those early days, Davis's mantra was "don't screw it up," a story he related with a big belly laugh.

Davis did nothing of the sort. Enough of an individualist to cast his own large shadow, Davis and his team have taken Maker's Mark to a whole new level.

Davis recalled the day Bill Samuels Jr. walked into a meeting, wrote the word "Yummy" in big letters, and then exited the room. Davis knew what Samuels wanted. He asked each member of his group what they could do as a team to make this new whiskey. "Bourbon is traditionally bitter," Davis told the *Houston Press*. "What yummy meant for us was to move toward something a little softer but still just as pronounced. We had to add a new element to the bourbon that was missing. Samuels Jr. wanted us to go further with it. He wrote that word down and left. We realized it was up to us to figure out what we could do to produce that. We had to figure it out from just that simple word. That's how it all started."

Davis called Brad Baswell, a fourth- or fifth-generation barrel maker, in to help push the project forward. The company tried more than 100 barrels before it hit upon the right one. Baswell brought in staves featuring differing toasts of French oak. These new woods brought out more of the stone fruit and vanilla notes in the bourbon. "When you smell the 46 you can smell the complex oak notes and the vanilla much more," said Davis. "We take 18-month-old French oak lined up using the radiant heat to penetrate all throughout the wood to caramelize all those wood chips. What you are trying to achieve is as you age it to take the bitterness out of it."

To further that, Maker's Mark has created a whole new business—the custom bourbon business. It has one new rickhouse built into the side of a hill. Inside it's all wood and glass and steel, and looks like something out of a James Bond film. Restaurants and stores can come in, buy a barrel's worth of bourbon, or more, and either re-oak it or direct the whiskey to a custom finish utilizing a combination of six French oaks of differing toasts. In beautiful, well-lit classrooms, customers sit with one of the team's distillers for a day, and blend and taste until they have their preferred flavor notes. The corresponding woods are placed in colder barrels (where the whiskey won't be pushed into the wood, but will instead rest on the char) and aged for another period of time (usually six months). This is cutting-edge stuff in bourbon country, and the results have been fantastic. Maker's 46 is suddenly the hottest part of its program.

Today, Davis sweats the small stuff, even down to admonishing guests to be careful not to step on newly painted places. He notices smudges and things left out. He handles everything with humor. And he is well-known for barbecuing on the distillery grounds. The smell of his grill wafts around the large campus like a giant reminder of who is in residence. And everyone wants a piece.

Section: 104

Part ID: 631 0783103-22222-24090

← FLOW

MB Roland Distillery

Located in the Christian County town of Pembroke, MB Roland Distillery was founded by Paul and Merry Beth ("MB") Tomaszewski in 2009 as Kentucky's first completely grain-to-glass craft distillery. Paul hails from southeastern Louisiana, and MB is a local native. They bought an old Amish dairy farm that came up for sale.

Paul named the distillery for his wife, MB Roland is her maiden name. She was at first incredibly pleased by what she saw as a romantic gesture. Paul told her no one would ever be able to pronounce Tomaszewski (he should have quit while he was ahead). The distillery quickly garnered a reputation as a cutting-edge craft distillery who produced quality spirits. That's something in the state of Kentucky. This stuff is good!

Originally Paul was the one and only full-time employee and distiller in 2009. They now have over a dozen employees. Even MB is a full-time distillery employee. The distillery is close to their local grain supplier, Christian County Grain. They use local white corn to hand make each of their products, ranging from their very unique "distillation & barrel proof" Kentucky Bourbon to their naturally-flavored moonshines made with corn and cane.

MB Roland Kentucky Straight Bourbon Whiskey (105-115 proof) is made using local, food-grade white corn, and bottled at barrel proof in the style of a pre-Prohibition bourbon. Each batch is a blend of 5 to 10 barrels. Bottles are hand labeled, numbered, and individually proofed. The whiskey is sold at the distillery, and is available in limited amounts through various distributors.

Each bottling of MB Roland Kentucky Straight Bourbon Whiskey Single Barrel (105-115 proof) is unique, uncut, and unfiltered. Rich and bold.

MB Roland Kentucky Straight Rye Whiskey (105-115 proof) is from a mash bill that blends a heaping of rye with the addition of local Christian County white corn. Sweet up front, but a backend of gingersnap and black pepper.

MB Roland Kentucky Straight Malt Whiskey (105-115 proof) is a hybrid whiskey made in a kind of single malt style, but they include white corn and rye to provide spicier, fuller flavors.

MB Roland Kentucky Dark Fired Whiskey (110-120 proof) is aged in used bourbon barrels. A little lighter than bourbon, but with all of the campfire notes for fans of smoky whiskey.

MB Roland Kentucky Straight Corn Whiskey (105-115 proof) is a corn whiskey mash aged in bourbon barrels.

The cane and corn line of moonshines is labeled MBR. MBR True Kentucky Shine (100 proof) is made using a recipe of white corn and sugar. Floral notes, citrus flavors, and a hint of apple peel. A quality cane and corn 'shine. MBR Kentucky Black Dog (90 proof) is a "dark fired" smoky, sweet 'shine made using "dark fired" corn, rye, and malted barley. They offer a whole line of naturally-flavored MBR 'shines.

MICHTER'S

By Richard Thomas

It's useful to think of Michter's in terms of "Old Michter's" and "New Michter's." The old company is the one that traces its semi-legendary roots back to Mennonite farmers in the 1750s and came to a final end when the Bomberger's Distillery closed in 1989.

The new company began when Joe Magliocco, founder of Chatham Imports, teamed up with former Wild Turkey president Richard Newman in the 1990s to resurrect the brand. Magliocco located his new company in Louisville, rather than the old Michter's home base of southeastern Pennsylvania. Although the choice upset some purists, as Magliocco often puts it, "Kentucky is where the whiskey business and its expertise are."

With help from Brown-Forman veteran Willie Pratt, the company acquired some excellent Kentucky whiskey stock, and began bottling and releasing whiskeys in 2000. They also began contract distilling under Pratt's supervision in 2003, "cooking in someone else's kitchen," as Magliocco described it, at which point Pratt became Michter's first master distiller. For a time, their bottling was handled by Kentucky Bourbon Distillers, now known as Willett.

Michter's kept growing, and produced some landmark whiskeys along the way. Citing just one example, according to Wine-Searcher.com, the esteemed Michter's Celebration Sour Mash Whiskey is America's third-most expensive whiskey (after Old Rip Van Winkle 25-Year-Old and A.H. Hirsch 20-Year-Old) and the most expensive in current, if irregular, production.

They opened their distillery in Shively in 2015, and in so doing became a middleweight fixture among the big Kentucky distillers. With the opening of their own distillery, Michter's began a period of transition from sourced and contract-produced whiskey to whiskey made in their own house. The journey to the day when every drop of whiskey in Michter's bottles will come out their own equipment and under their own roof will be largely overseen by Pam Heilmann, who succeeded Willie Pratt as master distiller in 2016.

Before coming to Michter's, Heilmann had put in 15 years at Jim Beam, including a stint as the distillery manager at the Booker Noe Distillery, Beam's less famous and much bigger plant. While there she worked under master distiller Jerry Dalton, a peculiar figure in Beam lore in that he was the only non-Beam to serve in that role at the company.

Because Michter's is arguably the largest and most important of the newcomers to Kentucky's whiskey industry, Heilmann's rise to the top distiller slot is quite emblematic of three whiskey workplace trends. First, by replacing Willie Pratt, she completed a changing of the guard in Kentucky bourbon that has been going on this past decade. It used to be typical to speak of master distillers as serving 20 or 30 years on the job, but now the longest-serving major distiller in Kentucky is Chris Morris at Brown-Forman, whose tenure began in 2003.

The most commented-upon trend, however, is how more women are coming to the forefront of the whiskey industry worldwide, as Heilmann joins Marianne Barnes in Kentucky and Maureen Robinson, Rachel Barrie, and Kirsteen Campbell in Scotland, among others. Less spoken of is how the boom-time expansion of the industry has created so many advancement opportunities in the first place. Becoming a master distiller in Kentucky used to require decades of patient work and was often a matter of family connections or dynasties, but the rapid expansion of the industry has created room for many bright talents to move over and up. Heilmann is an outstanding example of that. In 2019 Heilman became Master Distiller Emerita and her protégé Dan McKee was made master distiller. But there can be no denying Heilman's influence and importance.

Royce Neeley grew up in Owen County and graduated from Transylvania University, in Lexington in 2013. He then attended Midway University, in Midway, where he earned an MBA in 2017 in Bourbon Tourism and Event Management.

This descendent of a long line of moonshiners (11 generations to be exact) from Owsley County, Kentucky, he is now president, CEO, and head distiller of Neeley Family Distillery. According to local lore, the Neeley and Allen families share a long history of notorious feuds and shootouts. "One wall inside the visitors' center and tasting room features old newspaper accounts, family photos, and even an actual rifle and pistol used by his ancestors to shoot and kill their enemies back in Owsley County. There's also one of his great-grandfather's makeshift stills on display in the corner of the room," wrote local journalist Don Ward.

Royce's mother got suspicious when her son was at college and stopped asking for money. What college student doesn't need money? In a surprise visit, she found her son had erected a mini-distillery in his dorm room. She dismantled the still and made

him swear he would not make another drop.

After graduating, Royce was unimpressed with the job market. He kicked around selling insurance, worked for his father's construction company, and took a turn as a factory supervisor. Ultimately, his parents agreed to assist him in making the family business legal. The Neeleys bought a 10-acre plot near the Kentucky Speedway, and planning began.

The new Neeley Family Distillery was established in Sparta, in Gallatin County, in 2016, and the doors opened in 2017. And when they say family, they meant it. Roy and Michele Neeley help run the place both by book keeping and tasting room sales. Roy (a reformed former moonshiner) is now a successful general contractor, and built the rugged facilities. Royce's grandfather on his mother's side, Earl Sizemore, serves as assistant distiller.

"We think this location will be ideal for attracting race fans and to capitalize on auto racing's long history with moonshine runners down in eastern Kentucky. That's how NASCAR got started," Royce said. Neeley Family Distillery is now a member of and stop on the prestigious Kentucky Bourbon Trail Craft Tour and B-Line passport program.

Neeley Family Distillery has grown immensely in the last few years.

They do things the right way. They have grown, but with real forethought. Their fermentation room is outfitted with five, large old-fashion styled Cyprus fermenters, and fermentation is open top. In January 2020 they received four new Donna tubs for their new yeast room. Neeley Family is one of the few distilleries in the country that still "work" all of their own yeast on site. Royce is a sworn advocate of sweet mash (versus sour mash). And insists on using a pot still. Royce has come into his own as a distiller. The distillery now has a new rickhouse

KENTUCKY FEUDISTS FIGHT

Two Reported Killed and Six Wounded in Furious Battle at a Bean Stringing.

LONDON, Ky., Aug. 27.—It is reported that two men were killed and five men and a woman wounded in a fight at a bean stringing at the home of William Peters in Owsley County.

The fight is said to have occurred between members of the Neeley and Allen families, between whom there is a feud. Jesse Neeley and John Allen were killed, each being shot several times.

About fifteen persons were engaged in the battle, which took place in a small room while the party was at supper.

The dispute is said to have started between James Neeley and John Allen, who are rivals for the affections of a young lady.

Warrants have been issued for the arrest of Delaney Peters, Robert Allen, Arthur Lynch and a boy named Gumm.

full of bourbon whiskey in its stores, and is ready to make the next big jump. They have a new 500-gallon copper pot still from Vendome, more employees, and are ready to up their production. Their products are now in select stores, and they've even shipped internationally (Ireland).

Everything at Neeley is done by hand, so that means more work, more effort. But the results certainly seem worth it.

Neeley started out offering moonshine, while squirreling away as much in barrels as they could. All that said, their moonshine is good! Which of course is a portent of good things to come. Neeley offers two excellent unaged spirits.

NFD Authentic Kentucky Moonshine (120.2 proof) has been the family's bread and butter for over 100 years. This is Royce's great grandfather's original 1913 shine recipe, which he altered with the addition of sugar. A corn and cane product. Leonard Neeley, had a specific way he made his liquor back in the day. Royce's ancestor ran it through his still three times with a thump keg attached. Neeley Family uses the same method today on copper pot stills they custom built allowing them to operate like Royce's great

grandpa's still. Their moonshine contains all local grains, fresh Kentucky limestone water, and a unique yeast strand the family has been using for 150 years. Each label is hand written by a Neeley, where bottles and batches are individually numbered. Crystal clear moonshine so pure it attracts the eye. A nose of buttered popcorn, cotton candy, and Granny Smith apples. Super smooth!

Pawpaw Sizemore's Kentucky Bourbon White Dog (110 proof), the flagship Neeley bourbon recipe, is bottled unaged. Crystal clear. Sweet grain, cereal, and a little Kentucky hug. Corn lingers. Very nice. You might be lucky enough to spot a bottle in select liquor stores. Scoop them up if you like fine, unaged whiskey.

They also make two lovely bourbon cream liqueurs named Southern Dew. Southern Dew Chocolate Moonshine Truffle is a blend of Irish cream base with chocolate fudge, vanilla, and walnut flavors. Southern Dew Orange Moonshine Creamsicle blends Irish cream with orange cream flavors and their moonshine.

Neeley Family Kentucky Single Barrel Bourbon (approx. 100-105 proof) is based on the same recipe that James Neeley made

back in 1740. It's made using sweet mash made from fresh non-GMO local grains and pure Gallatin County limestone water. It is then fermented in open-top cypress at cool temperatures, allowing the yeast ample time to produce their great flavors. The whiskey is triple pot-distilled. Non-chill filtered, aged 18 months, and bottled at barrel proof right out of the barrel. Neely's Single Barrel comes with several flavor profiles, including Peppercorn Punch, Electric Yellow Rose, Maple Mocha, or Marshmallow Black Belt. Barrel Select won a gold medal in the San Francisco World Spirits Competition.

Neeley Family Kentucky Single Barrel Straight Bourbon Whiskey (approx. 100-105 proof) is made the same way as the whiskey, but it is aged for a minimum of 25 months in order to meet the "Straight Bourbon" labeling laws. It is differentiated by a black label.

DAVID-JAMES WHISKEY

Neeley Family Distillery is also the home of David-James Whiskeys. The idea for this whiskey was born in hilltops and hollers of 18th century Georgetown, Kentucky, and it is made from carefully selected sourced bourbon and whiskey. There are four partners. Richard "Doug" Linger, a pharmacist by trade, started Old George Town Spirits in 2017. Phillip A. Johnson, a fellow pharmacist, is also a partner. Mike "Gee" Gee is a longtime construction expert, and James R "Bo" Kelly is the man who brought Old George Town Spirits' partners together

Royce is the master distiller of this line. According to him, "Housing this brand allows us to have some of the best aged whiskey in the world on our shelf, while our bourbon and moonshine sleeps in their barrels for the next few years or so, until we deem our bourbon is ready for market."

The David-James products are sold at the Neeley Family Distillery, but the blends are also available elsewhere. This high-proof, high intensity brand was created for distribution to Southern and Midwestern states.

David James Straight American Whiskey (119.6 proof) is distilled in Indiana and aged 10 years in Indiana and Kentucky. Lightly filtered. Mingled at Neeley Family in a small batch of 21 barrels. Caramel, cherry, honey, vanilla, and oak. This is their best-selling whiskey and has won numerous awards.

David James Straight American Whiskey Platinum (111.2 proof) is distilled in Indiana, aged in Indiana and Kentucky. Aged 9 years and 7 months in American white oak barrels. Lightly filtered. Hand bottled at Neeley Family with handwritten labels. Creamy sweet vanilla with spice, hints of pepper and caramel.

David James Straight Bourbon Whiskey Gold (111.2 proof) is distilled in Tennessee and aged in both Tennessee and Kentucky. Aged 8 years and 10 months in American white oak barrels. Lightly filtered. Blended at Neeley in a small batch of 25 barrels. Hand bottled. Cherry, tobacco, chocolate notes.

David James Straight Bourbon Whiskey Platinum (93.66 proof) is distilled in Tennessee, aged in Tennessee and Kentucky. Aged 9 years and 5 months in American white oak barrels. Lightly filtered. Blended at Neeley and hand bottled. Dark caramel, cocoa, and peppercorn.

Neeley Family Distillery is every bit as good as some of the more chic, artisanal craft producers in Louisville and Lexington. They must be tried. Royce Neeley is one to be watched.

NEW RIFF DISTILLING

New Riff Distilling is an independent, family-owned, distillery. According to the company, it takes pride in its "freedom to innovate and collaborate, riff on the old and redefine the new." Ken Lewis is president and owner of this urban distillery that has caught the eye of industry insiders and aficionados with its a very serious, quality-driven focus.

Brian Sprance is the head distiller (who originally came by way of Boston Beer Company), and there are a whole host of employees pushing this place to a new level. It opened in 2014 in a state-of-the-art facility in Newport, right across the Ohio River from Cincinnati, Ohio.

Two large grain silos feed New Riff's two hungry stills. Its 500-gallon pot still offers an immense range of artisanal possibilities, from un-aged spirits to barrel-aged bourbon, whiskey, and rye. New Riff has collaborated with Bellevue's Ei8ht Ball Brewing to lay down a burgeoning single malt whiskey, as well. Rising almost 60 feet in the air, and with a 24-inch diameter, New Riff's column still can produce almost 700 gallons of spirits per day. Do the math, and the sky is virtually the limit for this new startup.

The shop downstairs is ample and cleverly outfitted. But the building goes on forever. In the upper floors there are super modern balconies for outdoor entertaining. And the top floor has a cool event space, with large bar, and more outdoor seating on both sides. New Riff is one of the hippest new distilleries to visit.

New Riff Kentucky Wild Gin is a fascinating blend of classic old world London Dry botanicals (coriander, orris root, angelica root, cinnamon, lemon, bitter orange, and, of course, juniper berries) with locally sourced botanicals that are native to the area (goldenrod, Kentucky's cheerful state flower; and a local native American juniper, the spice bush). This blend makes for an incredibly smooth gin, with zip, zest, and a flavor profile that isn't just different—it's spicy, it's local. New Riff Barreled Kentucky Wild Gin is aged in Kentucky bourbon barrels, and is equally impressive.

New Riff originally sold sourced whiskey under their OKI label. That has been retired. Now, all New Riff products are made from their own distillate. New Riff's Straight Bourbon and Straight Rye can be found in a wide range of stores, and distribution is growing.

New Riff Kentucky Straight Bourbon (100 proof) has a mash bill of 65% corn, 30% rye, and 5% malted barley, all non-GMO. Aged at least four years. Each bottle states date of distilling and date of bottling. The is a high-rye bourbon, complete with the big gingersnap finish. Lots of caramel, honey, oats, cereal, and butterscotch, but with a black pepper ending that leaves the mouth dry, with a pop. This is a rye-drinkers bourbon. This is the work horse of the line. Very, very drinkable. Stands up to ice.

New Riff Kentucky Straight Rye Whiskey (100 proof) has a mash bill of 95% rye and 5% malted rye. Aged four years in charred American oak. Non chill-filtered. Bottled in bond. This is a rye-lovers whiskey. Burnt orange peel. Caramel, molasses, tobacco, black pepper, hint of spices. A big bite at the end flavor wise. The alcohol doesn't make it hot. The flavor does. A big rye for those who want bold whiskeys. Another workhorse in the New Riff stable.

Available at the distillery is a series of truly exceptional single barrel expressions. New Riff Single Barrel Bourbon 16-11658 chosen by Jay Erisman, co-founder (quick on spice, polished, hints of smoke, dark

fruit, and clove); New Riff Single Barrel Bourbon 16-11637 chosen by Grover Arnold, brand ambassador (buttery caramel, brown sugar, honey pepper, lingering rye spice); New Riff Single Barrel 15-5258 chosen by David Miller, distiller (baking spices, caramel, apple, black cherry, tobacco); New Riff Single Barrel Rye 16-6588 chosen by David Sprance, distiller (raspberry, vanilla bean, black pepper, clove, dry citrus zest); and New Riff Single Barrel Rye 16-1151 chosen by Stephanie Batty, distiller (geranium, tangerine, sandalwood, vanilla, fruit). And the prices of these, comparable to their quality, are relatively inexpensive. Fantastic bottlings. More to come.

High quality and flavor from New Riff, a place to keep on your radar.

OLD POGUE

By Richard Thomas

Old Pogue is best known for its nine-year-old bourbon, which is such a hot ticket item that the most reliable way to acquire a bottle these days is to make the trip to the distillery. Those making that journey, far off the Bourbon Trail's beaten track to Maysville, are in for a treat beyond that prized bottle. Old Pogue is a delightfully picturesque, craft-scale distillery, located next to the historic family home and overlooking the banks of the Ohio River. What is more, its hometown has a good claim to being the founding location of the bourbon industry, as the earliest business-related reference to "Bourbon Whiskey" was in a Maysville newspaper, circa 1821.

So, if you want to do some bourbon tourism where bourbon began, don't go to Scott County looking for the stomping grounds of the semi-mythical Reverend Elijah Craig. Go to Maysville and Old Pogue.

Old Pogue entered the scene when master distiller H.E. Pogue bought the distillery that employed him in 1876. The distillery was shuttered during Prohibition, and H.E. Pogue III got out of whiskey trade altogether afterward. This had as much to do with his family's tragic legacy in the business as with the difficulties facing many distillers in restarting production after the forced 14-year stoppage: Pogue lost both his father and his grandfather in workplace accidents.

After discovering some antique bottles of vintage Pogue whiskey in the 1990s, H.E. Pogue's descendants decided to re-enter the whiskey business. Using a contract-produced bourbon based on a family recipe, Old Pogue was relaunched in 2004. The brand soon developed a cult following, and with annual production runs still limited to dumps of just 20 to 30 barrels at a time, Old Pogue bourbon has become almost unavailable outside of the distillery gift shop.

Foreseeing where the bourbon industry was headed, the Pogues opened their distillery in 2012, taking charge of their own production. The distillery reintroduced the Old Maysville Club brand as a 100% malted rye bottled-in-bond whiskey, giving fans of rye a mature version of an all-malted whiskey. Just recently they also released their first bourbon of their own make. Old Pogue's Master Select (91 proof) Old Pogue was the flagship product of the original H.E. Pogue Distillery in 1876 and is also the first product released by the modern Pogue Distillery. Straight Kentucky bourbon, limited availability.

OLD SALEM SPIRITS

It all began in 1917 when a Kentucky coal miner asked a Chattanooga Bakery traveling salesman for a snack "as big as the moon." Earl Mitchell reported back and the bakery obliged with a tasty treat aptly named MoonPie. It was filling, fit in the lunch pail, and the coal miners loved it. The rest, as they say, is history. A tradition was born, and a national treasure established.

According to Old Salem Spirits president Keith Spears, he and a friend first came up with the idea a few years ago. But they didn't have the cash to fund the whole idea. So they participated in an historic partnership. The Campbell family is fifth generation bakers of the iconic Chattanooga Bakery MoonPie. Paul and Stephen Beam are seventh-generation distillers from one of bourbon's most iconic families. Together the two families created MoonPie Moonshine. Eventually the Beams wanted to focus on their homegrown bourbons and ryes. The brand was eventually taken over by Keith Spears and Old Salem Spirits in 2018. This special collection of MoonPie Spirits is the ultimate "workingman's reward" that represents the marriage of two great Southern traditions. The moonshine, made in Frankfort, has the same flavor profile as the 100-year-old secret recipe of The Original MoonPie.

Old Salem Spirits is an alcohol branding company that offers exclusive and unique adult beverages centered around the entertaining and colorful history of spirit-making. They build brands through television and on-site promotions. Old Salem Spirits has no tasting room, but makes its current MoonPie Moonshine available to other tasting rooms, which serve as satellite shops. The moonshine is available in numerous tasting rooms as well as a large swath of retail liquor outlets. It is among the top ten most distributed moonshines throughout the country. "The tastings are a very important part of marketing our brand," says Spears. They are currently in more than a dozen states.

MoonPie Moonshine Vanilla is perfect for a mixer or to enjoy straight out of the bottle! Simple, sweet, vanilla, and smooth.

Chocolate was the original MoonPie flavor and MoonPie Chocolate Moonshine honors that tradition. This amber moonshine is decadent and sweet, and surprisingly chocolatey.

One of Chattanooga Bakery MoonPies most popular flavors is banana. MoonPie Moonshine Banana is a blending of banana and vanilla, almost like a banana cream pie. Get a box of Nilla Wafer, start sipping, and enjoy!

The bakery reintroduced coconut as a new variety in their line of baked goods in time for Mardi Gras. Moonpies are a big hit at the Mobile Mardi Gras in Alabama. The folks at Old Salem joined in on the fun with MoonPie Moonshine Mardi Gras Coconut.

Old Salem's

ALC 25% BY VOL (50 PROOF)

CHOCOLATE

MOON PIE®

MoonShine

GRAIN NEUTRAL SPIRITS WITH NATURAL FLAVORS

James E. Pepper Distillery

The Pepper family brand of whiskey dates back to the American Revolution and was produced through 1967. The family built and operated two main distilleries: the original distillery is now home to Woodford Reserve Distillery; the James E. Pepper Distillery in Lexington was built later. In the late 1960s the bourbon industry hit hard times, and both the brand and distillery in Lexington were abandoned.

In 2008, the brand was acquired by whiskey entrepreneur Amir Peay. Peay sought out relationships with the Lawrenceburg Distillery in Indiana and the Bardstown Bourbon Co. in Kentucky. The reclaimed brand used sourced whiskeys from these distilleries while Peay rebuilt the old distillery. Today some of the James E. Pepper whiskeys contain whiskeys distilled at those distilleries.

"I'm a history and whiskey nerd, and that led me to discover the whiskey brand started by Col. James E. Pepper," said Peay.

"We re-dug the limestone well and were able to study old drawings from 1934 to rebuild our still system. And we are going to build a small craft distillery here. The scale and the size of production would not allow us to make whiskey here and sell it for the same price as our current product line. So what we are going to do is we will probably start blending in some of the whiskey that's distilled here into the existing line. We will always continue to work with third parties for the existing line, but we will of course have new whiskeys, new product lines just from whiskey distilled here."

The distillery is named for Colonel James E Pepper (1850-1906), master distiller, who was a larger-than-life bourbon industrialist and flamboyant promoter of his family brand. He was actually the third generation to produce Old Pepper Whiskey, "The Oldest and Best Brand of Whisky made in Kentucky," which was founded in 1780 during the American Revolution. Back in the day, Pepper was among the largest distilleries in America.

Pepper was an avid horseman, and operated one of the finest stables in Kentucky. His thoroughbreds competed in the Kentucky Derby and in races across America and Europe. He traveled in an ornate private rail car named "The Old Pepper," which sported the famed whiskey label on the outside.

Pepper was even involved in the invention of the Old Fashioned cocktail A bartender at the Pendennis Club, a gentlemen's club founded in 1881 in Louisville, claims the cocktail was invented there by a bartender looking to honor Pepper. Pepper spent much time promoting his whiskey in New York, and stayed at the Waldorf Astoria Hotel, where he introduced the cocktail's recipe.

James E. Pepper 1776 Straight Bourbon Whiskey "1776" Straight Bourbon (100 Proof) is a non-chill-filtered whiskey with more than 38% rye in the mash bill. Lovely caramel and brown sugar up front, with honey and chocolate, and a lovely gingersnap finish.

James E, Pepper "1776" Straight Rye (100 proof) is a non-chill-filtered high-rye rye, with a mash bill with 90% rye. This is the workhorse of the Pepper line. A favorite among bartenders across the country. Notes of dark cherry, cocoa, cloves, eucalyptus, and honey. A big gingersnap finish. Stands up to ice, and mixes exceptionally well in cocktails. Great for Old Fashions and Manhattans.

James E. Pepper "1776" Straight Rye Barrel Proof (114.6 proof) has the same attributes of its workhorse brother, but packs a much bigger alcohol wallop and more intense notes of anise, spice, cloves, eucalyptus, chocolate, and honey. James E Pepper Old Pepper Rye is their single barrel selection of this whiskey.

Henry Clay Straight Rye Whiskey (86 proof) is named for gifted politician Henry Clay (1777-1852) who famously shipped barrels of whiskey from the Oscar Pepper Distillery to the Willard Hotel in Washington DC. Clay was an important national figure from 1811 until his death. Clay's tomb and estate, maintained and operated as a museum today, are located in Lexington. After Clay's death, the Henry Clay Distillery was built in Lexington in 1869, only to be destroyed by fire a few years later. It was Colonel Pepper who bought the destroyed distillery, rebuilding it on the grounds where it stands today. This whiskey is named in his honor. This is a Pennsylvania rye, meaning it is a high-rye content (more than 90% rye in the mash bill). Softer than its "1776" brethren. Affordable cocktail rye.

AARON SCHORSCH

Its hard not to like Aaron Schorsch. He's a hard-working guy who made it. After graduating from Indiana University Bloomington, he started off as a production operator at Seagram in the plant that is now known as MGP (one of the largest distilleries in North America), and eventually went along to join the Pernod Ricard merger. He was there for more than 10 years. He started out rolling barrels and then operating equipment. It was a huge place, but a great one to learn about distilling. According to him, he had every job you could have. He then put in a year-and-a-half at the Boston Beer Company, the maker of Samuel Adams, in their Cincinnati plant, where he was a brewing supervisor.

After that, Schorsch joined Jim Beam, where he was a distillery and warehouse supervisor for almost four years. He then made the jump to Archer Daniels Midland where he was the warehouse manager for more than three years. In October 2016 he landed at James E. Pepper where he became distillery manager and head distiller.

If all of that sounds exhausting, it should. But it completely prepared him for his role now. At Pepper he is a man on the move. The distillery mornings start early, and usually not without him. From emptying trucks filled with new barrels, moving equipment, to bottling and overseeing the mash and operating the still, Schorsch and his small band are the hardest working group in the distillery business, and Pepper has begun to make more and more whiskey. It's very exciting to watch.

"This place was left for dead," Schorsch recalled. "It was abandoned, used for storage and Lord knows what. The cops said at one point this was a bad place to come." He pointed out that the giant and impressive tasting room is where the old grain bins used to be. Their still room was the old mash room. The fermentor room is the old doubler and still room. And what is their storage and bottling room today was the old dry house.

"When I arrived, it was a construction site still. I ended up being a kind of general contractor, kinda distiller guy, I guess," he said with a smile. "I'm glad I got to do it, because there were a lot of things that I got to have a kind of say in."

Schorsch said new whiskeys will start releasing in 2020 that are made on site. They will be available in the tasting room only. Can't wait. The group they have running James E. Pepper are good, competent folks. Looking forward to some exciting bottles in the future.

LEXINGTON DISTILLING DISTRICT

The old James E. Pepper Distillery sat abandoned for years. It was Tony Higdon and Barry McNees who led the charge to start restoring the old Pepper Plant. But the site was so large, and the building so gigantic, that only a major producer could adequately fill it up. And, frankly, it would be cheaper to build a new plant for anyone of that size. So the developers chose a different tact.

They decided to split up the buildings, and begin a renewal. The final product is something like a mall of craft producers called The Lexington Distilling District. James E. Pepper in effect is the anchor business, and takes up the largest building. However, it's not the only craft beverage business located there. The old boiler house is now Goodfellas Pizza. The old administration building is now an ice cream shop. One of the other out buildings is a small microbrewery. The old warehouse is now home to a cidery, and two pubs. And another distillery and bar – Barrel House Distillery is in yet another out building.

The weekends are packed. All kinds of folks wander the grounds. Families. Groups of friends. Couples. The rehabilitation has been a success. And the town of Lexington has seen a historical piece of ground, that was a gruesome example of urban blight, suddenly blossom in the new craft beverage world.

Preservationist Distillery

Marci Palatella is the founder and owner of Preservation Distillery in Bardstown, Kentucky. Preservationist Distillery is located just off of the Bluegrass Parkway. It's a 40-acre farm, with 10 acres of cattle, and the rest planted to grains. This is a small shop. They mill their own grain for the estate whiskeys. They use only local grains. It's a small system for the estate whiskeys. The distiller runs two mash tuns, sixteen closed fermenters, and two copper hybrid pot stills. It's a thousand-gallon system for whiskey. Plus there's also two additional continuous column stills. All said, it's a 1 to 3 barrel system. Estate whiskeys have been laid down, but are still aging. In the meantime, Preservationist sell a series of blends.

Marci Palatella originally established this brand in 1986 for the Asian market when small batch bourbons were super hot. The original whiskeys were blended from sourced whiskeys from Old Commonwealth distillery and later Heaven Hill. The brand faded, and had not been available for years. Palatella revived the brand in 2018 when she founded Preservationist. Blended from sourced stocks, Very Olde St. Nick Ancient Cask 8-Year-Old Rye Whiskey (approx. 119 proof) is a barrel-strength rye, with a big nose, and nice notes of spice, caramel, black pepper, dried fruit, and honey.

Rare Perfection 14-Year-Old Canadian Whiskey (100 proof) is another of the brands developed by Palatella that she brought back with the founding of Preservationist. It's made from sourced whiskeys, and is a four-grain bourbon mash bill. A very lovely whiskey for those who like older bourbons.

Wattie Boone & Sons 7-Year-Old (94.7 proof) is another of Palatella's old brands that was reintroduced in 2018. It's named after Wattie Boone, who was the first person documented to have made bourbon in Kentucky, along the Beechfork just behind Preservation Distillery. This is a Tennessee whiskey aged for seven years in Kentucky. The color of golden honey. Baking spices, oats, caramel, vanilla, and lingering brown sugar. Lovely, straightforward whiskey.

Rabbit Hole
Distilling

This is all you really need to know. In the review of Rabbit Hole in *Modern Thirst*, co-founder Bill Straub wrote, "If you haven't heard of Rabbit Hole Distilling, don't worry. You will soon." It really doesn't get any better than that!

They began distilling in 2014, and began construction on their state-of-the-art Louisville distillery two years later. CEO and founder Kaveh Zamanian fell in love with a girl named Heather, who lured him away from his beloved scotch, turned him on to bourbon, and lured him to Kentucky. Now that is a love story.

Zamanian was a psychologist who had attended Northwestern University; he had a clinical practice for nearly 20 years and taught at Loyola University. He decided he wanted to go into the distilling business. When he told his wife, she lamented it was a mid-life crisis, that he was losing his mind, claiming that he would "take the whole family down the rabbit hole." That's exactly what he did, and the company name bares the evidence.

The distillery is like nothing you have ever seen. It's like something out of a

Bourbon is a verb.

KAVEH ZAMANIAN
FOUNDER & WHISKEY MAKER

James Bond film. According to Zamnian, he wanted the architecture to embody the Rabbit Hole philosophy of authenticity and transparency. The building does that. There are no walls in the distillation area, save the ones that guard against the outdoors (and those are glass). Pipes running under the floor are transparent, and the same is true of the floors. You can watch distillate and whiskey race back and forth between the distillation room and the bottling and barreling rooms. Even the spirit safe, which looks like a jewel box, puddles the distillate on a 3' by 5' stainless steel case, enclosed in glass, so more of it can be seen by the naked eye. The operation is a glass and steel funhouse built to accentuate and illuminate the art and science of distilling. It took Zamanian and the architects one-and-a-half years to design it, and one-and-a-half years to build it. As Zamanian likes to say, "Chemistry happens when passion and purpose align." He also likes to say, "Bourbon is a verb."

In truth, Zamanian thinks there's too much smoke and mirrors in the distilling business. He wanted his process to be honest and out in the open to the consumer. The only thing not available to the consumer are the rickhouses where they age the whiskey; those are in Henry County. Right now they make bourbon, rye, and they have a special single malt project in barrels, that won't be ready for some time. Rabbit Hole considers Kelvin Barrel to be a partner in the whiskey making process, and works very closely with them. They are also aging spirits in French oak and Japanese Mizunara (oak).

Rabbit Hole Cavehill Kentucky Straight Bourbon Whiskey (95 proof) is a four-grain whiskey. It has a mash bill of 70% corn, 10% malted barley, 10% malted wheat, and 10% honey malted barley.

Rabbit Hole Heigold Kentucky Straight Bourbon Whiskey (95 proof) has a mash bill of 70% corn, 25% malted rye, and 5% malted barley. A high-rye bourbon. This whiskey is named for a German immigrant

stonecutter Christian Heigold from the 1800s. It is made with German rye. Aged 3 years in new charred American oak.

Rabbit Hole Boxergrail Kentucky Straight Rye Whiskey (95 proof) has a mash bill of 95% rye and 5% malted barley. This is a rye-lover's rye. A big rye, with a huge floral nose and a gingersnap bite. However, its super smooth and sophisticated, more like a fine Highlands Scotch than a big, biting rye. This is one of their big sellers, and a hit with the awards judges and whiskey writers. And deservedly so. Exceptional high rye.

Rabbit Hole Dareringer Straight Bourbon Whiskey Finished in PX Sherry Casks (93 proof) has a mash bill of 68% corn, 18% wheat, and 14% malted barley. The whiskey was aged in Pedro Ximenez Sherry Casks from Spain's renown Casknolia Cooperage. The casks hold the sherry for two years, and then are sent back to Kentucky. It's sweet up front with a kiss of spice. This is also a Scotch lover's whiskey. Super refined flavor profile. Outstanding.

Rabbit Hole Founder's Collection Boxergrail Kentucky Straight Rye Whiskey (114.6 proof) is a limited edition, small-batch blend of Rabbit Hole ryes. Aged 6 years in the barrel at cask strength. Despite the high proof, there is little burn. Honey. Baked apple. The flavor is paramount. Taken neat the flavors are impactful, but never overpowering. This complex, well-balanced rye is graceful.

The plan is to produce two Founder's Collection releases a year – one in spring, around the Kentucky Derby, and one in fall. All will be small batch, limited editions.

These whiskeys are incredibly sophisticated. These are not big caramel bombs. They are not brawny or biting. These are incredibly complex spirits, much more akin to cognac, brandy, and Highlands Scotch. Stone fruits. Honey. A bite, but not stinging. Flavors of honey and orange zest linger. Rabbit Hole, in their packaging and flavor profile, are spirits made for a global market, part of the newer, more international style. And they are incredibly elegant. To steal an old line: I have seen the future of bourbon, and its name is Rabbit Hole.

Second Sight Spirits

Rick Couch, Carus Waggoner, and Dan Gibson founded Second Sights Spirits, a small, artisanal distillery in downtown Ludlow. They approach the business a bit differently than others, saying: "We believe everything we do should be good for the spirit. Our mantra not only guides us to use the best ingredients and techniques to create a premium spirit but directs the company to excite, engage, and entertain our customers." Couch and Waggoner both have backgrounds in mechanical engineering and industrial design, and created two of the largest shows in Las Vegas: Cirque Du Soleil's LOVE and Viva Elvis.

"What brings us the most joy is when we have a new idea and working off of each other to make it come to life," Waggoner said. "That's where we really get our joy, just making and creating."

The most unusual part of Second Sight Spirits is the still. It looks like a swami, and is similar to their eye-catching logo. The idea behind the still's design is to drive home the double entendre of the term "spirits." Except this one is mostly copper with highlights of stainless steel and glass.

Second Sight is interesting because for how little it is, the quality and inventiveness aren't hindered at all. Second Sight sells Villa Hillbillies Moonshine in their tasting room. But their big claim to fame is rum. Currently they produce five rums. Really inventive, really good rums. And one bourbon. "Coming up with a brand new bourbon is a really hard sell sometimes because there are so many great bourbon's in the state," said Waggoner.

For Second Sight Bourbon Barreled Rum (90 proof) they procure freshly emptied bourbon barrels from the finest bourbon makers in all of Kentucky to craft this unique aged rum. Exquisite white rum is transmogrified by placing it into bourbon-saturated barrels and aging it.

Second Sight Dark Rum (90 proof) is crafted using molasses from Louisiana and distilled and aged in Kentucky. An amazing dark rum.

Second Sights Oak Eye Kentucky Bourbon Whiskey (92 proof) is handcrafted in ultra-small batches from a mash bill of corn, rye, wheat, and malted barley.

SILENT BRIGADE DISTILLERY

Keith Bundy, a welder, and John Brown, an engineer, opened Silent Brigade Distillery in Paducah, Kentucky, in 2016. According to Bundy, "Silent Brigade Distillery was born from our passion to create the smoothest traditionally crafted bourbon . . . We started building copper stills and selling them. While we were in the process, we got a lot of questions, especially from the distillers, wanting to know what our stills are capable of. And so we were experimenting with them and found out we're actually pretty good at making whiskey as well."

The name "Silent Brigade" refers to a violent band of raiders that rose up out of the Tobacco Wars in Kentucky from 1900 to 1908.

Bundy told the press that their true goal was to make some of the top-quality bourbons in the region.

It started off with Silent Brigade Kentucky Moonshine (100 proof), a classic corn sugar wash with a mash bill of 50% corn and 50% cane sugar. This 'shine is straightforward and smooth. It also offers it in flavors such as apple pie, peach and apple, piña colada, blackberry, and chocolate coconut.

Silver Trail Distillery Explosion and Fire

On April 24, 2015, 26-year-old Kyle Rogers and 40-year-old Jay Rogers were hard at work at Silver Trail Distillery. Suddenly a violent explosion ripped through the small craft distillery, which is famous in western Kentucky for its moonshine. A raging fire then ensued. Both men suffered major burns and were in critical condition at Vanderbilt Medical Center.

Eric Gregory from the Kentucky Distillers Association (KDA) said distillers across the area were ready to offer any help necessary. "It's an industry of over 200 years, that's really been built on camaraderie and friendship. It's times of crisis in the industry where everyone pulls together and helps each other out," Gregory said. The KDA started the Lifting Spirits fund, while Copper & Kings, Glenns Creek, and MB Roland all held fundraising events. Local CFSB bank locations were accepting donations for medical expenses, and Taco John's in Murray donated a portion of all their sales to help defer the costly medical expenses.

Silver Trail owner and master distiller Spencer Balentine was not injured but was severely shaken by the injuries the two had suffered.

On May 12, 2015, Rogers lost his battle with the terrible injuries he sustained. His family issued the following statement through the KDA: "We are deeply saddened to report that our son, Kyle, passed away last evening. And yet, we take solace in the fact that he is in God's comforting hands and is being greeted by cherished loved ones. We know Kyle is at peace and free of the pain from the last two weeks. We cannot begin to express our thanks for the wonderful and caring medical team at Vanderbilt Hospital

and the tremendous outpouring of support from friends and loved ones, especially the family of Jay Rogers, who have stood by our side and shared in our prayers. We also would like to thank Spencer Balentine and all of Kyle's colleagues at Silver Trail Distillery. Kyle took so much pride in being a moonshiner, and we are grateful that he was able to work in a profession that he loved so much. It is now our turn to pray for all those who knew and loved Kyle, and to show our thanks through God that we were blessed to call him son, brother, and friend for 27 years. He will be with us always."

In a warm tribute, whiskey expert Fred Minnick wrote: "I am just picturing the time I met Kyle, his warm smile, a Kentucky swagger and a firm hand shaking my right hand and putting his moonshine in the left. We lost a good one, an up-and-comer with unlimited potential."

Balentine honored Kyle with a specially printed back label that was put on all bottles of the famous moonshine. The label honored the life of Kyle Rogers and included one of the last tweets he sent out, which read: "I didn't choose the moonshine life. The moonshine life chose me."

STITZEL-WELLER

Stitzel-Weller is as historic a name in distilling as there is in America. The original Stitzel-Weller Distillery was founded in 1935, after the merger of W. L. Weller & Sons (a successful distributor) and the A. Ph. Stitzel Distillery. The two companies had cooperated with each other for years, not the least of which was surviving Prohibition through the sale of medicinal spirits. After Prohibition ended, Julian Van Winkle Sr. founded the company in 1933 with partners Alex T. Farnsley and Arthur Phillip Stitzel. The actual distillery began operations on Derby Day in 1935. For many years it was known as the Old Fitzgerald Distillery, named for the king of American whiskey sales during the '40s and '50s.

The Stitzel-Weller Distillery produced such legendary labels as W. L. Weller, Old Fitzgerald, Pappy Van Winkle, Old Weller, and Rebel Yell, among others.

The company was able to store more than 25,000 barrels in its two warehouses when it opened in 1935. The company even invented the modern rickhouse we know today. In its heyday, Stitzel-Weller employed more than 220 workers, held 300,000 barrels in its 18 warehouses, and produced 800,000 cases of spirits a year. Will McGill was the famed first master distiller of Stitzel-Weller. A veteran of the industry who had spent time at Early Times and Tom Moore, he was the oldest distiller in the industry when he died in 1952 at the age of 87.

Due in large part to W. L. Weller, Stitzel-Weller was incredibly influential in championing the making of bourbon that uses wheat instead of rye, providing a slightly round, softer finish. However, due to the decline of whiskey and other brown spirits, and with no diversity in their portfolio, Stitzel-Weller was sold off in 1972, with its various brands and stocks bought up by the likes of Buffalo Trace, Heaven Hill, and what is now Luxco.

Diageo used its deep pockets to reopen the distillery campus in 2014. Larry Schwartz, Diageo's CEO, said in his grand reopening remarks: "We are the heirs of Pappy Van Winkle and certainly the great brands that were distilled here through the years."

in 1987. Tom Bulleit was a Kentucky lawyer whose great-great-grandfather Augustus Bulleit had developed a recipe back around 1830 and produced it for about 30 years. Augustus's original recipe called for approximately two-thirds rye and one-third corn. That would not qualify as a bourbon today. So Tom created a sourced whiskey that was high in rye and had a lengthy aging process. Today's mash bill contains 68% corn, 28% rye, and 4% malted barley. It is bottled at 45% ABV and remains popular among mixologists and consumers.

Seagram bought the small but solid brand in 1997. What followed was one of the greatest rebrandings since Marlboro cigarettes. The funky type, more New York than Kentucky, and the square bottle were discarded. Stealing a page right out of the Philip Morris playbook, the whiskey was placed in an antique brown bottle, and given a fresh makeover, calling it the Frontier Whiskey.

But more importantly, the whiskey was solid. Seagram moved production of the whiskey to Lawrenceburg, Kentucky, and by 1999 had national distribution. When Diageo bought Seagram, the brand continued to explode. On March 14, 2017, Diageo opened a brand-new Bulleit Distillery in Shelby, Kentucky. Diageo invested $115 million to erect the new production facility on a 300-acre lot. The new distillery has the capacity to produce 1.8 million proof gallons per year.

The distilling operations were moved to Shelbyville, where a new, state-of-the-art distillery is busy making whiskey. In a nod to the past, the Old Fitzgerald doubler from the original system was exhumed and installed at Shelbyville.

The newest incarnation of Stitzel-Weller includes the vaunted Bulleit brand. It also has such brands as I. W. Harper and Blade and Bow.

One visits the old Stitzel-Weller site as part of the Bulliet Frontier Bourbon Whiskey Experience. Your tour includes the Blade and Bow Room, Tom Bulleit's office, the old distillery museum, the small still area, one of the remaining Stitzel-Weller warehouses, and the tasting room and shop.

BULLEIT

Bulleit Bourbon is a high-rye bourbon that has soared in popularity over the last decade. The reincarnation of the Bulleit brand began

I.W. HARPER

The I. W. Harper brand of bourbon was started by Isaac Wolfe Bernheim. A successful businessman, his distillery and distribution business helped solidify downtown Louisville, making it a hub of the distilling industry. The Bernheim Distillery, which is owned by Heaven Hill, was built in 1992 and named in his honor.

Bernheim used his first two initials, I.W., but chose a more American-sounding surname for his bourbon, thinking it was more marketable. And thus, I.W. Harper was born. This was an incredibly successful brand, one of the most storied in the industry until Prohibition. With waning interest in whiskeys in the 1970s and '80s, the whiskey was only available overseas—where it was very popular. Diageo, now the owner, repackaged and reintroduced the brand in 2015.

I.W. Harper Kentucky Straight Bourbon Whiskey (82 proof) has a mash bill of 73% corn, 18% rye, and 9% malted barley. It features lots of caramel, wood, and spice, and is a lovely, smooth dram. The I. W.

Harper 15-Year-Old Kentucky Straight Bourbon Whiskey (86 proof) has a mash bill of 86% corn, 6% rye, and 8% malted barley, and was aged in oak for 15 years. This bourbon provides lots of sweetness upfront, and features big notes of caramel, raisin, baked apple, and vanilla. This wonderful whiskey was a limited edition. So if you see it, snatch it up!

BLADE AND BOW

Diageo began working on Blade and Bow in 2012 with an idea for a whiskey that paid homage to the old Stitzel-Weller Distillery site. The name refers to the parts of a key (the blade being the shaft or shank of the key, and the bow being the handle). Stitzel-

Weller has long used the "Five Keys" symbol to stand for the five key steps in making bourbon: grains, yeast, fermentation, distillation, and aging. The package is elegant, and a brass-colored key is attached to each bottle.

The intention of this bourbon was to utilize the last remaining original barrels of the old Stitzel-Weller bourbon stocks. Diageo has neither denied nor confirmed whether this is a four-grain whiskey (corn, rye, wheat, and malted barley), but it feels like one. In a five-tier solera, the oldest barrels are at the bottom. Only a small portion of liquid (maybe half or less) is drawn from the bottom barrels. The barrels are then refilled with slightly younger stocks from the barrel just above, and so on, and so on. This way the old Stitzel-Weller product stays in the whiskey for many years.

Blade and Bow Kentucky Straight Bourbon Whiskey (96 proof) is an easy-drinking bourbon. It's a lighter styled bourbon with notes of honey, caramel, stone fruits, and caramel, with hints of cream custard.

The 22-Year-Old Kentucky Straight Bourbon (92 proof) is a limited bottling that features whiskeys distilled in Louisville and Frankfort. This is an incredibly smooth whiskey. The nose evokes just-baked cornbread or vanilla cake, with hints of honey, caramel, pecan, and spice. All in all, it's one of the prettiest bourbons you will find.

ORPHAN BARREL WHISKEY DISTILLING PROJECT

According to the distiller, "The Orphan Barrel Whiskey Co. was started to share barrels of delicious and rare whiskey, hidden away and nearly forgotten in the back of rickhouses and distilleries. Stories of these lost whiskeys have become the stuff of legend. Our goal is to bottle these rare, small offerings for the world to try and for you to add to your whiskey collection. Every Orphan Barrel whiskey is hand-bottled in Tullahoma, Tennessee."

That was the idea in theory, but the line soon became so popular that the parent company started doing large production runs to satisfy the growing demand. Provenance was another issue early on, as some whiskeys from this brand are older and rarer than others. Regardless of their rarity, a majority of them are tasty. Here's three you should look for:

Lost Prophet Kentucky Straight Bourbon Whiskey (91 proof) sat in charred American white oak barrels that were nestled in a corner of the historic Stitzel-Weller rickhouses in Shively for 22 years. Honey, apricot, spice, and vanilla dominate this lovely whiskey.

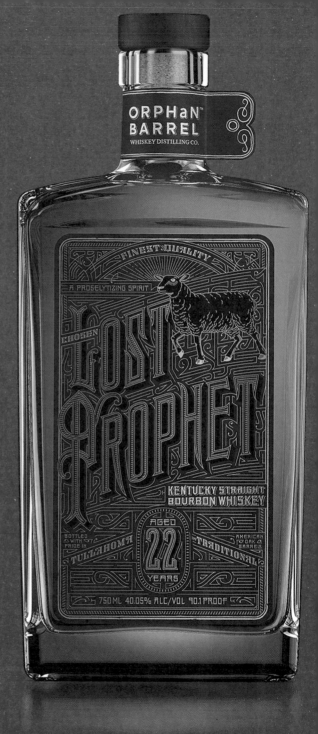

Forged Oak Kentucky Straight Bourbon Whiskey (90.5 proof) spent 15 years in charred American white oak barrels in a Stitzel-Weller warehouse. Maple, vanilla, caramel, and cocoa melt into corn, butter, black pepper, and more caramel in this one. Truly lovely.

Barterhouse Kentucky Straight Bourbon Whiskey (90.2 proof) was a small-batch run of 20-year-old, barrel-aged bourbon. The whiskey was made at New Bernheim with a mash bill of 75% corn, 13% rye, and 12% malted barley. The result features oak, caramel, dark fruits, rich figs, and allspice, with hints of piecrust and more caramel and vanilla at the end.

THREE BOYS FARM DISTILLERY

Three Boys Farm Distillery is family-owned and operated by Ross and Heather Caldwell and their three sons. It is a small craft distillery located on a lush 122-acre farm in Graefenburg. The family moved to Kentucky in 2010, and opened their distillery that same year. The whiskeys went into production in 2013. And let me tell you, they nailed it!

Ross is a dedicated distiller with a real passion. And this is truly craft distilling. Three Boys does everything by hand, from germinating and milling their own grain to distillation, barreling, and bottling. It's all made right in the barn, making Three Boys a truly artisanal product.

Like many other distilleries, they sold un-aged white whiskey and moonshine to pay the bills early on. Three Boys Farm's entry into the moonshine category is Foggy Dog Moonshine. They offer their traditional, un-aged moonshine, as well as flavors such as sweet tea, apple pie, cherry pie, peach pie, and blackberry cream.

The Three Boy Kentucky Straight Bourbon is the estate-made bourbon. A big caramel bomb with cherries, butterscotch,

pecans, but with sufficient snap. It is sold uncut and unfiltered. They even suggest you tip the bottle upside down to get whatever particulates are in the bottle moving around before you drink it. Hard core. But you gotta like it.

The Three Boys Kentucky Straight Rye (with a mash bill that that has risen to 90% rye from 66% previously) is an estate high-rye rye, and as impressive a rye whiskey as there is. It's a big gingersnap of a whiskey, with lots of spice and color but a surprisingly smooth finish. A must try, if you can find it!

Whiskey Thief Bourbon Whiskey comes in two strengths: 98.6 proof and 123 proof. The 123-proof edition is a bigger, dark caramel whiskey with lots of flavor. This is a very good bourbon that makes a bold, simple statement.

Here's another simple statement: Three Boys Farm Distillery should be on your list of go-to Kentucky distilleries!

TOWN BRANCH DISTILLERY

By Richard Thomas

Town Branch began when Alltech, the international animal feed giant started by Irish biochemist Dr. Pearse Lyons, bought the Lexington Brewing Company. Being attached to a corporate giant like Alltech helped the brewery weather the general failure of Craft Beer 1.0 in the Commonwealth, and they then became a trailblazer in bourbon barrel-aged beer with the introduction of their popular Kentucky Bourbon Barrel Ale in 2006.

As much as he liked his beer, what Dr. Lyons was really interested in was whiskey. Town Branch Distillery opened its doors and launched a line of sourced whiskey and liqueurs in 2012, and by doing it once again became a trailblazer, because they created one of the early "brewstilleries" in America.

Initially the two operations of making beer and whiskey remained separate, cross-pollinating only in the sourced barrels of Town Branch Bourbon going over to age Kentucky Bourbon Barrel Ale. As both operations have grown, they have become more and more intertwined, sharing equipment as well as casks. The brewstillery also cross-pollinates with its parent company, Alltech, in the department of the yeasts used in fermentation, yeast being a key and often distinctive ingredient that is usually overlooked by enthusiasts. A rye whiskey was added to the line in 2014, and nowadays everything that goes into bottles of Town Branch Bourbon, Rye, and Pearse Lyons Malt is made in-house.

Another feature setting Town Branch apart from other Kentucky distilleries is their stills. They are one of two distilleries in the state using pot stills, along with Woodford Reserve. But whereas Woodford Reserve uses an Irish-style, triple set of pot stills made (in the very Kentucky tradition) by Vendome, Town Branch follows the Scottish pattern: not only do they have two pot stills, but those stills were made in Scotland by Forsyths. It's especially ironic given that Dr. Lyons also owns an Irish distillery, and in a case of reverse expectations, that distillery uses equipment made by Vendome.

Town Branch Tasting Notes

Town Branch Bourbon (90 proof) has a mash bill of 72% corn, 15% malted barley, and 13% rye. Hints of caramel, brown sugar, cherry, and vanilla. Very smooth.

Double Oaked Kentucky Straight Bourbon Whiskey (94 proof) is a small-batch edition of Town Branch Bourbon (same mash bill) re-casked into a second round of new charred white oak barrels. Deep brown sugar and cherry. Lovely.

Town Branch Bourbon: Sherry Cask Finished (100 proof) has a mash bill of 72% corn, 15% malted barley, and 13% rye; this is a 9-year-old Kentucky straight bourbon whiskey from the early days of Town Branch Distillery. The bourbon is finished in Spanish Oloroso sherry casks for this limited-edition release. Notes of caramel, roasted pecans with dried plums and raisins. "Finishing this in the sherry casks for nine months imparted a dry finish that complements the natural caramel and vanilla notes in the whiskey, as well as a rich burgundy color," said Mark Coffman, master distiller at Alltech Lexington Brewing & Distilling Co. "We selected nine barrels of the best bourbon in our warehouse for this expression."

Town Branch Rye (100 proof) has a mash bill of 55% rye, 30% corn, and 15% malted barley. Big, floral nose, with hints of vanilla and oak. Lovely honey and pepper finish. Very smooth.

Town Branch Malt Whiskey (87 proof) is a non-chill filtered Kentucky single-malt whiskey. A sweet cereal nose, hints of molasses, vanilla, brown sugar, and spice. Lovely dried fruit and stone fruit at the end.

Kentucky Cask Strength Single Malt Whiskey (110 proof) with a mash bill of 100% malt. This is limited-edition bottling aged in freshly decanted Oloroso Sherry Casks for 11 years. Lovely deep color, with baked apple and pears, and dark fruits and cocoa coming across the palate. Lovely finish. Very pretty.

Town Branch Sundown (40 proof) is the distillery's entry in the ever-growing Kentucky Bourbon liqueur category. It is a blend of Kentucky bourbon, dark-roasted coffee, and sugar. Notes of mocha, chocolate, bourbon, and toffee. A lovely dessert liqueur.

BOURBON TOWN BRANCH™
KENTUCKY DISTILLERS' ASSOCIATION
PEARSE LYONS RESERVE
1
MALT HOUSE:
2
THE LAUTER TUN:
The grains are emptied into a roller mill where the husks are cracked to expose the starches before their release into the lauter tun. As the grain falls into the lauter tun, it is combined with the second ingredient: water. The grain and water are mixed together to create mash. The mash sits inside the lauter tun, activating the enzymes to convert the starches into sugars while the husks act as a filter.
3
6
SPIRIT STILL:
7
SPIRIT RECEIVER:
The final spirits are transferred to the spirit receiver and held until ready to be placed into barrels. When making Town Branch, the bourbon is reduced to 125 proof or less with demineralized water. It is required that Bourbon age at less than 125 proof.

Villa Hillbillies Moonshine

"It's a good-time drink for people who don't take themselves too seriously," said Dan Gibson, creator of Villa Hillbillies Moonshine. Gibson was getting frustrated at his job. And, apparently, he was getting on his wife's nerves. She told him he needed a hobby. Next thing he knew, he was watching the Discovery Channel's Moonshiners and Gibson thought he'd give it a try. "It's not too often your wife has a suggestion along those lines so I decided to hop to it."

As the old saw goes, his friends tried it. And their friends tried it. And so on and so on. Until he couldn't keep up with demand. He needed help and a bigger shop. "When I couldn't keep up any longer, I got the gumption to take it to the masses." In October 2015, Gibson agreed to a partnership with Second Sight Spirits in Ludlow, Kentucky. Second Sight Spirits, founded by Rick Couch and Carus Waggoner, is an artisan distillery focused on bringing the art of handcrafted distilling back to Northern Kentucky. "We just kind of backed into it," Gibson said. "They were nice enough to bring the brand to life." Villa Hillbillies is distilled and sold at the site. "I didn't think it would turn into this," said Dina Gibson, Dan's wife.

Villa Hillbillies Original (100 proof) is handmade in small batches. Clear. Super smooth.

Villa Hillbillies Apple Pie (40 proof) is handmade in small batches with eight different spices that are steeped in spirits. The flavored spirits are then mixed with apple juice. Smooth, flavorful.

Villa Hillbillies Fire Jack (60 proof) is a spiced moonshine.

Villa Hillbillies Honey (20 proof) is their original 'shine flavored with honey from a local farm, which gives this one it's unique color and taste.

WILD TURKEY

Wild Turkey is one of the most iconic brands in the liquor industry. It has a legion of fans, from literary mavericks to movie titans and music stars. It was journalist Hunter S. Thompson who immortalized the famous bourbon in his 1972 book Fear and Loathing in Las Vegas (the bourbon was also featured in the film adaptation) and the 1973 book Fear and Loathing on the Campaign Trail '72. Stephen King also mentioned it in his book It. David Foster Wallace made it the favorite bourbon of the family's patriarch in his novel Infinite Jest. The bourbon was also featured in such movies as Rambo: First Blood Part II, The Cassandra Crossing, Rush, Mystic River, In the Heat of the Night, Silver Bullet, Who Framed Roger Rabbit?, Bad Lieutenant, Barb Wire, The Eiger Sanction, Where the Buffalo Roam, and The Guardian. There was even a 1982 top-10 country single by singer Lacy J. Dalton called "Wild Turkey." Few bourbons and whiskeys have that kind of iconic brand placement.

As storied as Wild Turkey is, and for as old as the bourbon industry is, Wild Turkey is a relatively new brand. The legend of Wild Turkey is a simple one. In 1940, an executive named Thomas McCarthy brought some bourbon with him on a wild turkey hunting trip. The hunters were so delighted with the brown liquid that they started asking for "that wild turkey bourbon." McCarthy knew that their requests had a good ring to it, and his company, Austin Nichols, bottled the first batch of Wild Turkey in 1942.

The name most synonymous with Wild Turkey is master distiller James C. "Jimmy" Russell, who's been making whiskey for 60 years. Russell is the longest-tenured, active master distiller in the global spirits industry, and is the creator of brands and expressions like Rare Breed, Kentucky Spirit, and Russell's Reserve. He is in multiple distilling Halls of Fame, a Kentucky Colonel, and was honored with a special day by the Kentucky State Assembly. So great is his reputation that friends and peers call him the "Buddha of Bourbon" and "The Master Distiller's Master Distiller."

When Campari Group purchased the brand and distillery in 2009, they made a $100 million investment in the business and built a brand-new distillery on the space where the old bottling lines were, right next to the old distillery. The new distillery opened in 2011 and new bottling lines began to operate in 2013. A beautiful new $4 million visitor's center was opened in 2014 to showcase the bourbons.

Jimmy's son, Edward "Eddie" Freeman Russell, was named master distiller in January 2015. He has been distilling for more than 30 years and was the creator of Wild Turkey Spiced, Wild Turkey Diamond Anniversary, and, of course, the co-creator of Russell's Reserve. Eddie is the third generation of Russells to work at the distillery. According to his father, "When Eddie began working at the distillery, I made him do every job there was, even cutting the grass, so the other employees wouldn't think I was showing him favoritism. I was probably a lot harder on him than I needed to be, but it was all to help him." He's not kidding, that tough love made Eddie a Hall of Famer in his own right.

Wild Turkey is one of the top-selling whiskeys in the world, with annual sales nearing $2 billion. And the public isn't the only place where the distillery carries a lot of clout—writers, critics, and mixologists all love the Russell's Reserve. They are the largest single-location distiller in the region, and have 700,000 barrels stored in 28 rickhouses. Large batch bottlings of their mainline products may be comprised of liquid from as many as 1,000 barrels. Small batch bottlings will number no more than 100 barrels.

Wild Turkey basically only uses two mash bills. The bourbons such as Wild Turkey, Russell's Reserve, Kentucky Spirit, and Rare Breed all use the same recipe of 75% corn, 13% rye, and 12% malted barley. Russell's Reserve Rye and Wild Turkey Rye also share the same recipe, consisting of 51% rye, 37% corn, and 12% malted barley. Essentially, it's the aging and finishing that produce the differences between the products.

EDDIE RUSSELL, MASTER DISTILLER

By Richard Thomas

Although Eddie Russell officially took over for his father, living legend Jimmy Russell, as master distiller of Wild Turkey in January 2015, he had been serving as Jimmy's principal deputy for some time, and his fingerprints are all over the distillery's releases from the past several years. These include the bourbon-rye hybrid Forgiven, Wild Turkey Spiced, the Diamond Anniversary Bourbon released to honor his father, and at least some of the Russell's Reserve whiskeys.

Eddie's story is typical of a scion of a Kentucky bourbon dynasty. He started young doing menial jobs at the distillery, learning about everything that went on in the business step-by-step as he made his way up. After a couple of decades in lower- and mid-level jobs, he started serving as Jimmy's deputy and developing products, like the aforementioned Forgiven and Wild Turkey 81 Bourbon. Accomplishments like this got him inducted into the Kentucky Bourbon Hall of Fame in 2010, five years before he had even assumed the master distiller mantle.

After 60 years in the business, Jimmy is widely seen as a traditionalist, and the way I've heard him describe his idea of the sweet spot for making bourbon reflects Wild Turkey 101 very well; compared to other flagship bourbons, Wild Turkey 101 is slightly older and substantially stronger.

Eddie had already shown a penchant for going outside that flavor profile as much as he builds on it. In particular, the Diamond Anniversary Bourbon, Russell's Reserve 1998, and the original Master's Keep release are all quite old bourbons by past Wild Turkey standards. You can tell just from his whiskey that Eddie is both his father's son and very much his own man.

WILD TURKEY

Wild Turkey bourbon comes in a number of expressions, the most famous of which is affectionately known as Wild Turkey 81 in-house. Nationally, it is known as the original Wild Turkey Bourbon Whiskey (81 proof). The Wild Turkey 101 is a bit stronger than the original, at 101 proof, and is one of the brand's stars. Wild Turkey Decades Kentucky Straight Bourbon Whiskey (104 proof) is a blend of rare barrels between 10 and 20 years old. Wild Turkey Master's Keep (86.8 proof) is a blend of 17-year-old whiskeys that combine into something smooth and impressive. Wild Turkey Rare Breed Kentucky Straight Bourbon Barrel Proof is a barrel-strength, aged bourbon, and Wild Turkey Kentucky Spirit Single Barrel 101 proof (50.5% ABV) is a barrel strength, single barrel offering. Wild Turkey's standouts, aside from

the 101, are Wild Turkey Rare Breed and Master's Keep. These are both well worth their price, and the Master's Keep is one to roll out around the holidays

Wild Turkey offers only one blended whiskey, the Wild Turkey Unforgiven (91 proof). This is made in small-batch, limited editions and is a blend of high-proof, six-year-old bourbons and ryes. This whiskey is something of a rollercoaster. It starts off with notes of caramel and baked apple, hits you with a wallop of spice, and yet is able to retain a smoothness throughout.

Wild Turkey offers two ryes: Wild Turkey Kentucky Straight Rye Whiskey (81 proof), which is aged in #4 char, new American white oak barrels. They also offer a 101-proof rye, which is the better of the two—not that you can go wrong with either.

RARE BREED

Wild Turkey released two whiskeys and a repackaging of their Rare Breed label. Rare Breed are barrel proof whiskeys, bottled uncut and unfiltered. Wild Turkey Rare Breed Kentucky Straight Bourbon Whiskey (116.8 proof) has a mash bill of 75% corn, 13% rye, and 12% barley. There's no age statement on the whiskey, but it's known to be a blend of 6-12-year-old bourbon. It has notes of sweet tobacco and hints of orange and spice. Very smooth. Wild Turkey Rare Breed Kentucky Straight Rye Whiskey (102.2 proof) is a sma-ll batch blend of 4-year-old rye, uncut, unfiltered, cask strength. The nose and palate have spice, biscuits, hazelnuts, cocoa, dried dark fruit, and citrus. Caramel and baking spice with a nice, long finish. Both these whiskeys were very well received.

MASTER'S KEEP

The Master's Keep label was first introduced in 2015. Wild Turkey "Master's Keep" Kentucky Straight Bourbon Whiskey Aged 17 Years. Then two years later they released Wild Turkey Master's Keep Decades (104 proof) a blend of 10-20-year-old bourbons. In 2018 they released Wild Turkey Master's Keep Revival (86 proof) a blending of 12-to-15 year old barrels finished in Olorosso barrels, reviving a style Jimmy Russell worked on almost a generation previously. In 2019, they released Master's Keep Cornerstone (109 proof) a 9-year-old rye whiskey. And in 2020 the distillery released Wild Turkey Master's Keep Bottled in Bond (100 proof) a 17-year-old bottle in bond bourbon, one of the oldest "bottled-in-bond" whiskeys released in recent years

RUSSELL'S RESERVE

Jimmy and Eddie Russell co-created this line of fine, high-end, small-batch offerings from their best barrels. If that's not enough to entice you, know that this whiskey has more than 90 years of experience behind it!

Russell's Reserve is an expression of the Russells' favorite bourbons and ryes, made using the traditional house mash bills. "Every expression of Russell's Reserve—both the bourbon and rye whiskey—is matured in only the deepest #4 or "alligator" charred American white oak barrels," according to the Russells, which ensures richness of flavor and color.

Russell's Reserve was rolled out for the very first time in 2013. The idea was to produce a high-end, single barrel, non-chill filtration bourbon and rye to compete in the collectible, high-end spirits portion of the market. With that target in mind, it had to be of the highest quality. And it is.

Russell's Reserve Single Barrel Straight Kentucky Bourbon Whiskey (110 proof) is loaded with flavor. It's a big, rich whiskey with a smooth start and a lip-smacking ending. As great as this one is, it was outdone by its older brother, the Russell's Reserve Single Barrel 10 Years Old Straight Kentucky Bourbon Whiskey (90 proof).

"This is bourbon at its best," says Jimmy Russell. "What is incredibly special about the Russell's Reserve Single Barrel is that each barrel has its own personality, but still captures the rich, creamy toffee vanilla style of Russell's Reserve. This bottling celebrates what we love about Russell's Reserve, but takes it to another level."

Russell's Reserve Single Barrel Kentucky Straight Rye Whiskey and the Russell's Reserve 6 Year Old Kentucky Straight Rye Whiskey are both excellent and fulfill the goal of being seriously collectible. Some people prefer the single barrel, and some prefer the six-year-old. Regardless of one's taste, they are both big, rich, smooth, creamy, spicy, incredibly complex, and imminently drinkable. Do not hesitate to purchase if given the opportunity.

WHISKEY BARON COLLECTION

The Whiskey Barons Collection was debuted by Campari America as a "Nod to the Bourbon Barons of Yore." The idea was to breathe new life into labels long forgotten, mostly those that had disappeared with Prohibition, but that had been popular in the 1800s. So far three have been released. All of the bourbons were made using Wild Turkey's bourbon mash bill (75% corn, 13% rye, 12% malted barley) in Lawrenceburg. However, it was noted, that neither Jimmy nor Eddy Russell was involved in the creation of Old Ripy or Bond & Lillard. Nether carries the Wild Turkey moniker.

Bond & Lillard Kentucky Straight bourbon Whiskey (100 proof) is a blend with an age of 7-year-old bourbon. The Bond family had been distilling in Kentucky for much of the 1800s, but the Bond & Lillard brand was born in 1869 between William E Bond and Christopher C Lillard. The original bourbon was quite successful and won the Grand Prize at the 1904 World's Fair. Caramel, coconut, vanilla, and pecans dominate. Very pretty whiskey.

Old Ripy Kentucky Straight Bourbon Whiskey (104 proof) is a blend of 8-year-old and 12-year-old Kentucky straight bourbon, non-chill filtered. The whiskey was sourced from Wild Turkey. The original brand was established in 1868. Old Ripy was created by Irish immigrant James Ripy. It was made in Lawrenceburg, Kentucky, on the current site where Wild Turkey Distillery stands today. The label was discontinued in 1950. Back then, the Ripy family was ubiquitous in Anderson County's bustling distilling community. Vanilla, toffee, and oatmeal with spice and brown sugar.

W. B. Saffell Kentucky Straight Bourbon Whiskey (107 proof) is a blend of 6-, 8-, 10-, and 12-year-old bourbons. The whiskeys were aged in #4 char barrels and is non-chill filtered. The whiskey is named for William

Butler Saffell, a well-known distiller in Lawrenceburg in the mid-to-late 1800s. Saffell had been a successful executive in the whiskey business, and founded his own distillery in 1889. His whiskey was an instant success. But Prohibition silenced the brand. Vanilla, caramel, spice, dried fruit, ginger, and pepper. Lovely whiskey.

CHILL FILTRATION

According to Campari and Russell's Reserve, "Chill-filtration is a common process whereby the whiskey is chilled at temperatures below freezing and is passed through an absorption filter thus removing fatty acids and other flavor contributors such as esters and proteins. By avoiding the chill-filtration process, the whiskey is bottled with more flavor compounds and a deeper color, which is denoted by an impressive haze when ice or chilled water is added."

WILDERNESS TRAIL DISTILLERY

By Richard Thomas

A familiar story in the micro-distilling scene is how the founders got out of the white-collar rat race to make spirits. They often know about marketing, finance, and how to run a business, but much of the time, if they know anything about making booze, it's experience in brewing, not distilling. Folks with practical whiskey-making experience starting a craft distillery are not unknown, but certainly not the norm.

That was not the case for Wilderness Trail founders Shane Baker and Pat Heist. Baker is an engineer and Heist a micro-biologist, and together they founded a fermentation and distillation support company in 2006, Ferm Solutions. By the time they went on to start their own nano-distillery in 2013, they already had several years of fixing a wide range of other people's distilling problems under their belt.

They moved from their small rented space in Danville, a picturesque and out-of-the-way college town south of Lexington, to an outlying farm in 2014. Wilderness Trail had just installed a new still in 2016, but by 2017 they were already talking about expanding again. Content to wait for a properly matured product, they are focused on letting their sweet mash bourbon age until they are ready to make their initial release, described as a 4-year-old, single barrel, cask strength, which they released in 2019. With business booming at Ferm Solutions, Baker and Heist can afford to wait, another point that separates them from the pack.

Wilderness Trail Distilling makes Blue Heron Vodka and Wildreness Trail Harvest Rum Handmade with Kentucky Sorghum Molasses, as well as four whiskeys.

Wilderness Trail Kentucky Straight Bourbon Whiskey Single Barrel Bottled In Bond (100 proof) has a mash bill of mash bill is 64% corn, 24% wheat, and 12% malted barley using their own custom yeast strains. That is among the high-wheat content bourbons in Kentucky. Sporting a yellow label, this is a single barrel product and bottled in bond.

Wilderness Trail Small Batch Kentucky Straight Bourbon (100 proof) is bottled in small batches of 12 barrels each. Mash bill is the same as the single barrel. Aged in #4 char barrels, this is the workhorse of the distillery's line.

Wilderness Trail Single Barrel Kentucky Straight Rye Whiskey (100-105 proof) has a mash bill of 56% rye, 33% corn, and 11% malted barley. Aged in #4 char, 53-gallon barrels, aged on the upper floors of their rickhouses for a minimum of 4 years (regular expressions are expected to be between 6 and 8 years of age in future).

Silver Label Signals Wilderness Trail 6-Year Bourbon (100 proof) is a wheated bourbon with a mash bill of 64% corn, 24% wheat, and 12% barley. This 6-year-old bourbon is only available at the visitor center.

WILLETT DISTILLERY

Willett Distillery can be found just outside Bardstown, Kentucky. The site where the distillery was founded had been the family farm before that. There are two distinct businesses at this location. There's Willett Distilling and there is Kentucky Bourbon Distillers (KBD). The entire company is still privately held and run by the Willett family. They are makers and bottlers of bourbon and rye under their flagship name Willett as well as a slew of other labels. The whiskeys range from 2 to 27 years in age.

As you could probably guess, Willett is all about family. According to the distillery, John David Willett was born on December 26, 1841, in Nelson County. He was one-third owner and master distiller at Moore, Willett & Frenke Distillery. During his lifetime, John David was also the master distiller at four other distilleries in Kentucky. Aloysius Lambert Willett, who went by Lambert, was born September 23, 1883, in Bardstown. Lambert was in the Kentucky bourbon business from the age of 15, and served several distilleries across the commonwealth in various capacities.

Aloysius Lambert Thompson Willett, who went by Thompson, was born on January 27, 1909. He was the founder of the Willett Distillery in Bardstown.

Willett Distilling used grandfather John's bourbon recipes as a blueprint to create the whiskey that they would make into Old Bardstown. They made 30 barrels on March 17, 1937. The Willetts put their first barrel into storage in Warehouse A. By 1960, they had filled their 100,000th barrel.

Over the first 20 years or so, the distillery introduced several new labels, including Old Bardstown and Johnny Drum. However, the distillery fell on hard times, like much of the industry, and was shuttered by 1980.

In 1984, Even Kulsveen married Thompson's daughter Martha, and the couple took over the distillery's day-to-day operations. On July 1, 1984, Kulsveen bought the distillery and the property, and rebranded the business as KBD. KBD bottled and sold bourbon from the aging whiskey stocks in the Willett warehouses.

Eventually, Willett began to run out of whiskey, started buying bourbon from other houses and acted more like an independent bottling company. The distillery insisted it was all from Kentucky, but did not confirm the source. It has been suggested that Heaven Hill may have been the main supplier.

In the 1990s, Kulsveen introduced a portfolio called The Small Batch Bourbon Collection, featuring such labels as Rowan's Creek, Noah's Mill, Kentucky Vintage, and Pure Kentucky. By 2005 the Kulsveen children, son Drew and daughter Britt, had joined the business. Over the intervening years their spouses would also join the family business. The first Willett estate bourbons were released in 2008, as was the estate-bottled rye and the Willett pot still bourbon.

KBD remains a very large bottling company in Kentucky and has been nicknamed "the big daddy of bourbon and rye bottling." Among the brands they bottle are Old Pogue, Michter's, and Black Maple Hill.

With the explosion of interest in bourbon, KBD reintroduced the Willett name as a brand in 2012. Today Willett/KBD produces a dizzying array of small labels.

A very extensive rebuilding and expansion have transformed Willett immensely. In 2011 the visitor center and offices were remodeled and opened. The rest of the distillery also underwent incredible upgrades. These changes allowed Willett to run its first distilling tests in decades in January 2012.

Today, master distiller Drew Kulsveen oversees an operation that has three stills, including a column still with a doubler and a beautiful pot still. There are eight smallish warehouses on the original distillery grounds, which hold approximately 40,000 to 48,000 barrels in total.

Anywhere Drew turns in the distillery, he'll see a member of his family. His wife Janelle Kulsveen oversees the tasting room and customer experience, his sister Britt Chavanne is operations manager, and her husband, Hunter Chavanne, works sales and marketing.

In the meantime, huge landscaping projects have beautified the distillery grounds, and the company plans to have a series of exclusive, opulent country houses for vacationers to rent, so they can experience the bucolic farm as well as the rich smells of the distilling world.

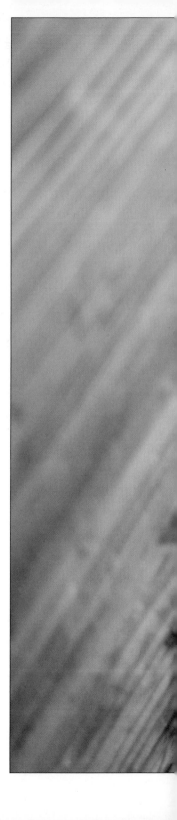

OLD BARDSTOWN BOURBON

Old Bardstown is named for a thoroughbred racehorse from the 1950s. He was a well-regarded horse in his day, but what was so fascinating about this horse was that he suffered severe ankle and hip joint problems. He was made a gelding and did not race until the age of four. However, he overcame this late start and had a successful four-year career. This "old" horse was retired at the age of eight, with lifetime earnings of $628,752. That's more money than 9 out of 10 of the Kentucky Derby winners of the 1950s earned in their careers. Old Bardstown died in 1972, at the age of 20.

There are three versions of bourbon available under the imprint: Old Bardstown Bottled in Bond (100 proof), Old Bardstown (90 proof), and Old Bardstown Estate Bottled (101 proof). Previously, these were all sourced whiskey, and the 90 proof with a black label was very solid stuff.

The Old Bardstown 90 proof with a beige label is now made start to finish at Willett. The mash bill is 72% corn, 13% rye, and 15% malted barley. It carries no age statement. The Bottled in Bond shares the same mash bill, and also features estate distillate aged on-premise. While all the whiskeys are good, the best of the Old Bardstown line remains the Estate Bottled.

NO.1
RECEIVING TANK
CAP. 1,760 GAL.
24.4 GAL. PER IN.

JOHNNY DRUM

Johnny Drum was introduced in the 1960s as a line made exclusively for a wholesaler in California. Johnny Drum comes in two different expressions including Black 4-12-year-old (86 proof) and Private Stock (101 proof). The Johnny Drum Private Stock is a standout, and many whiskey writers lament the disappearance of the 15-year-old version.

WILLETT ESTATE

Willett Family Estate Bottled Bourbon (proof and ABV vary, but generally in the 110 proof range) was a four-year-old bourbon first released on March 17, 2016, 79 years to the day (March 17, 1937) that Thompson Willett put his first barrels of Kentucky bourbon into Rickhouse A on the Willett property. The mash bill is 72% corn, 15% malted barley, and 13% rye. This bourbon was only offered at the Willett distillery gift shop. Blended from four barrels of the Private Barrel Selection program and bottled at cask strength, this whiskey was made start to finish at Willett.

Willett Family Estate Bottled Rye (109 proof) is a 2-year-old rye, and the first rye made and aged at the Willett Distillery in decades. This whiskey was a blend of Willett high rye (mash bill 74% rye, 11% corn, 15% malted barley) and Willett low rye (mash bill 51% rye, 34% corn, 15% malted barley). The result is a youthful but exciting rye. Very impressive, and well worth a try!

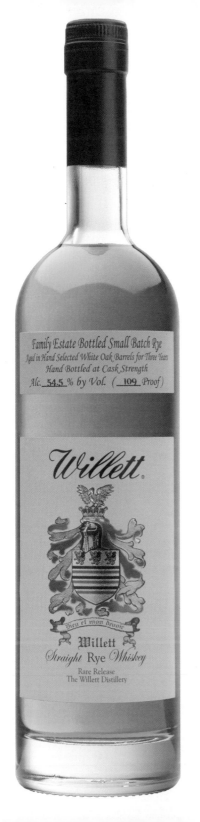

WILLETT POT STILL

Willett Pot Still Reserve (94 proof) was introduced in 2008. The sumptuous decanter-styled bottle, which actually resembles their pot still, offered a sourced, small-batch bourbon. Smooth, sweet, rich, and featuring caramel, pecan, yellow cake, and corn notes with a nice spicy finish, this is always a very popular bottle during the holidays. And it's always one of the first bottles to be finished.

SMALL BATCH BOURBON COLLECTION

Pure Kentucky XO Straight Bourbon (107 proof) is a small-batch, no-age-statement high-proof bourbon with limited release. To balance the higher alcohol, Willett offers a more aggressive oak profile. It is a spicy bourbon with hints of sweetness, without being too sweet. It has a nice, lingering finish, and provides great bang for the buck.

Noah's Mill Bourbon (114.3 proof) is a lovely no-age-statement whiskey that is rumored to contain all four grains, blend wheated bourbons with high rye bourbons, and use as many as four different mash bills. All that mystery can't overshadow the fact that this is one high-octane, spicy dram.

Rowan's Creek Kentucky Bourbon (101 proof) is a no-age-statement blend with a great, long-lasting finish. It stacks up well against the competition for proof, price, and flavor. This is the absolute keeper of the Small Batch Bourbon Collection, and one of Willett's most popular offerings.

Corner Creek Reserve Bourbon Whiskey (88.6 proof) is a no-age-statement sourced, lighter bourbon that features apple and pear notes and has a slightly floral nose. This is also a good value.

"Yes, I've had all my shots: bourbon, whiskey, and rye."

—Noah (the cat) of Willett Distillery

To understand what Woodford Reserve is really all about, one must go to Scotland. In 1993, The Balvenie, one of the distilleries in the William Grant & Sons portfolio, was established as a "boutique" scotch distillery, especially when it released David Stewart's famed Doublewood, which changed the distilling industry forever. It was the first scotch whiskey to be finished in another wood—port wood to be specific. With this release, William Grant & Sons established a showplace distillery that would be the jewel in the company's crown.

It was not a coincidence that Brown-Forman established Woodford Reserve not long after. Brown-Forman also owned the famed Jack Daniel's. The executives at Brown-Forman strategically positioned Woodford as The Balvenie to Jack Daniel's Glenfiddich.

Woodford is meant to be a sophisticated bourbon. Its flavor profile highlights brandy, cognac, and fruit. More so, master distiller Chris Morris is attempting to make a bourbon that is of a high-enough caliber to dominate internationally. If I were to liken Woodford Reserve to a famous scotch, it would be Glenmorangie. It has the same cognac, brandy, honey, and spice notes as the famed Highlands single malt, but the Woodford also has a big dose of caramel upfront. Its quotient of rye keeps it from being cloyingly sweet, making for a dryer bourbon without sacrificing its Kentucky heritage.

The distillery where Woodford Reserve stands now actually began its operational life in 1780, as the Old Oscar Pepper Distillery (which later morphed into the Labrot & Graham Distillery). The seemingly ancient buildings that house Woodford Reserve today, located near the town of Versailles in north-central Kentucky, were built in 1838, making Woodford, technically, one of the nine oldest distilleries in operation in Kentucky today.

The original distillery was founded by Elijah Pepper. He passed the operation on to his sons, who changed the name to the Oscar Pepper Distillery. In the mid-1800s, the famed Dr. James Crow worked to establish new practices and procedures that improved the bourbon making process, especially in the areas of sour mash fermentation, pot still distillation, and barrel maturation. In 1878 Leopold Labrot and James Graham bought the distillery and operated it until it was purchased by Brown-Forman in 1941. Brown-Forman ceased operations in 1968 and then sold the mothballed distillery in 1971.

When Brown-Forman decided to establish Woodford Reserve as their "boutique" bourbon distillery, they repurchased this shell of an old distillery in 1993 and released its first whiskey in 1996.

According to master distiller Chris Morris, Woodford didn't make a profit for 14 years. Luckily, money was no object, as the small distillery was transformed from a bunch of old, dilapidated buildings into one of the nation's premiere bourbon distilleries. It was Brown-Forman's long-range thinking that sought to establish Woodford as one of the premiere distilleries in the world, on par with the best of Scotland.

The storied Lincoln Henderson was Woodford's first master distiller. Henderson guided the company's first decade of production and releases before handing over the reins over to Morris in 2003. Morris began working as a chemist for Brown-Forman in 1976, and had served as Henderson's protégé during the distillery's early years.

CHRIS MORRIS
THE GRAND MAN OF BOUTIQUE BOURBON

Chris Morris is not your normal master distiller. He has grown up in this business from the time he was in high school. It's a lifetime spent casting about bins of grain and barrels of aging Kentucky spirits.

Morris is a once-in-a-lifetime figure. He is to the Tennessee and Kentucky distilling world what David Stewart represents in Scotland. Despite his sterling reputation at home, Morris has his eyes set abroad, where he has spent considerable time. During these tours, he befriended men like Stewart and Dr. Bill Lumsden, and saw a number of things that formed his opinions, tastes, and ideas.

Morris is a fastidious man. He dresses clean and simple. He is a gracious, extremely well-mannered Southern gentleman. But do not be fooled by this calm. He is as exacting as a scientist and demanding as a general. He walks slowly but with purpose. He always has a smile, but when his head jerks, his staff immediately starts buzzing around. There's no mistaking that Morris has high standards, and one gets the sense that behind the curtains there is hell to pay if something is out of place or not done with grace.

Morris has the staff do things the old-fashioned way. They still run the Scottish-made spirit safe by hand. And instead of using computers they keep large ledgers that look like something out of Harry Potter. This reverence for the past doesn't hold Morris in check, though—he was the first bourbon producer to finish his whiskey in chardonnay and cognac barrels.

He's been at the forefront of distilling in the United States for more than a decade. He was the first to offer bourbon pairing dinners in the region (an idea he picked up in Scotland). He started with bourbon and cheese pairings. Then dinners in 1991 and 1992. His own dinners hold such an esteemed place in his memory that Morris said, "I still have the menus."

According to Whisky magazine, "At Woodford Reserve, Chris developed the Master's Collection, Woodford Reserve Double Oaked, Rye and Distillery Series products, and in 2015 he was given the additional responsibility of Vice President of Whiskey Innovation for Brown-Forman. As a student of the industry, Chris authored the Society of Wine Educator's Certified Spirits Specialist program, introduced the use of taste notes for Bourbon in 1992 and developed the Bourbon Flavor Wheel in 2004."

And when the craft distilling wave began to rise it was Morris who hosted the fledgling industry at Woodford Reserve. He conveyed tons of information to these would-be distillers, and allowed for a trading of information amongst the participants.

Another feather in Morris's cap is serving as the mentor to Marianne Barnes, who was named the first female master distiller in Kentucky history, over at Castle & Key. For years she worked for Morris at Brown-Forman and Woodford Reserve, eventually rising to the position of master taster.

Of all the bourbon distillers in the region, Woodford was ahead of the curve when it came to bottling their own rye. Was Morris clairvoyant? Not really. They decided they would reach for 10% of the overall rye market at a time when the boom hadn't quite started yet. That goal was 9,000 cases. They are now doing 30,000 cases and still only hold 9-10% of the rye marketplace.

Morris insists that to achieve their unique flavor, all Woodford barrels are first toasted like wine barrels before they are charred, in order to find more of those stone fruit and cognac notes. He also intimates that the Master's Collection will continue to expand and roll out new ideas. The master still has a few tricks up his sleeve, and he smiles when asked about future expressions. He mentions chardonnay, pinot noir, four oak, and maple wood expressions that are in the works.

When asked what the toughest part of his job is, he answered quietly, but with a smile, "Patience." He hates waiting for new products to develop. And he is bullish on pot stills, insisting, like an old Scotsman, that they produce richer, more flavorful whiskey. When asked what else, his nose wrinkles, and his brow furrows. He's delicate on this point, but it's a personal rankle. Morris insists that there needs to be an estate bottled equivalent in the bourbon industry.

Obviously, Morris is among the most accomplished of men making whiskey in the United States. And if you're wondering what this giant likes to drink, it's bourbon. In the winter he likes the bigger, older expressions, sometimes neat, sometimes with some ice. In the summer, he prefers mixed cocktails.

Woodford Reserve Flavor Profiles

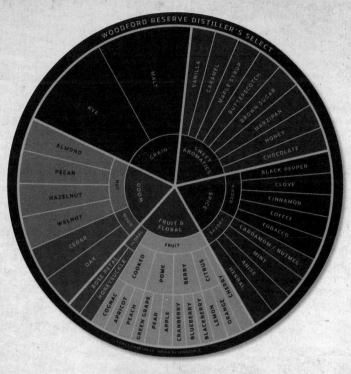

What makes Woodford so special? It begins with the approach of the famed distillery. The narrow, single-lane roads that lead to the company's impressive entry gate wind through some of the most beautiful horse farms in all of Kentucky. Beautifully manicured pastures, framed by meticulously maintained white horse fences, wind their way through beautiful bluegrass hills, with magnificent horse stock, before gently landing you at Woodford's opulent entrance.

Woodford Reserve is the Augusta National of the distilling world. With its neatly manicured lawns bursting with flowers and the impeccably maintained retail shop and buildings, Woodford Reserve sparkles like some of the best country clubs in America. In 1995 it was listed on the National Register of Historic Places, and in 2000 it was designated a National Historic Landmark. Knowing that it had plenty to show off, Woodford was the first distillery to start offering tours.

But its beauty is not just superficial. It is one of the hardest working distilleries in the region. The buildings are beautifully restored and outfitted with fastidious care. As one tours the many buildings, there is no question Henderson and Morris designed their distillery to reflect the best of the classic Scottish style. The old stone buildings house giant fermentation tanks made from oak and banded in wrought iron. Their spirit safe is an authentic 19th century Scottish apparatus! Everything is done by hand, the old-fashioned way.

Even the packaging was a major decision. According to Morris, it was imperative that the bottle stood out and that its profile and silhouette were absolutely unique. In the end, they wanted something more akin to a cognac bottle than a whiskey bottle, signifying to the consumer that it contained a more refined, more elegant spirit.

Henderson and Morris experimented with varying fermentation times of five, seven, and nine days, seeking the fermentation that would extract the most flavor. They settled on five days, which is still among the longest cook times in this illustrious distilling region. Their insistence is that this longer fermentation adds many more of the stone fruit flavors that they seek.

Even the yeast was a trial and error process. Woodford maintains its own unique cereal culture yeast. It took 20,000 yeast generations to develop the Woodford strain of yeast. Even today, in order to keep the strain pure, all yeast at the distillery is destroyed once a quarter, and a new, purer strain (kept isolated in their lab) is brought out.

The distillery also focuses on quality by utilizing five giant pot stills to augment their large column still, more pot stills than any other bourbon maker in Kentucky. Pot stills create a better, more flavorful whiskey, and pass on many more of the traits Henderson and Morris were looking to capture.

Woodford Reserve Kentucky Straight Bourbon (90.4 proof) has a mash bill of 72% corn, 18% rye, and 10% malted barley. The bourbon is aged an average of seven years in charred new American oak barrels. Woodford Reserve Distiller's Select Bourbon consists largely of pot still whiskey. Some amount of column-distilled bourbon from the Brown-Forman Distillery in Shively is blended in, resulting in a magnificent bourbon filled with honey, caramel, stone fruit, yellow cake, and gingersnap.

Woodford Reserve Kentucky Straight Rye Whiskey (90.4 proof) is a special, Baltimore-styled rye, with a decent dollop of corn to smooth out the spiciness. The mash bill is 53% rye, 33% corn, and 14% malted barley.

Honey, apple, and pear hit you on the nose and palate. Caramel and vanilla follow, and it closes with a lovely, spicy gingersnap finish. It's easily one of the best ryes on the marketplace, and is sure to impress your guests.

Woodford Double Oaked (90.4 proof) is the same as Woodford Reserve but it undergoes a unique barreling process. According to the company, this is a "twice-barreled bourbon . . . uniquely matured in separate, charred oak barrels—the second barrel deeply toasted before a light charring." This second barreling intensifies the flavors in the whiskey, creating a softer and sweeter dram. For those who like woody whiskeys and are looking for a bigger flavor statement without the extra alcohol usually associated with such finishes, this is the clear choice.

Woodford Reserve Kentucky Straight Wheat Whiskey (90.4 proof) has a unique mash bill with wheat as the dominant grain at 52%, 20% malt, 20% corn and 8% rye. This deep amber whiskey has a uniquely floral nose, but has the smooth vanilla bean and brown sugar one would expect. A hint of white pepper on the finish.

NEW VISITOR'S CENTER
WOODFORD MASTER'S COLLECTION

According to the distillery, "Woodford Reserve Distillery's Master Collection honors the pioneering work of Pepper and Crow, applying their handcrafted methods to a variety of grain recipes, fermentation styles, and maturation processes to create a range of unique whiskeys." This is meant to be a homage to Oscar Pepper and former master distiller James Crow, whose discoveries and innovations in bourbon making "are credited with refining and defining key processes such as sour mashing, yeast propagation, copper pot distillation, and the maturing of whiskey in new, charred oak casks."

These bourbons are high-end expressions and every one is an absolute winner. The most beautiful finishes that I have tasted in this group are the 1838 Style White Corn and the Four Wood Selection. But all are simply spectacular. If you like fine bourbon, every single one is worth its price. They deliver like few other houses can. Impeccable!

The offerings from the Master's Collection are as follows: 2019 – Chocolate Malted Rye; 2018 – Oat Grain & Select American Oak Bourbon; 2017 – Cherry Smoked Malt Bourbon; 2016 Brandy Cask Finish; 2015 1838 Style White Corn; 2014 Sonoma-Cutrer Pinot Noir Finish; 2013 Double Malt Selection; 2012 Four Wood Selection; 2011 Rare Rye Selection; 2010 Maple Wood Finish; 2009 Seasoned Oak Finish; 2008 Sweet Mash (First International

MASTER'S COLLECTION

WOODFORD RESERVE®

BATCH PROOF

123.6 PROOF

KENTUCKY STRAIGHT BOURBON WHISKEY
61.8% ALC/VOL (123.6 PROOF) | 750mL

Release); 2007 Sonoma-Cutrer Chardonnay Finish; 2006 Four Grain (National Release); and 2005 Four Grain (Kentucky Release).

BACCARAT EDITION

Woodford has long been a leader among the bourbon scene. Several recent releases have confirmed their and master distiller Chris Morris's place in the hierarchy of Kentucky distilling. The most recent accomplishment was the release of the Woodford Baccarat Edition. Not sure which is more remarkable – the whiskey or the packaging. Woodford Reserve Baccarat Edition (90.4) is crafted by uniquely finishing Woodford's best barrels of bourbon to be re-barreled in select XO Cognac barrels. Each barrel has seen three seasons of cognac before being filled with Woodford Reserve. The whiskey is presented in a bespoke Baccarat decanter.

Baccarat Crystal is a French manufacturer considered to be one of the finest crystal producers in the world, and is located in Baccarat, France. The founding of the original glass works in 1764 was granted by permission of King Louis XV of France. They began crystal production in 1810.

"Woodford Reserve Baccarat Edition is a celebration of history, a celebration of the connections between France and Kentucky -- and a celebration of the finest flavors of bourbon and cognac," said Morris.

The finished product features the high points of both worlds. Caramel, brown sugar, stone fruit, figs, vanilla, honey, orange zest, and orange blossom, and a creamy, smooth finish. This is sophistication usually reserved for the world's greatest Scotches. The American distilling industry should hold its collective breath – for sophistication of product and presentation, Woodford and Morris have done it again. They have both thrown a gauntlet down in the name of American whiskey and by doing so, have stretched the value of it as well.

DISTILLERY SERIES

Woodford Reserve Five Wood Bourbon Whiskey Finished in Port and Sherry Casks (90.4 proof) is a Woodford Reserve's bourbon matured in new American oak, and then finished in Tawny and Ruby port wood, and Oloroso and Amantillado sherry wood casks. Five woods. A limited edition, this whiskey features figs, stone fruit, caramel, and brown sugar, with a super smooth finish that lingers forever. Elegant. Complex. Incredible! Tasting room only. The terrifying thing? Is super reasonably priced.

Woodford Reserve Four Grain Blended Whiskey (90.4 proof) is a blend of Woodford Reserve bourbon, rye, malt, and wheat whiskeys. Each whiskey was aged in new and used charred oak barrels. This is a lovely whiskey with a rich nose of grains, cereal, oats, caramel, vanilla, brown sugar, and a pinch of ginger snap. Textured, layered, chewy, yet absolutely stunning. It's only available from the tasting room.

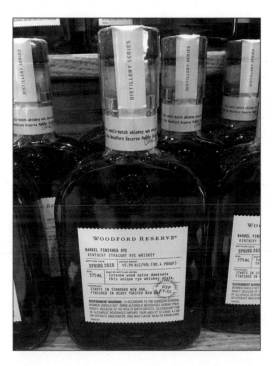

ELIZABETH McCALL

Woodford Reserve assistant master distiller Elizabeth McCall, CSS (Certified Specialist of Spirits) is the second generation of her family to work in the bourbon industry, and one of the youngest female distillers in the United States. She followed in her mother's footsteps, starting as a sensory expert and working in the quality department. McCall has a master's degree from the University of Louisville and has been a member of Brown-Forman's R&D Department since 2009.

She was jobless and a friend suggested she apply for an entry-level job at Brown-Forman. She knew nothing about distilled spirits at the time. "It's unique that I am a woman in this role, just given the history of the titles in the industry," McCall said. "But at Brown-Forman, I've always been surrounded by women. It's never been weird for a woman to have a seat at the table and to voice her opinions."

Now, she works directly with master distiller Chris Morris on innovation and the development of new products within Woodford Reserve. Additionally, she works directly with consumers through personal barrel selections and education on sensory methodology. She also works to define the quality sensory standard to which every drop of Woodford Reserve must live up to.

"It's how our industry goes. I had a master who I was trained under, and I'm the seventh master distiller at the company," Morris said. "We really respect that lineage. You learn all of these secrets and processes that are handed down from generation to generation. What I'm doing with Elizabeth is passing that legacy onto her."

"It feels like a huge amount of responsibility," McCall said of her job. "But I also have so much pride and understanding of the big picture of it all. I'm extremely honored and humbled to be taking on this role. I almost don't have the words to really describe it. It's very surreal. I get choked up and emotional thinking about what's ahead."

TENNESSEE

Show Me The Money!
Distilling in Tennessee

In the movie *Jerry Maguire*, Cuba Gooding Jr. shouts "Show me the money!" In *All the President's Men*, Hal Holbrook urges Robert Redford and Dustin Hoffman to "Follow the money!" Both are right—and the evidence of this is very clear in Tennessee.

For the uninitiated, Tennessee is a battleground state, and we're not talking politics. We're talking whiskey. Tennessee whiskey! There is big money on the table, and for those playing, they're betting that Tennessee whiskey is the next big thing.

There are new distilleries popping up everywhere. Some are small mom-and-pop, craft distillers. Some are larger distilleries, like Old Dominick, Nelson's Green Brier, Chattanooga Whiskey Company, SPEAKeasy Spirits, Old Glory, Ole Smoky, and a slew of others that count banks and industry players like Sazerac and Constellation among their investors.

As the popularity of craft whiskey grows, large conglomerates are looking for new ways to satisfy the public's thirst for brown spirits worldwide. Numerous brands are being established and marketed and it is absolutely awesome to watch the ingenuity, excitement, and entrepreneurial spirit that is skyrocketing the industry forward.

The amazing thing is that Tennessee was once the leader in distilling. The state passed statewide Prohibition in 1908, 12 years before the national law went into effect. The rugged terrain of the Tennessee landscape was a great place to hide stills and escape, or pay off, the law. Corruption exploded. Things were so dire that even Jack Daniel's moved to Kentucky for about 10 years!

Today, the landscape is filling up fast with incredibly fascinating players. From moonshiners and white lightning producers, to those who are hoping to create lasting brands and working to craft extremely fine spirits, Tennessee is suddenly teeming with the bold and talented.

In 2009, there were only three distilleries in the state: Jack Daniel's, George Dickel, and Prichard's. Today, there are more than 30 and the number is growing. There is even a Tennessee Whiskey Trail.

Fortunately, the evidence of considerable investment is everywhere. From huge new distilleries to massive overhauls and upgrades at Daniel's and Dickel, everywhere you look, expectations are sky-high.

With so many options to choose from, try as many of these distilleries as you can. There are some terrific people out there making everything from moonshine to bourbon to Tennessee whiskey, not to mention some great gins, vodkas, and other spirits.

TENNESSEE WHISKEY TRAIL

Despite the fact that the largest single brand of American whiskey, Jack Daniel's, is just south of the border in the neighboring state, it's Kentucky that has always held itself in high regard in terms of distilling.

In this sense, Tennessee has always played second fiddle. It is time for Tennessee to be the star. The Tennessee Whiskey Trail was announced in July 2017. Headlined by the two largest manufacturers in the state—Jack Daniel's and George Dickel—the new association featured 25 small and large distilleries.

With the craft distilling boom swelling the state's rolls, it is now time to flex their muscles and proclaim Tennessee whiskey second to none. Tennessee has a proud history of distilling. "Distilleries in Robertson County date back to the early 1790s, when settlers Thomas Woodard and Arthur Pitt established small stills on their property," wrote historian Teresa Biddle-Douglass in *The Tennessee Encyclopedia of History and Culture.*

Jasper "Jack" Newton Daniel (born 1848) got into the whiskey business at 15. And he struck out on his own 22 years later, establishing a 5,000-acre facility in his hometown of Lynchburg in 1886. George A. Dickel also established his distilling operations during this time and the rest is history.

Today, Jack Daniel's is the best-selling brand of whiskey. In 2016 they sold 12.5 million cases worldwide. Dickel is the second-largest distiller in the state making Tennessee whiskey (with its special mellowing process) one of the hottest whiskey styles out there.

The new boom in Tennessee distilling has boosted the tourism industry and increased the number of exports. With the federal authorities allowing the term "moonshine" to be applied to white whiskeys, there is a whole new industry bubbling up in still columns around the state—the moonshine boom.

The classic Tennessee whiskey has even been codified. Tennessee governor Bill Haslam signed House Bill 1084 on May 13, 2013, which requires charcoal filtering using maple wood (known as the "Lincoln County Process") as well as attaching the already existing laws for bourbon. This ensures "Tennessee whiskey" remains a consistent product in order to make it a distinct category. New distillers such as Prichard's, Nelson's Green Brier Distillery, Corsair Distilling, Nashville Craft, Collier and McKeel Distillery in Nashville, and Tenn South Distillery in Lynnville are all producing Tennessee whiskey and many others are setting up production.

With all the quality spirits out there, there has never been a better time to tour Tennessee!

The History of Distilling in Tennessee

Tennessee has a long history of distilling—and we're talking about legal distilleries established as proper spirit producing companies. This is not to be confused with moonshining.

As Teresa Biddle-Douglass writes in *The Tennessee Encyclopedia of History and Culture*, "Tennessee's natural limestone springs, ample timber, and fertile soil for growing grain have made the state an ideal location for whiskey production." She continues, "Whiskey was an important part of frontier life as both an easily portable diet staple and a medicinal drug."

The earliest known distilleries, dating all the way back to the early 1790s, were originally located in Robertson County, when settlers Thomas Woodard and Arthur Pitt established small stills on their property. Their sons continued the operations and developed whiskey production into a prosperous business. Wiley Woodard

inherited his father's farm and distillery in 1836 and had doubled his whiskey sales by 1841. Soon, he was shipping large quantities of whiskey throughout Tennessee and other southern states," according to Biddle-Douglass. Soon competitors such as Nelson's Greenbrier arose and became distillers of national prominence.

Other distilleries also blossomed, such as Jasper "Jack" Newton Daniel's distillery in Lynchburg in Moore County. Jack got into the distilling business at the age of 15 and by 1866 he owned the company. George A. Dickel was a successful Nashville merchant during the same time. He established a partnership that began to sell whiskey sourced from several local distillers. Dickel eventually bought the distillery which became one of his most popular suppliers, Cascade Creek in Coffee County. Dickel's Tullahoma distillery is still making whiskey today.

Journalist Jason Wolf wrote in *The Tennessean*, "Looking back to the early 19th century, the state has had a complicated relationship with alcohol." He continues, "Tennessee passed the first prohibition law in the United States on Jan. 26, 1838, making it a misdemeanor to sell alcoholic drinks and delighting the religious-minded temperance societies that had grown in political clout."

, The American Temperance Society was founded by Marcus Morton in Massachusetts in 1826. The Tennessee affiliate was formed three years later in Nashville. The 1830s and 1840s saw a rise in the movement to eradicate alcoholic beverages for consumption. It was at their first convention in 1853 that a complete statewide temperance ban in Tennessee was first mentioned.

According to the Tennessee Whiskey Trail, "Tennessee was a leading producer of distilled spirits even prior to the Civil War.

In fact, Tennessee made so much whiskey, that the then Confederate government of Tennessee outlawed whiskey production in order to field and supply the army. This was the nation's first act of prohibition. Following the Civil War, Tennessee quickly rebuilt its distilled spirits industry."

In 1885, there was an attempt to ban the manufacture and sales of distilled spirits in all of Tennessee, but it failed to pass through the Tennessee state legislature. Other efforts included the creation of the Anti-Saloon League in 1895 as a response to saloons that had been operating since 1831

The early temperance efforts focused on tighter regulations and controls of alcohol, as well as restricting the sales of these legitimate businesses. For example, sales were restricted by their proximity to schools, hospitals, and churches. More restrictions were slowly added to the state statutes.

The death of Edward Carmack was a pivotal moment in Tennessee's prohibition history. Carmack, the temperance candidate of the Anti-Saloon League and the Women's Christian Temperance Union, was murdered while running for governor. In Tennessee he became something of a martyr for the cause, but his death was only marginally related to Prohibition. This inspired temperance forces to work with a new intensity, as if the "murder" of their candidate proved the iniquity and sinfulness of spirits.

By January 1909, Senator O. K. Holladay of Putnam County submitted a bill that "forbid the sale of liquor within four miles of any school in the state; an identical bill was introduced in the House," wrote W. Calvin Dickinson. Then Governor Malcom Patterson assailed the proposed law, thundering, "For a State...to attempt to control what the people shall eat and drink and wear...is tyranny, and not liberty." Regardless, the measure was approved and Patterson's veto was overridden. A follow-up law prohibiting the manufacture of spirits was passed shortly thereafter.

In 1908 Tennessee contained hundreds of registered distilleries across the state," claims the Tennessee Whiskey Trail. Only two survived Prohibition: Jack Daniel's and George A. Dickel. Jack Daniel's reopened soon after the law permitted in 1940 while George A. Dickel, after some retooling, reopened in the 1950s. These two distilleries formed the cornerstone of Tennessee distilling for the next 40 years.

NELSON'S GREEN BRIER DISTILLERY
The SOUNDTRACK of AMERICA
MADE IN
TENNESSEE®
TENNESSEE WHISKEY TRAIL

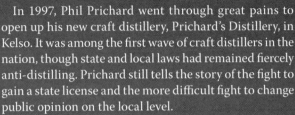

In 1997, Phil Prichard went through great pains to open up his new craft distillery, Prichard's Distillery, in Kelso. It was among the first wave of craft distillers in the nation, though state and local laws had remained fiercely anti-distilling. Prichard still tells the story of the fight to gain a state license and the more difficult fight to change public opinion on the local level.

In 2009, a cadre of ambitious entrepreneurs attempted to ease many of the restrictions on distilling in the state. With the craft distilling boom exploding across the nation, Tennessee now lagged behind substantially. Among this group were Heath Clark, of Heath Clark Distilling; Mike Williams, of Collier & McKeel; and Darek Bell, of Corsair Distillery. These three were instrumental in the legislative effort.

On July 5, 2009, the Knoxville News Sentinel put out an article with the headline: "Ground Zero for Whiskey: Law Allows Production of Distilled Spirits in State." The accompanying article, written by Cynthia Yeldell, noted, "Under the new law, about 44 counties are now eligible for distilleries. Manufacturers will be allowed in any county where both retail package sales of liquor and liquor-by-the-drink sales have been locally approved. Some 10 counties, including Cocke—with its reputation for moonshining—opted out of the legislation. Knox County hasn't had any discussions of opting out, according to Knox County Commission Chairman Thomas 'Tank' Strickland."

This opened the floodgates and by 2017, there were 30 to 40 distilleries crafting authentic Tennessee whiskey. Today, the future for Tennessee whiskey is as bright as ever. Somewhere, Jack and George are toasting a glass to Tennessee!

TENNESSEE WHISKEY IS ALL GROWN UP

Jeff Arnett, Jack Daniel's master distiller, speaks passionately about producing the best-selling American whiskey in the world. He is proud of the brand he represents and wears his passion for the product on his sleeve.

Arnett talks about the importance of setting standards for Tennessee whiskey as a product, not just a brand. With the announcement of the new Tennessee Whiskey Trail and the rise of the craft distillers, he has serious concerns about what will happen to the world-famous style of Tennessee whiskey.

Tennessee whiskey is different from bourbon in that it is first filtered through charcoal (which Jack Daniel's refers to as "mellowing") before going into the barrel. This softens the whiskey, taking off the rough edges making it a consequential step.

Many distillers were anxious that bourbon was suddenly being made all over the United States, including New York State, which produces seven or eight bourbons. The TTB and the federal government specified the steps required to put bourbon on your label, ensuring the consumer of what they are getting.

Arnett says the lack of a standard for single malt whiskey in the United States underscores his worries about Tennessee whiskey. He and state authorities have talked to the TTB about setting a national standard, but because of the name "Tennessee whiskey," the TTB kicked the can down the road to the state liquor authority, claiming it was a state issue instead of a national one. It was up to the Tennessee liquor authority to set a standard for the whiskey their state has become world famous for.

George Dickel & Co. brand ambassador Brian Downing is in complete agreement with Arnett. With craft distilling exploding in the state, he is worried that having no set standard will adulterate what Jack Daniel's and Dickel have built over the course of a century.

Bourbon has national regulations that distinctly set it apart from Tennessee whiskey. The state of Kentucky has erected even stricter regulations in order to label something "Kentucky bourbon." No such stringency exists for Tennessee whiskey, despite Arnett's and Downing's desire for it. With these stricter laws directed to protect quality for beer, champagne, and even wines from Napa, they feel the time is ripe for a definition and regulation of what Tennessee whiskey really is. It is about preserving their distillery's century-plus heritage, as well as ensuring consistency and quality in any product using the "Tennessee whiskey" designation.

There is a whole slew of craft distillers chomping at the bit to make Tennessee whiskey and people will be watching and waiting for the explosion. The only problem? It takes time to make quality whiskey.

Lincoln County Process

While you're in Tennessee and you're trying Tennessee whiskey, you will hear the term "Lincoln County Process." This is the step that separates Kentucky bourbon from Tennessee whiskey. As they say at Jack Daniel's, bourbon comes out of the still, but Tennessee whiskey goes into the barrel.

All whiskey—with the exception of Prichard's—is made using the Lincoln County Process.

In most cases, the whiskey is processed in the same way as most bourbons. The mash is cooked, yeast is added, the distiller's beer is poured down the still, and what emerges is essentially the same spirit. The only difference is that Tennessee whiskey must be passed through a charcoal filter before it is barreled. This filtering is called the "mellowing process," or the Lincoln County Process.

The degree to which the spirit is exposed to the charcoal beds varies greatly. Jack Daniel's puts their spirit through massive, 10-foot-high tanks while George Dickel uses 13-foot-high tanks. On the other hand, some of the other distilleries pass the distillate thorough fish tank-sized charcoal filters. There is no minimum, but there is the legal insistence that the process be followed.

Jack Daniel's burns $1 million worth of maple each year and employs their own small fire department to keep up with their manufacturing demand.

This process helps filter impurities out of the whiskey. It has been conjectured that this strips the distillate of flavor, but there is also a belief that the final product is somewhat smoother than non-filtered products (similar to Irish whiskey being lighter and softer than single malt Scotch).

READ THE LABEL

A label's wording can be confusing, especially where Tennessee whiskey is concerned. It must say "Tennessee whiskey." If it says "Tennessee straight whiskey," that means it was made in Tennessee, but it didn't go through the Lincoln County Process.

Thirteen Great Tennessee Whiskeys

Here are 13 Tennessee whiskeys available on the market right now. They are available for sale or for tasting in Tennessee. But in the next five years the number will triple. Tennessee whiskey is the next big thing in brown spirits!

1. **Jack Daniel's Tennessee Whiskey Barrel Select 100 Proof**
2. **George A. Dickel Tennessee Whiskey Barrel Select**
3. **H. Clark Distillery Tennessee Whiskey**
4. **Ole Smoky Whiskey Straight Bourbon Whiskey**
5. **Corsair Tennessee Single Malt**
6. **Sweetens Cove Tennessee Straight Bourbon Whiskey**

Moonshine In Tennessee

In *The Tennessee Encyclopedia of History and Culture*, William E. Ellis writes, [Moonshine] is untaxed liquor, furtively produced quite often by the light of the moon, or at least out of the immediate reach and oversight of law enforcement." Ellis continues, "Nicknamed 'corn likker,' 'white lightning,' 'white mule,' 'mountain dew,' and numerous other local appellations, the typical moonshine is clear in color and potent, usually approaching 100 proof, or 50 percent alcohol by volume."

Most moonshine is sold clear in mason jars at 80 to 100 proof (40%–50% ABV). In recent times it has become very popular to sell the moonshine with added flavorings. The most popular flavor offered is the apple pie moonshine, usually mixed with fresh sweet cider and cinnamon. Other favorites have blended in lemonade, sweet tea, or berries. These have proven to be popular with young adults, and great for barbecues as well. Many other flavor combinations are also available, including a cream version.

The word "moonshine" has never been thoroughly confirmed, but it is felt that the term is closely derived from the early English term "moonrakers." The idea was that in order to avoid detection by revenue or tax collectors, moonshiners brewed, fermented, and distilled by night, under the light of the moon. Until recently, the term "moonshine" was always associated with clandestine and elicit production, distribution, and sale of such spirits.

Most moonshiners operated in the back country and woods, a tradition that continues with modern hoochers to this day.

Moonshine was an important part of Appalachian culture here in America. In

the late 1700s and throughout the 1800s, Scottish and Irish descendants who settled into the mountains' craggy peaks and hidden dales brought their whiskey making techniques to the region and flourished. Throughout the 1800s, especially during Prohibition, whiskey became an important source of revenue and income for otherwise insolvent families.

As a study of farmers in Cocke County, Tennessee, once reported, "One could transport much more value in corn if it was first converted to whiskey. One horse could haul ten times more value on its back in whiskey than in corn."

A 2006 article in the *Los Angeles Times* reported, "To many Tennesseans, Cocke County is the place their parents warned them about, the butt of hillbilly jokes, the last redoubt of an old, untamed Appalachia. For decades this poor and dramatically beautiful area, north of Great Smoky Mountains National Park, was a haven for moonshiners and bootleggers who evaded federal tax agents by hiding in its rugged hills and hollows." Times reporter Richard Fausset wrote that County Mayor Iliff McMahan Jr. "who counts a few illicit whiskey makers among his forebearers— said a wariness of federal power was deeply ingrained here. 'In the old days' McMahan said, 'moonshiners were rarely considered criminals—just people trying to feed their families. When they were busted by federal revenuers those families often went hungry.'"

"In my time on the bench, we have obviously had a tremendously greater devastation from OxyContin and prescription pills than we ever had with moonshine," Circuit Judge Rex Henry Ogle told the *Commercial Appeal* newspaper. Ogle presided over Sevier County (previously a dry county) and conceded that moonshine had always been part of the community's culture. Ogle's father had told him stories of that illicit trade from back in the 1940s. "He had driven up English Mountain and...he kept hearing shotguns go off. [The neighbors] were letting those making the liquor know somebody was coming up the mountain," Ogle said.

There are several types of spirits sold as moonshine. Classic 'shine is usually made of 100% cane sugar. Corn whiskey is mostly corn and cane sugar. Some distillers use a classic recipe of "Corn & Cane," which is predominantly cane sugar mixed with a small amount of corn. There are other white spirits sold as white whiskey, featuring classic bourbon or Tennessee whiskey mash bills. These are sold as immature or unaged whiskey, identical to Tennessee whiskey which is run through the Lincoln County Process and sold white and unaged.

Today, the Federal Alcohol and Tobacco Tax and Trade Bureau has approved of the term "moonshine," allowing it to be labeled on a legally made jar or bottle of moonshine. Many whiskey experts agree that due to white whiskey or 'shine's long history and popularity within the craft distilling industry, it should be recognized as a category unto itself. Moonshine deserves its place on the top shelf given its history in Tennessee.

That said, illegal moonshine is still made in Tennessee. *Moonshiners*, a series on The Discovery Channel, follows the exploits of illegal distilling operations throughout the South. Several of the stars even went on to make legitimate 'shine with legal distilleries.

BOOTLEGGERS DISTILLERY

Bootleggers Distillery was founded in February 2015 in Hartford, Tennessee. After exploring a number of different occupations, founder Darrell Miller decided to return to his roots. His mother's side of the family contains a long line of moonshiners, dating all the way back to William Mullins, who was said to be the only passenger on the Mayflower that wasn't part of their religious sect.

"It's just an itty-bitty country place," says Miller, claiming that Bootleggers is that smallest batch distillery in the US. "We do not brew in hundred or even thousand gallon tanks. We brew in 25-gallon pot stills so that we can maintain a closer more regulated quality." The smaller the batch, the more control you have over the product. I will never do it any other way."

Miller started with his original corn-and-cane moonshine recipe, calling it "the straight-up, down-to-earth, no flavor added white lightning!" Bootleggers soon branched out into other flavors, including apple moonshine, peach, salted caramel, pineapple, hot toddy, lemon drop, mocha, cinnamon, and many more. They also produce a straight silver rum, a coconut silver rum, and have a line of cocktail mixes as well as a cherry moonshine that is packed with maraschino cherries.

Bootleggers Whiskey Select (86 proof) is a small batch whiskey made right there at the distillery. There have been two bottlings a year. This is very small-batch. It sells out quickly and their customers rave about it.

The Old 15th Whiskey Small Batch Continuously Mellowing (95 proof) unaged whiskey is bottled with a piece of charred oak in the bottle. The idea is that the whiskey ages in the bottle, not in the barrel, and the consumer gets to play cellar master, choosing when to open the whiskey. The consumer then has the option of aging the whiskey with one stick, two stick, or three sticks for either light, medium, or heavy oak flavors. The bottles will range from 95 to 110 proof and make for a very unique offering and a great gift for the real whiskey lover in your family.

Big River Distilling Co.

Big River Distilling Co. (also known as B.R. Distilling Company) is a brand-new distillery in North Memphis, Tennessee, just across the street from the Mississippi River. The distillery belongs to three childhood friends Alexander Folk (Director of Operations), McCauley Williams (President) and JB Blancett (Sales Manager) "We're Memphis guys through and through," Blancett told *Edible Memphis* magazine. "This truly is a premium Memphis product."

They started out as only a local product, in Memphis, but have expanded to have statewide distribution. All the bottles are hand filled and hand labeled.

"We've seen the craft brew movement really take off here and how proud Memphians are to call these beers their own," said McCauley. "We wanted to provide the same thing overtime with spirits."

Blue Note Juke Joint Whiskey Straight Bourbon Whiskey (93 proof) is unfiltered, made in Kentucky, and aged and blended in Tennessee. It has a mash bill of 70% corn, 21% rye, and 9% barley. The age of the whiskey is 3 to 4 years and it receives its name from Memphis, Tennessee's claim to being the home of the blues. This is the workhorse of the line. Sweet corn, cherry, allspice, and oak on the nose with vanilla, allspice, apricot, and pear coming across the palate. Pear, cherry, and vanilla on the finish. Very smooth.

Blue Note Straight Bourbon Whiskey Aged 9 Years (93 proof) is a premium small-batch whiskey. Blue Note is a proprietary blend of two mash bills 84% corn, 8% rye, and 8% malted barley and 70% corn, 22% rye, and 8% malted barley. Less than 1,000 bottles were produced (five barrels). Maple and butterscotch on the nose with maple, caramel, and vanilla across the palate, and a lingering hint of vanilla.

"We wanted to bring to Memphis a high-quality bourbon product that we blend here," said Folk. "A bourbon is a very unique product and has very different elements that really go into creating a quality blend."

Another product they've put out more recently is the Riverset Straight Rye Whiskey (93 proof),a high-rye rye made from 95% rye and 5% barley. A small-batch rye, the whiskey is aged for four years in barrel and finds inspiration from the Mississippi River across the street. Vanilla and spice on the nose with hints of apple, cinnamon, vanilla, and oak. A finish of vanilla, spice, and black pepper.

Riverset Straight Rye Whiskey Single Barrel (123 proof) is a high-rye with a mash bill of 95% rye and 5% malted barley. It's an unfiltered, barrel strength, four year old whiskey Vanilla and spice on the nose. Apple, cinnamon, vanilla, and oak on the palate. Vanilla, spice, and black pepper on the finish

"We want them all to be something that we can really hang our hat on, and that the Memphis market can be proud to call their own," Williams said of their whiskeys. It seems like Memphis has barrels of things to be proud of.

Brushy Mountain Distillery

Brushy Mountain Distillery is located at the old Brushy Mountain State Penitentiary in Petros, Tennessee, in Morgan County. From 1896 to 2009, it was the end of the line for hardened criminals. It is a prison for housing infamous inmates both real and fictional, having been set in novels by Thomas Harris and Cormac McCarthy. It is considered one of the most notorious prisons in America.

In 2013, local citizens came together to turn the prison into a tourist attraction by developing it into a commercial real estate center. It reopened in 2018. It is a popular attraction and within its confines is a distillery–Brushy Mountain Distillery.

Chattanooga entrepreneur Pete Waddington envisioned the distillery while touring the old prison years before. He and a partner founded End of the Line Moonshine in 2017. Today, the distillery offers End of the Line Moonshine, Frozen Head Vodka, Brimstone and Copperhead Cinnamon Moonshine and Liqueur, and Double Barrel Whiskey.

Employing locals as their distillers, the Bushy Mountain Distillery's End of The Line moonshines are made from farm to still, using local grains and water from the mountains' natural springs. This is true Tennessee Moonshine. They offer Apple Pie, Blackberry, Butterscotch, Cinnarum, Frosted Orange, Honey, Peach Cobbler, and Scared Straight.

Brushy Mountain Double Barrel Whiskey (117 proof) is made from the best corn and natural mountain spring water available. It's aged 6 years and finished in Caribbean rum barrels. It's bottled it at cask strength right there in Petros, Tennessee. A big nose of caramel and butterscotch notes is balanced by a hint of vanilla in this wonderful craft sipping whiskey.

Believe me, you'll enjoy doing your time at Brushy Mountain.

Cascade Hollow Distilling Co.

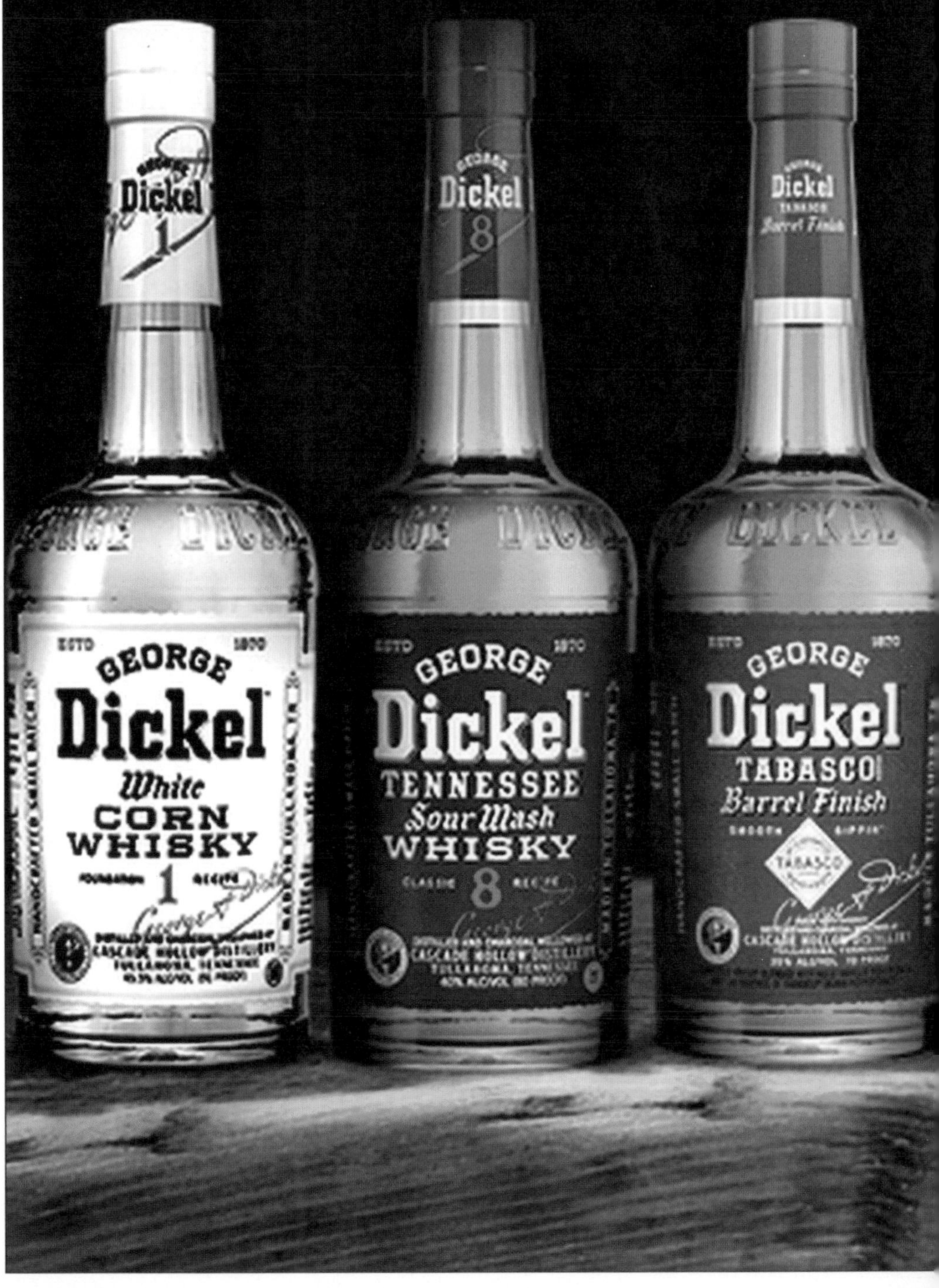

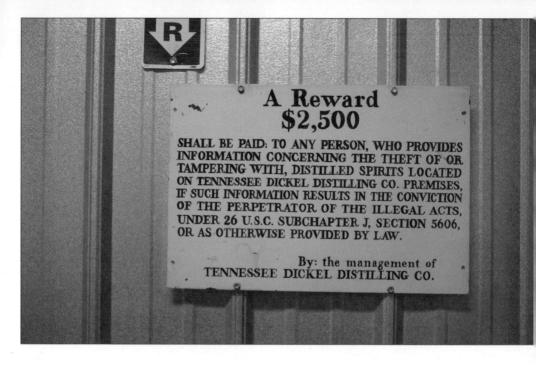

Cascade Hollow Distilling Co. was formerly known as George Dickel Distillery. The name was changed in March 2018 as part of a rebranding by its parent company, spirits conglomerate Diageo. The distillery is still the maker of George Dickel Whiskey, their main brand.

Born in Germany in 1818, George A. Dickel arrived in the United States in 1844. He settled in Nashville and opened up a retail store in the 1850s. By 1861, he was selling liquor. After the Civil War, he established the wholesaling company George A. Dickel, wherein he purchased whiskey from various distillers, and sold it to other retailers in barrels, jugs, and bottles. As the company started to grow, Dickel took on his brother-in-law Victor Emmanuel Shwab and Meier Saltzkotter as partners.

Dickel's biggest and best supplier in the 1870s was John F. Brown and F.E. Cunningham in Cascade Hollow, near Tullahoma, Tennessee. After Matthew Sims bought out Brown in 1879, McLin Davis entered the picture as the head distiller. It is Davis who more than likely came up with the recipe George A. Dickel & Co. still uses today. By the 1890s, Cascade "Mellow as Moonlight," a reference to the mash being cooled at night to produce a smoother whiskey, was one of the best-selling whiskeys in the region.

As Dickel's health declined, Shwab took on more and more control. By 1916, he had consolidated his positions at both Dickel and Cascade. He used this power to move the company to the Stitzel Distillery in Kentucky when Tennessee enacted statewide prohibition in 1908.

The brand remained in the Bluegrass State until 1956 when Ralph Dupps reconstructed the Cascade Hollow distillery about a mile from the old site. The new distillery drew its water off the Cascade Branch and took advantage of the classic Lincoln County Process. The first batch came off the still on July 4, 1959, and was not bottled until 1964. The distillery and brand changed hands several times in the intervening years and is now owned by Diageo.

Today, George A. Dickel & Co. remains the No. 2 distiller in the taste of Tennessee, behind only Jack Daniel's. They are also the second-largest producer of Tennessee whiskey in the world. With the rebirth of brown whiskeys, Dickel has seen the popularity of the brand growing immensely. The distillery has gone through a facelift in the last few years and the newly renovated retail shop is an absolute eye-catcher.

And, ever mindful of tradition, Dickel remains the largest, non-computerized distillery in the United States.

The distillery's barrels are made from eastern Tennessee wood because it's local and contains slightly less sap, which will flavor the whiskey less. The mash bill is 84% corn, 8% rye, and 8% barley. They use Tennessee corn grown within 30 miles of the distillery. The rye and barley are from the Dakotas and Wisconsin and the company has nine fermenters that hold 22,000 gallons each. These behemoths produce 500 barrels of spirits in a day. The whiskey is chill-filtered at 40 degrees in 15-foot-high charcoal tanks.

Interestingly, Dickel's barrels are toasted to #4 char, but the heads are only toasted to #2 char. Since it uses single-story rickhouses, the distillery has 14 warehouses that contain up to 250,000 barrels of whiskey at any one time.

George Dickel White Corn Whiskey No. 1 (91 proof) is an un-aged whiskey finished with the signature Dickel "Chill Charcoal Mellowing" process. It is one of the best white whiskeys available on the market. Complex, elegant, and smooth with rich

corn bread and vanilla flavors, alongside hints of buttered popcorn.

George Dickel Rye Whiskey is the only rye that's finished using the chill-filtered, Lincoln County Process in the United States. The rye whiskey is sourced from Lawrenceburg, Indiana, and is made from 95% rye and 5% malted barley. The charcoal can't mellow out this super spicy, super smooth rye.

George Dickel Tennessee Sour Mash No. 8 (80 proof) is the signature Tennessee whiskey from Dickel. This blend is often thought of as a value-priced sour mash, but it is an excellent whiskey with great quality and flavor. Though I like some of Dickel's other products better, this is a very, very solid whiskey, perfect for sipping or cocktails! Sipping it brings corn bread pancakes with pecans, butter, and maple syrup to mind.

George Dickel Tennessee Sour Mash No. 12 (90 proof), a blend of 7- to 9- year Tennessee whiskeys, packs a little more punch. There is a lot of butter pecan, salted caramel, and black pepper in this one, which becomes incredibly aromatic with just a few drops of water. This one's the go-to whiskey in my liquor cabinet.

George Dickel Tennessee Whiskey Barrel Select (86 proof) is a small batch Tennessee whiskey bottled from 10 barrels at a time from whiskey that is nine-and-a-half years old on average. In the distiller's opinion, the esterification is complete at this age. On the nose and palate, the cognac notes come through big and loud with stone fruit appearing upfront and remaining throughout. This is not only one of the best Tennessee whiskeys on the market, it is one of the best whiskeys in Kentucky and Tennessee—period. It's also a great value, making it a good bottle to trot out over the holidays!

NICOLE AUSTIN
THE REAL
WONDER WOMAN

Nicole Austin isn't your normal Kentucky or Tennessee master distiller. She's not from the region and she learned her trade out of town—in New York City.

In 2006, Austin graduated with a bachelor's degree in chemical engineering from Manhattan College in Riverdale, New York. She then began her career in environmental engineering. "I thought I was going to be the next Erin Brockovich. That was one-hundred percent my plan," says Austin.

She fell in love with whiskey while out on a date and went to work at King's County Distillers in 2010. "I didn't have the right last name to work in Kentucky or the right degree for Scotland, so I was like, 'What am I going to do?'" Austin said. "In 2010, Kings County got the license to distill ... and I basically knocked on their door and was like, 'I'm going to work for you now. I'm done asking, I'm telling.'" She was 27 years old when, as master blender, she created a rye whiskey that eventually won double gold in 2015.

"It's rare as a distiller that you actually get to touch every part of the process," she said. "But the first time Kings County made rye, I actually touched every part of the process."

"What is maturation of this spirit like? What does it taste like when it's new? What does it taste like when it's two years old, three years old, four years old? I feel like that's where it all starts. It's the liquid first," Austin said.

In that same period, Austin helped co-found the New York State Distillers Guild and the American Craft Spirits Association (ACSA). She established a standard for Empire Rye, a New York State codified standard for rye made in the state. On behalf of the industry, Austin worked hard to get the excise taxes lowered which endeared her to the crafters, as well as the big boys. "There are so many craft distilleries out there who are going to become profitable this year because of this legislation. It's the first time in the history of this country that the tax on distilled spirits has been reduced, ever," Austin said.

She began working for Dave Pickerell, the famed flying master distiller and industry legend. Austin then went on to work for William Grant & Sons, one of the largest distillers in the world, as the commissioning engineer for Tullamore Dew, the famed Irish whiskey.

At the age of 33, in March 2018, Austin was named the master distiller of George Dickel in Cascade Hollow, Tennessee.

"Nicole is absolutely perfect to lead Cascade Hollow Distilling Co. because she brings so much to the table," Sophie Kelly, senior vice president of North American Whiskeys for Diageo, said in a statement. "Not only is she an established chemical engineer and distiller, she has a real business mind, an entrepreneurial spirit, and a true vision for the future of the company, its brands, and the category."

"You can still respect tradition and innovate. Innovation doesn't mean it has to be something that's completely out there. You can respect the tradition, respect the history and respect the legacy and still bring something new to the world," Austin said of her new role at Dickel.

By May 2019, she released George Dickel 13-Year Old Bottled In Bond (100 proof), a mash bill of 84% corn, 8% rye, and 8% malted barley. Being a Tennessee whiskey, it was charcoal mellowed using the Lincoln County Process. "We wanted George Dickel Bottled in Bond to be rooted in authenticity, quality, and truth, reflective of the values we feel are most important when making Tennessee's finest whiskey. The aged stocks we have access to here at Cascade Hollow are absolutely beautiful and it's important to me that we create whiskey that's sure to be a great value for the quality you're getting," Austin said at the whiskey's release.

Sweetens Cove

Owners of the Sweetens Cove brand include football great Peyton Manning, tennis legend Andy Roddick, sportscaster Jim Nantz, and singer-songwriter Drew Holcomb. Among others are the co-owners of the Tennessee golf course Sweetens Cove, a dream course which they purchased in 2019. They decided they wanted to have a house brand of whiskey to offer their members. That idea went even further.

Sweetens had no clubhouse, but it had traditions. The "wonderfully organic tradition" was: newcomers had to have one shot of whiskey before hitting off the first tee. "People would drop off or leave bottles and it became part of the lore and experience." explained co-owner Mark Rivers.

"We wanted a Tennessee product that reflected the nature and story of Sweetens Cove. In some ways, this first release is a love letter to Tennessee. Whiskey was a part of the Sweetens ritual and is certainly a part of centuries of legacy in this state. It was a natural." Rivers told Nino Kilgore-Marchetti of WhiskeyWash.com.

First, they hired Marianne Eaves, who had been at Woodford and Castle & Key before striking out on her own as a consultant. She in turn found some sweet 13-year old Tennessee whiskey to blend and bottle. Approximately 100 barrels. The whiskey was bottled at barrel strength and only 14,000 bottles were produced. Four barrels were held back for a special 2020 reserve release.

Many in the industry had loudly opined that there was only one place to get that much whiskey that is so old – Dickel's. Neither company would confirm the source of the whiskey.

"I always look for ways to create balance while celebrating what the barrels have to offer," Eaves told industry insider Fred Minnick for Forbes.com. "It was great juice and through blending, I was able to come up with some really fun flavor profiles. All five batches are different, celebrating the age of the bourbon and highlighting the nuanced flavors they managed to present, even above the oak after all that time."

That said, the whiskey got some great reviews and a hole-in-one for the golf course and Eaves.

Marianne Eaves

Marianne Eaves's career has been nothing short of amazing. A meteoric rise through the world of bourbon and she's doing it as a woman in an old boys' game—and winning.

Bourbon's history is filled with names. Jack Daniel's. Jim Beam. George Dickel. So who was Kentucky's first woman distiller? Marianne Eaves. She was born in Tennessee and raised in Kentucky. She went to the University of Louisville where she earned a degree in chemical engineering. "Right out of college, I could have built an efficient ethanol plant," Eaves told the Daily Beast, "but it wouldn't have tasted very good."

She went to work for Brown-Forman, starting out as an intern and then indispensable assistant to legendary master distiller Chris Morris at Woodford Reserve. She rose to the position of master taster and she made numerous contributions to Woodford and Brown-Forman.

"Women do have a more sensitive palate," Eaves told the *Daily Beast*, "Women should be able to create more nuanced spirits."

Eaves was recognized in *Whiskey Advocate* as "The Next Generation" for the bourbon industry. She has been honored by *Forbes* and included in the 2015 Food & Drink "30 Under 30" list.

When Eaves was named Kentucky's first woman master distiller in 2015 at the age of 28, the news went national. Eaves was the first woman ever to be named master distiller in modern distilling history. There have been prominent women in the industry, but none in memory were awarded the honor of master distiller. Morris made note of how proud he was of Eaves and how sad he was to lose her.

As she stepped into the role of master distiller herself, taking on the herculean restoration project of Castle & Key Distillery, Eaves was recognized by *Wine Enthusiast* as one of America's "Top 40 Under 40 Tastemakers."

From the very beginning, Eaves helped create and build Castle & Key.. After starting whiskey production, the next goal was to create a signature London Dry style gin. Eaves told Imbibe magazine, "We also believe that gin is a growing category and hope that our Kentucky-style gin using a bourbon or rye mash base will appeal to a more diverse set of drinkers."

As for the bourbons and whiskeys? Eaves insisted on using all Kentucky grown and bred grain and corn. According to Imbibe writer Emma Janzen, "Eaves worked with a local farmer to resurrect the endangered Hickory King corn, an 1800s-era heirloom variety that would have been similar to the kind used for original production of Old Taylor. It will take three years to propagate enough seed to fulfill the amount required to make the whiskey." Eaves worked with the Halcomb family of Walnut Grove Farm in Adairsville, Kentucky, to grow a non-GMO white corn.

"For our proprietary recipes, we will be using this grain exclusively," Eaves said at the time. "I have been out in the field, planting and harvesting with the Halcombs to evaluate the fields and review their approach to fertilization so that we get the right starch content and flavor."

Eaves abruptly left in 2020, leaving the industry buzzing once again. Just as her whiskeys were maturing, especially the Pinhook line which she helped craft. Industry journalist Fred Minnick opined, "Eaves left Castle & Key and embarked on a consulting career that could very well reshape the whiskey industry's cottage segment of consulting."

Minnick was right. The famed Dave Pickerell, the industry's star consultant and equivalent of the wine industry's Michel Rolland, had passed away in late 2018. The industry suddenly lacked an experienced flying distilling consultant.

"The project building Castle & Key was a tremendous opportunity to meet people and have people reach out to me. I'm just really grateful for my time there. They have a great team. They have a strong desire to improve the industry and to be a leader," said Eaves. "My opportunity is to take my expertise beyond bourbon and beyond Kentucky and try to spread the gospel a little bit and extend a helping hand to folks. One thing that I've found I'm really passionate about is sharing the technical expertise that I brought with me to Castle & Key from Brown-Forman."

And that's exactly what she's doing.

Her first release as a consultant was the Sweeten's Cove Tennessee Bourbon. Currently, she's working on a rosé vermouth with Lindsay Hoopes at Hoopes Vineyard in Napa, California. She's also a consultant to the highly-acclaimed boutique St. Augustine's Distillery. She has worked for Sonoma County Distillers as a technical consultant for their expansion. Eaves also hopes to produce the first premium whiskeys from scratch in China with Judy Chan, who revolutionized the wine industry in China with her vision at Grace Vineyards.

"Marianne is well poised to be the 'next big thing' in the craft whiskey world," said St. Augustine Distillery co-founder Michael K. Díaz. "Her education, experience and work ethic all combine to provide a real benefit to the craft distiller.

To borrow a line: Marianne Eaves's future is so bright she needs to wear shades—and you'll think she's pretty cool, too

Chattanooga Whiskey Company

Chattanooga used to be a hotbed of distilling. By the end of the 19th century, there were more than 30 distilleries in the city; more than any other city in the state. Unfortunately, Tennessee's statewide prohibition began a full decade before the national "Great Experiment" which all but shut down the distilling industry.

There was no distilling in Chattanooga until almost 100 years later. In 2009, Joe Ledbetter and Tim Piersant established the Chattanooga Whiskey Company.

However, their road was not an easy one. Though the state of Tennessee was willing to grant them a license, Hamilton County was not one of counties allowing distilleries to operate. After a long battle, via social media and the courts, the question "Would you drink Chattanooga whiskey?" was put to the public. In November 2012, the "Vote Whiskey" campaign came to a head when the Hamilton County Commission approved the new distillery. In spring 2013, Governor Bill Haslam signed a bill

allowing it to go forward and in March 2015, the Chattanooga Whiskey Company was established.

The distillery has gone through some changes since its inception. The original distillery, known as the Chattanooga Whiskey Co. Experimental Distillery, is across the street from Terminal Station, which is famous for its association with the Glenn Miller song "Chattanooga Choo Choo." The distillery's custom-made still is affectionately called "Doc." It was fabricated by Vendome Copper & Brass Works and the head distiller is Grant McCracken. According to Piersant, the distillery is "part experiment and innovation lab, part museum and all good." This remains their bread-and-butter retail shop.

The main distillery is a sleek black machine a few miles away. Clad in black, it is a combination of a sleek ultra-mod show room and a down-to-earth brass tacks distillery. This is a state-of-the-art mid-sized distillery with power and room to spare and what's

going on here is nothing short of spectacular.

Chattanooga Whiskey Co. 1816 is one the brands the distillery distributes.

The three expressions of barrel-aged whiskey currently available for purchase are all high-rye bourbons made using a mash bill of 75% corn, 21% rye, and 4% malted barley.

Chattanooga Whiskey Co. 1816 Reserve (90 proof) has a mash bill of 75% corn, 21% rye, and 4% malted barley, and is solera barrel finished. Caramel, honey, brown sugar, and vanilla notes with a lovely hint of spice.

The Chattanooga Whiskey Co. 1816 Cask (113.6 proof) has a mash bill of 75% corn, 21% rye, and 4% malted barley. This is a blend of barrels between 2 and 10 years old. This is a big, barrel-strength bourbon with a slightly darker color. It offers lots of burnt caramel, vanilla, baked apple, and toffee flavor with a big, bold spicy ending of gingersnap and a slight, slight hint of cinnamon. It's a big and warm dram.

There was also a limited-edition Chattanooga Whiskey Co. 1816 Single Barrel (106 proof) release. It was highly prized, highly coveted, and sold out quickly. Additionally, there was a Chattanooga Whiskey 1816 Native Beer Barrel Finished (100 proof). It has a mash bill of 75% corn, 21% rye, and 4% malted barley and is a blend of 2 and 10 years old whiskeys.

For the 1816 Native, the distillery partnered with local craft breweries, giving them bourbon barrels to age and add complexity to their unique beers. Those barrels were returned to finish the 1816 Reserve. The result was a match made in barrel heaven—eight barreled bourbons layered with unique flavors from the traces of beers and whiskey that came before them. 2018 breweries included Heaven & Ale Brewing Co, Oddstory Brewing Co, Terminal BrewHouse, Hutton & Smith Brewing Company, Chattanooga Brewing Co, Moccasin Bend Brewing Company, Three

Taverns Craft Brewery, and Big River Grille & Brewing Works. Some of the most unique whiskeys were made in either Kentucky or Tennessee by either a big or craft producer.

Then there's the High Malt series with three different finishes. Chattanooga Whiskey Straight Bourbon Whiskey (91 proof) Tennessee High Malt is now one of the big workhorses of the distillery. It has a four grain mash of yellow corn, malted rye, caramel malted barley & honey malted barley. The mash bill experiences an extended 7-day fermentation. Distillers feel that this emphasizes the fruit complexity and high-malt character. The whiskey is aged in two different charred and toasted white oak barrels. After aging more than 2 years, the distillery uses a Solera finishing process—involving more than 100 barrels into a 4000-gallon charred, white oak Solera finishing barrel, which must be empty. Tasting notes include dried apricot, sweet tea, and honeyed toast. It's an easy drinking, craft bourbon and fantastic whiskey that is getting more and more publicity and distribution.

The Chattanooga Whiskey Straight Bourbon Whiskey Unfiltered Barrel Strength (111 proof) goes through the same process but is bottled at barrel strength. A small-batch whiskey, it's slightly harder to come by aged a minimum of two years and full of character and flavor.

Chattanooga Whiskey Straight Rye Malt Whiskey (99 proof) is a four grain whiskey with at least 51% rye), including a blend of slow toasted and drum roasted rye malt. Aged more than 3 years, each batch is 6-10 barrels each. Tasting notes of sweet and savory notes of candied fruit, herbs, and spice. An excellent, smooth rye.

There is also the Experimental Series, a limited collection of whiskeys and spirits born from their original 100-gallon Experimental Distillery in Downtown Chattanooga. Each batch utilizes a multitude of grains, barrels, techniques, and unique ingredients to create one-of-a-kind whiskeys. This series is a whiskey geek's dream!

The Chattanooga Whiskey Batch 16 (75-77 proof) is a whiskey infused with coffee. It's a 2-year and 7 months-old whiskey infused with a special blend of Ethiopian and Colombian coffees, citrus peel, vanilla bean, and cane sugar. They released three barrels worth in Fall 2020.

The Chattanooga Whiskey Batch 14 (102 proof) has a mash bill of ten grains. Aged 2 years and 8 months, the 4 barrels were finished with South American Demerara Rum and Barbados Rum for an additional 11 months. It was released in April 2020.

Other Experimentals include: BATCH 013 Bourbon Barreled Gin; BATCH 012 Mead Barrel Finished; BATCH 011 Maple Syrup Barrel Finished; BARREL 91 Tennessee High Malt; BARREL 75 Tennessee Double Barrel; BARREL 63 Tennessee Double Malt; BARREL 50 Tennessee Single Malt; BARREL 42 Tennessee Rye Malt; BARREL 51 Wheated High Malt; BARREL 62 Scottish Style High Malt; BARREL 55 Native Barrel; BARREL 52 Smoked High Malt; BARREL 32 Tennessee High Malt; BATCH 010 Tennessee Double Barrel; BATCH 009 Tennessee Double Malt (high corn); BATCH 008 Tennessee Single Malt (Barleywine finish); BATCH 007 Tennessee Rye Malt (3 varieties of malted rye); BATCH 006 Native Barrel (Wheated), and many more.

Chattanooga is gaining fans. The word is spreading and rightfully so. Chattanooga distills some of the best craft whiskeys in any state and soon they won't be the little craft distiller who could. Chattanooga Whiskey Co. is full steam ahead and only a fool would miss this train!

The Chattanooga Tasting Experience

I have been to a lot of wine, beer, spirits, and cider tasting rooms. It's what I do for a living and every so often, a tasting experience makes a huge impression. None more so than that at the Chattanooga Whiskey Co.

First off, tastings happen at the bar. I like that because it's a beautiful bar with wood staves, copper, and black iron which adds just the right touch of steampunk. The barrel staves woven throughout the space , crafted from reclaimed wood from a local factory, are from their own barrels. Architect Thomas Palmer and carpenter Matt Sears of Haskel Sears Design and Construction helped set the bar very high for this tasting.

For Piersant, the goal of the tasting is "to allow us to get creative with techniques and showcase our current product." Each tour concludes with a full tasting of Chattanooga Whiskey and locally-produced Dr. Thacher's Cocktail Syrup.

The tasters sample three whiskeys—the 1816 100, 1816 Reserve, and 1816 Cask. They are served alongside the cocktails made with those bourbons using the local Thacher's cocktail mixes. It's a smart, clever, and informative tasting that's done extremely well in a beautiful, relaxing setting.

EXPANSION, BUT STAYING LOCAL

The downtown Experimental Distillery is a small production facility that Chattanooga has been using to chug along since the early days—similar to Apollo 11 where one side was used as a life raft until it was time to jet home. It will continue to be the experimental section of distillery operations. However, Chattanooga Whiskey Co. purchased an old Chevrolet dealership location and is turning it into a state of the art distillery in downtown Chattanooga. Less than a few miles away from the tasting room, a massive new plant is under construction. The interior of the building

was gutted, reconstructed, and is now being filled with massive fermenters, two stills (a very large column still and a pot still), and huge barrel rooms.

The distillery will produce six different recipes for both their bourbons and their Tennessee high malt. They are already at work on a four-grain bourbon as well. The new distillery features an immense event space with a cavernous production area. These guys are serious and it's a great sign of things to come.

CORSAIR

Corsair is one of the most famous and most accomplished of American craft distilleries.

From the moment you step into a tasting room at Corsair Distillery and see the labels on each bottle, you know there is something different about the place. The labels feature three men in black-and-white suits, reminiscent of Quentin Tarantino's iconic film *Reservoir Dogs;* they look as if they're about to walk right off the bottle. That's just a hint of the place's bold attitude.

Of all the most impressive whiskey makers in Tennessee and Kentucky, few compare to Corsair. Corsair is a mad whiskey scientist's dream. In one visit we tasted almost a dozen different whiskeys, everything from nine-grain bourbon to quinoa whiskey to two types of hopped whiskey. Even the most dyed-in-the-wool curmudgeons grudgingly admit that Corsair is one of the most interesting distilleries in the entire United States. Everyone within the Kentucky and Tennessee whiskey communities have an eye fixed on Corsair.

In a world of Vermeers attempting to emulate the grandmaster bourbons, Corsair wishes to be Van Gogh. The rules that guide most of the bourbon whiskey world in Tennessee and Kentucky suddenly disappear when one comes into contact with Corsair. It's as if these folks stepped into a time machine and set the controls for one or two decades ahead. The idea of a bourbon made simply with corn, rye, and barley seems absurd here. Nothing is too sacred to be experimented with and no technique seems too crazy.

Granted, there is still an appreciation for the fundamentals. Corsair prefers to make their own beer or mash and they age their bourbon in new American oak. Beyond that, it's a giant playground.

DAREK BELL:
FOUNDER, OWNER, DISTILLER,
PUSHER OF BOUNDARIES

Darek Bell, a Nashville native, is the founder
and owner of Corsair Distillery. Bell began
fiddling around as a homebrewer and
winemaker (even dabbling in sake) before
he attended the Siebel Institute in Chicago
and the Bruichladdich Distilling Academy
in Islay, Scotland. He is dedicated to one
thing—pushing the envelope and always
seeking ways to push past the accepted
wisdom of distilling. He focuses constantly
on new recipes, using alternative grains,
unconventional smoked grains, and unusual
botanicals. This daring way of distilling
prompted *Spirits Business* magazine to
name Bell one of the "10 Most Pioneering
Distillers." Bell is the author of two books:
Alt Whiskeys and *Fire Water*.

According to the company's website: "Childhood friends Darek Bell and Andrew Webber began homebrewing beer and wine in Darek and Amy Lee Bell's garage. They hit a snag while working on a prototype bio-diesel plant, causing Andrew to remark that making whiskey would be much more satisfying."

Andrew Webber (who holds an MBA) is head distiller and the distillery's president, a job that entails running day-to-day operations, bean counting, janitorial work, lecturing, and serving as brand ambassador. Amy Lee Bell is a co-owner and leads the marketing side of the business, serving as a brand ambassador, as well as the copywriter and publicist. Together, these three make magic.

In 2008, Corsair opened its first tasting room and distillery in Bowling Green, Kentucky. The Marathon tasting room location in Nashville was opened in 2010. And their new headquarters, on Merritt, was opened in 2016.

Each location has its own distiller. Aaron Marcum is the head distiller at the Bowling Green location, Colton Weinstein is the head distiller at the Marathon location, and Clay Smith is the head distiller at the headquarters on Merritt. Each distiller makes a special number of recipes. Some are very specific and particular to one person. Occasionally, whiskeys from one part of the Corsair empire are blended with those produced at another location. Each distillery makes something unique and different and all of them make whiskeys that may be blended at another location.

Not long after Corsair opened their products and experiments started garnering immediate attention from writers and spirit historians, as well as media hotspots like *Food & Wine, Saveur, Imbibe, Whisky Magazine, Whisky Advocate, The Atlantic, Time Out New York*, and Maxim.

While Corsair has a reputation for experimentation and small production,

their three facilities make their whiskeys much easier to find than ever before. Ryemaggedon, Triple Smoke, Dark Rye, and Oatrage can all be found in discerning shops, or at can be ordered by your local purveyor.

I visited the Nashville headquarters on Merritt where they have an 800-gallon pot still, two column stills, and six healthy-sized fermenters. Smith is friendly, helpful, and proud of what he and the company produce. As you would expect, he is also a beverage freak who loves all wine, beer, and spirits.

That love helps Corsair make some wicked cool whiskeys. Their two biggest sellers are the Triple Smoke, their version of a single malt, and their Ryemageddon, which is truly an outrageous rye whiskey.

The Triple Smoke American Malt Whiskey (80 proof) is a malted barley whiskey made from three smoked batches—cherry wood, peat, and beechwood—pot distilled and barrel-aged in new charred oak. Essentially a single malt whiskey, it is rich with notes of caramel, brown sugar, vanilla, and smoke. It's very good, especially for those who like things a little smoky.

The Ryemageddon (92 proof) is an American high-rye made from chocolate rye and malted rye. It has a mash bill of 88% rye—80% malted rye and 8% chocolate rye and is aged in oak for eight to nine months. While some may not like rye for its spiciness, this is a wonderful new twist on rye whiskey. The chocolate malt adds a big, rich flavor to the caramel and toffee up front, but doesn't take away from the lovely gingersnap finish so often associated with a traditional rye. It is an absolute winner and among my favorite rye whiskeys in both states.!

There is also a Ryemagedon Single Barrel cask strength boasts a 123.5 proof (61.75% ABV).

Corsair Tennessee Single Malt (90 proof) is a 100% two row malted barley American single malt, first aged in American oak casks. The whiskey is finish in ex-Caribbean rum barrels. Sweet, dark rum, bold oak, and mild malt tones on the nose. Rum, honey, and malt come across the palate.

Corsair Dark Rye American Rye Malt Whiskey (85 proof) has a mash bill of 61% Malted rye, 4% malted chocolate rye, and 35% malted barley. Unlike many other rye whiskeys, Corsair does not use corn to fill up our grain bill. Corsair Dark Rye is technically both a rye whiskey and a malt whiskey. Big notes of pepper, chocolate, and oak. This big, chewy, artisanal craft rye is not for the faint of heart.

Corsair remains at the forefront of craft distilling and in a single visit, you'll have the chance to taste a whole world of amazing and experimental whiskeys that continue to push boundaries.

CUMBERLAND CASK TENNESSEE WHISKEY

Manuel Eskind was an important individual in Tennessee whiskey, though few know his name today. He was instrumental in helping to reopen the shuttered George Dickel Distillery in 1933. With Eskind in mind, his descendants established Capital Distilling Company in 2012, and announced their Cumberland Cask Tennessee Straight Whiskey in 2013.

Manuel Eskind was an important individual in Tennessee whiskey, though few know his name today. He was instrumental in helping to reopen the shuttered George Dickel Distillery in 1933. With Eskind in mind, his descendants established Capital Distilling Company in 2012 and announced their Cumberland Cask Tennessee Straight Whiskey in 2013.

While it says "Tennessee Straight Whiskey" on the bottle, this is a whiskey made in Tennessee and not a Tennessee whiskey, as it is not made using the famed Lincoln County Process. The bottle statement has caused some confusion, but the company has been clear in its messaging otherwise. All Cumberland Cask whiskeys have been distilled and aged in Tennessee and bottled in Nashville. The folks at SPEAKeasy Spirits crafted this whiskey and it's gotten some nice attention.

Cumberland Tennessee Straight Whiskey First Expression: Modern Expression (92 proof) is a boutique, small batch blend of six-and-a-half-year-old and eight-and-a-half-year-old whiskeys with a mash bill of 70% corn, 25% rye, and 5% malted barley. A big corn whiskey, it notches nice notes of caramel and sweet white cake with honey, vanilla, and a lovely smokiness.

Cumberland Cask Second Expression: Barrel Cut (118 proof) uses the same mash bill as the First Expression, but is bottled at barrel strength, providing a bigger shot of flavor, smoke, and alcohol. "Barrel Cut is a cask strength, uncut, unfiltered, hand crafted whiskey, just like Manuel used to sell," the distillery states.

Cumberland Cask Third Expression: Ruby Cut (90 proof) is the first and only port wine-finished whiskey made in Tennessee. The distillery aged their classic six-year-old whiskey in four California ruby port-styled dessert wine barrels "for a full Nashville winter to allow the whiskey to contract and squeeze all the port wine in the wood out into the whiskey." The whiskey aged a full six months in barrels resulting in a deep amber color and a unique sweetness. The whiskey was then dumped and stored in stainless steel. The same four port barrels were then refilled immediately with a new batch of six-year-old whiskey and rested for six months, this time through a Nashville summer. Once the second batch had aged for six months, it was dumped and blended with the stored winter whiskey. All reports claim that the Ruby Cut was fantastic, but it was difficult to get a hold of. If you're struggling to do so, the Barrel Cut is a nice consolation prize. It's a very tasty whiskey that benefits from just a splash of water.

The company went through a period when product was scare, but a new reorganization and a repackaging of the company will lead to a relaunch.

Doc Collier Moonshine

In April 2014, Doc Collier Moonshine opened their doors in Gatlinburg, Tennessee. Each bottle of moonshine is made from four classic elements—sugar, corn, yeast, and fresh English Mountain Spring Water—and features a family recipe that is more than 100 years old.

"According to local legend, the owner's great-great grandfather, William 'Doc' Collier, once traveled through the Smoky Mountains on horseback delivering his moonshine 'before moonshine was even a word,'" journalist Jessica Bookstaff Doppelt wrote. The distillery receives as much as 300 to 600 gallons at a time from the English Mountain Spring Water Company for fermenting and distilling.

The Doc Collier Moonshine Original Recipe (125 proof) is their "straight off the still," high-proof, unfiltered moonshine. The Doc Collier Unaged Corn Whiskey (80 proof), a straight "Corn Liquor" made solely from corn, water, and yeast. There's the classic Doc Collier Heritage Shine (80 proof), which, according to the distiller, is as close as you can get to traditional, old-fashioned 'shine. It is "like something you would get from a truck or trunk here in the Smokies" according to the distillery. Doc Collier also features a number of flavored shines, including 'Shined Cherries, Peach, Blackberry, Sweet Tea, Greenbrier Apple, Root Beer Float, Smoky Mountain Sunrise, Firecracker, and Buckeye, as well as seasonal offerings.

For whiskey enthusiasts, the Doc Collier Unaged Corn Whiskey is one that's worth trying.

EAST TENNESSEE DISTILLERY

East Tennessee Distillery, the home of Roberson's Tennessee Mellomoon moonshine, is situated in the hills of Piney Flats. Master distiller Neil, "Tiny" Roberson, is a former Navy chemist who was trained with the difficult task of turning seawater into drinking water. After his service, he worked for more than 12 years as a lab technician and analyst for two very large companies.

As a hobbyist, Tiny made small batches of craft "liquid sunshine" in his garage. His homemade 'shine became a fast favorite with friends and family. Around that same time, Tennessee began licensing small craft distilleries and Tiny gained legitimacy in August 2011, and the distillery opened its doors in 2012.

"It really took an act of faith because the way the laws and everything are set up, we had to have all the equipment in place and ready to go before we could apply for the permit at the federal level," Tiny told the *Johnson City Press*. "If anyone thinks they can take on this kind of business on a shoestring budget, they might want to rethink it."

Roberson's Tennessee Mellomoon Fine Tennessee Sippin' Shine (100 proof) is clean and easy to sip, both straight or on ice. It's also great for a cocktail or punch. Roberson's Tennessee Mellomoon 150 Proof is a 'shine that is as close as commercial moonshine can get to those that came off the old stills. The high alcohol content is great for those who like their moonshine hot. The East Tennessee Distillery also features 'shines with flavors like Apply Pies, Banana, Butterscotch, Coconut, Caramel, Grape, Peach, Honey Ginseng, and Strawberry. Tiny's award-winning 'shines are available in Tennessee, South Carolina, Florida, and Ohio, so keep an eye out whenever you're in those parts.

"What whiskey will not cure,
there is no cure for."

—Proverb

H Clark distillery

In 2014, Heath Clark told *The Tennessean*, "Five or six years ago, I made a list of things I needed to do to make whiskey. And Roman numeral No. 1 was to get permission." However, the paperwork and filings alone took far longer than Clark thought. Once completed, Clark stated, "Now that the time is here, the distillery looks like I hoped it would. It's in an old grain barn, a pretty rural structure, with all the necessary infrastructure. It looks exactly like a place whiskey should be made."

H Clark Distillery, established on August 1, 2014, was the first legal distillery in Williamson County in more than 100 years. A micro-distillery, they currently produce the company's handcrafted Tennessee Bourbon, Gin, New Whiskey, and Black & Tan Whiskey. Clark, his wife Becky, and a handful of friends and employees craft these incredible whiskeys one small batch at a time. The beautiful 400-liter Hoga still is an alembic-styled copper pot still that sits comfortably on a brick pedestal with its long, elegant neck curving into a copper rectifier. It's as pretty as it is practical and says a lot about the man who is trying to make quality spirits in this neck of the woods.

STEP INTO MY LAW OFFICE

Heath Clark is a master distiller forty hours a week, but he has another full-time job: he's a lawyer—and a fairly popular one, too. Clark has a unique and specific distinction—he is the only practicing attorney-for-hire to have his law offices located in a distillery!

Clark worked as operations counsel for one of the nation's leading privately held owners of community-focused hospitals. He consulted on legal issues and operations in Arizona, Florida, Louisiana, Nevada, Tennessee, and Utah. He now provides advice and counsel for hospitals, physicians, imaging centers, and other forms of health care.

In 2009, Clark was also instrumental in passing some of the laws that allowed small craft distilleries to mushroom in Tennessee. On the wall of his office, Clark displays a photo of numerous distillers and himself with the governor of Tennessee as the new laws were signed.

If there's one thing you can be sure of—Clark's spirits come from a man with impeccable judgment!

We started off our tasting with H Clark Tennessee Dry Gin (88 proof). Clark and company tried 26 different botanicals including sassafras and honeysuckle. The resulting gin packs a big wallop of juniper upfront, a punch followed by big shots of evergreen and black pepper. This nicely balanced gin is aromatic and delicate without any wilting.

H Clark New Whiskey (80 proof) is a white whiskey made from 40% malted barley, 11% chocolate malt, and 49% malted oats. The result is reminiscent of a distilled oatmeal stout. While corn whiskeys often have notes of corn bread and popcorn, this one is a big oatmeal cookie. It is very well-balanced and a real standout in the growing field of oatmeal-influenced whiskey.

H Clark Black & Tan (80 proof) is a blend of new and one-year malt whiskies. It's a lighter styled whiskey, with oak and caramel giving way to a nice, spicy ending. It's as smooth as the aged whiskies from Scotland, but with more toffee flavor.

H Clark Tennessee Bourbon (90–100 proof) is a four-grain bourbon made from 70% corn, 15% malted barley, 7.5% wheat, and 7.5% rye. It's aged in newly charred, 25-gallon American white oak barrels for two years. First released in December 2016, the very first bottle of this lovely bourbon was auctioned off to raise money for those impacted by the fires that devastated East Tennessee in 2016.

This is a big, big chocolaty malt with notes of dark caramel, burnt sugar, toffee, and salted caramel. It's big and robust, with hints of vanilla, cocoa, and sweet, dark bread.

I loved this whiskey which fares well with a splash of water. In my opinion, it's the best bourbon in Tennessee and one of my favorite craft bourbons anywhere.

H Clark Tennessee Rye is made from 100% rye and aged for two years in charred new American white oak. The mash bill is 80% unmalted rye, and 20% malted rye, so you're sure to get plenty of spice in this one.

Heaven's Door Distillery

Heaven's Door Distillery was planned to operate as a distillery and art center in a former church building in downtown Nashville. Heaven's Door teams Marc Bushala (CEO of Heaven's Door Spirits) and other unnamed investors with Bob Dylan. Bushala said he and Dylan had raised $35 million from investors for the project. Bushala's HDS Distilling Co. owns the property where the distillery will be built. Bushala is known as the CEO of Spirits Investment Partners (SIP), the company that is partnered with Dylan on this project. HDS investors include Nashville-based entrepreneur and distiller Darek Bell of the iconic Corsair Artisan Distillery. It was suggested that Corsair and Heaven's Door would likely have a symbiotic relationship on the project.

Bushala said they were "focused on creating something unique and enduring. We also have around six years-worth of amazing aged whiskey, so we have plenty of runway." The facility will include a distilling operation, a concert venue, a restaurant, and whiskey library, as well as an art center, featuring paintings and metalwork sculptures created by Dylan. The distillery will operate within the church which was built in 1860 and will now also be a boutique hotel. Burshla said, "Our most likely course of action is to renovate the church proper as the art center and open it first."

Four whiskey expressions were released in April 2018, all from sourced whiskey. "I've been traveling for decades and I've been able to try some of the best spirits that the world of whiskey has to offer. This is great whiskey." Dylan said.

The design on the bottles from Heaven's Door mimic one of Dylan's sculptures. Heaven's Door Tennessee Bourbon (90 proof) has a mash bill of 70% corn, 25% rye and 5% malted barley and aged for 8 years in new charred American oak. Tasting notes include strawberry, vanilla, baking spice, caramel, cereal, cocoa and spice. A real keeper!

Heaven's Door Double Barrel Whiskey (100 proof) is finished in cigar barrels from Vosges, France. Heaven's Door Tennessee Bourbon 10 Year Old (100 proof) is a low-rye whiskey that has gone through the Lincoln County Process. Notes of strong dark cherry, maple, caramel, cereal, biscuit, and pineapple.

Heaven's Door Straight Rye (92 proof) is more of a Baltimore rye. It's very smooth with notes of gingerbread at the end and soft hints of anise, clove, caramel, and pecans.

HOOK & LADDER DISTILLERY

Located in downtown Kingsport, Tennessee, Hook & Ladder Distillery was founded by Drew Draper who claims that he has been distilling moonshine since he was 17. After teaming with his father Keneth, a fire captain with 26 years of service, the Hook & Ladder finally gained legitimacy. The tributes to firefighters don't stop with the name—Hook & Ladder's very cool tasting room is festooned with all kinds of awesome firefighting paraphernalia.

Drew and Kenneth use an old, thumper-style still to make high-proof 'shine. Their smooth and simple Hook & Ladder Original Recipe has since been accompanied by a number of different flavors, as well as a high-octane 140-proof version.

"Too much of anything is bad, but too much good whiskey is barely enough."

—Mark Twain

Jack Daniel's Distillery

Jack Daniel's is the best-selling whiskey in the world with more exported product than Johnnie Walker. It is also the best-selling Tennessee whiskey in the world—and it's located in the dry county of Lynchburg!

Jack Daniel's has grown every year over the last 25 years. Its sales grew exponentially through the whole vodka, gin, and tequila, "we-want-it-clear" craze. This is not true of any other Tennessee or Kentucky distillers and in 2013, the distillery went through

extensive improvements with a $100 million expansion, designed to keep up with the world's demands.

Total sales top more than $4 billion with sixty-five percent of all Jack Daniel's exported to more than 160 countries around the world. Jack Daniel's sports five main distilling lines and three smaller ones. They run 13 different bottles 24/7 at the distillery and produce more than 200,000,000 bottles a year. They have one day off from

cooking each week. Jack Daniel's uses US No. 1 Corn-grade sweet corn with zero tolerance for foreign material, discoloration, damage, worms, disease, smut, decay, or any other defects. Only whole-kernel corn is used, most of which comes from western Kentucky, Indiana, and Illinois.

They also use lactic acid to clear the mash and make it sterile. The yeast is grown at the distillery in a 1,700-gallon fermenter. Jack Daniel's has 64 40,000-gallon fermenters where they make their distiller's beer. That's 2.56 million gallons of beer a week! Each fermentation takes six to seven days with the majority cooking for six days.

Jack Daniel's has six constantly working stills, four column stills, and two pot stills. Everything is 100% copper, true to the Jack Daniel's tradition because copper produces a cleaner spirit. It comes out of the doubler as bourbon and comes of out the charcoal tanks as Tennessee whiskey. They fill

approximately 2,000 barrels a day which amounts to nearly 100,000 to 150,000 gallons of spirits. The distillery uses a proprietary toasting process on their new American white oak barrels. One-third of all Scotch is aged in former Jack Daniel's barrels.

Jack Daniel's has 89 rickhouses throughout Lynchburg and with an operation this huge, it's no surprise that the distillery has its own burn station where charcoal is made for the "Mellowing Process." During the process, it takes one gallon three days to trickle through 10-foot-high, slow-flowing tanks. Approximately $1 million of maple trees are burned each year in order to make enough charcoal for their whiskey production. Four firemen are assigned to do the work and operate in a very carefully controlled setting.

Fine dust is always a danger as it is as flammable as the alcohol vapors, but the distillery has an on-site fire team with plenty of equipment and around six million gallons of water.

Their water source is a huge cave spring. The discharge is filtered and returned to the creek once it is safe; 70% of their silage is sold wet to local farmers (master distiller Jeff Arnett recommends mixing in a little hay with it).

Jasper Newton "Jack" Daniel, born in 1850, was of Scots-Irish, Scottish, and Welsh descent. The youngest of 10 children, he learned how to make whiskey in the 1850s from a preacher/grocer named Dan Call and Call's slave, Nearest Green. In 1875, Daniel and Call established a distillery and by 1884, Daniel owned the company outright and purchased the land where it now resides. He began using Daniel's iconic square bottle in 1897.

Daniel died in Lynchburg on October 10, 1911. He passed away due to blood poisioning, although there was an apocryphal tale that his death resulted from an infection that sprouted after he kicked the safe in his office. His nephew, Lemuel "Lem" Motlow, ran Jack Daniel's for the next 36 years and built it into one of the biggest brands in the country.

The company was sold to the Brown-Forman Corporation in 1956 and in 1972 Jack Daniel's Distillery was listed on the National Register of Historic Places.

CHRIS FLETCHER

THE MAN IN WAITING ASSUMES THE THROWN

Chris Fletcher was assistant master distiller under master distiller Jim Arnett for the final six of Arnett's twenty-year tenure at Jack Daniel's. Arnett relied heavily on Fletcher and had immense confidence in the young man. Fletcher, the grandson of legendary Jack Daniel's master distiller Frank Bobo (1968–1988), loved the job and found his footing quickly. He'd already earned the respect of famed whiskey expert Chuck Cowdery, which was not an easy thing to do. Cowdery wrote, "Fletcher is an ideal fit for Jack Daniel's. He has the heritage and authenticity of Jack as his birthright, but also brings a fresh approach to product innovation."

Fletcher had an easy style to him. He was confident, smart, and most of all, he loved whiskey. Even spending a short amount of time with him told you a lot about how things were.

And thus it came to pass in 2020, at the age of 39, Fletcher became the master distiller at Jack Daniel's when Arnett retired. Fletcher was only the 8th person ever to assume the role.

"It's an honor to be named master distiller here at Jack Daniel's and join a line of folks who've made the best whiskey in the world," said Fletcher.

"Over the last 17 years, I've been able to learn and work alongside so many talented whiskey makers and I am very grateful for the mentors I've had; including Jeff Arnett who taught me so much. Our distillery and team here in Lynchburg are the best in the business, and I cannot wait to continue working with them crafting the world's favorite Tennessee whiskey."

Fletcher graduated from Tennessee Technical University in 2003 with a BS in chemistry. He worked for eight years at Brown-Forman as a chemist in research and development.

"Our distillery operates in the most traditional method I've seen," he said. "The possibilities are almost endless, we don't have to rely on outsourcing to create new-to-world offerings."

The changing of the guard was obvious. "Our newest Single Barrel Special Release is a barrel proof rye whiskey – I think that says it all." Fletcher said. That release signals a shock wave through the industry. Jack Daniel's was all-in on the super-premium market and now a new voice is at the helm of the largest whiskey brand in the world. Raise a glass, this is going to be fun.

Acknowledging a Debt: Nathan "Nearest" Green

While visiting with Jeff Arnett and Chris Fletcher, we were told the story of Nearest Green.

In Mr. Jack Daniel's old office, there is a picture of the great founder himself taken with the distillery crew. "What makes the portrait so intriguing is the gentleman sitting immediately to Jack's right, an African-American worker. Given the time period when this photograph was taken—around the 1900s—and the racial divide that permeated the American South, it's intriguing to see an African-American man seated beside the proprietor of a business. Their proximity to one another in this photo underscores the remarkable relationship that is at the heart of how Jack came to make whiskey," states the company. "The man in the photograph, we have reason to believe, is George Green. Along with being Jack's friend, George was also the son of Nathan 'Nearest' Green. And it's Nearest Green, along with the Reverend Dan Call, who taught Jack Daniel about making whiskey at a still owned by the Lutheran minister."

When Jack Daniel was a child in the 1850s, he went to work for Dan Call, a local preacher and grocer. Legend has it that the doting Call taught Daniel how to work a still and make whiskey, but Daniel's real teacher was Nathan "Nearest" (sometimes incorrectly referred to as "Nearis") Green, one of Call's slaves.

Green stayed on with Call even after he had been freed in post-Civil War Tennessee. Allegedly, Call told Daniel, "Uncle Nearest is the best whiskey maker that I know of." He then told Green, "I want [Jack] to become the world's best whiskey distiller—if he wants to be. You help me teach him."

"Uncle Nearest" had at least three sons who eventually worked at the Jack Daniel's Distillery—George Green, Edde Green, and Eli Green all worked there. Four of Green's grandchildren also worked at the distillery—Ott, Charlie, Otis, and Jesse. Seven generations of Green's descendants have worked at the distillery with three members employed by the company today.

This story underscores a very important point. Not just about Jack Daniel's and not just about whiskey. This story shines a spotlight on the incredible contributions African-Americans have made to the distilling industry over the last three centuries.

In *The New York Times*, Clay Risen wrote, "Slavery and whiskey, far from being two separate strands of Southern history, were inextricably entwined. Enslaved men not only made up the bulk of the distilling labor force, but they often played crucial skilled roles in the whiskey-making process."

George Washington was once America's biggest distiller with six slaves that ran the distillery. The rumored inventor of bourbon, Elijah Craig, owned 32 slaves. The Pepper family owned 25 slaves. In fact, a slave is thought to have recorded the first whiskey recipe in America.

Whiskey historian and authority Fred Minnick echoed, "We may never know the full contribution of slaves in American whiskey. But with each passing year, I and other researchers find more about their contributions. Let's hope these men and women get the credit they rightfully deserve."

EVERY DAY WE MAKE IT, WE'LL MAKE IT THE BEST WE CAN

Jack Daniel's Unaged Tennessee Rye Whiskey (80 proof) is an un-aged Tennessee rye whiskey made with a mash bill of at least 70% rye. This is a rich, rich whiskey and easily one of the best un-aged whiskeys made in America. There are big hints of spice right up front that are evened out by hints of vanilla and corn bread. This whiskey is good neat, but with one cube of ice it becomes a

stunner. Big and bold, this white whiskey is made for serious whiskey drinkers and an absolute joy to drink.

Jack Daniel's Tennessee Straight Rye Whiskey (90 proof) has a high-rye mash bill with 70% rye in it. It possesses all the earmarks of a fine rye with nice copper/amber color, caramel and burnt sugar upfront, and a spicy finish. There's also that Jack Daniel's touch of smoothness at the end. This isn't a bracing rye, but if you like the flavor without all that bite, this is a wonderful option.

Jack Daniel's Old No. 7 Tennessee Sour Mash Whiskey (80 proof) is the classic Tennessee whiskey with a mash bill of 80% corn, 12% barley, and 8% rye. Caramel, honey, vanilla, and spice make up this very smooth and sexy dram. It's the world's most popular whiskey for a reason. This stone-col classic is great neat or with ice.

Gentleman Jack Double Mellowed Tennessee Whiskey (80 proof) was a gift from former legendary Brown-Forman master distiller Lincoln Henderson. Gentleman Jack is run through the classic Lincoln County Process before it goes into the barrels and is then run through one more time before being bottled for an extra smooth taste. An immediate hit upon its release, this whiskey has gone on to become a massive success.

JACK DANIEL'S SINGLE BARREL COLLECTION

In 2020, Jack Daniel's repackaged and debuted their Single Barrel Collection. It was acknowledged as the distillery's official foray into the quality whiskey market and was met with much fanfare and approval. First introduced was the Jack Daniel's Single Barrel Select (94 proof) which they pronounced as their "signature single barrel offering" of their classic Tennessee whiskey.

Jack Daniel's Single Barrel Rye (94 proof) was the first new grain bill the distillery had introduced since Prohibition. With a 70% rye, 18% corn, and 18% barley mash bill, this was a big step for the distiller. A smooth deep rye with dark fruit, caramel, and black pepper.

Jack Daniel's Single Barrel, Barrel Proof (125-140 proof) was the first cask strength whiskey introduced by the distiller. Notes of vanilla, caramel, toasted oak. Robust, but not overpowering.

There is also Jack Daniel's Single Barrel 100 Proof (100 proof) Tennessee Whiskey Bottled-in-Bond. Available Duty Free Only. This is the quality Tennessee whiskey only Jack Daniel's could make

JUNCTION 35

In early 2020, Trey and Summer Saylor opened Junction 35. Trey is the master distiller while Summer handles marketing and sales. The young couple founded the new distillery and restaurant in the Smoky Mountains of Sevier, Tennessee. At Junction 35 Spirits, they hope to create unique spirits and delicious signature dishes.

"We are very excited for what's in store for Junction 35. Distilleries are a popular business in our area and we hope to bring a new approach to the industry with our project," says Trey, an as effusive and bubbling a distiller as I have ever met. He loves what he is doing. The Saylors are good people.

The large spacious bar, retail location, and restaurant are dominated by the brand's railroad theme. Their beautiful design pays homage to the hard-working men of the railroad as well as some of the most famous train stations in America, like Grand Central Terminal.

Make no mistake, you can come for a great meal, but there are plenty of very good spirits to stay for and all are small batch and hand-crafted.

Junction 35 Moonshine Original (100 proof), their "white dog whiskey," hits with the base notes of vanilla and some heat that has hints of cinnamon. It is very smooth, and very good. Their moonshine comes in a number of other flavors including

HANDCRAFTED SMALL BATCH

JUNCTION
35
SPIRITS

Junction 35
Straight Bourbon
Whiskey

35

45% ALC./VOL. 90 PROOF 750 ML

Peach, Apple Pie, Blackberry, Strawberry, Margarita, and Sweet Tea, and are all available at 70 proof.

Junction 35 Rum (80 proof) is a small batch Puerto Rican-style rum with hints of citrus, vanilla, and sugar cream.

Junction 35 Gin (80 proof) is a lovely, light-styled floral gin, with notes of orange peels and botanicals. Definitely a quality craft gin, but not overpowering. Flavorful. Junction 35 Gin Barrel-Aged (80 proof) is barrel rested in used charred oak barrels for six months. Not overpowering on the oak, this whiskey has a nice flavor profile that's perfect for cocktails.

Junction 35 Vodka (80 proof) is a non-GMO corn, wheat, and barley product. The spirit is distilled five times and then filtered twelve times. This all-grain spirit is one of their best sellers. Their Junction 35 Vodka Jalapeno (80 proof) is a smooth, well-balanced vodka, perfect for cocktails and with just a touch of flavor and kick at the end. Their Junction 35 Citrus Vodka (80 proof) offers lovely hints of lemon, lime, and orange.

Junction 35 makes a series of whiskeys. Their most popular is the Junction 35 Honey Flavored Whiskey (70 proof) which is a nice whiskey with a slightly sweet tint. Other flavors include Cinnamon Whiskey and Caramel Apple Whiskey.

Junction 35 Straight Bourbon Whiskey (90 proof) is a wheated whiskey that is aged for more than 2 years in American oak. It's a dark gold/copper color with hints of cereal, vanilla, and white pepper on the end. It has a lovely smooth and slightly sweet lingering finish.

Junction 35 Straight Rye Whiskey (90 proof) is barrel-aged 3 years. It has notes of dark fruit, a hint of cereal, and a gingersnap finish.

Junction 35 is solid stuff that guarantees a great time.

KING'S FAMILY DISTILLERY

Justin and Cara King are the owners of King's Family Distillery in the foothills of the Great Smoky Mountains. They founded the distillery in 2018. Though Justin started in the whiskey business in less-than-legal ways, he eventually became a master distiller at Ole Smokey Moonshine Distillery. He traveled extensively as the face of the brand, propelling the moonshine into all 50 states (and eventually to 60 countries).

Cara began her career in the whiskey industry in 2008, starting out in the grain business. Her family's grain farm, including rye, has been a part of the whiskey industry for more than 60 years. She worked in Louisville, Kentucky, for almost a decade. Cara knows the lands and the families that lovingly produce each and every barrel of grain.

These are two industry professionals who know what they are doing. They know grain and they know distillation. It's a great pairing for people who like whiskey.

The pair make the super smooth King's Family Vodka (80 proof) that is six times distilled corn-based vodka. They also produce King's Family Ginger Vodka (80 proof) which is super clean, with a lively gingersnap finish.

King's Family American Blended Whiskey (80 proof) is a blend of bourbon and light whiskey, each aged at least two years. This is a light, sweet whiskey with notes of honey, caramel, and vanilla. It's balanced with spice, pear, and oak. This is a lovely light whiskey that goes down super smooth and is a little too easy to drink.

King Family Bourbon Kentucky Straight Whiskey (87 proof) is a 99% corn bourbon, aged in new bourbon barrels about 4 years. They only bottle one barrel at a time which makes it a true small-batch whiskey. In Justin's point of view, it's a sweet and smooth whiskey that appeals to the folks who come

to this part of the country. Notes of corn, vanilla, fig, and date all come through. It's a fantastic and unique sipping whiskey, as well as the flagship and the workhorse of the King's Family line.

King's Family Wheated Bourbon (100 proof) is a wheat-forward mash bill. It's a sourced whiskey, about 4 to 5 years old with a lot of complexity to it. This lovely soft whiskey offers notes of chocolate, toffee, and apple on the nose. On the palate there's toffee, orange, and spice.

The King's Family Rye (90 proof) mash bill is 51% rye, 45% corn, and 4% malted barley. It's a super smooth rye with a soft beginning and hints of sweet nuttiness, cherry, and orange zest. This is Cara's favorite, especially when you consider her family's ties to the grain.

King's Family Distillery is a lovely place that's putting out quality whiskey. With a very talented husband and wife team, you'll want to be a part of this family.

KNOX WHISKEY WORKS

By Emily West

Inside Knoxville's first distillery since Prohibition, Miranda White is leading the charge to create corn whiskey and bourbon.

Nestled in an older part of town inside a 100-year-old warehouse, Knox Whiskey Works opened its doors back in 2015. Crafting small-batch liquor, the group creates whiskey, gin, vodka, and a coffee liqueur. Out of that lineup, it offers nine different products.

"We knew that it would be an interesting business undertaking," she said, noting their first 300-gallon still came from a Craigslist purchase. "So far it's been fantastic. We have the support of the community for sure."

White first started making larger batches of whiskey in larger barrels, ones that were not quite ready to pull for bottling. Today, she makes much smaller batches in -5 to -10 gallon increments which ages faster for consumption. It takes 12 hours for their product to go through distillation and it ultimately goes through three distillations before it's even inside a barrel.

Farm to bottle, Knox Whiskey Works products are made from ingredients sourced about 30 miles away. Its corn comes from an heirloom variety in Jefferson County.

"The farmer grows this type of corn just for us," White said. "The mantra we are trying to keep here is locally sourced and organic if we can get it. We use a pure corn mash bill. The fact is that it's a true mash and we went the extra miles to make it that way."

WHISKEYS TO TRY:

Old City Heirloom Corn Whiskey—bottled at 43.25% ABV, 86.5 proof by volume

Jackson Ave Gin—bottled at 45.5% ABV, 91 proof by volume

Tennessee Valley Vodka—bottled at 43.25% ABV, 86.5 proof by volume

Cold City Old Brew Coffee Liqueur—bottled at 20% to 25% ABV, 40 to 50 proof by volume

Marble City Pink Gin—bottled at 43.25% ABV, 86.5 proof by volume

Fleur de Vie Liqueur—bottled at 20% to 25% ABV, 40 to 50 proof by volume

Tennessee Tailgate Orange Flavored Vodka—bottled at 33% to 36% ABV, 66 to 72 proof by volume

Silver Release Bourbon—bottled at 45% ABV, 90 proof by volume

Deals Gap Dragontail Habanero Flavored Whiskey—bottled at 35% ABV, 70 proof by volume

Rye 95 Whiskey Distiller's Select - Limited Reserve Single Barrel Rye 95% Rye mash bill, aged in American Oak bottled at 47.5% ABV, 95 proof by volume

LEATHERWOOD DISTILLERY

Leatherwood Distillery is a small operation in Pleasant View, Tennessee. It's owned and run by retired Master Sargent Andrew Lang, a veteran with 24 years of active-duty service in the United States Army; 16 of which came in the 5th Special Forces Group (Airborne). Leatherwood Distillery is Lang's spirited tribute to the 5th Special Forces Group, nicknamed "THE LEGION."

Lang's partners include Ashland City's Johnny Lindahl who acts as the business and marketing advisor, as well as Chicagoans Mike Collins and Bill Havle. During Lang's tour of Afghanistan in 2011 he met Masoud Rezai, who was working as a local interpreter for the US Armed Forces. They formed a fast friendship and reunited again during Lang's final tour of duty in 2014. Rezai "was given the opportunity to come to the United States with a special immigration visa, due to his work with the U.S. government. Once here, he received his green card," wrote Amy K. Nixon of The *Tennessean*. Rezai, who works at the distillery full time also owns a percentage of the business. Today, the two work hand-in-hand making incredible 'shine.

The distillery opened in 2017. Lang makes an old-fashioned sugar moonshine which is all sugar with no grain to add flavor. Each label at Leatherwood features a different story from Lang's career in the military. The classic 'shine, Leatherwood Midnight Extraction (80 proof), is a classic white sugar 'shine. Other flavors in the line include Georgia Peach, Apple Pie, Mango Tango, and R&R Red. Lang is also working on a classic Tennessee straight whiskey.

Leatherwood Snake Eater Bourbon Whiskey (85 proof), a smooth, small batch bourbon has grain, oak, dried fruit, vanilla, caramel, and allspice on the nose. On the palate, fruity grains and savory spice come through.

Leatherwood Check Point Rye Whiskey (80 proof) has notes of freshly baked rye bread, vanilla, and caramel on the nose. Sweet and spicy grains on the palate with honey, vanilla and a hint of dried fruit. Nice touch of spice and black pepper at the finish.

Leiper's Fork Distillery

"Leiper's Fork Distillery is recapturing the lost art of small batch production, using local ingredients and pouring our heart and soul into every drop we produce to bring a premium Tennessee spirit from grain to glass," says Leiper's Fork Distillery owner and master distiller, Lee Kennedy.

Upon meeting Lee and his wife, Lynlee Kennedy, it's very clear very quickly that the two intend to make quality whiskeys. Lee, who grew up in Tennessee said, "Everyone knew who made the best moonshine and where to quietly get it. It was not a mass-marketed fad, but just a part of everyday life. Most of our fathers drank bourbon, not because it was trendy, but because they wouldn't contemplate drinking anything else."

At Leiper's Fork Lee and Lynlee are focused on two things: Tennessee whiskey and bourbon. They use locally grown grain, limestone-filtered water, and classic, traditional techniques when making their small-batch whiskeys. They also age them in traditional, 53-gallon charred white oak barrels for five to seven years.

The distillery's tasting room is in a 200-year-old cabin that once served as a refurbished dogtrot. Their stillhouse is a 5,000-square-foot timber-frame building with a 500-gallon swan neck whiskey still and old-fashioned cypress fermentation tanks.

Leiper's Fork lies along the historic Natchez Trace, a forest trail that runs from Natchez, Mississippi, to Nashville,

Tennessee, (approximately 440 miles) and connects the Cumberland, Tennessee, and Mississippi Rivers. Meriwether Lewis, of the Lewis and Clark Expedition, died while traveling along the Trace.

Lee and Lynlee established their distillery on 30 acres and started distilling in April 2016. All the grains they use are either sourced locally from the county or within the state. They believe that whiskey has terroir and based on what they've produced, it's hard to argue with them.

Matt "Pops" Mayo is hailed as one of the best front of house men in Tennessee whiskey.

Experienced master blender Ashley Barnes (formerly of Four Roses and Buffalo Trace) was brought in to help with the blending of their burgeoning warehouse in order to create a consistent blend for the distillery's bottlings. Her deft hand is exactly what this small artisanal house needed and the spirits are high-quality.

Old Natchez Trace Tennessee White Whiskey (90 proof) is made from a classic bourbon mash bill of 70% corn, 22% rye, and 8% malted barley. This is easily one of the best white whiskeys produced in the region with corn, honeysuckle, and other sweetness upfront, as well as a hint of butter and popcorn.

Old Natchez Trace Rye White Whiskey (90 proof) is made from the same mash bill and is similarly impressive. It has notes of white pepper, spice, a hint of nuttiness, a touch of anise, and a slap of gingersnap. Add a touch of water and a hint of petrol enters the picture as the other flavors intensify. It's super smooth and incredibly exciting.

Colonel Hunter's Select Barrel Tennessee Bourbon Whiskey (95 proof) is a 9-year-old bourbon bottled from 20 barrels and made from a sourced bourbon in Tennessee. The mash bill is 72% corn, 20% rye, and 8% malted barley. This lovely, light, and complex dram features buttery caramel, brown sugar, and a chewy nuttiness that gives way to a bit of ginger.

Colonel Hunter's Select Barrel Tennessee Bourbon Whiskey (100 proof) has a mash bill of 84% corn, 8% rye, and 8% malted barley. This bourbon is a 9 years, 5 months, and 11 days old. It has lovely complexity and balance, with lush vanilla and caramel notes and a soft finish.

Colonel Hunter's Single Barrel Tennessee Bourbon (95 proof) has the same mash bill as the other two Colonel Hunter whiskeys, but occasionally the distillery chooses special barrels for bottling.

Leiper's Fork Straight Rye Whiskey (95 proof) is also available (green and gold labels). The first barrels of rye were made using seven different grain bills from a Baltimore/Maryland-styled rye (55% rye) to more of a Pennsylvania high-rye (85% rye). This is a blend of the original 13 barrels of rye the distillery made.

Leiper's Fork also releases limited single barrel, cask strength bottlings with no chill filtration. The whiskey is robust, full bodied, and flavorful.

Leiper's Fork Tennessee Whiskey (100 proof) is 70% corn, 15% rye, and 15% malted barley. It's a small-batch bottling that was aged for four years in new American oak charrred barrels.

Leiper's Fork has fulfilled its promises, passing the eye test, the nose test, and the taste test.

SHELBY'S RESERVE

WHISKEY

MASH BILL	BATCH	
64 % CORN		
22 % WHEAT	BOTTLE	
12 % BARLEY		
48% ALC/VOL	96 PROOF	

AGED AT LEAST 2 YEARS

750ML

SHELBY'S RES

STRAIGHT

BOURE

WH

MASH BILL	BATCH	
60 % CORN		
30 % WHEAT	BOTTLE	
10 % BARLEY		
45% ALC/VOL	90 P	

AGED AT LEAST 2 YEARS

750ML

Lost State Distilling

Joe Bianchi and his son Nick, founded Lost State Distilling in July 2019. In 2020, the distillery was named Best New Craft Distillery by a panel of experts in *USA Today*.

"Especially being in small town," said Joe. "It goes to show we have a little bit of people everywhere voting for us, so it's very good. Especially since we beat out distilleries in Denver, California, so being in Bristol, that's a big thing."

The State of Franklin was an unrecognized and autonomous territory in eastern Tennessee from approximately 1784 to 1788. The distillery is named for that lost state. The Bianchis bought the abandoned Bristol Supply and Equipment Co. building, across from the Bristol Train Station, for $375,000 in April 2018.

Their goal was not to compete with other moonshiners in that region (of which there are many), the goal was to make a 4-year-old Tennessee whiskey using local corn. "There's a lot of spirits other distilleries have not heavily touched," Nick said. "We hope to get in and experiment."

Nolichucky Jack Silver Rum (80 proof) is a crystal-clear rum with notes of vanilla and light hints of butterscotch. The rum is very smooth and made with panela, an unrefined whole cane sugar.

Franklin Four is the largest label thus far and their Franklin Four Single Barrel Straight Bourbon Whiskey is a hand-selected barrel with a limited release of no more than 350 bottles.

Franklin Four Whiskey is a blend of two wheated bourbons. It's smooth with big caramel on the nose. In very small limited releases, there's the Franklin Four Cask Strength Single Barrel Bourbon and the flavored Franklin Four Cinnamon and Maple (60 proof).

There are two Shelby's Reserve whiskeys. Shelby's Reserve Whiskey (101 proof) is a wheated whiskey with a mash bill of 64% corn, 22% wheat, and 12% barley. The whiskey is aged at least 2 years in new American oak charred barrels.

There's also the Shelby's Reserve Straight Bourbon Whiskey (90 proof), a wheated-bourbon with a mash bill of 60% corn, 30% wheat, and 10% barley. This whiskey was aged at least two years in new American oak charred barrels.

All in all, Lost State Distillery shows barrels of promise.

Nashville Craft Distillery

NASHVILLE CRAFT DISTILLERS
Bruce Boeko began building Nashville Craft Distillery in the Westwood-Houston (WeHo) section of Nashville in October 2014. His first distillations occurred in March 2016 and the distillery opened two months later. There are currently two brands being sold by the distillery—Nashville Craft and Fugitives.

The numerous spirits Nashville Craft develops are all incredible concoctions created by Bruce himself. Fugitives is a co-

branded, cooperative label with an outside brand team. The tasting room and distillery are urban chic and industrial, reminiscent of a mad scientist's laboratory. All that comes together to assure visitors that they are about to be rewarded with great whiskey and exciting innovations. Boeko is one of the most passionate and talented people in Tennessee whiskey and he's someone to watch in the future.

BRUCE BOEKO
SCIENTIST AND
DISTILLING GEEK

Here's why I liked Nashville Craft Distillery's owner and master distiller Bruce Boeko: Right off the bat, he is so passionate about distilling that when the Tennessee Whiskey Trail was initially opened, he was the first person to visit every distillery on the trail. I love that kind of whiskey geek!

Boeko is big on science as he was previously a DNA laboratory director. He insists on making his craft spirits using almost solely local and regional ingredients and resources. A homebrewer and biology major in college, Boeko was inspired by Louis Pasteur to become a research scientist and eventually found work at a DNA testing lab in North Carolina. He started his own lab in Nashville in 1996.

Boeko's love of craft beverage making got the better of him and in 2013 he attended Moonshine University where he was hooked. He then took more in-depth classes at Kothe Distilling Technologies in Chicago and decided distilling was for him.

Boeko embraces both tradition and the new age, forward-thinking outlook of the craft distilling movement. In essence, he's a mix of Darek Bell of Corsair and Woodford Reserve's Chris Morris. He makes a classic bourbon-styled mash bill for his Tennessee whiskey, but the grains are local. He makes a rum, but it's with locally-grown, Mennonite sorghum. Despite these innovations, Boeko follows the old-line processes and traditions by rote. He's a distiller's distiller and he's got the passion of a street corner preacher, plus all the talent and discipline of a portrait artist.

Chris Weber, Hemingway's Bar and Hideway

Nashville Craft Distillers are Boeko's singular creations. Nashville Craft Distillers Naked Biscuit (90 proof) is a rum made with sorghum. The first batches were made using 100% pure sorghum syrup from Muddy Pond Sorghum Mill, located in the Tennessee hills midway between Nashville and Knoxville. According to the distillery, "Sweet sorghum cane has been grown in Tennessee for generations. Unlike sugar cane, it is well adapted to our state's climate." Sorghum has been a traditional substitute for sugar in tough economies throughout history and continues to be an ingredient in many locally baked goods. It's also a wonderful rum for cocktails.

There's also Golden Biscuit Sorghum Spirits (90 proof) which is bourbon barrel-aged.

Nashville Craft Spirits Crane City Gin (80 proof) is a fabulous, aromatic wheat and malted barley gin mixed with some lovely botanicals. The name is a nod to the city's recent building boom. This is a wonderful gin with notes of wintergreen, pepper, and citrus.

Nashville Craft Traditional Bourbon Whisk(E)Y (93 proof) is a handmade spirit mashed, distilled, aged and bottled at 514 Hagan Street. It's made from a mash bill of 80% corn, 10% rye, and 10% malted barley. The first batch was bottled on December 7, 2019. The whiskey has a nose of caramel, cherry, and vanilla. Sweet dark fruit comes across the palate with hint of oak and spice.

Nashville Craft Original Bourbon Whisk(E)Y (93 proof) is a wheated bourbon made from a mash bill 60% corn, 30% wheat, and 10% barley. This is a made-from-scratch whiskey launched on May 11, 2019. The whiskey has a nose of caramel, vanilla, and. Fruit is followed by oak on the palate, finishing with warm spice.

FUGITIVES

Fugitives Tennessee Artisan Spirits is a brand owned by Jim Massey and Darren Briggs that celebrates Tennessee's local agricultural traditions, and craftsmanship. The idea is to make craft spirits in small batches, especially "artisan whiskey and spirit distillations featuring locally raised organic and heirloom grains. Farmed, fermented, distilled, and bottled locally, Fugitives Spirits offers a True Taste of Tennessee Terroir," according to the company. Each batch is copper pot–distilled at Nashville Craft Distillery.

Fugitive Spirits has grown since its beginning. Though they can be found in a half dozen states, including New York, it remains a quality whiskey which means it's usually found in the stores with better whiskey collections. Nashville Craft Distilleries' fan base of writers and industry influencers continues to grow. According to a local distributor, the New York connection grew out of a food and spirits writer who was effusive in his praise.

Massey especially wants to be known as a whiskey man, but some of Fugitive's best customers prevailed upon him to make vodka. One of the highly-anticipated new releases of 2021 was the Briggs & Massey Vodka (80 proof) made from non-GMO corn. It's glutenfree, crystal clean, and super smooth with real flavor. The vodka bears his and his partner's names.

Corn Breeds and Whiskey Terroir

Jim Massey stresses that they are forced to do limited releases for the next few years because it's not always easy to find a farmer who will grow what he wants. The farming practices have to be sustainable, nearly organic, and the farmers need to raise the heirloom corn variety he prefers, which may not be as productive as more popular corns that are being grown.

Massey is clear: he doesn't just want non-GMO corn, he wants specific breeds. Most importantly, the corn must be from Tennessee, according to Fugitives Spirits. Even further, Massey is big on transparency about his corn and grains, such as growing traits and yields of Tennessee Red Cob versus Hickory Cane.

"Here in Tennessee, we have arguably the best-known agricultural product in the whole world—Tennessee whiskey," he said. "Yet until recently, it hasn't been made with just Tennessee grain in decades. I'm glad to be a part of the first big step in revitalizing Tennessee agriculture in our small way." Fugitives Spirits is not the only small, craft distillery that uses local corn. There are a handful of artisan crafters who insist on it. He's a little more vocal about it, though.

Because Tennessee whiskey has to undergo the Lincoln County Process by law, the growth of the category has been slow, but steady. "The effect of these constraints has kept 'paper tiger' brands from hijacking and repackaging hundreds of variation brands on industrial bourbon and calling it 'Tennessee Whiskey'," said Massey. "While the marketplace is flooded with repackaged bourbon brands all carrying the same juice, Tennessee whiskey has held steadfast and true. There are only a handful on the market, so we've ended up being the true rare find."

Massey is quick to tell you that he knows and works with his farmers. He points to Alfred and Carney Farris (they grow rye and the heirloom Jubilee corn) whom he has contracts with at their Windy Acres organic farm in Orlinda (about a half-hour from Nashville). His Hickory Cane corn comes from Jennifer and Frank Nicely's farm in Strawberry Plains, near Knoxville.

"In terms of flavor, the grain is affected by the soil it's grown in, arguably as much as by the type and variety. For instance, Hickory Cane grows well in rockier soil and has more intense flavor when it struggles a bit. When you do a double pot distillation like we do, we are able to bring out all the great nuances of that corn," he said. "What we put in the barrel has a more robust grain profile from the start and that begins with the dirt."

Massey believes in whiskey terroir. It is a notion in the industry that is picking up steam. He's passionate about it.

"I pay my farmers a living wage to grow specialty grains and I like to say the best way to preserve green space is to make farming profitable," said Massey.

Finding farmers who would cooperate with the company's demands were hard to find, but slowly that is changing. "Farmers ask me, 'I heard you're paying for corn.' We're building this path a little at a time," Massey said.

Currently, Fugitives is laying down 100 to 200 barrels a year. Each bottle of Fugitives is made only with local corn. In the beginning, it limited what they could produce, but now things are starting to move forward. Currently, it's the grain that's been slowing

them down. Their aim is 1,000 barrels a year, but the goal is not to be the biggest, most well distributed Tennessee whiskey, says Massey, it's to turn Fugitives into the best Tennessee whiskey, period. That starts with the corn and where it's grown. Grandgousier will always be a small batch, true Tennessee whiskey.

Fugitives Grandgousier Tennessee Whiskey (96 proof) is small batch whiskey that is made with local, sustainably grown heirloom "Hickory Cane" corn. The mash bill is 89% corn and 11% malted barley and also takes four days to ferment. This whiskey, which is subjected to the Lincoln County Process, is an exceptional product that you should absolutely seek out. The Grandgousier is a lovely dram that begins with caramel and toffee, and has hints of rich vanilla cake, hot pancakes, syrup, black pepper, and exotic spices.

Fugitives also offers Grandgousier Tennessee Whiskey Single Barrel (94 proof) made with sustainably raised Tennessee heirloom corn and the finest Irish malted barley. This whiskey is a blend of two bourbon mash bills distilled in Tennessee, celebrating the local land, grain, and spirit. This small-batch whiskey is a limited release, providing hints of fig and chocolate with a big finish of warm sweet caramel.

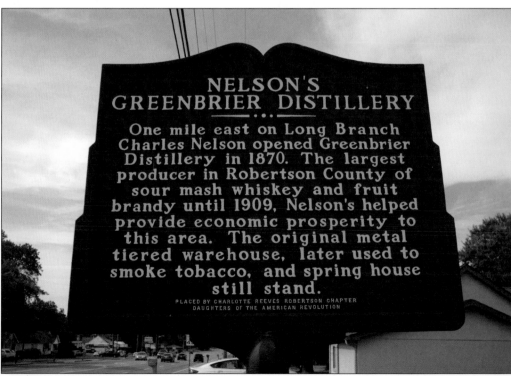

NELSON'S
GREENBRIER DISTILLERY

One mile east on Long Branch
Charles Nelson opened Greenbrier
Distillery in 1870. The largest
producer in Robertson County of
sour mash whiskey and fruit
brandy until 1909, Nelson's helped
provide economic prosperity to
this area. The original metal
tiered warehouse, later used to
smoke tobacco, and spring house
still stand.

PLACED BY CHARLOTTE REEVES ROBERTSON CHAPTER
DAUGHTERS OF THE AMERICAN REVOLUTION

Nelson's Green Brier Distillery

Nelson's Green Brier Distillery is located in downtown Nashville, in an old, turn-of-the-century industrial building. The second you enter the place, you know you are in a craft distillery that is catching on. It has the look of the already arrived—because it has!

Nelson's line of Belle Meade bourbons is available nationally today, thanks to the help of Constellation Brands. The conglomerate bought a small share in the distillery back in 2016, and in 2019, they bought a majority share. That is a success story for a young, craft distillery.

The two bothers who own and run this distillery, Andrew and Charles Nelson, are hell-bent on becoming the next big brand of Tennessee whiskey. Based on the quality of spirits, the branding, and the investment behind them, Nelson's Green Brier Distillery seems like they are poised to take this next step.

It's amazing that Nelson's Green Brier has been resurrected. One of the earliest distilleries in the state, contemporaries of Jack Daniel's and George A. Dickel, it suffered one of the period's most horrific afflictions: Prohibition. Fortunately, its resuscitation by the Nelson brothers has brought back a huge chunk of Tennessee whiskey's history and heritage, as well as a whole new flock of fans. This is a serious whiskey company and they intend to return the brand to national prominence.

The brothers are both happy with codification of Tennessee whiskey and believe in it as a fledgling whiskey category. They believe in protecting the integrity of what Tennessee whiskey means and in the unique qualities the Lincoln County Process lends to their whiskey. Charles even testified during the statewide hearings on the subject.

HISTORY SET SAIL:
CHARLES NELSON AND HIS GREEN BRIER DISTILLERY

According to the distillery, "Charles Nelson was born July 4, 1835 in Hagenow, a small town in the Mecklenburg-Schwerin state of northern Germany. He was the eldest of six children whose father, John Philip Nelson, owned a soap and candle factory. When Charles was 15, his father decided he wanted to move his family to America for a better life. He sold his soap and candle factory, converted all of the family's earthly possessions to gold, and had special clothing made to hold all of that gold on his person during the journey. In late October of 1850, he gathered his family and boarded the Helena Sloman to set sail for America. On November 19 of that year, intense storms and gale force winds sent many of the nearly 180 passengers overboard. John Philip Nelson was one of those unfortunate souls and, weighed down by the family fortune, he sank directly to the bottom of the Atlantic Ocean. Luckily, the rest of the family arrived safely in New York, but with only the clothes on their backs and a 15 year-old Charles found himself man of the house."

In need of money, Charles and his brother began making soap and candles. After saving enough, the Nelsons moved to Cincinnati, Ohio, where a 17-year-old Charles opened a butcher shop. He was then introduced to spirits and learned how to distill and sell his concoctions. Just before the start of the Civil War, Charles moved to Nashville and opened a grocery store. He instantly became known for three things: coffee, meat, and whiskey. The whiskey side of his business quickly exploded.

Charles gave up on the store business and bought the distillery in Greenbrier that made his whiskey. He received a "patent for improved distillation and expanded the production capacity in order to keep up with demand."

By 1885, Charles was producing and selling 380,000 gallons of Nelson's Green Brier Tennessee Whiskey in markets ranging from Florida to California to France, making the brand No. 1 in Tennessee at that time. The company insists it was Charles who was among the first to sell his whiskey by the bottle rather than the jug. In the early days, the distillery was commonly known as "Old Number Five," since it was registered as distillery number five and was located in the fifth tax district.

Charles Nelson died on December 13, 1891. His wife Louisa ran the business until 1909, and was the only woman to run a distillery for a number of years. In 1908, Prohibition reared its ugly head in Tennessee and forced Louisa to close the distillery's doors which would not open again for another 108 years. The new distillery is located elsewhere, but the property is now listed on the National Register of Historic Places and the ruins of the grain house and a barrel warehouse still stand.

LOUISA NELSON: WHISKEY PIONEER

Louisa Nelson's story had all but disappeared, until her great-great-grandsons revived her legacy. Louisa was Charles Nelson's second wife (the first passed away at a young age). He married Louisa Rohlfing on March 4, 1863. The two lived in Cincinnati briefly and then moved to Nashville. It is said that "All that cultivated taste could suggest or wealth provide were to be found in this beautiful home. In all family matters he would, with knightly grace, defer to his beloved wife whose word to him was law. Seldom do we find a happier more perfect home than this one," the *Daily American* newspaper reported of the Nelsons years later. "Mr. Nelson, accompanied by his wife and children, has several times visited Europe, and on each occasion, he paid his native town a visit."

After Charles died in 1891, Louisa ran Nelson's Green Brier Distillery, the largest in Tennessee at that time, from 1892 to 1909. "Miss Louisa," as she was known on the distillery campus, is the first woman to run a large distillery of that kind and more than held her own against the biggest names in the business.

"In her honor, the Nelson brothers have actually named the beautiful copper still in their Clinton Street facility 'Miss Louisa.' Every barrel that comes off that still (about one per day) is produced in her memory," wrote Chris Chamberlain in *Nashville Scene*. "Now the Nelsons have decided to go even further spreading Louisa Nelson's story and recognizing her role in the business and in the entire industry. They have inaugurated the first annual Louisa Nelson Awards, an 'accolade honoring women of achievement, inspiration and vision in Nashville who show exemplary successes in their field and leadership in the community.'"

KINDRED SPIRITS
THE NELSON BROTHERS

William Nelson invited his sons Andy and Charlie to Greenbrier, Tennessee, on a summer day in 2006. The trio met at a butcher shop and the boys began peppering their father with questions about the old Nelson distillery they had heard of. The butcher, Chuck, excitedly told his visitors, "Look across the street over there. Your granddaddy built that warehouse. This street is Distillery Road, you know, and that spring, it's never stopped running. It's as pure as pure can be."

Bill, Andy, and Charlie eagerly explored the ruins and met with the Greenbrier Historical Society whose curator showed them two original bottles of Nelson's Green Brier Tennessee Whiskey.

Charlie and Andy stared at the perfectly preserved bottles and looked at each other: "This is our destiny."

The brothers did three years of painstaking research and planning before reforming the old company.

Both brothers graduated from Loyola Marymount University with degrees in the humanities. They're also both history buffs which proved useful as they researched, sought capital, and crafted brands from Charles Nelson's original recipes. They went through state archives, old newspapers, Robertson County records, and Greenbrier Historical Society materials. One of the brothers even wrote his senior college thesis on Prohibition saloons and distillers.

"Stuff pops up still," according to the brothers. "People reach out all the time. A woman from Spokane, Washington, called us with stuff she found at an old estate sale." Today, Andy is in charge of the distilling and Charles is the sales and marketing guru.

BELLE MEADE BOURBON

Belle Meade Bourbon is loosely named after the famous Belle Meade Plantation, located in Belle Meade, Tennessee. The house was built in the 1820s and remodeled in 1853 into the estate that stands today. In 1953, the state purchased the mansion and its 30 acres and it is now operated by the Association for the Preservation of Tennessee Antiquities.

Among other things, Belle Meade produced many successful racehorses and studs, including Bonnie Scotland, Enquirer, and Iroquois.

Belle Meade Bourbon was one of the signature lines of the old Nelson Green Brier Distillery. Nelson had been engaged to create a line of bourbons named after the old, famous plantation and stud farm by Sperry, Wade & Company in 1879. They continued to sell the whiskey until the distillery closed in 1909.

One of the newest vintages of this bourbon is the Belle Meade Bourbon Sour Mash Straight Whiskey (90.4 proof). This is made from sourced whiskey that has been aged six to eight years and blended with high-rye bourbons (30% rye). Referred to as the "classic," this is a non-chill filtered, small-batch bourbon bottled from four-barrel batches. The whiskey is floral with notes of caramel and lots of spice, pepper, brown sugar, and ginger.

Belle Meade Single Barrel Cask Strength Bourbon (109.3 proof) is a bottling of 9-year-old, high-rye bourbon at barrel strength. The original fill date is handwritten on each bottle and the bottles are numbered. There are three barrel-finished expressions: Sherry Cask Finished, Cognac Cask Finished, and Madeira Cask Finished. The Belle Meade Sherry Cask and the Belle Mead Madeira Cask were among my absolute favorites, providing the softer, more complex bourbon I prefer.

Nelson's Green Brier Tennessee White Whiskey (91 proof) is made in the "Miss Louisa" copper pot still with a mash bill of 70% corn, 16% wheat, and 14% barley. The distiller's beer ferments for four days and is then run through a charcoal mellowing stage in line with the Lincoln County Process. This is a lovely white whiskey with flavors of corn bread, buttered popcorn, and lots of vanilla.

Nelson's Green Brier Tennessee Sour Mash Whiskey (91 proof) originally released a mash bill of 70% corn, 16% wheat, and 14% malted barley when they poured their first experimental Nelson's 108 whiskey. Today,

they remain more secretive about it and one can only assume the recipe is not far from that mark. They were, and remain, adamant that they were not following the wheat trend, but were attempting to stay true to the original family recipe. Aged in new American oak charred barrels, the whiskey is 3 years old in the bottle, and will most likely finalize at 4 years of age by 2022. This is one of the best Tennessee whiskeys out there and the 2019 bottling has been nothing short of fantastic. The outstanding whiskey has a big nose of caramel, ripe apples, cereal, and dried fruits, along with a creamy honey and vanilla finish.

Tennessee Whiskey is Going National!

Nelson's Green Brier has grown tremendously. By June 2020, they were in nearly a dozen states and by 2025 it's safe to say that their goal is to distribute their whiskey across 48 contiguous states. Their bottles were front and center in the burgeoning Tennessee whiskey category throughout Tennessee, Kentucky, and a number of other states. Their Belle Meade bourbons are already nationally distributed and growing in popularity as well.

I asked Andy Nelson if Nelson's Green Brier had any plans to add different finishes to their Tennessee Sour Mash. He replied, "We definitely want to do more interesting stuff, but at the same time we don't have any timeline for that. Building this brand the way we want to do it, we're trying to focus on what we need to do. And that's sticking with just Tennessee whiskey for now." Andy adds that he'd love to play with finishes, but that timeline has not been established yet.

What's happening at the Nelson's Green Brier Distillery is impressive. It is on schedule to experience double digit growth each year for the next few years and they are easily the fastest growing whiskey in the category.

That kind of growth has impacted the distillery in terms of how much grain the distillery is taking in, even compared to a couple of years ago. "The grain has gone particularly quite smooth fortunately. You get the right farmers, who you can work with, and they're the ones who make it easy for us."

Andy points out that the biggest issue is the difficulty maintaining their signature flavor profiles as demand evolves and increases. "It's the matter of the constant sort of inventory Tetris, so to speak, where you're looking and making sure you're getting a certain amount because you want to make sure your blend profile remains consistent in the bottle as the aged inventory continues to evolve and get older."

One of the benefits of aging stock is the amount of time the whiskey stays in the barrel.

How does that affect the age of their Tennessee whiskey? Andy explains, "The first stuff we ever put in a bottle was two-year old and five-year old whiskey." By 2021, he points out, "The youngest stuff will be three years old," and by 2022 "it will be nothing before four-years old."

That's the inventory Tetris he refers to. "There's so many moving pieces."

The other problem is warehouse space. They've been renting warehouse space for a while now. Tennessee whiskey has to be aged in Tennessee, but the bourbons are scattered where they can rent space.

As for Belle Mead, the demands are huge. As Nelson's Green Brier Tennessee Whiskey and Belle Mead Bourbon grow, the lines will remain focused. The numerous fancy (and delicious) finishes available in the Belle Mead line will no longer be available nationally. They will only be available in their gift shop and the emphasis will remain on the core products, i.e., the classic and the reserve. In 2020, Bell Mead released a Single Barrel and a Mourvèdre Cask and both were only available within their tasting room. Andy excitedly mentioned that they have a good-sized number of exceptional finishes coming up in the future and he was emphatic that they were not stopping their experimentation anytime soon.

Currently, it seems like there's no stopping Nelson's Green Brier—and that's great for Tennessee whiskey lovers.

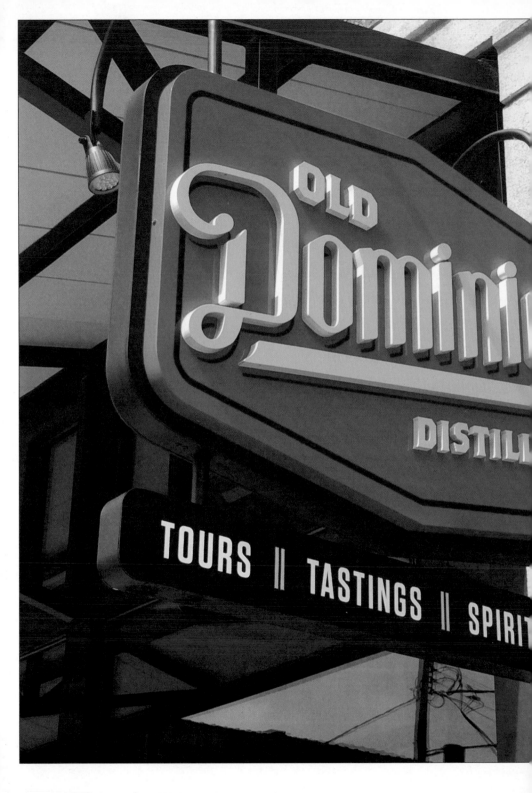

Old Dominick Distillery

Domenico Canale, an immigrant from San Pietro di Reveneto, Italy, established himself in Memphis in 1860, at the end of that town's first big boom. By the time Canale arrived, the town had experienced 1,200% growth and immigrants were responsible for more than one-third of the population.

By the mid-1860s, Canale was operating his own fruit cart and eventually opened his own store. Despite the war, Domenico's business thrived and as Memphis exploded after the war, Canale & Bros.—a prosperous wholesaler, confectioner, and whiskey purveyor—opened in 1866.

Old Dominick bourbon appeared and the business continued to thrive until 1909 when Tennessee's own prohibition law shuttered all whiskey operations.

Almost 100 years and five generations later, D. Canale's extant family spent $10 million and three years building a state-of-the-art new distillery with the aim of resurrecting the old brand. They intended to bring back old products and establish several new ones.

Cousins Chris Canale and Alex Canale opened the newest incarnation of Domenico's legacy in May of 2017 and the distillery has flourished since.

ALEX CASTLE
MASTER DISTILLER
OF MEMPHIS

Old Dominick's head distiller is Alex Castle. She grew up near Covington, Kentucky, not far from Cincinnati, and graduated from the University of Kentucky with a degree in chemical engineering.

"I really loved chemistry and calculus and physics. I wanted to go into something that used those subjects but wasn't teaching," Castle told the *Memphis Daily News*. Her mother suggested she try her hand as a brew master or a master distiller and she found her calling "I said, 'Okay. Done. I'm doing one of those.'"

She has worked at Alltech's Lexington Brewing and Distilling Co. and Town Branch Distillery, finishing as a distillery supervisor at Wild Turkey, before moving down to Memphis. Currently, she lives in the downtown section of the city with her husband and their dog, Whiskey.

"I've never been one to sit at a desk all day, so I definitely love the hands-on aspect of being a maker—but I also love the creativity that I can have when developing a new product," she told *Edible Memphis*. "When you spend an entire day producing enough distillate just to fill a few barrels and then have to wait several years to finally enjoy that product, you definitely learn to appreciate the work and effort that goes into anything artisanal. Patience. With spirits, you have to be patient. You can't rush the process at all. The whiskey will be ready when it's ready."

The pride and joy of the early line was the Old Dominick Memphis Toddy. They use the high-rye bourbon and then steep a blend of spices and fruit to flavor the whiskey. The flavored whiskey is sweetened to taste and bottled at 60 proof. The nose is rich with clove, cinnamon, black pepper, cardamom, and orange peel. This is a lovely, lovely liqueur that is perfect for the holiday.

HULING STATION SERIES

In 1866, Domenico Canale's spirits business was booming. Rail cars bearing oak-aged whiskeys rolled in and out of the D. Canale & Co. warehouse at Huling Station. Any bottle bearing the Old Dominick brand was known far and wide to be fine whiskey. More than 150 years later, Huling Station Straight Bourbon is an homage to the whiskeys of 1866 Memphis. These whiskeys are starting to see some nice distribution.

Huling Station Straight Bourbon (100 proof) is a high-rye bourbon with a mash bill of 52% corn, 44% rye, and 4% malted barley. The average age of the whiskey is 4 years in new American #4 char barrels. This whiskey has notes of caramel, dried apple, and vanilla with a gingersnap finish.

Huling Station Straight Wheat (90 proof) is made from a mash bill of 83% wheat, 12% corn, and 5% malted barley. This sweet, soft whiskey, is approachable with an easy finish of honey and vanilla.

Huling Station Blend (100 proof) is a 50/50 blend of their wheated whiskey and their bourbon. It opens soft and warm with hints of cereal, touches of vanilla, oak, and caramel, as well as a slight twang of gingersnap at the end.

Old Dominick is not only prepared to dominate the Memphis market—it is built to compete with the big brands in Tennessee and beyond.

The distillery is located in a cavernous, revamped old machine works. Brick, spit-polished stainless steel, copper, and glass enhance the old building, including a very mod tasting bar, an outdoor tasting patio, and a 13-foot high neon sign featuring the famous Dominick rooster, America's oldest breed of chicken.

The distillery has two Vendome stills, one for whiskey and other potables, and the other for vodka. They also have six large 1,800-gallon stainless steel fermenters and even mill their own grain. They currently have two large grain silos and have planned to build two more. The fermentation of their mashes is generally three to five days.

Their plain, silky smooth vodka uses the same mash as their Tennessee whiskey. They also have a Honeybell Vodka, which is flavored with real honeybell oranges. The nose is outrageous and the flavor is completely dry, yet incredibly refreshing.

Released in 2020, Formula No. 10 Gin (95 proof) is made with eight different botanicals. It's a lovely craft gin, aromatic, and perfect for martinis or other mixed drinks.

OLD FORGE DISTILLERY

Old Forge Distillery in Pigeon Forge is all about history. According to the distillery, "Mordecai Lewis was granted a 151 acre plot of land by Governor William Blount [in 1790]. Rich with natural resources and located along the banks of the Little Pigeon River, the area was ideal for building the forge and the mill. Iron-making was one of Tennessee's first true industries. The iron forge was built by Isaac Love [in 1817]. [In 1830,] William Love, Isaac Love's son, built the Old Mill. Listed on the National Register of Historic Places, it has been in continuous operation stone grinding corn, wheat, rye, and buckwheat." In 1910, they built a grain supply warehouse and farm store—and that's just the beginning.

Fast-forward to July 2014, Old Forge Distillery, located in a 100-year-old former farm supply store, opened their doors. They get their corn from a 184-year-old mill right next door—the same one built by William Love.

Old Forge specializes in moonshine. They make three different kinds using the freshly ground grain. They also make rum, vodka, gin, infused spirits, and truly fantastic bourbon.

Old Forge Blended Bourbon Whiskey (100 proof) is aged for 9 years in white American charred oak barrels and non-chill filtered. The whiskey is mellow and smooth with nice oak, caramel, and vanilla flavors. "Chilling a whiskey during the filtering process can increase efficiency but can also alter the flavor by removing natural proteins and fatty acids," head distiller Keener Shanton explains.

Old Forge Cyclone Jim Tennessee Bourbon Single Barrel (110 proof) is a limited edition, 12-year-old, single barrel , non-chill filtered Tennessee Bourbon. "Describing Cyclone Jim as a limited edition isn't marketing hype," says Shanton.

"You simply can't age a whiskey that long without nature shrinking the supply. But the taste makes it all worthwhile!" About this incredible 110 proof whiskey, Shanton says, "The high proof enhances the flavor profile without sacrificing smoothness. Devoted bourbon fans will love sipping Cyclone Jim." The whiskey has lovely notes of toffee, caramel, vanilla, and oak.

Old Forge Cyclone Jim is named after the horse who powered the clay grinding mill for Pigeon Forge's original pottery enterprise, now known as Pigeon River Pottery. The beloved Cyclone Jim was in charge of cleaning the freshly harvested clay taken from the Pigeon River. As Cyclone Jim's popularity spread, he and the pottery store became the first tourist attraction in Pigeon Forge. After Cyclone Jim retired, every horse that took on the job took his name. "I thought it was a great name for a single barrel bourbon," Shanton says, "Because every bottle is a signature expression of a great spirit."

KEENER SHANTON AND THIN MASH TECHNIQUE

Previously a fireman with a penchant for home brewing, Old Forge head distiller Keener Shanton specializes in a thin mash technique (a combination of no-cook and cooked processes) that he insists "results in a smooth spirit with a deep grain flavor."

Shanton operates the 100-gallon batch still that produces three different recipes—No. 001, No. 007, and No. 008. The 1830 Original Recipe No. 001 is made from 100% corn. Recipe No. 007 is 70% corn, 25% rye, and 5% malted barley. Recipe No. 008, called Miller's Blend, is a wheated blend with a mash bill of 70% corn, 25% wheat, and 5% malted barley.

"Once the corn is ground and it's gone through the tempering and blending with Shanton, the resulting moonshine will be ready to bottle...The spring water used to make the moonshine comes from Dandridge and hasn't seen the light of day until it gets here," Kris Tatum, the distillery manager, told Melanie Tucker in *The Daily Times*.

This is real geek stuff, but if you're talking distilling, you better know brewing. In Shanton's, and a number of brewer's eyes, the thickness of the mash is everything.

In John Palmer's whiskey bible *How to Brew*, Palmer writes, "The grist/water ratio is another factor influencing the performance of the mash. A thinner mash of [greater than] 2 quarts of water per pound of grain dilutes the relative concentration of the enzymes, slowing the conversion. [This] ultimately leads to a more fermentable mash because the enzymes are not inhibited by a high concentration of sugars." Palmer continues, "A stiff mash of [less than] 1.25 quarts of water per pound is better for protein breakdown and results in a faster overall starch conversion, but the resultant sugars are less fermentable and will result in a sweeter, maltier beer." Palmer explains, "A thicker mash is more gentle to the enzymes because of the lower heat capacity of grain compared to water. A thick mash is better for multi-rest mashes because the enzymes are not denatured as quickly by a rise in temperature."

In layman's terms, Shanton is doing his best to manage carbohydrates and sugars, protein breakdown, and mash temperature. If this trifecta can be achieved, the results will yield a more flavorful distiller's beer and a more flavorful whiskey.

MOONSHINE

Old Forge Distillery 1830 Original Unaged Corn Moonshine (100 proof) is made using the famous recipe No. 001 which has a mash bill of 100% corn. Smoke and eucalyptus do come across as promised with hints of exotic fruits and a light, sweet, and smooth finish.

Old Forge Distillery 1830 Original Distiller's Blend (100 proof) is made from recipe No. 007 with a classic Tennessee corn, rye, and barley mash bill. Hints of corn bread and malt, sweet corn, stone fruits, come through and a smack of gingersnap precedes a smooth finish.

Old Forge Distillery 1830 Original Miller's Blend (100 proof) is a wheated un-aged whiskey made from a mash bill of Tennessee corn, wheat, and barley. Creamed corn, cereal, pancakes, butter, and lots of vanilla come across in this one.

The moonshines also come in such flavors as Chocolate, French Toast, Coffee, Blackberry, Lemon, Apple Pie, Cinnamon, Vanilla Bean, Bananas Foster, Oatmeal Cookie, Kettle Corn, Pumpkin Roll, and many, many others. All three of the "original recipes" series are very good, high quality, un-aged whiskeys, but I found the corn and wheated versions to be the best.

There is also an Old Forge Rum made from a traditional molasses mash bill, their very clean, grain-based Old Forge Vodka, and a series of high-end, mixologist-friendly, artisanal flavor-infused neutral spirits. These spirits are made with natural flavors such as orange, rosemary, ginger, lemongrass, cherry, and basil.. Of special note is the Old Forge Tennessee Root (92 proof). This is a grain spirit gin made with locally hand-selected botanicals and juniper and aged in former bourbon barrels. This is a spectacular barrel-rested gin for gin enthusiasts.

The Old Forge Reserve Single Barrel Bourbon (89 proof) is a single barrel, 9-year-old sourced bourbon. This nice whiskey offers hints of caramel, honey, apple, and gingersnap.

OLD GLORY DISTILLERY

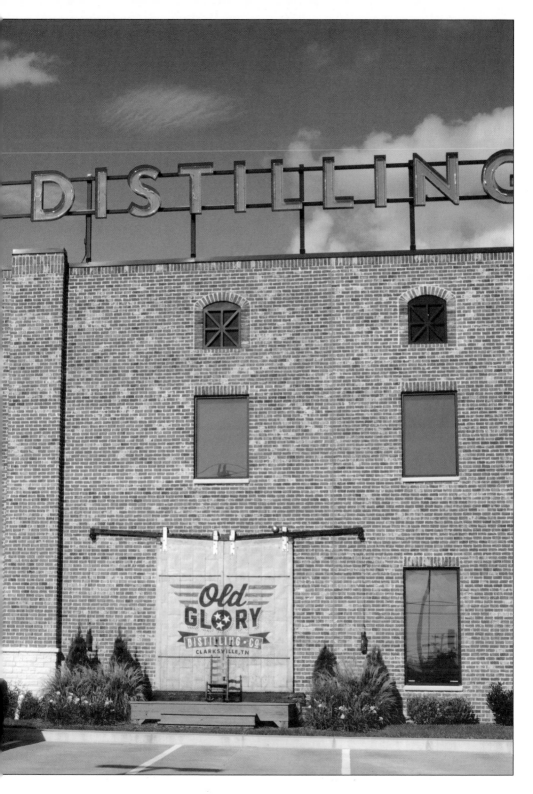

At the young age of 26, Matt Cunningham already has a brand-new distillery the size of a large grammar school. He came up with a label and an idea and then went out and sold it. There was barely any funding, so Cunningham turned to Kickstarter and set a $25,000 goal, eventually raising $37,632!

"In the years it's taken this venture to go from concept to reality, I've been referred to a few too many times as Mr. Cunningham. Mr. Cunningham is my dad. And my dad will even disagree with that and tell you Mr. Cunningham was my grandfather. Regardless, I'm 26 years old, and I'm simply Matt," says Cunningham.

A lifelong Clarksville native and University of Arkansas graduate, he became interested in the craft distilling after college, but became a fireman. But soon Cunningham busied himself with turning his dreams of distilling into reality.

Old Glory started out making moonshine and vodka but it's very evident that Cunningham has much bigger plans. He's laying down Tennessee whiskey and bourbon every chance he gets and building up a position on barrel-aged whiskey. Cunningham is dedicated to becoming a player in the Tennessee whiskey business and his distillery is already humming with conference rooms, rental bars, and a massive wedding space, making it one of the most popular event spaces in Clarksville.

Old Glory doesn't have any Tennessee whiskey or bourbon right now, since Cunningham refuses to bottle sourced whiskeys under his label. He'll wait. He's got hundreds of barrels aging right now. And he's making more every day. Old Glory Tennessee whiskey is made from a mash bill of 70% corn, 20% wheat, and 10% malted barley and is passed through Tennessee maple charcoal for mellowing. Old Glory bourbon is made from a mash bill of 73% corn, 19% rye, and 8% malted barley. Both

are being aged in small, 30-gallon charred new American white oak barrels. Other whiskeys are being aged in larger barrels for a longer-term maturation.

They bottle their moonshine, rum, and vodka. "We've got a lot of industry here, but a lot of it is stuff people have a hard time putting their hands on. We wanted to bring something here that you could come see exactly how it's made, from start to finish, and actually take a product that we made home with you," Cunningham told *Clarksville Now.*

Old Glory Bourbon Whiskey Small Batch (90 proof) is made from the mash bill of 73% corn, 19% rye, and 8% malted barley. This is small batch whiskey making right now. This whiskey is a blend of their in-house bourbon, roughly half of which has been aged in 25-gallon and standard 53-gallon barrels. This whiskey has a big sweet nose of caramel and dried fruit with hints of vanilla and white pepper on the finish

Old Glory is a family endeavor. "My dad [Tom Cunningham] was the general

contractor for the project...My mom [Tammy Cunningham] is my biggest fan and she does a little public relations work for me...My grandfather hand-painted the Old Glory logo on the sliding loading dock doors on the front of the building. He's a retired sign painter...My uncle, Scott Harrison, built the open-face Old Glory Distilling Co. neon sign that sits atop the building. So, this truly is a local, and family-oriented project," Cunningham told *The Leaf-Chronicle.*

Old Glory Smooth Shine TN Moonshine (80 proof) is made from a mash bill of 70% wheat and 30% sugar, rather than corn. This shift results in an incredibly smooth, malty 'shine with honey, vanilla, and yellow cake flavors.

Old Glory Tennessee Vodka (80 proof) is made from 100% non-GMO corn, finished in their copper pot still, and filtered through the same sugar maple charcoal they use for their Tennessee whiskey. This vodka is super clean and extra smooth.

Old Glory Jumper's Stash is a white rum made from 100% molasses. It is named for the brave men and women of the 101st Airborne Division (Air Assault), the Night Stalkers of the 160th Special Operations Aviation Regiment (Airborne), and the 5th Special Forces Group (Airborne). Their home base Fort Campbell is located just a few clicks away from the distillery. This smooth, easy-to-drink dram is sure to bring them pride.

Old Glory White Hat Whiskey (80 proof) is their small batch bourbon that was released in December 2017. Their high-rye mash bill makes an excellent, smooth, and spicy whiskey.

Old Tennessee Distilling Company

In 2015, Old Tennessee Distilling Company opened up in Kodak, Tennessee. They debuted their first bottled spirits at the Smokies Festival that June. Old Tennessee Distilling is known for producing moonshine, whiskeys, vodkas, ryes, rums, infused fruits, and gin.

The distillery was originally named for the 1950s Robert Mitchum film *Thunder Road*, but in 2019, the company had a change of direction. History is important to Old Tennessee and their spirits are made on-site by master distillers, Old Tennessee's farm-to-bottle products are handmade and homegrown from the bounties of local fields and the fertile minds of their forebears. The goal was to respect the past while living for the moment. Many of their products are named for historical figures, important events in the history of Tennessee, like Cal F. Johnson, the Treaty of Dumplin Creek, and Tuckaleechee Caverns. Thus, they arrived at Old Tennessee Distilling Company.

Jason Franklin was born and raised in Sevierville, Tennessee, and represents the next generation of distillers. He attended Tennessee Institute of Electronics and studied information technology, remaining in the electronics industry for a more than a dozen years. In 2003, Franklin became very interested in the process of making moonshine and over the next few years, he built a series of progressively larger stills which ultimately led him to his first distilling job. Then he got his first job in distilling. In 2015 he was hired as master distiller and began setting up the distillery, experimenting, and creating the many products they have there now.

Dwight Bearden has more than fifty years of whiskey-making under his belt. Born and raised in Dahlonega, Georgia, Bearden's family has been making liquor for at least four generations. He started making 'shine at the wise age of 6 with his father. School wasn't as fun or fascinating as bootlegging and he had his first still at 17. At Old Tennessee Distilling Company, where Bearden's first still now resides, the old-school distiller likes to make corn whiskey, moonshine, and the occasional apple brandy. He's an entertaining fellow and if you're lucky, he has a few stories he's happy to retell.

The lineup of moonshines produced by Old Tennessee are under the Dumplin Creek name. Tennessee Frost 100 Proof (50% ABV) is a classic corn and cane Tennessee unaged 'shine made from ground corn and sugar. Smooth and straightforward with some good corn flavor. Other flavors in the Dumplin Creek line include Apple Pie, Autumn Maple, Bananashine, Blackberry Bramble, Cinnamon Bonfire, Little River Lemon, Pumpkin Patch, Red Haven Peach, Salted Caramelicious, S'mores Moonshine, Summer Strawberry, Toasted Mango, Watermelon Falls, and Orange Dreamsicle.

Under the Dumplin Creek brand they also produce Dumplin Creek Gin 90 proof (45% ABV) and Dumplin Creek Vodka 90 proof (45% ABV). Another of the key products is their Renegade Rum 92 Proof (46% ABV), which also comes in a barrel-aged version and a coconut flavored version.

They also produce Cal F. Johnson Black Mountain Rum 84 proof (42% ABV) and Cal F. Johnson Black Mountain Spiced Rum.

Old Tennessee Straight Bourbon Whiskey 13 Years Old (86% proof) is a 13 years old bourbon aged in American charred oak. This very nice whiskey produces hints of caramel, fruit, cereal, sweet corn, buttered popcorn, dried apple, spice, and a hint of white pepper.

Butcher's Bourbon Prime Cut Tennessee Straight Bourbon Whiskey 12 Years Old (92 proof) was aged in American charred oak barrels for 12 years. This is a very nice bourbon, great for sipping and stands up to ice.

Old Tennessee is popular for their very good moonshine, but their whiskeys are also quite impressive.

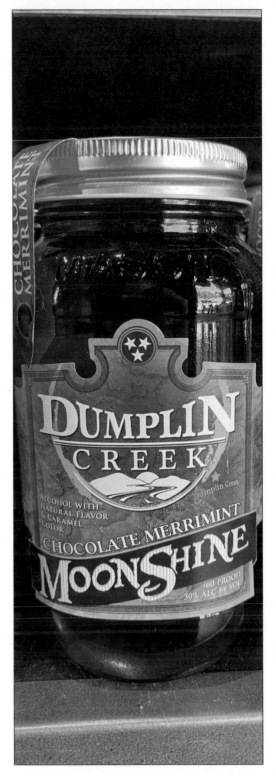

OLE SMOKY DISTILLERY

If there is an instant success story in Tennessee that resulted from the changing of the distilling laws in 2009, Ole Smoky Distillery is it. Ole Smoky became the first federally licensed distillery in the history of East Tennessee and was only the fourth distillery licensed in the state when it opened on July 4, 2010. At the time, only Jack Daniel's, George Dickel, and Prichard's were open and Ole Smoky quickly became the poster child for craft distilling, proving the market for moonshine was ripe for the picking.

The original distillery was located in Gatlinburg where Joe Baker founded the company and, using his marketing genius, proffered his family's 100-year-old family recipe. Since then, dozens of distilleries claim such heritage for their recipes, but Baker was first in and made it stick. The current recipe was tweaked with the help of legendary master distiller and consultant Dave Pickerell, who was previously the master distiller at Maker's Mark.

Ole Smoky was an instant media darling, featured on the Today show and on Martha Stewart Living radio. The brand was smartly positioned and the market was hungry for novelty. Today, Ole Smoky is among the bestselling moonshines in the United States and the brand is now available in 49 states and Canada. The original distillery is still located "up the hill" from Gatlinburg, ready to snap up visitors to Dollywood and the Great Smoky Mountains.

The Gatlinburg distillery, which is also known as "The Holler," is America's most visited distillery. It's a unique experience, a shop, and distillery all in one! The smell of cooking and fermenting grains hits visitors right as they approach the entrance where they have the opportunity to see the distillers at work. The original staff of seven employees swelled to more than 300 in just six years and the small batch process gave way to making more than 1,000 gallons a day!

Just like the old-time moonshiners, Gatlinburg's moonshine was sold in old-fashioned mason jars with lids. They were among the first to start offering numerous flavored moonshines and they now have more than 26 available.

Ole Smoky Original Moonshine (100 proof) is a spicy, smooth 'shine, with lots of buttered corn, sweet creamed corn, and a little spice at the end. It has a smooth, smooth finish.

In October 2014, Ole Smoky opened a second location called Ole Smoky Barn at The Island,

Pigeon Forge. The Ole Smoky Barn has approximately 6,000 square feet of public space with an on-site still and tasting area. It echoes the design of the original "Holler," using reclaimed, local barn wood, fixtures, artwork, and other elements. Moonshine made at the "Barn" is jarred, labeled, and sold on-site. Joe Baker said, "It's a great destination that offers a memorable experience for families visiting the area." They now have four locations. Two in Gatlinburg (The Holler and The Barrel House), The Barn in Pigeon Forge and 6th & Peabody in Nashville.

In February 2016, Ole Smoky launched a new, aged whiskey line after it purchased Davy Crockett Whiskey and rebranded it Ole Smoky Tennessee Whiskey. They turned the old Davy Crockett Barrelhouse in Gatlinburg into a third Ole Smoky location and paired the strengths of Crockett's very high quality whiskey products with their own already very strong and highly-recognized brand name. At the Ole Smoky Barrelhouse, visitors are able to see firsthand how aged whiskey is made.

"Having two categories under Ole Smoky's name is a huge win for the company and we hope it will be a great opportunity to increase our fan base," said Robert Hall, CEO of Ole Smoky. While locals were sad to see the demise of the Crockett label, experts in the field applauded the move as it increased Ole Smoky's reach and breadth in an age where brown spirits have moved to the forefront of the liquor industry.

Ole Smoky Whiskey launched with four expressions: Ole Smoky Straight Tennessee Whiskey, Ole Smoky Blended Whiskey, Ole Smoky Salty Caramel Whiskey, and Ole Smoky Tennessee Mud. The company has since moved to add flavored whiskeys, echoing the trend among big whiskey producers. The other flavors include Honey, Cinnamon, Pecan, Salty Caramel, Root

Beer, Mango Habanero, Peach, and Salty Watermelon.

Ole Smoky Blended Whiskey (80 proof) is the distillery's take on a blended whiskey. Very smooth, approachable whiskey with sweet notes of cereal , caramel, and spice. It's an easy sipper that's great with just ice ice or for cocktails

Ole Smoky Tennessee Straight Bourbon Whiskey (80 proof) is the classic whiskey of the line, aged in charred new American white oak barrels. It is said to be aged for approximately four years, though no age statement is proffered on the label. Despite that, this is a solid whiskey with notes of caramel, honey, pecan notes, light brown sugar, and a hint of spice at the end.

PostModern Spirits
By Emily West

In the summer of 2017, Eric McNew took the dive into making multiple spirits while waiting on his whiskey to age at PostModern Spirits.

"As most start-up distilleries go, you either source from another product or you have to be really innovative to come up with cool ideas until you have an aged product," McNew said.

McNew's bourbon, aged in a cherry wood barrel, is akin to a Highland scotch. "We were committed to not sourcing products and do authentic products."

Each week, PostModern Spirits picks up 600 gallons of mash from a nearby brewery. McNew brings that back to ferment for five days until distilling it over the weekend. "With the current bourbon craze, we wanted to do something different," McNew said. "That's what we are aiming to do with our single malt and not trying to emulate other flavors."

In the meantime, McNew also creates five different spirits that range from a corn whiskey vodka to flavorful liqueurs. He also makes a variety of gins which he hopes give a spirited twist to cocktails.

"We wanted great things to mix with those and other spirits," he said. "That's why we wanted to do the liqueur line. We have a clear vision of where we want to go with authentic products and really trying to be genuine in what we do."

Post Modern Spirits American (Single) Malt Whiskey (90 proof0 is made from locally-crafted beer partnered with Crafty Bastard Brewery to create this American (Single) Malt Whiskey. The mash bill is 100% malted barley. There's a sweet, smoky character with a delicate aromatic finish.

Post Modern Spirits hi(rye) Whiskey (90 proof) has more than 50% rye in its mash bill. "This rye whiskey is truly a first for Knoxville," said head distiller Ron Grazioso. "No one has fermented, distilled, and aged a rye whiskey in the modern era in Knoxville. The rye grain is notoriously difficult to work—some say rye whiskey is made from the tears of distillers. We had a great time collaborating with our friends from Elkmont Exchange on this whiskey."

PRODUCTS

KORE Vodka

Giniferous Gin

Empirical Dry Gin

Chamomile Liqueur

Elderberry Gin Liqueur

Currently barreling
American Single Malt
Whiskey + UpRoot Gin

PRICHARD'S DISTILLERY

Phil Prichard was born in 1939. "At that time, there was no Austria on the map," he wryly points out. At 78 years old, he is still an imposing man, virile, and in possession of a booming, gruff voice.

"I grew up in Memphis, Tennessee, and in 1980, I moved to Vermont where I purchased a small farm. My wife, Connie, and I married in 1982 and in addition to our real jobs, we began to import horses from Norway. In 1987, we moved from Vermont to upstate New York where we purchased a beautiful farm overlooking the Mohawk River valley, a place where we could pursue the raising and breeding of our Norwegian Fjord horses. It just so happened that a Christmas gift shop was included with the purchase of the farm. It was a good business," recalled Prichard for GotRum.com.

Eventually, the taxes more than doubled and the Prichards were in need of a new line of work.

A friend casually mentioned the idea of making rum in Tennessee from locally-grown sorghum molasses. "Now that was an interesting thought!" said Prichard. They moved back to Tennessee and he started making rum with sorghum molasses. An old high school friend, Victor Robilio, eventually tasted this rum, and said, "Phil, you are producing one of the finest rums in the world. If you do not pursue this as a commercial venture, you are going to make a serious mistake."

With that little push, Prichard opened Prichard's in 1997.

Prichard's Distillery is the third-oldest distillery in the state and was one of the first 10 craft distilleries in America. Prichard himself counts men like Fritz Maytag and pioneers like Anchor Steam Brewing and Distilling among his friends. He is so persuasive that when the local planning board had its final roll call on his distillery, Dimple Gyser (a presumed teetotaler who was known to be tough on any new changes in the community) gave an enthusiastic "Yes!"

Prichard named the enterprise after his grandfather who operated an open distillery (illegally) for many years in the 1880s.

In 2000, Prichard's bought an old schoolhouse in Kelso, which had been turned into a community center. The distillery slowly expanded but it needed immense work. Prichard could have built a new building but his work paid off at his unique distillery. The immense bottling line is in the old gymnasium, the old school office now operates as one of the two stores, and the old trophy case now holds gleaming bottles of Prichard's liquors.

They also operate a lovely second tasting room known as Prichard's Distillery at Fontanel. Fontanel is also the home of The Mansion, the 40-room, 33,000-square-foot log cabin formerly belonging to Barbara Mandrell. They established this satellite location in 2014 and installed a classic lambic copper still, the result of Prichard's trips to The Hague, Frankfurt, and Cognac. "I called Vendome and asked, 'You ever build one of these?' And they said 'No.' I said, 'You better learn!'" The still at Fontanel is one of the most beautiful in Tennessee. A big, pear-shaped copper still with a long swan neck, it sits gracefully at the center of the distilling room floor. When asked what he was making with it, Prichard gave a sideways glance. "Brandy. We're going to make fine brandy. And cuts are critical in brandy." Prichard's plans to release small, limited-edition brandies yearly for the holiday season.

A Soldier's Child Foundation

If there is one thing Phil Prichard is passionate about, other than his own business, it's his involvement with A Soldier's Child Foundation (ASCF). Prichard's Distillery is a proud corporate sponsor of this organization.

The inspiration for ASCF came while Daryl Mackin, the fonder and executive director, was preparing for his six-year-old son's surprise birthday party. Like most parents, he was easily caught up in all of the "chores" required to pull off the celebration.

"I quickly lost sight of the joy of the moment," says Mackin. "I was sitting at my computer at work where I have a memorial of Staff Sgt. Marc Golczynski on my wall. Marc was the son of my previous neighbors, Henry and Fay Golczynski, and a fallen soldier of the Iraq war. I also have a very moving picture of Marc's son Christian receiving his father's flag." The award-winning photo by Aaron Thompson was reprinted all over the world. "As I finished typing out my son's invitations and gave a big sigh of frustration, I looked up at my wall and was immediately convicted in my spirit for my negative attitude. My heart turned to Christian Golczynski, who will never be able to have a party planned by his dad.

"There are many children like Christian that will never receive another birthday gift from their parent because they gave their life while defending our freedoms. Likewise, the fallen soldier will never be able to give their child a surprise birthday party, a bicycle for their son, a necklace for their daughter, or financial assistance for their child's first car or pursuit of higher education."

The ASCF's mission is to serve the children of military personnel who have lost their lives while defending the United States of America. ASCF has three points of service for the children of our fallen: birthday celebrations up to the age of 18; mentorship programs for children in Journey Camp (for ages 10 to 16), and Leadership Development (for ages 17 to 25); and college scholarships through the Fallen Patriots Foundation and Folded Flag Foundation.

A portion of every bottle of Sweet Lucy sold by Prichard's Distillery goes to this fund.

Prichard's is proud of their copper pot still, the first one used to make a Tennessee whiskey. The company ages their product in everything from 15-gallon to 53-gallon charred American white oak barrels and they're famous for three things: rum, whiskey, and liqueur. The rum is iconic and sold in a myriad of flavors, including Fine Rum, Crystal Rum, Peach Mango Rum, Key Lime Rum, Cranberry Rum, and Private Stock Rum. The bottle is modeled off an old, iconic 19th century one with a crooked neck. I loved the two classic rums.

The Prichard's Fine Rum (80 proof) is modeled after the classic rums of the Colonial period, made with molasses and barrel-aged for a minimum of three years. It is a big, rich, delicious rum with notes of caramel, honey, vanilla, and spice.

If you're a rum enthusiast, you'll want to try Prichard's Limited Edition Private Stock Aged Rum (90 proof). This is a blend of aged rums, some as old as 13 years, in small, 15-gallon barrels. Packaged in what looks like a perfume bottle, this is rum done as fine cognac or old Highlands Scotch. This is not just a drink, it's a dram. Caramel, figs, dark honey, baked apple, pear, and vanilla all come through in this aged gem.

Prichard's is also well-known for their bourbon and Tennessee whiskey. They offer the Lincoln County Lightning, Double

Barreled Bourbon, Double Chocolate Bourbon, Tennessee Whiskey, Tennessee Malt Whiskey, and a Rye Whiskey. There is no question that Prichard's Double Barreled Bourbon Whiskey (90 proof) is among the better bourbons being made in the United States. The sourced whiskey is aged for 9 years and has a mash bill of white corn, rye, and malted barley. According to the distillery, "Bourbon is generally barreled at a relatively high 125 proof. However, the final bottle proof may be as low as 80. Our bourbon is taken from 120 proof to 95 proof and re-barreled in new charred oak barrels to reinforce the barrel notes that bourbon is so famous for." In fact, the bourbon is barreled twice, a technique and name Prichard trademarked. In a not-so public fight, Prichard spent hundreds of thousands of dollars defending his trademark successfully against one of the big boys from Kentucky. The rich opulent taste of the double barrel is hard to beat. Thick with caramel, burnt sugar, brown sugar, and hints of toffee, baked apples, and pears, this is an exceptional bourbon that even Jim Murray has given consistently high scores.

Prichard's Tennessee Whiskey (80 proof) is the only Tennessee whiskey made in the state that does not use the Lincoln County Process. The whiskey is made using white corn, rye, and malted barley, and then aged for 10 years in heavy charred American white oak and used rum barrels. The flavors of dark honey, sweet corn, vanilla, and spice make this rare whiskey one that you'll want to seek out.

Prichard's is also known for their line of liqueurs. Most notable among them is Sweet Lucy (70 proof). Sweet Lucy was the proverbial name for a flask of homemade sweet liqueur that duck hunters brought with them up and down the Mississippi River. Prichard's bourbon-based version is flavored with oranges and apricots and is one of the best-selling bourbon liqueurs on the market. They also offer a Sweet Lucy Cream Liqueur (36 proof).

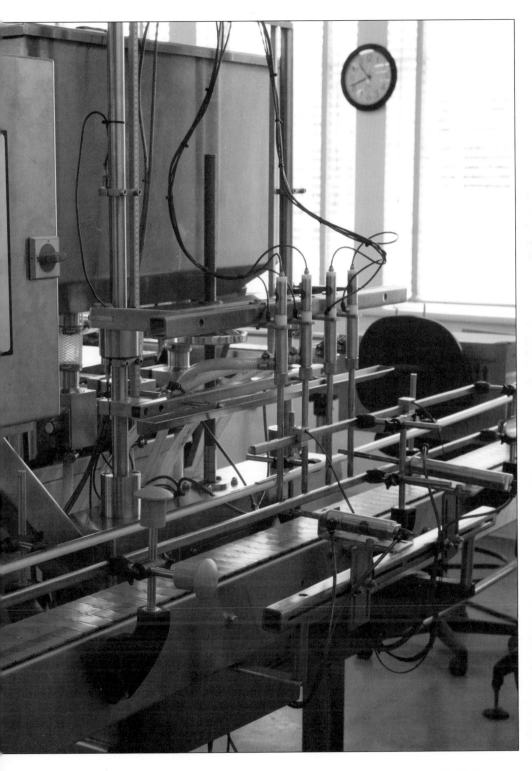

WHOSE "TENNESSEE WHISKEY"?

In the attempt to codify "Tennessee whiskey" as a category whiskey, Jack Daniel's and George Dickel initiated a movement to establish rules similar to those created for bourbon. Most successful categories in wines, beers, and spirits eventually codify, but there was a lone dissenter.

"This is all about my rights. And when you take away any of my rights, I'm going to fight you tooth and nail on it," Phil Prichard told *The Washington Post*. "Last year, a lot of those rights got taken away from me through a process that was abetted by an employee of Jack Daniel's for the benefit of Jack Daniel's. If I wanted my whiskey to taste like Jack Daniel's, I'd make it like Jack Daniel's."

An angry Prichard, who had already been making popular "Tennessee whiskey" for years, testified against the bill in 2013, but despite his protests, most other distillers signed on to the new definition of Tennessee whiskey.

"The only corn we grew in Tennessee in the 18th century was white corn, and we only used pot stills," said Prichard. "If I had the power and influence Jack has in this state, and I told everyone that Tennessee whiskey was made with white corn in pot stills, how would distillers feel about that?"

Prichard was able to reach a compromise and was awarded an exemption that made the distillery the only one in the state that did not have to use the Lincoln County Process.

"If I subscribe to this rule that Jack Daniel's has imposed on us all, then I would then be paying homage to Jack Daniel's and not paying homage to my grandfather Benjamin Prichard," he said over the phone.

SAMUEL T. BRYANT DISTILLERY

Samuel T. Bryant was in the tree removal business for more than a dozen years. He sold his business and then started casting around for something else to do. "I studied chemical engineering in college and was already making wine," Bryant told *The Jackson Sun.* "So I figured that would be something that would be viable. I sold the tree business in 2011 and we officially opened the distillery July 1, 2016."

According to Bryant, he presented the idea of opening to a distillery to Ron Acree and Joel Newman of the Tennessee Small Business Development Center. "I talked to [Newman] and Ron [Acree] at the Jackson Chamber, mainly Joel, and we put a plan, an estimate together...and we were thoroughly wrong. What we budgeted was much less than the actual cost, but we still wanted to keep going." Luckily, Bryant has a good enough sense of humor to laugh about it now.

It's very much a family affair and on any given day you will see Samuel T. Bryant and perhaps his father, Pete. Samuel T. Bryant makes an unconventional lineup of liquors and liqueurs. They are one of the few Tennessee or Kentucky distilleries that make a grappa. Grappa is moonshine made with leftover pressed grapes, stems, and cane sugar. It's the Italian version of white lightning. Their grappa is distilled from local grapes from Crown and Century Wineries.

TNKilla (80 proof) is Bryant's version of a tequila. This is an agave-based distilled spirit, but since it's not made in Mexico, it cannot be called tequila. It's a very nice take on the classic spirit and a big favorite of the distillery's fans.

Samuel T. Bryant Tennessee Moonshine (80 proof), which is made with corn, rye, malted barley, and sugar, is a classic grain-and-cane 'shine. It is a smooth, un-aged white whiskey with a lovely nose and an easy finish. They also make several flavors of 'shine, including Blueberry and Coconut.

Samuel T. Bryant Tennessee Sam (80 proof) is "Sam's take on whiskey made in Tennessee." This isn't officially recognized as "Tennessee whiskey" (it has not gone through the Lincoln County Process), but it is his classic 'shine aged in charred American white oak barrels. This is a smooth, easy-drinking light whiskey and a very nice version of a barrel-aged 'shine.

When discussing Samuel T. Bryant Tennessee Pete (80 proof), Sam likes to ask, "What if bourbon and Scotch had a baby?" As he jokes, they can't call this a Scotch because it is made in Tennessee. It has all the sweet notes of bourbon, but it has all the smoky qualities you would expect from a good Scotch.

ALLISA HENLEY
TENNESSEE'S FIRST
FEMALE DISTILLER

It was big enough news when John Lunn left George Dickel for Popcorn Sutton, but when Allisa Henley followed him, the whiskey industry took notice. Henley, Tennessee's first female master distiller had left the safe shade of the Diageo umbrella for Popcorn Sutton.

All hell broke loose. Sazerac bought the Popcorn Sutton distillery (the Popcorn Sutton brand was retained by the owners in Ohio), but Lunn and Henley remained with Sazerac. Since 2017, the team has been firing their pot stills every day and making Tennessee whiskey at Sazerac's Newport distillery. A move was announced in 2018 that the distillery would move operations to Murfreesboro, but delays in 2020 sidelined the timetable. In the meantime, the two distillers keep building their Tennessee whiskey inventory.

"Allisa worked for more than 11 years in a variety of positions at George A. Dickel, including most recently as the facility's master distiller. During her time with George Dickel, Henley was instrumental in the launch of George Dickel's Barrel Select Tennessee Whiskey, Rye Whisky and Single Barrel products. She is also credited with the creation and operation of the brand's consumer experience center and most recently, with the discovery and launch of a rare 17-year-old limited edition Tennessee Whiskey," stated Popcorn Sutton.

Of the consumer experience center, Henley told Coed.com, "I essentially had to write a tour script from scratch and you can't write about it unless you know what you're talking about. I firmly believe you can learn more on the job than you ever can in a classroom."

According to Sutton, "Allisa did her undergraduate work at the University of Tennessee-Chattanooga and then earned her MBA from Lipscomb University. She studied at the Stave and Thief Society Executive Bourbon Steward program and is accredited as a Master of Whiskey. Henley has [led] and participated in numerous distillery training classes, whiskey educational seminars, and industry panel discussions throughout the world."

The Tennessee whiskey world is excited about what will come out of Newport/Murfreesboro. Only time will tell.

SHORT MOUNTAIN
DISTILLERY

SHORT MOUNTAIN DISTILLERY

By Emily West

When Tennessee laws changed—granting whiskey creation outside of just three counties— Billy Kaufman decided he would try his hand at making spirits on his 400-acre farm in Woodbury. Before 1920, Cannon County had 18 distilleries that closed due to Prohibition. After the law changed in 2009, Short Mountain Distillery became the state's sixth distillery.

"What people like to know about us is Al Capone bought alcohol from this land during Prohibition and our farm was the pick-up site," Kaufman said. "It's also the same spring that made the products of Capone and we can trace that back."

Kaufman and his brothers David and Ben conduct a farm-to-bottle process and make organic whiskey and moonshine. The liquid is aged in white oak barrels, following the Lincoln County charcoal process to create the Tennessee spirit.

"I think making traditional spirits is sometimes unique enough," Kaufman said. "We don't have to go out on a limb to get people excellent spirits. We don't have to go crazy. We use our case spring water to make the quality of distilling that we strive for. I like to think of us as a sustainable green distillery."

Short Mountain Distillery sees nearly 20,000 visitors a year, Kaufman said. His site is unique with a full restaurant cafe and the occasional transition into a wedding venue.

The distillery even has a private barrel program where customers can buy smaller amounts down to 5-gallon barrels with personalized labeling.

"We don't predict when our barrels are ready," he said. "They are ready when they taste right."

They also produce a classic Shine (105 proof), a Shiner's Select (100 proof), an Organic Shine (100 proof), and a number of other flavors.

Short Mountain Green Thumb Organic Tennessee Whiskey (100 proof) is the first of its kind, an authentic Tennessee whiskey made with 100% organic malts and grains. It has the classic smoothness with the subtle complexity unique to the category Tennessee is famously known for. Ripe fruit, dry hay, and vanilla are on the nose with tobacco, dried mango, and caramel on the palate, finished with spice, a hint of smoke, and a touch of white pepper.

Short Mountain Tennessee Bourbon Whiskey (100 proof) has a mash bill of yellow corn, oat, rye, and brewer's malts. It was crafted in small batches, and aged for more than 4 years in new American white oak barrels charred at a level three. This whiskey offers sweet hints of vanilla and caramel with just a tinge of black pepper and touches of maple, vanilla, and orange zest.

Short Mountain Red Pecker Rye Whiskey (100 proof) is made with cherry wood-smoked chocolate rye malt. It's crafted in small batches and aged more than 4 years in new American oak charred barrels. Campfire, vanilla beans, black-strap molasses, and cordial cherries are on the nose with bittersweet chocolate, roasted coffee, and smoked pecan on the palate. It finishes with marbled rye bread and English walnut.

Sevier Distilling Co.

Chris Yett founded Sevier Distilling in 2015 in Sevierville, Tennessee, after he'd been in banking and real estate for more than a decade. "At my distillery we make all of our alcohol through fermentation. I don't buy anyone else's alcohol to make our own. I specialize in whiskey (both moonshine and barrel-aged), vodka, rum, gin, and distilled spirits specialties. I also produce grain-to glass bulk artisan spirits for craft distillers," says Yett.

Working behind Yett is a great team of guys. Chad Cooper is the man with the plan when it comes to being the right-hand distiller and he seems to have the golden touch. Kenny Sweet is also there as well as general manager Doug Branham. They play hard and they work hard.

The Sevier Distilling Company traces its roots all the way back to the genesis of Sevier County. Yett's family tree goes back to the families who settled the mountains of Appalachia of the East Tennessee region, including the patriarch, "The Immigrant" Valentine Sevier, and his son, "Col." Valentine Sevier, brother of the first Governor of Tennessee, and John Sevier. Beyond a few touches, the distilling techniques and recipes that Yett uses today are the same ones that the Sevier family used in 1750—but that doesn't stop them from being innovators, especially Cooper. Sevier is one of the more elegant and individual distilleries in the state.

Hidden Cove Rum (80 proof) is a 100% sorghum based rum. TenneKeela (80 proof) is an agave-tequila-like spirit (they're not allowed to call it tequila). Branham says of the Lime Tennekeela (80 proof), "We took our Tennekeela and infused it with organic limes for a taste that is outstanding. It's an 80 proof margarita, just add the salt and lime!"

The TennOdka (80 proof) is a super fine, 25-times distilled vodka from Appalachian corn and regional grains.

The Yenoh (82 proof) which is pronounced "Ya Know" (honey spelled backward) is the pride and joy of Sevier Distilling. Sevier claims Yenoh is the world's first honey liquor as its unique recipe is distilled from 100% honey. The nose is outrageous with

honey and big floral notes. It tastes lovely with citrus coming through and is perfect for cocktails, especially citrus martinis!

Sevier Distilling Real Deal Shine (100 proof) is truly an artisan moonshine. It's an un-aged corn whiskey. Smooth, sweet notes of Appalachian corn. It's super clean, super smooth, and one of the best 'shines in the state.

Southern Pride Distillery

In March 2012, Southern Pride Distillery became a small-batch artisan distillery in Fayetteville. Owner Randy Trentham (a born and raised local boy) and distiller Tim Shavers cut the ribbon in November 2014. The opening had been delayed because of tornadoes in the region, but Trentham & Co. would not be deterred.

Trentham is an accomplished building contractor, he even worked at Jack Daniel's. At Southern Pride, they use an old family recipe but with a little twist. According to the company, "Our story starts with a great grandmother and her Bible with the family recipe tucked safely inside the cover. Preserved by family members as all family secrets are." Now that's whiskey as religion!

Southern Pride uses a copper pot still to make its products, sources local cornmeal from Pearl City, and sources water from a spring on the property. The company found immediate success within the state and its bottles are now available in approximately a dozen states.

Southern Pride Original Moonshine (90 proof) is twice-distilled and made from cane, corn, and barley. This is a very good 'shine, with a lot of corn bread, cereal, sugar, and honey in the nose. There are also a number of other options, including Peach, Apple, Blackberry, Green Apple, a Double-Barreled Charred 'Shine, and a Double-Barreled Cinnamon.

Southern Pride White Whiskey (80 proof) is a classic un-aged Tennessee white whiskey with a bourbon-like mash bill. This small-

batch, barrel-aged whiskey is very pretty and shows real promise for brown spirits at Southern Pride.

As does Southern Pride Double Barrel Whiskey (80 proof), which is barrel-aged and then re-barreled into another charred new American white oak barrel. The Tennessee line of whiskeys (which also features peach and cinnamon flavors) is very strong here and should gain some notice once distribution widens (they are only available at the distillery).

Take it from me, the Tennessee Whiskey and the Double Barrel Whiskey are worth taking home.

SPEAKeasy Spirits Distillery/ Pennington Distilling Co.

SPEAKeasy started as a liquor marketing company in 2011. It was a consulting firm that specialized in content, presentation, public relations, and advertising. They were the marketing department you could never afford to hire in-house.

Today, SPEAKeasy Spirits Distillery/ Pennington Distilling Co. produces more than 140,000 to 160,000 cases of distilled spirits annually, including their own brands and the brand they co-pack. The distillery offers product formulation, private labeling, bottling, rectifying, and processing services to the alcoholic beverage industry, as well as marketing, product design/packaging, distribution, and consulting. They are one of the largest craft distilleries in Tennessee. Unfortunately, because they don't do bourbon and rye (yet), they have flown somewhat under the radar.

SPEAKeasy Spirits was founded by Jenny and Jeff Pennington. Jenny and Jeff had plenty of contacts when they decided to start the distillery, but they still sought advice from such distilling veterans as Greg Davis and Bill Samuels at Maker's Mark, Jim Rutledge at Four Roses, and several folks at Jack Daniel's. They started distilling in 2014 and another partner, Tommy Bernard, joined the distillery soon after. His arrival brought two major things: an incredible understanding of the liquor distribution

business, especially in Tennessee, and money that allowed for the purchase of a large column still.

They found a new home, an old call center and construction company garage, reminiscent of an old airplane hangar in the middle of downtown Nashville. With Jesse Meeks (formerly of Popcorn Sutton) as master distiller and Carter Collins as plant manager, they have quickly assembled an all-star team.

General fermentations last three to five days and are made in cypress mash tubs in 1,000-gallon batches. They cook and strip five days a week and run the still twice a day. They also have a full-time chemist and lab. Between their own brands and their co-packaging operations, SPEAKeasy/Pennington's sends shipments to more than 33 states, Canada, and Mexico. Slowly, the company is evolving from SPEAKeasy Spirits to Pennington Distilling Company.

Their rise was meteoric, as Jen Todd wrote near the end of 2015, "In three years, SPEAKeasy Spirits Distillery has invaded bars, restaurants, liquor stores and homes with four brands." Those brands were Pickers Vodka, Whisper Creek Tennessee Sipping Cream, Pennington's Flavored Rye Whiskey, Collins Cordials, and Walton's Vodka.

Pickers Vodka (80 proof) is a classic, clean vodka made with non-GMO white corn from western Tennessee and filtered four times before it is blended with premium Tennessee water. What results is a clear, smooth vodka. The vodkas also

come flavored, with such exotic profiles as Blueberry, Blood Orange, and Pineapple.

Walton's Vodka (80 proof) begins with 100% Tennessee red winter wheat. After being pot distilled in small batches, it is then run through the distillery's new, advanced column still and drip-filtered four times before being cut. This is an excellent wheated vodka and definitely worthy of your attention.

Pennington's Flavored Ryes are a line of extra smooth rye whiskeys that come in three flavors: Vanilla, Peach Apricot, and Strawberry. Their popular Vanilla tastes like maple syrup with booze in it. The idea was to balance the spiciness of the rye with the flavors, making a cocktail right out of the bottle. It's also great as a cocktail mixer.

Their best-selling line is Whisper Creek Tennessee Sipping Cream (40 proof). "This was the first bourbon sipping cream to break out of Tennessee commercially. Whisper Creek features premium-aged, charcoal-mellowed Tennessee whiskey made at SPEAKeasy Spirits," say Jeff and Jenny.

"The results are a rich taste and a smooth, less oily mouth feel than more traditional cream liqueurs. It has a different taste profile, emphasizing the natural whiskey elements, instead of the chocolate and coffee tastes predominant in the current market's numerous Irish creams," raved *Nashville Lifestyles* magazine. They also have such flavors as Mocha, Pumpkin Spice, and Peanut Butter Chocolate.

The distillery makes Collins Cordials, a line of flavored brandies and liqueurs aimed at mixologists and home bartenders alike. Flavors include Triple Sec, Blue Curacao, Amaretto, Sour Apple, Sour Watermelon, and many others.

SPEAKeasy/Pennington has also been laying down serious bourbon, rye, and Tennessee whiskey.

DAVIDSON RESERVE WHISKEY

Davidson Reserve whiskeys are made with local corn. They appreciate transparency so they always share the varieties they use, as well as who grew them. It's a very important aspect of their distilling program and has garnered great praise for quality, as well as taste. These are some of the better whiskeys coming out of Tennessee and they are gaining in reputation and respectability nationally.

Davidson Reserve Tennessee Sour Mash Whiskey (100 proof) is made with a mash bill of 70% Tennessee white corn, 25% Tennessee white cereal rye, and 5% barley, milled on-site using a hammer mill. The whiskey is aged for 4 years before bottling. Sweet aromas of freshly made maple cookies, strawberries, and crème brûlée on the nose. Caramel, graham crackers, pineapple, stone fruit, peach cobbler and toasted marshmallows on the palate with a spice finish.

Davidson Reserve Small Batch Bourbon (100 proof) is made with a mash bill of 60%

Tennessee corn, 22% Tennessee red winter wheat, and 18% malted barley. This is a wheated bourbon. The whiskey was barrel-aged 4 to 6 years. Creamy banana pudding, graham cracker, honey almond, maple syrup, dried apricots, toasted marshmallow, dried mango, brown sugar, bubble gum, cinnamon, vanilla bean as well as notes of toasted pecans, nutmeg, allspice, raisin, fig, apricot, vanilla bean, sweet cream, and a lovely dried citrus fruit on the finish.

Davidson Reserve Tennessee Straight Rye Whiskey (100 proof) is a 100% Tennessee White Cereal Rye. This whiskey was created from a recipe of 100% rye from Renfroe Farms, a third-generation family farm in Huntingdon, Tennessee. Rye forward with hints of maple, spices, and snickerdoodle on the nose. More rye and fresh apples, caramel, white pepper. This is an exceptional, remarkably drinkable rye worthy of a search.

Davidson Reserve Four Grain Tennessee Straight Whiskey (100 proof) is made from a blend of their three different Davidson

Reserve whiskeys: Tennessee Straight Rye Whiskey, Tennessee Straight Sour Mash Whiskey, and Tennessee Straight Bourbon Whiskey. Every batch of this lovely whiskey consists of a unique breakdown of each whiskey creating a new, distinct taste profile with each release. Dark caramel with hints of fresh vanilla bean, with dried dates, raisins plums and milk chocolate come across the palate.

Davidson Reserve Genesis is the first whiskey that they distilled and was put into barrels to age on October 14th, 2014. Made with a mash bill of 70% Tennessee corn, 25% Tennessee rye, and 5% barley, they only release 1,017 bottles of this incredibly special, silky smooth whiskey each year in October. Sweet sugar maple and toasted pecans on the nose with a creamy caramel and sweet vanilla bean on the palate and a lovely spice at the end.

SPEAKeasy/Pennington is meant to continually keep expanding. They have expanded several times over the last three years. With their popularity and marketing genius, they won't just need more space, they'll need a whole new distillery!

Sugarlands Distilling Company

Sugarlands Distilling Company opened its downtown Gatlinburg distillery in March 2014. A producer of quality moonshine and whiskey, the distillery offers tours and tastings, and features an Appalachian storytelling oral history program. The company has partnered with TAG USA, one of the most respected beverage marketing/sales organizations in the country.

Ned Vickers is the CEO and owner of Sugarlands. A former consultant who simply enjoyed home brewing, he spent a year researching moonshine recipes before he and his team found a recipe they were happy with. The idea has always been for Sugarlands to set itself apart by using quality ingredients, like white corn grown in Tennessee. The Gatlinburg tasting room distillery boasts a large copper pot still and a bunch of 750-gallon cypress wood fermenters.

"Sugarlands opened in 2014 after a legal tussle with Gatlinburg. The town

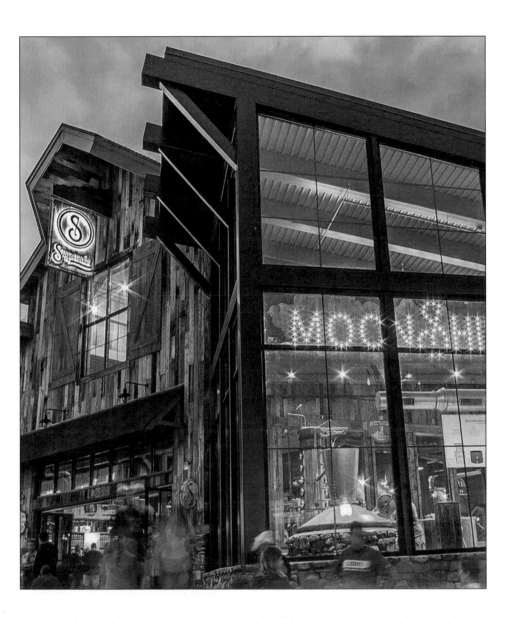

attempted to block it opening by invoking an ordinance that required liquor sellers to be at least 1,000 feet apart. Sugarlands is just a few doors down from Ole Smoky," reported *The Wall Street Journal.* "The state legislature eventually overrode that ordinance."

"We have seen incredible growth over the past three years," said Vickers in 2017. "Our company is locally owned and operated and we are deeply involved in our community. We believe in the 'mountain way,' which means lending a hand and giving back when you can. We take pride in helping spread that idea as far as we can." Sugarlands is now one of the most visited distilleries in America.

MOONSHINE

If you like good 'shine, or at least famous 'shine, Sugarlands Shine is for you! This is one of the bestselling lines of moonshine in the entire industry. The Sugarlands Silver Cloud Moonshine (100 proof) is a classic cane-and-grain 'shine. This is an easy drinking 'shine with flavors like Blockader's Blueberry, Butterscotch Gold, Appalachian Apple Pie, Old Fashioned Lemonade, and Southern Sweet Tea, among many others. Sugarlands previously did a series of Shine Sipping Creams with flavors like Electric Orange, Dark Chocolate Coffee, and Butter Pecan.

MOONSHINER'S GO HOLLYWOOD!

Moonshining went from the backwoods to the television screen...and the moonshiners went Hollywood. The Discovery Channel created a reality TV series titled *Moonshiners*. It focused on the lives and lifestyles of moonshiners who distilled (illegal) moonshine in the Appalachian Mountains of North Carolina, South Carolina, Tennessee, and Virginia. It captured the danger and drama involved in the making of illicit whiskey, as well as transporting it. It even covered law-evading techniques. The show made stars out of many of its participants, especially Marvin "Popcorn" Sutton. It premiered on December 6, 2011 and was a huge success, running for four seasons and spawning a spin-off series. There is no question that the popularity of moonshine and the show catapulted 'shine into the national marketplace, spurring sales and viewership.

In 2014, Sugarland partnered with The Discovery Channel to bring out four great moonshines featuring some of the most famous moonshiners and their most unique recipes. "The Legends Series is a product line that celebrates authentic moonshine craftsmen like Mark and Tickle," said Brent Thompson, director of marketing for Sugarlands Distilling Company.

Jim Tom's Signature Moonshine Unaged Rye (100 proof) is from Jim Tom Hedrick, a legendary moonshiner, and this rye 'shine is unique and amazing. Smooth as silk, but still spicy.

Another is Danville, Virginia, native Steven Tickle's Dynamite Cinnamon Moonshine. According to Sugarlands, "He experimented with recipes on his own ten-gallon still using a turkey fryer, jelly jars for double-thump kegs, and a shotgun condenser."

Another famous moonshiner is Mark Rogers, a long-time hunter, fisherman, and woodsman. "He has made moonshine most of his life, learning the trade from his 12 uncles when he was only 8 years old." His offering was Mark Rogers' American Peach Moonshine.

Then there's the team of Mark Ramsey and Digger Manes. Ramsey was introduced to moonshining when he was a young man enjoying the great outdoors in eastern Tennessee. Manes has spent almost his whole life around the still and learned from a local moonshine legend in Cocke County. They have two recipes: Mark and Digger's Hazelnut Rum and Mark and Digger's Apple Rye.

WHISKEY

Sugarlands also produces a serious aged whiskey, Roaming Man Tennessee Straight Rye Whiskey (122.9 proof). This began as Jim Tom Hedrick's Unaged Rye, one of the Legend Series 'shines. It was made with a mash bill of 51% rye, 45% corn, and 4% malted barley and then aged for two years in charred American white oak barrels. It is a cask strength whiskey and one of the best whiskeys being made in Tennessee right now. It's a big chewy whiskey with lots of caramel, burnt sugar, cream, vanilla, and black pepper, plus a heavy dose of gingersnap. This award-winning dram has turned a lot of heads and impressed even the most dyed-in-the-wool skeptics. The only problem? It's made in extremely limited quantities and only available at the Gatlinburg tasting room. If you can get your hands on this unicorn whiskey, it's worth every penny!

TENNESSEE HILLS

Tennessee Hills Distillery is the dream and vision of founder Stephen Callahan and his wife Jessica Curtis Callahan. The distillery is located in Jonesborough, Tennessee, and housed in a Civil War-era historic Salt House building constructed in the1840s, complete with the town's oldest elevator cranked by hand.

The building has gone through a very rigorous renovation process, with a fun retail area and a small but quickly growing distillery, complete with mashing/fermenting and hand-made copper stills. The motto here is "Embracing Heritage," which they apply to everything they do. And if you're visiting, hopefully you'll meet company mascot, Jack, who is easily the coolest distillery dog ever. This is a young distillery, and the well-packaged goods do very well on liquor store shelves.

The distillery offers classic styled spirits such as Hellcat Gin and Spitfire Vodka. Then there is a line of smartly designed moonshines and other potent potables with a corn liquor base, including Coconut, Lavender Lemon, Pecan Pie, Pineapple Upside Down, and Dark Roast. Two of the most popular products are Angry Pecker (70 proof) a classic clear rum and Red Hot Pecker (70 proof) rum made with cinnamon but not super sweet. Not to be missed by aficionados is Tennessee Hill's Corn Liquor (102 proof) a smooth as silk corn whiskey with a wonderful nose of corn bread and vanilla. Super easy to drink.

Tennessee's Hill's whiskey brand is S. E. Callahan's. This line of sourced whiskies is the company's bread and butter, and has wide distribution for such a small distillery. The brand has proved to be very successful. The SE Callahan's Straight Bourbon

Whiskey (90 proof) is a 3-year-old high-rye bourbon. The nose starts with fresh baked corn bread, baking spices, toffee, and mint. The palate starts with caramel and baked apple, with hints of mocha, orange bitters, and a lovely smack of white and black pepper at the end. The label offers two flavored whiskies, SE Callahan's Blood Orange and Honey, SE Callahan's Oatmeal and Spice.

SE Callahan's Straight Rye Whiskey (90 proof) is a smooth elegant rye, with lovely notes of apple and pear, notes of caramel, a hint of wintergreen, molasses, vanilla, and a good-sized pop of gingersnap at the end. A lovely drinking rye.

"Always carry a flagon of whiskey in case of snake bites. Furthermore, always carry a small snake."

—W.C. Fields

TENN SOUTH DISTILLERY

Tenn South began when Blair Butler, a radiologist, and Clayton Cutler, an engineer, decided they wanted to make quality whiskey. After a period of investigation, the duo bought 28 acres in Lynnville in 2011 and began to build their distillery. They acquired state distillery license No. 12 and began production in 2013.

Tenn South makes three products: Clayton James Tennessee Whiskey, Big Machine Platinum Filtered Premium Vodka, and All Mighty 140 Shine. There's nothing sourced here and it's all good. They use local Giles County white corn and grind it themselves. Mashing, fermenting, distilling, barrel aging, and bottling are done right in the distillery. They have two main stills, a classic copper pot still with a stripping column, and a vodka column.

SHINE

Tenn South makes several different 'shines, but the original was the All-Purpose Shine (100 proof), a classic grain-and-cane 'shine. This 'shine is made using only Giles County white corn, sugar, and water. Just like old moonshiners, Tenn South says, "We don't cook the mash. We just mix it, let it ferment and distill it." They will leave it out in the sun which may take three to seven days depending on the ambient temperature. This is an easy drinking moonshine with cornbread, buttered popcorn, vanilla, and yellow cake flavors. The distillery also offers the All-Mighty 140 Shine, for those who like their 'shine a bit bigger, as well as Apple Pie and Peach Pie flavored versions.

BIG MACHINE PLATINUM VODKA

Big Machine Label Group President and CEO Scott Borchetta announced the launch of Big Machine Platinum Filtered Premium Vodka in 2017, making the music label's first noise in the spirits business. Big Machine Label Group is home to superstars such as Florida Georgia Line, Reba McEntire, Rascal Flatts, Thomas Rhett, and Brantley Gilbert. "Over the past 11 years Big Machine has provided the soundtrack to millions of fans worldwide," said Borchetta. "With the launch of Big Machine Premium Vodka, we are now offering a superior product that perfectly complements the music we take such great pride in."

Big Machine Platinum Filtered Premium Vodka (80 proof) is an all-grain vodka that comes through a wild, space-aged, Fritz Lang-inspired vodka column with 25 plates and eight copper rings for cooling. It utilizes the popular Russian and Ukrainian method of Platinum filtration. The result is an incredibly smooth, excellent, and clean vodka.

ABERNATHY GIN

There's also Abernathy New American Gin (86 proof) and Abernathy New American Barrel Reserve Gin (86 proof) available at the distillery. The New American Gin is a London Dry-style, very citrus forward and fragrant, made with nine botanicals including juniper, coriander, cassia, citrus peels, and pecans. The Barrel Reserve gin is aged in freshly emptied "Clayton James Tennessee Whiskey" barrels. According to the company, "We also add a single Tennessee cherry stave and allow these flavors to mingle, enhancing some and minimizing others, for just a few months."

CLAYTON JAMES TENNESSEE WHISKEY

Clayton James Tennessee Whiskey (90 proof) is made with a mash bill of 74% Elton white corn, 13% malted barley, and 13% hard red winter wheat. It is made in a pot still before going through the Lincoln County Process. Tenn South does that differently, instead of running their whiskey through a charcoal filter and risking stripping out some flavor, the spirit is stored in containers of sugar maple charcoal for about a week. "We allow our spirits to acquire a unique, sweet maple smokiness from the charcoal," the distillery says. "This signature step serves to differentiate Clayton James Tennessee Whiskey from all other Tennessee Whiskeys." Each batch is then barreled in one 53-gallon barrel, two 25-gallon barrels, and four 15-gallon barrels. The youngest barrel is written on the back label.

Meanwhile, some of the newest whiskey stocks are resting in 53-gallon cylindrical, heavily charred barrels that offer easier storage. Cutler has the barrels custom made for him in middle Tennessee and he received a patent for the design in August 2017. Clayton James remains one of my favorite Tennessee whiskeys.

Instead of a big rickhouse, Cutler chose to store his barrels in old 40-foot shipping containers which approximate the extreme temperatures present on the seventh floor of a traditional rickhouse. This serves to accelerate and enhance his whiskeys. It's hard to argue with the results which instantly catapult Clayton James into the conversation for best Tennessee whiskey on the market. This is an absolute winner with a beautiful mouthfeel, caramel, brown sugar, vanilla wafer, and baked apple notes, as well as a smooth, easy finish. Tenn South also offers the Clayton James Single Barrel Cask Strength (112 proof), which spends 36 months in heavily charred oak.

One thing was clear visiting this distillery: Tenn South is doing a lot of things right.

Tennessee Legend Distillery

Nestled in the foothills of the Smoky Mountains, Tennessee Legend Distillery is a producer of moonshine, flavored whiskey, vodka, and cream liqueur Nestled in the foothills of the Smoky Mountains. There are two locations in Sevierville, Tennessee: one on Winfield Dunn Parkway, and the other on Newport Highway. The Newport Highway location is the original distillery and tasting room which opened in mid-2015 and the Winfield Dunn location is a satellite store. So far, they have a very loyal and growing following.

The Tennessee Legend Tennessee White Lightning Moonshine (100 proof) is an un-aged corn whiskey without a lot of added sugar. This 'shine has a very serious following, as do the Grape and Blackberry offerings.

Tennessee Legend Vodka (80 proof) is a small batch spirit distilled six times and carbon-filtered to provide an extra smooth finish.

Tennessee Legend also offers a line of cream liqueurs for sipping. The Tennessee Legend Crème Bruleé (40 proof) is a popular one along with other flavors including Ora`nge Creamsicle, Dirty Cream, and Root Beer Float (which is a combination of rum and neutral spirits).

Tennessee Legends Canebreak Bourbon Whiskey (85 proof) is a small batch whiskey aged in American oak charred barrels. A lovely, light bourbon and easy sipper that's perfect for cocktails.

Tennessee Legend Kingsnake Bourbon (90% proof) is made and barrel-aged in Sevierville, Tennessee. Small-batch distilled and aged for two years in brand new American charred oak. Smooth with hints of caramel, cereal, oak, and vanilla.

Tennessee Legends Kingsnake Straight Bourbon Whiskey Single Barrel (120.2 proof) is aged for 2 years in new American charred oak barrels. Notes of caramel, sweet corn, oak, and vanilla.

TENNESSEE SHINE COMPANY

Tennessee Shine Company is a small-batch distiller of moonshine and whiskey with locations in Sevierville and Pigeon Forge. The company was established in 2015 and was formerly known as James Creek Distilling and Tennessee XXX. Their small-batch whiskeys start with corn and malted barley and are then stored in small barrels. They use a 250-gallon still to distill each batch of moonshine which features a family recipe that's been handed down through the generations. They even offer specialty flavors and seasonal limited editions to cater to their growing audience. Well-known for their 'shine, the distillery just recently released a line of flavored corn whiskey. They also carry Moon Pie 'shine.

Tennessee Shine Co. Small Batch Corn Whiskey (100 proof) is a quality, small-batch, un-aged corn whiskey that has earned an artisanal reputation. Notes of buttered popcorn and cornbread, as well as wafts of cotton candy and vanilla make this an excellent, basic 'shine.

The distillery also offers crowd-pleasing flavors such as Muscadine, Green Apple, Coffee, Honey-Do-Me, Small Batch Rye, Caramel, Cream, Cinnamon, and the ever-popular fruity Tennessee Shine Co. Blue Houdini (50 proof).

The distillery also offers two straight whiskeys and some flavored whiskeys. Tennessee Shine Co. Southern Craft Corn Whiskey (100 proof) is a whiskey made with more than 51% corn and aged in American charred oak barrels. This is a light, creamed corn whiskey with nice hints of oak, spice, caramel, and vanilla. It's an easy drinking whiskey so if you're looking for something to take home to the serious whiskey drinker in your life, this is the one.

Other corn whiskey flavors include S'mores, Caramel, Cinnamon, and Espresso.

The Tennessee XXX Tennessee Straight Bourbon Whiskey (80 proof) has a classic bourbon mash bill with more than 51% corn. It's aged in new American charred oak barrels. Hints of caramel, apple, oak, and spice.

UNCLE NEAREST DISTILLERY

Perhaps no new distillery's debut has received as much attention as Uncle Nearest. The distillery is named for the previously little known—but now celebrated—Nathan "Nearest" Green (c. 1820 – 1890). Born into slavery and emancipated after the Civil War, Green was a head stiller, commonly referred to now as a master distiller, who was the moving force behind the founding of Jack Daniel's. It was Green who taught distilling techniques to Jack Daniel, founder of the Jack Daniel Tennessee whiskey distillery. Green was hired as the first master distiller for Jack Daniel Distillery and he was the first Black master distiller on record in the United States. His contributions to whiskey were obscured by time, but he has become celebrated over the last decade.

The idea behind Uncle Nearest Distilling was simple – to pay tribute to the man who invented Tennessee whiskey. Enter Fawn Weaver, bestselling author and entrepreneur, who first learned of Green's story in 2016 while on vacation in Singapore. Discovering Green's ghosted fate was "jarring," she told the press. Green had been largely forgotten in the showdown of Daniel's showmanship. There was no question that Green's labor and technique were essential ingredients behind the world's most iconic brand and Weaver was determined to address it. Within a month, she was living in Lynchburg, Tennessee, and whiskey would never be the same. Collecting thousands of documents and interviewing Green's descendants drew a more well-rounded understanding of who Green was and what he accomplished. She made his story known.

Weaver decided she was going into the whiskey business in 2017 and on September 14, 2019, the welcome center of Uncle Nearest (as he was affectionately known by his family) opened their doors with Weaver as CEO. "What was amazing when I first started in the whiskey business is that I didn't realize that this was the first American spirit ever to commemorate an African-American. Ever. Can you imagine? We've been here 400 years, and ours is the very first," said Weaver.

The new distillery is located in Shelbyville. "Every day, there are people that wanted to come out and visit the grounds—they didn't care whether or not we had an actual distillery," Weaver said. "So, we began really speeding up the process because of the number of requests of people coming. We wanted to be able to deliver something real to them."

Even more revolutionary, was the executive suite. Weaver assembled four incredible trail-blazing women at the helm of Uncle Nearest. It is the first major American spirit brand to have an all-female executive team. Alongside Weaver, Katharine Jerkens,the SVP of Global Sales, has overseen every aspect of growth from inception forward; Sherrie Moore,the Head of Whiskey Operations who, with over 35 years in the Tennessee whiskey industry, became the first woman to oversee operations for a major American whiskey brand in 2002; and Victoria Eady Butler, the first Black woman master blender of a major spirit brand.

With these powerhouse women leading the way, Uncle Nearest Distillery is now the most awarded American whiskey owned by women in US history.

Uncle Nearest sources whiskey from multiple sources, mostly from Tennessee. At the same time, they are laying down as much whiskey as quickly as possible as they start providing their own stocks in a bottle. Currently, the distillery offers three whiskies.

Uncle Nearest 1856 (100 proof) is a blend of premium-aged whiskeys between 8 and 14 years old. This elegant whiskey has a deep golden hue. On the nose, is pumpkin seeds, stone fruit, spice, and caramel corn. On the palate, sweet caramel and maple, and oatmeal raisin cookie. Vanilla and a hint of gingersnap linger for a long time.

Uncle Nearest 1884 Small Batch Whiskey (93 proof) is a small-batch blend of the whiskeys. Super smooth and mellow. It's rich and very pretty.

Uncle Nearest 1820 Premium Whiskey Aged 11 Years (117.2 proof) is a single barrel whiskey that's aged a minimum of 11 years. It has limited releases throughout the calendar and sells out quickly. It's impressive, big, robust, and flavorful.

Uncle Nearest was instantly a hit, both with the press and in sales. They have skyrocketed and their whiskeys have won dozens of gold medals with *Whisky Magazine* naming them Distillery of the Year in 2019. People will undoubtably know who Uncle Nearest is from now on.

Nearest & Jack Advancement Initiative

In June 2020, the Jack Daniel's Distillery and the Nearest Green Distillery announced the Nearest & Jack Advancement Initiative which is meant to further diversity within the American whiskey industry. Both companies are supporting it equally with an initial combined pledge of $5 million to help create the Nearest Green School of Distilling, develop the Leadership Acceleration Program (LAP) for apprenticeships, and establish the Business Incubation Program (BIP) focused on providing expertise and resources to Black entrepreneurs entering the spirits industry. This joint initiative will be guided by an advisory board with members from both organizations.

Motlow State College, the fastest growing college in Tennessee, has worked with leaders from both companies for the past year to develop a curriculum for the Nearest Green School of Distilling. The STEM-based and employable skills focused program has passed Motlow State requirements and is now awaiting approval from the Tennessee Board of Regents to begin moving toward accreditation by the institutions accrediting body SACSCOC. The certificate program may be offered as early as Fall 2021.

The Leadership Acceleration Program (LAP) will offer apprenticeships specifically to Black people already in the whiskey industry who have aspirations of becoming a head distiller, head of maturation, or production manager. The inaugural apprentices have already been identified and will begin shadowing at top distilleries throughout the country.

The third arm of the Nearest & Jack Advancement Initiative is the Business Incubation Program (BIP) that will offer Black entrepreneurs mentorships in all areas of the distilling business. They'll have access to top marketing firms, branding executives, and expanded distribution networks, as well as other assets and opportunities to grow their spirits businesses.

"Generally, when companies talk about the need to improve diversity, few immediate action steps follow," said Fawn Weaver, CEO of Uncle Nearest Premium Whiskey. "Our group is different. We are doers and we all agreed to work together to improve diversity in our industry, specifically, a way to get African Americans into top positions within our industry. Nearest Green taught Jack Daniel how to make Tennessee whiskey and we're incredibly proud our companies are joining forces to further their legacies of excellenceand to make distilling and the whiskey industry we love more diverse."

"Given our deep commitment to diversity and inclusion, I am thrilled we are coming together in this way today," said Lawson Whiting, President and Chief Executive Officer of the Brown-Forman Corporation, the parent company of Jack Daniel's. "This collaboration allows the extraordinary friendship of Nearest and Jack, and the hope they embodied during racially divided times in our country's history to help us advance the next generation of African American leaders in our industry."

FAWN WEAVER
FIRST BLACK WOMAN
MASTER DISTILLER & CEO

Just listing the number of things Fawn Weaver has accomplished in her lifetime can leave you breathless. Most notably, she has authored three *USA Today* and *New York Times* bestselling books. Weaver also founded the blog HappyWivesClub.com and overnight, the blog exploded into an international online club with more than 1,000,000 members in more than 110 countries. Books, videos, and worldwide celebrity followed.

"For me, as an African American, it was mind-boggling," she said. "We know that African Americans have been involved in so many brands over the centuries, but we've never been able to pinpoint to one and say: This person actually had a name and this person had a significant role."

Her conversion from author to master distiller was an "Aha!" moment. She came to Lynchburg in the hopes of writing a book or making a documentary about Nearest Green. She began interviewing his descendants when suddenly, it happened. "After that, my focus shifted from a book and a movie being the big pieces of the story to that bottle sitting on the shelf. That's what cements his legacy. Literally no other medium can make sure that a hundred years from now people will still know his name and his story. And so that's where we shifted to not just building a brand for a bottle that is commemorative, but building a brand that is meant to last for every generation to come."

Weaver has used her celebrity to help push the brand—and it doesn't hurt that the whiskey is very good. She has been a tireless promoter and has made Uncle Nearest one of the fastest growing brands in the industry. And Uncle Nearest hasn't even scratched the surface in terms of international sales. Fortunately, Weaver is popular around the world and it's just another challenge to keep this amazing woman going.

Wheeler's Raid Distillery

Founders Anthony Amico, Ryan Thomas, and Partner Brian Waller run Wheeler's Raid Distillery. In 2016, Thomas wanted to take his passion for whiskey to the next level and Wheeler's Raid was a fascinating battle. General Joseph Wheeler led his troops to intercept a wagon wheel supply line cutting through Nolensville, Tennessee. While raiding the wagon wheel supply line, soldiers learned that several of the wagons were stocked with whiskey! Wheeler's Raid Distillery is meant to invoke this local history.

Thomas has been in technology for 23 years and has served as an executive in several large companies. Amico has been a restaurateur for more than 30 years and has owned, operated, and sold several successful restaurants Waller, COO, was an investor, but was asked to come on to oversee product operations, including production, R&D, supply chain, and inventory management.

"We wanted to create a community like Jack Daniel's and bring it to Nolensville," Amico said. "I've been a resident of Nolensville for the last 10 years and I've got other businesses in Nolensville and this is just a tight-knit community that's something special."

The distillery is located in an industrial park in Nolensville, Tennessee. It has a large, spacious tasting room and bar with an easy and relaxed atmosphere. They have created a number of bottlings, some are extremely small batch and only available at the tasting room while

others can be found through distribution in Tennessee and Kentucky.

Wheeler's Raid Original Blend 01 (100 proof) is a 3-4 year-old bourbon finished with hand selected double toasted American oak staves.

Wheeler's Raid Cask Strength 02)118.4 proof) is a limited-availability small batch whiskey, with bottlings of 6 to 8 barrels of 5 to 6 year-old bourbon. Bottled at cask strength, it's spicy with some black cherry, vanilla, and hints of caramel, and a creamy finish.

Wheeler's Raid French Oak 03 (105 proof) is a blend of bourbons between 4 and 6 years old and hand finished with medium toast

French oak staves. A hint of that dryness and a slight vanilla essence of the French oak at the finish. The distillery hopes to make this available year-round.

Wheeler's Raid Original Blend Rye 04 (90 proof) is a rye-blend and it will be a hand-selected set of 4 to 8 barrels per bottling. A high-rye rye in small batch with a Caribbean-style finish.

Wheeler's Raid Cask Strength Rye 05 (105.6 proof) is a limited availability whiskey, cask strength, hand-selected rye.

Wheeler's is making some impressive whiskeys and we're all looking forward to more from this small, quality house.

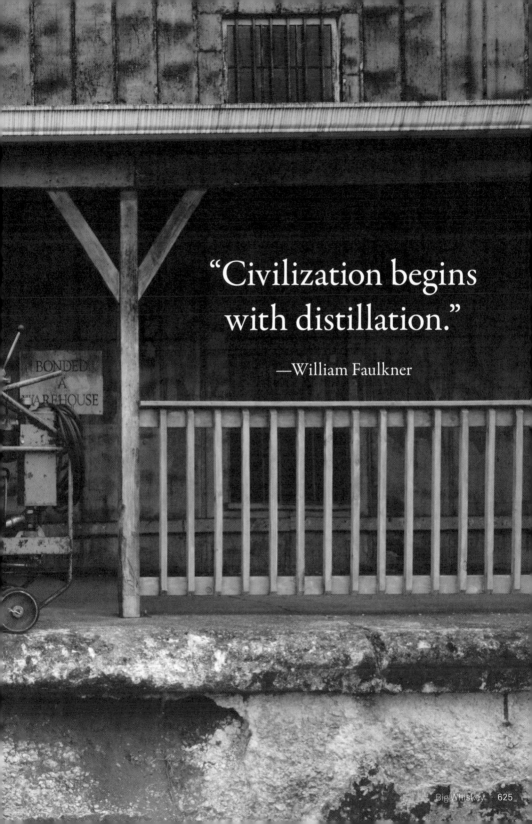

"Civilization begins with distillation."

—William Faulkner

Acknowledgments

Any author of such an effort owes a great debt of gratitude to those who went before him. During the course of my research, I poured over more than 1,000 sources, including letters, interviews, and articles, from various websites, blogs, newspapers, and magazines. Special thanks and appreciation for their constant beat coverage (both news stories, reviews, and books) of the Kentucky and Tennessee whiskey industry would be Chuck Cowdery, Fred Minnick, Nino Marchetti, Eric Burke, Brett Atlas, Carla Harris Carlton, Clay Risen, Susan Reigler, Lew Bryson, Maggie Kimberl, Josh Peters, and many, many others.

I would, of course, like to thank John Whalen of Cider Mill Press Book Publishers, who helped make this book a reality. Were it not for his excitement, enthusiasm, and faith in me, I might have given up under the weight of this massive project. Also, it was tremendous fun and his photography is so incredible. Such a talented photographer. I also owe a huge debt of gratitude to Cider Mill staffers Buzz Poole, Hannah Kinsey, Steve Cooley, and any others who helped mold a rather large manuscript into readable shape. Thanks to my boon travel companion and sometime driver Richard Srsich.

Special thanks to Richard Thomas, Jim Myers and Emily West for their contribution and opinions. Not only did they contribute writing to the final book, but their writings on the whiskies of Kentucky and Tennessee were invaluable research resources.

Thank you for those who took time for me in Kentucky, including Tiffany Slone, Sarah Bessette, Katie Farley, Chris Morris, Andrew Buchanan, Kristie Wooldridge, Freddie Johnson, Kyle Henderson, Deja Lawson, Jennifer Cissell, Britt Kulsveen Chavanne, Drew Kulsveen, Lauren Cherry, Bernies Lubbers, Al Young, Ashley Farmer, Greg Davis, Royce Neeley, Rebekah Sue Neeley, Kaveh Zamanian, Steve Nally, Col Mark W. Erwin, Jacob Call, Caleb Kilburn, Steven Beam, John Rempe, Keith Spears, Aaron Schorsch, Paul McLaughlin, Jeff Mattingly, and Robert Sherman among many.

Thank you for those who took time for me in Tennessee , Meaghan Regan, Charlie Nelson, Andy Nelson, Phil Prichard, Kelley Cureton, Tim Piersant, Matt Cunningham, April Weller Cantrell, Kim Peterson, Heath Clark, Bruce Boeko, Jenny Pennington, Carter Collins, Kristin Anglin, Alex Castle, Clay Smith, Ashley Shaffner-Fletcher, Jeff Arnett, Chris Fletcher, Meg Sellers, Brian Downing, Marianne Eaves, Jim Massey, Dara Carson, Chris Yett, Chad Cooper, Kenny Sweet, Doug Branham, Stephen Callahan, Jessica Curtis Callahan, Fawn Weaver, and Trey Saylor, among many.

Finally, thank you to the countless publicity, marketing, sales, and tasting room individuals who helped me and put up with my endless questions and harassment. Thank you.

Contributors

Richard Thomas is the owner and managing editor of The Whiskey Reviewer.com. Thomas's opinions and advice on whiskey have appeared on ABC News, Discovery Channel programming, *Style* magazine, and elsewhere. He is the author of P*ort: Beginners Guide To Wine*, American Whiskey, and contributed to *The New Single Malt Whiskey*.

Emily West is a journalist who currently writes for *The Tennessean*. She covers spirits, business, and local news in the Nashville, Tennessee, region. She has written numerous features for other local newspapers and magazines in the region, as well.

Image Credits

John Whalen: pages 3, 4-5, 6, 8-11, 16, 18, 21-26, 28-29, 31, 33-34, 36-47, 51, 75, 84-88, 91-93, 95, 104-109, 115-119, 126-128, 130-131, 133, 144-145, 150-151, 153, 156-157, 160-161, 167-169, 180-181, 186-187, 196, 201-206, 210-211, 216, 218-220, 222-223, 224 (bottom), 226-227, 229-231, 244-250, 252-258, 264-271, 273-274, 276, 278 (top), 284-286, 288-295, 297-299, 303, 308-309, 318-323, 325, 328-334, 340-345, 347, 358-359, 361, 366-367, 372-373, 378-379, 381, 383, 388-390, 392, 396-399, 403-407, 409-410, 412-420, 422-423, 434, 438-439, 444-447, 449, 452-453, 458-462, 468-473, 478-481, 484-486, 490, 510-515, 519-522, 525, 527-530, 535-536, 538, 545-549, 552-553, 561-563, 565, 569, 578-582, 583-589, 598-607, 609, 624-625, 627, 638-639.

Carlo De Vito: pages 49, 57-58, 61-62, 64, 67, 69, 71, 98, 100, 102-103, 121, 122, 125, 132, 136-137, 159, 176-177, 182-183, 195, 199, 207-208, 217, 259-261, 275, 279, 300-301, 306, 310, 313-314, 316-317, 327, 350-351, 368, 370, 376-377, 384, 400-401, 424, 426-427, 435, 440, 450, 476-477, 482, 403-404, 508, 523, 532-533, 556-557, 567, 610-611, 614.

Page 53 courtesy of the Library of Congress.

Pages 110, 112-113, 238-240, 315, 371, 374-375, 411, 596 used under official license from Shutterstock.com.

Michael Thornton: page 158.

All other images courtesy of the respective distilleries.

Index

About Cider Mill Press Book Publishers

Good ideas ripen with time. From seed to harvest, Cider Mill Press brings fine reading, information, and entertainment together between the covers of its creatively crafted books. Our Cider Mill bears fruit twice a year, publishing a new crop of titles each spring and fall.

"Where Good Books Are Ready for Press"

Visit us online at
cidermillpress.com
or write to us at
PO Box 454
12 Spring St.
Kennebunkport, Maine 04046

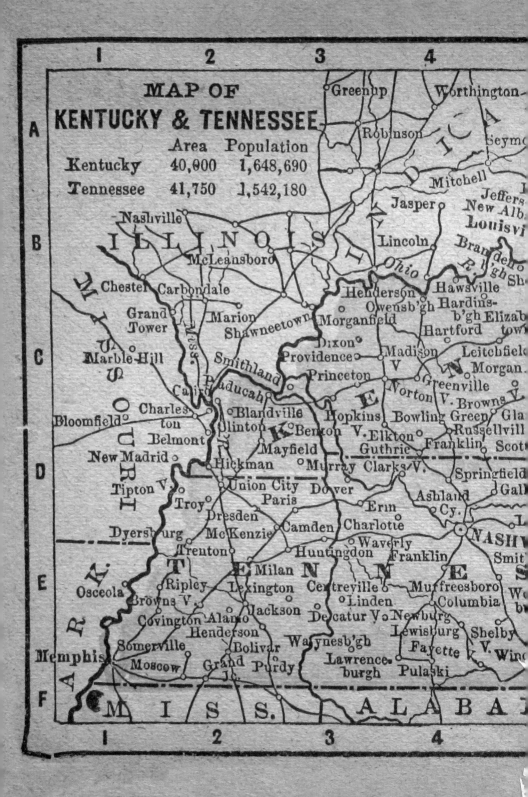

MAP OF
KENTUCKY & TENNESSEE

	Area	Population
Kentucky	40,000	1,648,690
Tennessee	41,750	1,542,180